The Politics of Regional Trade in Iraq, Arabia, and the Gulf 1745–1900

SUNY Series in the Social and Economic History of the Middle East
Donald Quataert, Editor

Issa Khalaf, *Politics in Palestine: Arab Factionalism and Social Disintegration, 1939–1948*

Rifa'at 'Ali Abou-El-Haj, *Formation of the Modern State: The Ottoman Empire, Sixteenth to Eighteenth Centuries*

M. Fuad Köproülü, *The Origins of the Ottoman Empire,* translated and edited by Gary Leiser

Guilian Denoeux, *Urban Unrest in the Middle East: A Comparative Study of Informal Networks in Egypt, Iran and Lebanon*

Zachary Lockman, ed., *Workers and Working Classes in the Middle East: Struggles, Histories, Historiographies*

Palmira Brummett, *Ottoman Seapower and Levantine Diplomacy in the Age of Discovery*

Ali Abdullatif Ahmida, *The Making of Modern Libya: State Formation, Colonization, and Resistance, 1830–1932*

Ayşe Buğra, *State and Business in Modern Turkey: A Comparative Study*

Donald Quataert, ed., *Manufacturing in the Ottoman Empire and Turkey, 1500–1950*

Samira Haj, *The Making of Iraq, 1900–1963: Capital, Power, and Ideology*

Hala Fattah, *The Politics of Regional Trade in Iraq, Arabia, and the Gulf, 1745–1900*

The Politics of Regional Trade in Iraq, Arabia, and the Gulf 1745–1900

HALA FATTAH

STATE UNIVERSITY OF NEW YORK PRESS

Published by
State University of New York Press, Albany

Printed in the United States of America

For information, contact State University of New York Press, Albany, NY
www.sunypress.edu

Production by Bernadine Dawes • Marketing by Bernadette LaManna

Library of Congress Cataloging-in-Publication Data

Fattah, Hala Mundhir, 1950–
The politics of regional trade in Iraq, Arabia, and the Gulf, 1745–1900 / Hala Fattah.
p. cm. — (SUNY series in the social and economic history of the Middle East)
Originally presented as the author's thesis (Ph.D.)—University of California at Los Angeles.
Includes bibliographical references and index.
ISBN 0-7914-3113-4 (alk. paper). — ISBN 0-7914-3114-2 (pbk. : alk. paper)
1. Arab countries—Commerce—History. 2. Arab countries—Commercial policy—History. I. Title. II. Series.
HF3866.F38 1997
382'.0917'4927—dc20 96-42069
CIP

This volume is dedicated to

my father and mother

Contents

Acknowledgments		ix
Introduction		1
1.	A Regional World: 1745–1900	13
2.	The Structure of the Regional Market of Iraq, Arabia, and the Gulf	63
3.	Regional Trade, Ottoman Centralization, and the British Economic Challenge: The Background to Economic Conflict in the Nineteenth Century	91
4.	River Routes	123
5.	The Grain Trade	139
6.	The Horse Trade	159
7.	The Growth of Regional Market Towns in Iraq, Kuwait, and Arabistan	185
Afterword		207
Notes		211
Bibliography		243
Index		251

Acknowledgments

This book was originally a Ph.D. dissertation submitted to the History Department at the University of California at Los Angeles. It has undergone many permutations since, and benefited from a great deal of thoughtful and insightful advice offered by a number of friends and colleagues. I want to thank the Chair of my doctoral committee, Professor Afaf Lutfi al-Sayyid Marsot, for her unstinting assistance and support during and after my years at UCLA, Professor Rifaʿat ʿAli Abou-El-Haj for the many far-ranging and thought-provoking sessions he chaired as head of *Ḥalqat al-Arbiʿā,* and Professors Mahmood Ibrahim, Mahmud AbuSwa, Dina Khoury, Sherry Vatter, Edward Mitchell and Fatma Atike for their trenchant criticism as well as for their camaraderie. I owe Dina Khoury a double debt for her scrupulous reading (and re-reading) of the entire revised manuscript prior to publication. Among the many other scholars who read and commented on this manuscript in the years since, and who helped me in clarifying a number of key issues during my research, I would like to acknowledge the memory of Mr. Albert Hourani at Oxford, and to thank (in no particular order) Professors Peter Gran, Michael Morony, Robert Fernea, Carl Trocki, William (Bill) Young, Bradley Smith, Thabit Abdullah and Sarah Shields; as well as Messrs. Ibrahim al-ʿAlī, Ata Abdul-Wahhab, Lahab Abdul-Wahhab, Yasser Alwan and Ms. Natana De Long-Bas. Before the work was accepted for publication, I received the very generous assistance of Professors Donald Quataert, Suraiya Faroqhi and Fred Lawson whose incisive comments helped immeasurably in restructuring the book. Needless to say, any mistakes in the text are purely mine.

In addition, I wish to thank the Social Science Research Council for awarding me a postdoctoral grant in 1988–89 to revise my dissertation for publication. I am also indebted to a number of research institutions and libraries for help in collecting the data for this work, starting with the Middle East Center and the Bodleian library at Oxford, the British Library in London, the Public Record Office at Kew, the India Office Library in London, the Majmaʿ al-ʿIlmī in Baghdad, the libraries at UCLA, the Library of Congress in Washington D.C, the library at Georgetown University, and the library of the University of Jordan. I would like to register a special note of thanks to shaikh Muhammad Bahjat al-Athari and Messrs. Khairi al-Umari and Husain Jamil in Baghdad, Mr. Dunning Wilson of UCLA, and Dr. Nawfan al-Hmoud and Mustafa Hamarneh at the University of Jordan. I am also indebted to Mr. and Mrs. Fakhri Bakir and their family of Potomac, Maryland; Mr. Nameer Jawdat of Chevy Chase, Maryland; Ms. Isgouhi Kassakhian of Los Angeles, California; Ms. Georgia Harb of Wilmington, Delaware; Malik and Rula AbiSaab of Binghamton, New York; and Mr. Hassan Shukri, Ms.Reem Kattan, Ms. Sahar Kattan, Ms.Hala E. Nasser and Ms. Zena Sati of Amman, Jordan. Finally, I am very appreciative of the combined efforts of SUNY press, and especially grateful to Mr. Clay Morgan and Ms. Bernadine Dawes for their unstinting advice and assistance.

This book would have remained half-finished had it not been for the tireless encouragement and constant support of my father, Munther Nuri Fattah Pasha. I owe him more than I can say. Not only did he he read every single word, he also designed the map, converted the different currencies of the nineteenth century, and touched up the language when it threatened to become pure verbiage. I thank him for his good counsel, immense patience, and great confidence in me.

For kindly granting permission to reprint from their publications, I thank the following publishers:

The passage from *Four Centuries of Modern Iraq* by Stephen Helmsley Longrigg is reprinted on page 94 by permission of Oxford University Press. Copyright © 1925 by Clarendon Press.

The passage from *Merchants, Markets and the State in Early Modern India,* edited by Sanjay Subrahmanyam is reprinted on page 3 by permission of Oxford University Press in India. Copyright © 1990 Oxford University Press.

The passage from *The Economic History of the Middle East, 1800–1914,* edited by Charles Issawi is reprinted on page 212 by permission of University of Chicago Press. Copyright © 1966 by University of Chicago Press.

The passage from *Politics and Society in Early Modern Iraq: Mamluk Pashas, Tribal Shaykhs and Local Rule Between 1802 and 1831* by Tom Nieuwenhuis is reprinted on page 210 by permission of Kluwer Academic Publishers. Copyright © 1982 by Martinus Nijhoff Publishers.

The passage from *An Historical Geography of the Ottoman Empire* by Donald Edgar Pitcher is reprinted on page 32 by permission of E. J. Brill. Copyright © 1972 E. J. Brill Publishers.

The passage from *The Old Social Classes and the Revolutionary Movements of Iraq: A Study of Iraq's Old Landed and Commercial Classes and its Communists, Baathists and Free Officers* by Hanna Batatu is reprinted on page 205 by permission of Princeton University Press. Copyright © 1978 by Princeton University Press.

The passage from *Iraq and Iran: Roots of Conflict* by Tareq Y. Ismael is reprinted on page 31 by permission of Syracuse University Press. Copyright © 1982 Syracuse University Press.

The passages from "Natural Frontiers Revisited: France's Boundaries since the Seventeenth Century" by Peter Sahlins, appearing in *The American Historical Review,* vol. 95 are reprinted on page 15 by permission of The American Historical Association. Copyright © 1990 The American Historical Association, Washington, D.C.

The passage from *Imperial Meridian: The British Empire and the World, 1780–1820* by C. A. Bayly are reprinted on page 7 by permission of Longman Group Ltd. Copyright © 1989 Longman Group Ltd.

The passage from *Foreign Office Confidential Print: The Affairs of Kuwait,* Edited by Robin Bidwell is resprinted on page 26 by permission of Frank Cass Publishers. Copyright © 1971 Frank Cass Publishers.

The passages from *Islams and Modernities,* by Aziz al-Azmeh are reprinted on pages 49–50 by permission of Verso Press. Copyright © 1993 Verso Press.

Introduction

In the mid-eighteenth to early nineteenth centuries, several districts in central and eastern Arabia, lower Iraq, Kuwait, Arabistan (present-day south-west Iran) and portions of the northern Gulf formed a regional market that bought, sold and shipped goods to India. While some present-day historians have argued that the origins of the regional market can be traced as far back as the advent of Islam, which, according to the historian of the Indian Ocean, K. N. Chaudhuri, gave the Indian Ocean an unparalleled spatial and temporal unity,[1] it is undeniable that by the 1700s, a long-standing regional trading bloc had emerged in Arabia, Iraq and the Gulf that tied remote districts in Najd to cosmopolitan towns such as Bombay by means of barter, credit and cash. The historic forces shaping the regional market's operations in the Gulf throughout the mid-eighteenth to early nineteenth centuries allowed it to assume a certain organic structure which was to withstand all exterior challenges until the 1860s, when European trade finally managed to subsume regional operations into the wider context of the world economy.

The existence of a broad trading region encompassing Iraq, Arabia, and the Gulf has been overlooked by the majority of scholars interested in the eighteenth and nineteenth century socioeconomic history of the area. Proceeding from the assumption that the economic history of the Ottoman provinces necessitates the study of each province on its own, as distinct from the region of which it formed a part, historians have consistently imposed barriers on regions that had none. Thus, the trend has been to study nineteenth-century Arab provinces and Gulf shaikhdoms as if they were distinct and self-sufficient entities, sustained by national economies and demarcated by national borders.[2] No attempt has been made to discuss the same provinces or Gulf principalities in the context of a broader economic region, or to analyze the social and commercial links that sustained the region in the face of exterior challenges.

And yet the issues pertaining to the structure, development, and resiliency of regional economies across Asia, Africa, and Latin America is one of considerable moment. The regional dynamic that spurred disparate districts and territories to cohere into transnational networks of trade cannot be easily dismissed, particularily when the claim has been made that

> Trade communities of merchants living among aliens in associated networks are to be found on every continent and back through time to the very beginning of urban life. They are . . . one of the most widespread of all human institutions over a very long run of time, yet limited to the long period of human history that began with the invention of agriculture and ended with the coming of the industrial age.[3]

In fact, this book argues that, insofar as Iraq, Arabia, and the Gulf are concerned, trade networks may have endured, and even resisted the coming of steam transport and rail technology until other factors colluded to diminish their influence. But this is getting ahead of ourselves. In order to understand the nature of trans-regional networks of trade, and their impact on Iraqi/Gulf society in the mid-eighteenth to early nineteenth centuries, it is imperative to provide a socioeconomic context for their emergence, efflorescence, and eventual demise. One way of reinvigorating the historiography on pre-industrial trade and commercial networks in the Ottoman Arab provinces, as well as in Arabia and the Gulf, is to draw on new insights and arguments, largely emanating from similar regions across Asia. In this respect, the burgeoning literature on Indian Ocean trade provides a good introduction; so it is to the historiography of Asian commercial networks that we now turn.

THE STRUCTURE OF TRADE IN THE INDIAN OCEAN PRIOR TO THE MID-NINETEENTH CENTURY: A HISTORIOGRAPHIC SURVEY

Close to fifty years ago, scholars of disparate disciplines and diverse historical interests began to develop a number of interlinked theories with regard to the overland and seaborne trade of the vast region bordering the Indian Ocean. For the most part, these theses had to do with the development of European (especially Portuguese and British) commercial expansion in the Gulf, Arabian Sea, and Indian Ocean, in the aftermath of what historians of the period considered to be Vasco de Gama's landmark sea passage in 1498.[4] For a time, the history of the Indian Ocean revolved around "naval and land warfare [between European trading Companies], diplomatic and dynastic intrigue . . . and wars and conquest."[5] Then a radical change came about with the publication of several economic histories of India, and the study of the Indian Ocean, properly speaking, was born. From the 1950s onwards, historians have been primarily concerned with two perspectives. One group has focused on the macro-history of the region, drawing upon large, comparative themes and analyzing continuities across time, while the other group has sought to uncover the specifics of local and provincial societies by studying one region in depth. Although the combined research of the two groups has weakened the old paradigmatic structure of Indian Ocean studies and largely jettisoned the Eurocentric perspectives of an earlier generation,

> the study of what M. N. Pearson has termed the "glamour routes"—the conspicuous routes on which the high-value commodity movements were carried on—still exercises a great fascination, as do Great Merchants, Great Ships and Great Ports . . . [6]

Nevertheless, change is in the air. For one thing, the field is wide open, especially with regard to comparative history. While at least one conference has been held on Ottoman, Safavid, and Mughal approaches to the study of state and peasants,[7] the more radical breakthrough has taken place in the works of *Annales*-inspired historians of the Indian Ocean. Thanks to the innovative books of K. N. Chaudhuri and others,[8] students of coastal India, southern Iraq, the Arabian littoral, and the northern Gulf, as well as those from Sri Lanka, Malaysia, Burma, Thailand, and China are now able to construct a theoretical framework that analyzes and assimilates the history of their respective trading networks within a large, varied and complex region. At the same time, researchers whose narrow focus on specific areas in the Indian subcontinent seemed to obviate the need for a larger canvas are now faced with a vast array of evidence on the regional history of agricultural production, land relations, pastoral systems, building and construction, shipping technology, food, fashion, and state bureaucracies not only in India but across the Islamic world and China. While Chaudhuri's portrayal of the Indian Ocean as a regional unity has been criticized as being overly ambitious in scope, and somewhat uncritical of European sources,[9] his pioneering studies are still the best introduction to the what has come to be known as the "Asian trading system."

Relying on a large corpus of primary and secondary materials, Chaudhuri emphasizes the systematic growth of ports of trade, their merchant component, the frequently uneasy relationship between merchants and the early modern state, as well as the eruption of "armed trading" brought on by the Portuguese in the Indian Ocean. Moreover, he pays special attention to issues normally passed over by other historians, such as the cultural dimensions of trade and the symbolic importance of certain commodities in some societies; the fact that preindustrial societies from Iraq to China not only traded in luxuries but in heavy goods such as dates, sugar, building materials and timber; and the legal structure often put in place by centralized governments who, while often at odds with merchant communities, found it provident to furnish emporia trade with the necessary continuity required to face massive disruptions of a military, political, or ecological nature. More significantly, Chaudhuri shows that within the large, seemingly uniform structure of Indian Ocean trade, there was unity in diversity. Thus, he believes that "the Indian Ocean was an area of social and cultural diversity rooted in four different civilizations: the Irano-Arabic, the Hindu, the Indonesian, and the Chinese."[10] In his book *Asia Before Europe,* the author carries these themes a step further by describing the symbolic "signifiers" of certain foods, architectural styles, clothing, and production régimes of nomadic/agricultural societies, pointing out that the unities and disunities of Asian civilization created important tensions which themselves provided the essential dynamic for this great zone of socioeconomic activity, the Indian Ocean.

Complementing Chaudhuri's books are a number of pivotal articles that shed further light on these issues. Edmund M. Herzig has pointed out that, contrary to the thesis that the European companies' diversion of the spice trade from the Gulf to the Cape route brought about the immediate decline of Asian trade, the fabled sixteenth-century port of Hormuz fell not because regional merchants and their commercial networks were "uncommercial" and "uncapitalistic" in their operations, but because

> [Hormuz] was too weak politically to hold off Safavid Iran, and because it ceased to provide the secure and economical entrepôt facilities that had attracted merchants to its port. Trade shifted to equally traditional but more profitable channels. This regional trade, of which Hormuz had for so long been the centre, continued to flourish for as long as the shipping and caravan routes remained open, and the Mughal, Safavid, and Ottoman empires continued to provide the peace and security needed for commodity production and supply. The European commodities found this "country" trade very hard to break into, and their agents repeatedly lamented their inability to compete with the Asian merchants whose overheads were insignificant compared with those of the companies, and who continued to carry the bulk of the regional trade throughout the seventeenth century. . . . If any broad truth is revealed in the story of Hormuz, it is not the failure of the traditional Asian systems and structures before the impact of "modern" Europe, but the older and simpler wisdom [that] . . . , "if merchants are hindered by one route, they find another, like water, and they never cease seeking a way that will bring them more profit."[11]

In other words, the "very considerable" regional trade emanating from Hormuz continued to expand throughout the area, tying the Far East and Southeast Asia to the Mediterranean and the Gulf ports, even after the trade in spices was largely monopolized by the Europeans. Because regional merchants traded in a wide variety of goods, and were not entirely dependent upon luxuries such as spices and silks, they could fall back on hardy perennials such as dried fruits and preserves, horses, dyes (alum and madder) cereals, dates, salt, and pearls from Iran, Iraq, and the Gulf ports, in return for which they received cotton piece-goods, sugar, rice and iron from India.[12]

Moreover, new research on south-west Indian ports in the seventeenth century (when the Portuguese were still fairly dominant on the coast) bears out

Herzig's contention that the spice trade has been over-inflated in most historical accounts of the Indian Ocean; and that one of the significant but lesser-studied aspects of the regional carrying trade between southern India and the Gulf involved not only the trade in manufactures, but that in food-grains, especially rice.[13] One of the interesting aspects of Subrahmanyam's description of the rice trade from Basrur is the delineation of the three groups involved, namely, the Portuguese *Estado da Índia,* private Portuguese and *mestizo* traders, and finally the Asian merchants. Unlike traditional histories, the author shows that on several occasions local merchants were able to circumvent the Portuguese grip on coastal trade and, in some cases, to play havoc with Portuguese restrictions on local traffic. In the 1630s, for instance, local traders, disturbed by excessive Portuguese coercion of local shipping, by-passed the important Portuguese station of Goa altogether, and actually brought about near-famines in the town.[14]

The fact that local merchants were capable of diversifying their "portfolios" and trading in a wide number of different goods has come in for sustained research on the part of historians of the Indian Ocean. Portfolio capitalists—defined as "entrepreneur[s] who farmed revenue, engaged in local agricultural trade, commanded military resources (war animals, arms and human labor), as well as on more than the odd occasion had a flutter in the Great Game of Indian Ocean commerce"[15]—are considered to have made their appearance in India in the sixteenth and seventeenth centuries.[16] In southern India, these large merchants were supported by tax-farms, while in northern India, important networks of merchant bankers (some of Persian origin) dominated the Mughal economy. Invariably, these rich merchants attracted the jealousy of local princes who saw them as competitors in a crowded field; they were also vulnerable to the fragility of large-scale credit operations, on which many of them had made their fortunes. The slow decline of Indian portfolio capitalists thus begins with the eighteenth century, as they were edged out of power by British and French private traders who combined the same sort of "complex enterprises, combining seaborne trade, overland and fluvial commerce, farmed commercial crops, and . . . private monopolies"[17] as their Indian counterparts, with the added advantage of Company support to assist in their operations.

One of the important points of this article is the authors' careful analysis of who was, and who was not, a merchant in Mughal India, a question that invariably dogs every researcher of the pre-modern Asian economy, and poses broad implications for the socioeconomic differentiation of various societies in the Indian Ocean region. Dina Khoury's article elaborates on this point, uncovering important differences between merchants and "sellers of protection" in sixteenth and seventeenth-century Iraq.[18] The latter are described as "entrepreneurs . . . who extracted protection rent from merchants [and] . . . had access to the means of organized coercion. They derived their power from their ability to provide merchants with "safe conduct," and perhaps more importantly for the smooth flow of trade, with an element of predictability in foreign terrain."[19] Whether these groups were composed of tribal leaders extracting the *khuwwa* or "protection money" in rural districts, or town officials collecting urban taxes, both were in essence merchants whose importance to the wider economy of the Indian Ocean, Arabian Sea, and northern Gulf lay in their redistributive functions. While the distinction between merchants and sellers of protection is frequently blurred in the sources, the author believes that the subtle, sometimes great differences between the two groups' relationship with the early modern state in Iraq, as well as with the political economies of its constituent parts (Basra, Baghdad, and Mosul), makes it imperative to reexamine the phenomenon in light of continuing questions concerning the debate about the nature of merchant capital in pre-industrial Asia.

In much the same vein, Anne Pérotin-Dumon shows that there was sometimes very little to distinguish between state merchants and pirates; in fact, the critical difference between "legal" and "illegal" trade seems only to have come about with the rise of the nation-state, the emergence of protectionism and "exclusivism," and the consolidation of international law.[20] Above all, the term reflected the realities of power. Thus, in the sixteenth and seventeenth centuries, newcomers in the Indian Ocean such as the Portuguese denounced the Malabar sailors who resisted them as "pirates" even though the latter were but defending the Mughal state's interests; similarly, in the Mediterranean, Venetian traders, who had long dominated the region, treated as pirates any new European competitor. The nineteenth century brought about a new development: the governments of centralized nation-states, who in the past had tolerated piracy from their own subjects because it provided access to new sources of wealth or new colonies, began to prosecute "their" pirates because the latter now posed a threat to the nation-building efforts of state elites. As a result, pirates were either warred upon or inducted into the state as government-sponsored merchants. Finally,

> at the Paris peace conference ending the Crimean War in 1856, privateering was "abolished." The British delegate thought that "our state of civilization and humanity required that an end should be put to the system which no longer belongs to our time." Although the decision . . . closed off about two centuries of established privateering, or *guerre de course*, between "civilised" nations of the Western world, at the same time it legitimated the campaigns the same nations would undertake against indigenous "pirates" in the second push of imperialism that was underway. . . .[21]

The historic collision between Europe and Asia has perhaps received the most attention of all. Adding a fresh perspective to the question, C. A. Bayly attempts to reconstruct the context of "the Second British Empire," that is, the period between 1780 and 1830, in which British expansion abroad first came into contact with Asian societies.[22] Unlike traditional histories, however, the author proposes a schema by which socioeconomic unrest and political change in eighteenth century Asian empires—chiefly the Mughal, Ottoman, and Safavid—inexorably drew in British energies, and refashioned the global map in the process. Thus, according to Bayly,

> The sequence of historical change ran perhaps like this: commercial growth and the changing balance of power between the centre and province led to growing regional autonomy. The imbalances of power and wealth so created led in turn to tribal invasion, conflict between the successor states and internal battles between elites over labor supply, trade, and revenues. New rulers arose in the mid- and latter half of the century who sought to create more compact armies and monopolize trade and production, which though buoyant in some regions, had been damaged by such conflicts . . . it was at this point that the role of the West, previously of secondary importance, became critical. . . .[23]

One of Bayly's important points concerns the use of commercial and agricultural monopolies by local elites in the pursuit of state-building in Asia. Thus, "trade monopoly, like religious patronage, was an act of incorporation by rulers of their subjects."[24] It involved the expansion of state patronage at the same time as the enlargement of territories taxed by the state apparatus. Monopolies may have been geared towards the assimilation, or incorporation of state subjects, but they were also a means of defense against expansionist foreign mercantile interests; eventually, by tying the subject closer to his sovereign, they may have paved the way for a form of Asian proto-nationalism that became apparent only much later on.

In sum, what this literature suggests is that there are different ways of conceptualizing the historical development of merchant empires, and the role of regional merchants in long-distance trade. Rather than focusing on the rise of the West, and the subordination of the Ottoman, Mughal, and Safavid empires to European material civilization, there is mounting evidence that the economies and societies of Asia operated on a dynamic that was peculiarly their own, and for a long time held the forces of an expansionist Europe at bay. Thus, the emergence of alternative or secondary markets, the transport of bulk goods as well as luxuries, the socioeconomic differentiation of merchants and their increasing occupational specialization, the establishment of commercial monopolies as an arm of new regional elites, and most significant of all, the unity of commercial networks over vast distances—all these features of the preindustrial economy existed prior to 1750, and have been commented upon at length by the revisionist scholarship of the Indian Ocean.

This book aims to provide a contribution to this on-going research by concentrating on the eighteenth and nineteenth-century history of the regional market that grew up around Iraq, Arabia, and the Gulf. Many of the theoretical points discussed above could equally be made for the commercial zone that spanned the Arabian peninsula, Kuwait, southern Iraq, and Arabistan (now Khuzistan). Here, too, local ports and market towns formed the backbone for a strong regional trading network that bought, sold, and transshipped goods to India. The mercantile community was diverse, grouping everything from poor tribesmen taking one horse to market to landed merchants living in grandiose mansions on the Basra riverfront, and trading in pearls, slaves, and dates. The organization of long-distance trade followed the seasons—especially the monsoon months, during which sailing to India and back became feasible—but it also incorporated local shipping technology, maritime contracts, compacts of partnership, long-distance credit, an assortment of local and international currencies and barter. The relationship between merchants and the state was just as complex. Although the state loomed as a threat in many merchants' eyes (particularly when its agents confiscated merchant fortunes or imposed forced loans on the mercantile community) it could also be a partner, and a facilitator in commercial operations. What, then, was the underlying dynamic of mercantile societies in Iraq, Arabia, and the Gulf in the eighteenth and nineteenth centuries, and what were the methods by which preindustrial trade networks survived in a highly competitive, and sometimes hostile environment?

The answers to these, and other questions, must lie in a reformulation of the whole nature of regional trade in the Indian Ocean. This book is itself a preliminary attempt in the reconceptualization of the socioeconomic history of one corner of this region. Its chief premise is that during the eighteenth and nineteenth centuries, regional networks of trade tied tribal markets in Najd to the markets and port of lower Iraq (Sūq al-Shuyūkh, Zubair, Khamīsiyya, and Basra), which in turn provided most of the foodstuffs and articles of clothing necessary for Kuwait and Arabistan (Ḥuwaiza and Muḥammara); that this network stretched all the way to western India and formed a major part of the commerce of the Indian Ocean region, and that as a result of the interconnection of disparate and far-flung districts from eastern Arabia to India, regional merchants sustained a large economic region with a wide array of local, regional and international goods, and were in turn provided with the funds and markets required to conduct their extensive business on a transnational basis.

Up to a few years ago, the prevailing opinion in scholarly circles was that pre-industrial trade networks in Asia were not able to cohere into a viable economic system because of physical, environmental, or political reasons. For instance, long-distance trade frequently came to a halt because of climatological problems connected with land and sea passage, recurrent epidemics of cholera or plague, or arbitrary government exactions all along the chief trade routes.[25] Merchants faced droughts and swarms of locusts that destroyed crops, tribal raids that fleeced them of capital, or governmental monopolies of scarce resources. Nonetheless, they fought back. While it is undoubtedly true that floods, famines, and military invasions incurred huge costs for merchants in terms of lost capital, commodities, or labor, the elasticity of pre-modern trade can be gauged by such widely practiced traditions as assimilating "protection" costs levied by state agents in mercantile operations, or decentralizing production so that more regions attained self-sufficiency.[26] Above all, the flexibility of commercial networks is apparent in the creation by merchants of alternative routes of trade, or secondary markets.

The interconnection of land and sea routes in the mid-eighteenth to nineteenth centuries was due in part to the rise and development of strategically placed market towns and trading centers, themselves the result of historically strong commercial links spanning a wide economic region. That market towns were the prime movers for the integration of trade on a regional scale is clear from their dual function. On the one hand, regional centers of trade afforded merchants opportunities to make profits; on the other, in their guise as free ports, they served as refuge from oppressive governmental taxation, and provided access to scarce commodities as well as ready channels for the transfer of blocked goods. While they initially may have been built to take advantage of thriving commercial routes, these markets were nonetheless easily abandoned by their regional clientele when the same routes declined, or were obstructed for a variety of reasons. This leads us to suggest that one of the strategies of this trading region involved the active rerouting of trade from blocked markets to alternative venues.

Besides the integrationist tendencies of regional markets, a second facet of trade was the establishment of family firms over a wide region. The local literature of the period records instances of merchants amassing large personal fortunes in regional trade even though problems in infrastructure (lack of passable roads and bridges, for instance), chronic plagues, and governmental interference cut into their profits.[27] Merchants were able to survive adversities through family alliances and the posting of relatives to areas as distant from one another as India and central Arabia. By means of a personal stake in the family business, representatives of merchant houses were sometimes able to control and to redirect trade to their own advantage. Even though merchant houses in Aleppo, Najd, or Bombay were often directly allied to the parent firm by kinship and marriage, their interests were not completely parochial in nature. Because of their regional ties and the fact that family members were scattered over a wide economic region, necessity decreed that these interests become regional over time, tied neither to a specific country nor to a set government but ultimately to an international trading community that commanded the access routes from central Arabia to India.

By the early nineteenth century, the commercial ties that consolidated the region's long-distance trade were coming under attack from outside forces, chiefly embodied in the Ottoman governments of Baghdad and Basra, and the emerging alliance of British consuls, merchants, and shippers in Iraq. Thus the second point made by this study concerns the subtle, and frequently covert strategies of communal resistance devised by regional merchants to regain control of transregional trade in the face of the concerted socioeconomic challenges thrown up by Ottoman or British agents from the middle of the nineteenth century onwards. Whether this resistance consisted of urban boycotts, contraband, or rural insurrections, it nonetheless emerged from the very diversity and flexibility of the regional market spanning Iraq, Arabia, and the Gulf. Again, the strategies devised by local merchants to retain some influence over the processes of regional trade have been passed over by the majority of scholars of Iraq and the Gulf, who prefer to continue dwelling on the phenomenal rise of the region's seaborne exports to India and Britain from 1864 onwards, and the "dynamic" revitalization of the local economy by means of the upsurge in foreign trade.[28] While the whole, convoluted issue of the impact of foreign trade on the developing economies of the region requires further examination, one aspect in particular urgently needs redefinition. Until very recently, most historians did not question the *process* of the incorporation of the economies of the periphery into the world market, preferring instead to dwell on the aftereffects of the Western impact on the developing societies of the Middle East, Latin America, and Africa. Their interest was confined to explaining the rapid transformation of these economies *after* the impingement of an industrializing West in search of raw materials, a free supply of labor, and cheap markets.[29] And yet, it is obvious that the manner and degree in which the economies of the periphery were suborned to the world market is as important an issue as the fact of their eventual (and very uneven) incorporation. By analyzing the crucial period between 1840–1860 in which British attempts to penetrate regional networks of trade met with resistance, and, in some cases, outright insubordination, this book attempts to function as a corrective, laying stress on the resiliency and endurance of regional networks of trade in a century in which local initiative has all but been written off, and in which the internal history of Asian trade has been submerged in the larger global threnody of the "impact of the West."

The organization of the book is as follows. The Introduction begins by situating the book squarely within a historiographic survey of the literature on Indian Ocean trade, and delineates the central arguments of the book. The first chapter then attempts a definition of core concepts used throughout the work, such as "region," and "borders," both according to the secondary (i.e., American and European) sources, and the primary scholarship, that is, the Arabic sources of eighteenth and nineteenth-century Iraq and Arabia. Regional frontiers were bitterly fought over by merchants and migrating tribes in Arabia, the Gulf and Iraq, as local notables and officeholders struggled to retain control of frontier zones in the face of powerful new religious-political movements (the Wahhabis) and the centralizing Ottoman Empire. Chapter 2 analyzes the structure of the regional market; it situates the component parts of the market within a regional framework of production and trade and discusses the specific contributions of each locality to this transnational trading network, whether this consisted of grain, dates or horses. Chapter 3 analyses the growing influence of the two external powers in the area, the Ottoman Empire and Great Britain. It revolves around the question of state centralization, and the transformation of Ottoman relations with the provinces of Iraq as well as with the Arabian littoral and the shaikhdoms in the Gulf. Although the core of the chapter consists of an appraisal of the policy of active Ottoman interference in the regional market's operations, an attempt has also been made to understand the local dynamics of Ottoman government in the provinces of Iraq, where it was a central facet of daily life. This chapter also traces the rising importance of British commercial designs on the economies of Iraq, Arabia, and the Gulf. It deals extensively with the effects, or non-effects, on the provinces of Iraq of what has traditionally been viewed as a major landmark in the commercial history of the region, the Anglo-Turkish Convention of 1838. That the regional market was able to make a shambles of the treaty was due in no small part to the still-influential role of local merchants in regional trade.

Chapters 4 to 7 investigate in detail the rise and fall of local commodities, trade routes and market towns. Chapter 4 studies the manifold attempts by tribes inhabiting the banks of the Tigris and Euphrates to control commercial access to the two rivers. An age-old method of circumventing Ottoman as well as British interference on the twin rivers of Iraq was to delimit areas of tribal hegemony in which foreign intruders were forced to pay imposts. By the mid-nineteenth century these duties served as an excuse for the first serious British attempt to apply the articles of the Anglo-Turkish Convention on riverine trade in Iraq. Eventually British consuls and shippers won the day, and riparian taxation was "reformed" under European duress. Chapter 5 details the struggle over the grain trade in the provinces of Iraq, as Ottoman governors and regional merchants fought to retain control of the sources of grain, and to thwart British efforts to gain access to supply. Although local traders and their Ottoman allies were able to maintain a tenuous domination of the trade in food grains until the late 1850s, by the last quarter of the century, the world market had succeeded in making substantial inroads into the regional supply, thus destroying local control. Chapter 6 analyzes the development, and eventual demise, of the horse trade with India. In contrast with the grain trade, the trade in horses remained important only through the nineteenth century; for after gasoline began to power automobiles and lorries, military transport no longer hinged on the sale and shipment of Arabian horses to British India. Nonetheless, the struggle over the control of the sale of horses occupied a significant place in the annals of British-Ottoman trade history. Finally, Chapter 7 investigates the continuing phenomenon of shaikhs/regional merchants building alternative market towns in southern Iraq in order to reorient trade away from burgeoning centers of foreign trade, such as Ottoman Basra. Although the institution of secondary markets was an eighteenth as well as nineteenth-century commercial tradition, by the 1870s and 1880s Ottoman governors had entered the fray, building towns around compliant shaikhs who had agreed to settle "their" tribesmen in return for an Ottoman title, customs house and military garrison. With the institution of state-sponsored towns in the Muntafiq and northern Iraq, a vital regional tradition came to an end, ushering in a period fraught with tensions that affect us still.

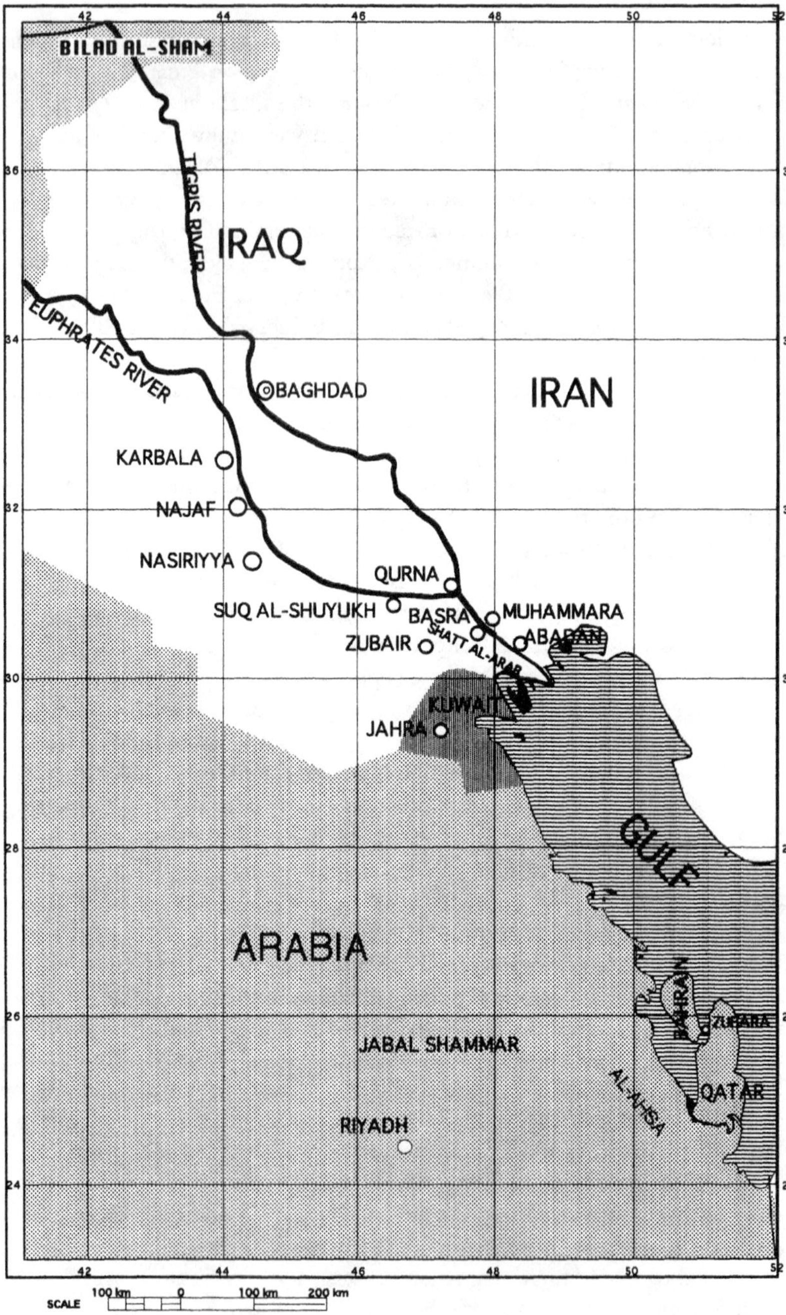

Map of Iraq, Arabia, and the Gulf

-One-

A Regional World: 1745–1900

Historically, the region encompassing southern Iraq, Kuwait, eastern and central Arabia, and Arabistan (Khuzistan) was interlinked by a number of distinct and sometimes contradictory impulses. On the one hand, it was home to a number of different ethnic, religious, and sectarian communities, most of whose inhabitants had developed broad ties of trade and exchange with each other, which allowed them to cross and re-cross each other's space in order to pursue their business. On the other hand, it was host to frequent social, economic and political tensions, emanating from the very configuration of settlement patterns, religious attitudes, and economic activities that characterized the region as a whole.

Any examination of these contrary, but not mutually exclusive, impulses must begin with a proper appreciation of the principal features of the period, the overwhelming dynamic that gave the region its coherence in spite of the many vicissitudes that periodically threatened to tear it apart. In the case of societies in Iraq, Arabia, and the Gulf, that dynamic sprang out of the realities of the shifting frontier. The notion of a frontier society connotes fluidity, permeability, access and acculturation—all characteristics that permeated the region at one level or another. It also suggests flux and impermanency, the natural by-product of societies constantly in the throes of formation, making and remaking themselves to suit the particular circumstances of the moment.

Although the region in question possessed no real frontiers or borders in a modern, jurisdictional sense, frontiers certainly existed in Arabia, Iraq, and the Gulf. Unlike the early Islamic period,[1] however, the concepts of *thughūr* or *ʿawaṣim* (which Arab geographers used to connote frontiers in the period of the first Islamic conquests) were rarely used in the historiography of the eighteenth century, even though by the mid-nineteenth century the term, *ḥudūd* (frontiers) had begun to make a comeback in the literature of Ottoman Iraq.[2] Nevertheless, even while the terminology of frontiers may have been in temporary abeyance in the eighteenth century, regional shaikhs, merchants, and commanders continued to draw and re-draw the contours of regional society by creating physical frontiers across a large area. It is quite possible, therefore, that the concept of frontiers was articulated in a different manner than in the earlier centuries, and focused more on creating new facts on the ground than on erecting ideologically-generated barriers between *dār al-ḥarb* (the realm of war) and *dār al-Islām* (the realm of Islam).[3] For instance, merchants throughout Arabia and the Gulf carved out economic zones defended by tribal irregulars, and obliged all but their allies to pay imposts to use their facilities; *ʿulamāʾ* (scholar) warriors such as the second generation of leaders of the Saūd family in Arabia forced submission on defeated tribes by making them pay the *zakāt* (alms tax); and Mamluk military commanders in eighteenth-century Iraq widened their revenue net by confiscating horses or grain from tribesmen in undemarcated no-man's-land between Ottoman Iraq and Safavid Persia. In each of these instances, frontiers were created that had to be defended at all costs; whether they were labelled as such may ultimately not be that significant an issue.

How was the dynamic of frontier-making played out in the eighteenth and nineteenth centuries? What were the circumstances that impelled certain merchant families, religious leaders, or military commanders to overturn existing frontier arrangements and create their own territorial order? What were the resource bases of these new frontiers-in-the-making, and what religious or moral sanction legitimized these undertakings? Since there is no real methodology of frontiers or regions in either the secondary or primary Arabic materials, perhaps the best way to substantiate, and contextualize the notion of an Iraqī/Gulf region is to draw on the ideas and insights of an earlier generation of American and European historians whose contributions to the literature on frontiers and regions occupy pride of place in the historiography on space, nation-formation and state-building. This historiography can be divided into two trends. On the one hand, William H. McNeill's pioneering studies on the European and American frontier[4] propounded the idea of a global, shifting frontier based on the spread of trade or cultivation, the scarcity of labor in the frontier areas, the development of slavery or peonage as a consequence of the frontiersman's urge to exploit his patch of wilderness, and the resulting stratification of society into the propertied few and the landless majority. On the other hand, another tradition exists, largely central to European historiography, of frontiers delimiting amorphous, protonationalist entities such as France or middle Europe. Authors such as Peter Sahlins and R. J. W. Evans have traced the various permutations in the ideology of the frontier from the Middle Ages to the beginning of the twentieth century, and have concluded that the idea of the frontier in Europe shifted radically in response to political, economic, and demographic factors.[5]

FRONTIERS, BORDERS, AND BOUNDARIES: A REVIEW OF THE LITERATURE

Sahlins believes that the evolution of the concept of natural frontiers was tied as much to the exigencies of French state policy (especially in its expansionist seventeenth-century phase) as to an officially-sponsored "idea" of France. Natural frontiers were those delimited by mountain ranges, indented trees, streams or even stones. Even though a consensus existed on what the concept meant in certain periods of French history, at other times its meaning shifted dramatically, especially from the seventeenth century onwards. To begin with, there was a linguistic differentiation between the term, "frontiers" and that of *limites* (boundaries); the first dated from the thirteenth century when

> the French monarchy began to take account of the "frontier" of the Kingdom as distinct from the jurisdictional boundaries of its suzerainity. The frontier was that which, etymologically and politically, "stood face to" an enemy. This military frontier, implying bellicose expansion and a zonal defense, stood opposed to the linear boundary or line of demarcation—the *limites* of jurisdictions or territories.

While an earlier generation had viewed natural frontiers as a limiting force, enclosing French space within distinct and defensible markers such as streams, trees or even trenches, with the advent of French expansionist policy in the seventeenth century, the philosophy of natural boundaries changed. As a result, rivers or mountains were no longer viewed as insurmountable barriers but as

> obstacles to be conquered—and passageways to be controlled—by establishing strongholds beyond them. As such, the idea of natural frontiers helped determine short and long-term policy decisions. . . . Natural frontiers were important to the French crown not as boundaries but as passages, and it was the plenipotentiaries of the empire who insisted on the Rhine as marking the separation of France from the empire.[7]

Eventually, the principle of natural frontiers was recognized by the Treaty of Utrecht in 1714 and took on all the appurtenances of law. By the end of the eighteenth century, a line of fortresses was established, separating France from Germany, and marking the first attempt at creating a linear frontier between the two countries. Even though France's "national" borders had not yet been completely demarcated by that period (for the provinces of Lorraine and Savoy had yet to be annexed to the rest of the country), the creation of France's first defensive border pushed the country onto the next stage of frontier-making, that of internal consolidation. Because of the competition between local powers and the embryonic French state, France's frontiers were "riddled with enclaves, exclaves, overlapping and contested jurisdictions, and other administrative nightmares."[8] The centralizing state had to reorder its internal frontiers before it could even think of outward expansion. With state interest supporting their venture, cartographers now came into their own, and mapmaking became an arm of French policy, as a result of which France was finally thrust into the position of demarcating its national frontiers. Although these territorial frontiers were to be challenged in the last decade of the eighteenth century (with the French Revolution adopting a "minimalist" position on state expansion), by the middle of the nineteenth century, the ideology of France's natural frontiers had become "a given," an unquestioned and absolute fact which was taught to French school children as if it required no excuse or explanation.

Adding definition to Sahlins' argument, and basing himself on the history of central Europe, R. J. W. Evans contrasts the meaning of the term "frontier" with that of "border" and "boundary." According to him

> A frontier is, etymologically, what "fronts" on another territory, or on the wilderness, with the strong implication in present-day parlance of a major, national, inter-state demarcation. But the meaning subsumes lesser, more localized meanings, and the whole terminology of the subject is correspondingly overlapping and imprecise. . . . Whatever the term used, the idea of a border was at once fluid and firm. On the one hand, the frontier was a vague and perhaps shifting no-man's-land, essentially imprecise, and frequently associated with topographical barriers of mountain, forest, or swamp. On the other hand, it was physically bound, from the large-scale *limes,* dyke, or row of prominent stones, to small and inconspicuous local markers. . . .[9]

Frontiers may have initially developed out of ecclesiastical concerns (such as "those French dioceses which derived from provincial organization in Roman Gaul"[10]) or out of legal, social or cultural matters (such as village law-codes or jurisdictions). Most of all, the author believes that they took shape because of economic factors such as agricultural patterns or aspects of production and trade. Even though "state" frontiers possessed a certain flexibility, at times subsuming "lesser borders" while at other times changing radically because of "war, inheritance, or exchange"

> local boundaries and lesser jurisdictions usually remained intact. . . . We can think of the whole development as a palimpsest of civil and ecclesiastical borders, whose lowest layers were almost always long-standing and broadly accepted (even when fiercely disputed in detail). . . .[11]

Evans echoes Sahlins' point by asserting that as European authorities developed a more centralized, military frontier, and sought to strengthen their hand against local potentates throughout their realm, natural frontiers gave way to artificial frontiers. The act of drawing arbitrary lines on a map, instead of following the contours of a rocky slope, solved a number of problems for centralizing governments, rationalizing state operations by doing away with the shibboleths and obsolete traditions that were behind most of frontier ideology in seventeenth-century Europe, and acting as strategic depth for military campaigns.[12] In fact, the military-strategic factor became an important issue, and figured prominently in the Treaty of Carlowitz between Ottoman Turkey and the Hapsburg Empire in 1699. As a result of the treaty, a whole new frontier was created and adapted to military requirements and

> The entire area along and behind the inter-state demarcation on the Austrian side became an official *Militargrenze,* directly subordinated to the needs of the army and ignoring the social and administrative structure of the customary manorial system; and it really meant business, enforcing strict quarantine for travellers from Turkey. . . . Here was the most formidable frontier which Central Europe had probably ever seen, at least since the days of the Romans, and one organized on novel principles, with strong central control . . . most of the arrangements endured, with further modifications, until the 1870s. . . .[13]

During the French Revolution and the Napoleonic era, two concurrent developments took place: the internal reorganization of France's domestic boundaries (the *départements)* on rational lines, and the mapping out of France's external frontiers.[14] This was finally followed in 1848, with the emergence of the "ethnic frontier." Whereas prior to the nineteenth century, ethnicity had never been significant in frontier-making, the rise of "linguistic identity" reshaped the European frontier as nothing else before.[15] Ethnic identity and language became the principles which undergirded the emergence of the nation-state in late nineteenth century Europe and, for that reason, became the all-consuming passion of the period after the First World War. One important difference remained, however. Evans points out that even as it functioned as the ideology of nation-states throughout Europe, and eventually the rest of the world, ethnicity remained *only* an ideology that states paid lip service to in times of national crisis; it was ultimately disregarded in favor of the more concrete military and strategic principles that were the true shapers of the early twentieth-century European frontier.

While Sahlins and Evans clearly trace the many permutations of the idea of "the frontier" in European history, the main problem of this genre of frontier studies is that it is too narrowly focused on the rise of the modern nation-state. As a result of this concentration, the whole issue of frontiers is ineluctably viewed through the prism of state-centered history. Nowhere is there an appreciation of the almost seasonal contention over pasturelands or agricultural districts that characterized most of the pre-industrial frontier-making of an earlier age. This last development is considered almost vestigial, and an anachronism that naturally gave way to the overwhelming superiority of the national frontier. Thus even while both Sahlins and Evans assert their belief in the concept of a fluctuating frontier conditioned by ideological, socioeconomic and political factors not entirely under state control, their studies actually gloss over the significance of the pre-industrial frontier, and consign it to primeval impulses that soon withered away with the coming of nationalism.

While Sahlins and Evans analyze the frontier principle only with respect to Europe, McNeill uses the whole world as his canvas, and propounds a truly global vision of the frontier by extrapolating from his research on central Europe to analyze frontier societies in North and South America, and China. Starting with his *Europe's Steppe Frontier* and terminating with *The Great Frontier,* McNeill proposes a schema whereby the Eurasian steppe frontier—an "empty" no-man's-land alternating between nomadism and cultivation, minor, polyethnic kingdoms and large land empires, sabres and guns, and freedom and compulsion—underwent a series of expansions and contractions that finally fixed it by the eighteenth century. Beginning with the premise that a thinly-populated frontier could never be a credible line of defense, he suggests that as soon as peasant communities in the agricultural rim of Europe were able to organize themselves into a successful bulwark against horse-nomads such as the Crim Tartars and later on, the Ottoman cavalry, the frontier began to assume shape.[16] The author cautions us that the creation of what was to become the central European frontier was a slow and unquestionably violent process, proceeding through fits and starts, and provoking intra-European strife as much as it stirred anti-Ottoman energies. Thus, the turmoil within Europe was just as ruinous as the off-and-on wars with the Ottoman armies; with Christian warlords in Hungary concentrating their attacks on their own peasantry at the same time as they arrayed themselves against Ottoman soldiers, and Moldavian princes preferring to recognize Ottoman suzerainty rather than succumb to either Hungary or Poland.[17] After the seventeenth-century "time of troubles" subsided, a period which saw the exhaustion of the "Ottoman expansive capacity," and the frittering away of military and political gains in Austria, Poland, Russia, Wallachia, Moldavia, a newer, tighter constellation of European alliances restructured the frontier to suit their interests.

Despite McNeill's rather unsubtle description of the Ottoman Empire as a collossus which foundered on its own inadaptability,[18] the rest of his thesis is on sturdier ground. The seventeenth century is taken as the starting point for the entry of two new forces: the emergence of a more compact, better-organized army in Austria, Hungary, and Transylvania, which established an alternative model to the heretofore-organized anarchy of the Cossack brigades on the Russian and Polish frontier; and the rise of autocratic government in Russia. These two developments had the effect of concretizing the frontier into a more or less defensible line, around which military autocracies and standing armies could take up firmer positions. At the same time as the military authority of the competing states on the border became more entrenched, a more novel educational system began to expose the ruling class of central and northern Europe to a more egalitarian world-view. Thus, nearly everywhere in Europe, more rigorous schooling was instituted, usually at the behest of an active Jesuit priesthood; and while this form of education catered in the main to the upper classes, the middle classes and in some instances even the peasantry were inducted into this Catholic-inspired educational system. The inference here is that eventually a near-universal educational system sowed the seeds for a more "national" curriculum in the schools, and reshaped the idea of the frontier even further.

Moreover, with the end of the massive Ottoman campaigns that had embroiled the central and northern European states in an almost-permanent state of siege, the frontier zone "became once more capable of sustaining settled agricultural populations."[19] New standing armies replaced undisciplined frontier irregulars; taxes, not plunder, became the base of the professional army and commercialized agriculture and trade brought more revenue to the state, which redistributed it to the army and the new, centralizing bureaucracy in the Hapsburg Empire and later on in Russia. With the growth and consolidation of the "limitrophe" empires (Austria under the Hapsburgs and Russia under Peter the Great), it was only a matter of time before the "interstitial polities" (Hungary, Transylvania, the Ukraine) were subsumed into one of the large empires, thus marking an end to the independence of the border regions in central and northern Europe, and demarcating the frontier once and for all.

DEPICTIONS OF THE FRONTIER, AND OF THE OTHER IN THE HISTORY OF IRAQ, ARABIA, AND THE GULF

Where the Sahlins/Evans scenario diverges from McNeill's is over the conceptualization of the frontier. The former view it more as a military-strategic line on the map than a region. McNeill's frontier, on the other hand, is composed of multi-ethnic zones where people are constantly rubbing shoulders and socializing with one another, only to find themselves on different sides as unwilling draftees in other peoples' armies. His frontier is a bustling and busy place, constantly being replenished by a diverse population and forever at the mercy of the expansionist designs of various leaders, whether Tartar,

Hungarian, Transylvanian, Austrian or Russian. In this respect, McNeill's contentious frontier, in which a host of different regional principalities and empires-in-the-making assert and re-assert their tenuous control over large, poorly-inhabited zones of grasslands and subsistence agriculture, is a model that fits in well with parts of the central Arabian and Iraqī landscape. The most important thing about it is its assumption that, throughout the fifteenth to nineteenth centuries, both in Europe and in other parts of the globe, there was never one frontier but many different frontiers. In the main, these were untidy clusters of settlements contiguous to other, equally sprawling but poorly-inhabited zones of population, whose inhabitants were never completely independent of one another, even though they may have been moulded by different regimes of production, social norms, and political structures. Although at times violently intrusive upon one another, the occupants of these frontier societies also influenced each other to a great degree. McNeill's frontier is therefore a permeable, cross-cultural passage, a middle ground in which socio-cultural and technological acculturation continues to take place until the beginning of the twentieth century.

Although the secondary literature on frontiers and on the workings of regional societies in Iraq, Arabia, and the Gulf is nowhere as explicit, nor even as voluminous as the European or American historiography on the subject, the primary literature in Arabic suggests that some of McNeill's, Sahlins', and Evans' theoretical points do in fact clarify a number of features pertaining to this large region abutting on to the Indian Ocean. In particular, the notion of a frontier as a defensive belt of territory "fronting" onto another jurisdiction is important; it implies that all frontier-making, whether entered into by shahs or sultans, provincial governors, tribal merchants or cultivators, possessed a common military-political dimension which translated into notions of inclusion/exclusion. Thus, in the eighteenth century, tribal irregulars secured the frontiers of desert settlements in central Arabia; was that any different from the organized armies sent out to defend the Iraq-Iran frontier in the sixteenth century? Both aimed at excluding foreign elements from their territory, and both sought to contain the inhabitants of their respective domains within well-defined territorial spheres as tributaries of the "state." While there is a school of thought that continues to see imperial frontiers, i.e., the military-strategic zones carved out by the Ottoman and Safavid empires in the sixteenth and seventeenth centuries, as radically different from the "borders" or "boundaries" demarcated by tribal shaikhs and local office holders, it may be that the similarities between both notions of frontier-making far outweighed the differences. For even though Ottoman or Safavid armies secured the outermost frontiers of their empires at the behest of imperial rulers, and even though the bureaucracy of these empires registered these frontier zones as revenue-producing districts from which stipulated taxes were to be paid to the imperial treasury, the only real difference between imperial frontiers and local ones may have been a difference of perception.

While a fuller explanation will be attempted later on in the chapter, suffice it to say that when the history of the region is viewed from the perspective of tribal merchants or shaikhs, there were no "lesser" borders or boundaries in Iraq, Arabia, and the Gulf; there were only constantly evolving frontiers that were defined from within the region according to the socio-economic and military-political context of the moment.

A reading of the literature of the period reinforces this depiction of frontiers as polyglot, ethnically diverse regions. It suggests that most of Iraqīi/Gulf society coalesced around a region of shifting frontiers that stretched from central Arabia to western India. This is evidenced by the fact that a substantial number of the local histories written in eighteenth and nineteenth-century Iraq, Arabia, and the Gulf were of a transregional nature, written most often by ʿulamāʾ whose places of origin may have been almost incidental in the larger scheme of things, but whose real contribution lay in the description of the other districts and regions that formed the body of their work. Because of their frequent journeys in search of knowledge throughout the Islamic East, their histories bore all the imprints of the travelling scholar; their insights and observations therefore can be used to reconstruct a partial picture of the social and political context of the region. This is particularily true with regard to merchants; for even while some ʿulamāʾ thought trade a lowly occupation, and considered merchants unworthy of biographical notices (a particular idiosyncrasy of certain "high" ʿulamāʾ in the towns of the interior, who confined themselves instead to recording the obituaries of governors, religious scholars, and town notables),[20] other ʿulamā,ʾ especially those from Basra, Arabistan, and Najd, included merchant biographies in their histories almost as a matter of course.

Because direct references to regions, frontiers, and borders are rare in the Arabic primary literature, any theory that attempts to encapsulate the workings of an identifiable region must take its cue from McNeill's "empty" frontier and infer the existence of a region-in-the-making from scattered textual allusions to zones of material and cultural exchange situated in or around centers of agricultural settlement, places of worship, or ports of trade. Best conceptualized as swaths of territory that functioned as passages instead of barriers, the permeable and fluctuating frontiers that emerged as a result eventually demarcated zones of settlement at the interstices of former military camps (Basra), near the burial ground of Muslim saints (Zubair) or on the edge of coastlines (Kuwait). Taking this as our point of departure, we can then deduce the importance of an integrated region from the very methodology employed in the historical texts. For instance, Najdī literary sources mention events not normally within the purview of central Arabia proper as if they had a direct bearing on the society's development. Thus, factional struggles in Iraqī towns or villages are sometimes inserted in the middle of narratives concerning Najd, as if they naturally belonged in the same narrative sequence.[21] Plagues in Baghdad and Basra are given long, horrific descriptions by Saūdī historians, just as the Persian siege of Basra in 1775 is detailed in depth.[22]

However, the interesting thing is that most of these accounts are interspersed between references to Saūdī campaigns in central Najd. From a literary point of view, it would seem that the events recorded by Najdī historians may be more than incidental allusions to noteworthy events; they could well be clues to the practical reality which underlay these regional histories. In effect, eighteenth and nineteenth-century Najdī historians conceptualized a large region in which events occurring in neighboring societies were of more than passing interest, for very often these same events, in Iraq or Kuwait or elsewhere, may have significantly affected the daily lives of Najdīs. In much the same way, historians of Basra normally included events in Najd, Kuwait, and Muhammara in their chronicles. As a result, regional market towns in Arabistan and Najd were sometimes given more importance than Baghdad, and historians of Basra seemed to be more conversant with the names of Kuwaiti landholders in south Iraq than with those of Mosul in the north.[23] On very rare occasions, the parameters of the region were even widened to include merchants from India; admittedly, however, local historians only seemed to refer to India-based merchants when the latter transgressed social norms (such as taking refuge in saint's sanctuaries in Wahhābī Arabia).[24] As time went on, popular culture assimilated this social reality, and gave voice to it through poetry and other forms of oral expression. One Najdī proverb sums it up best in the following manner: "Al-Hindu Hinduka᾽ idhā qalla mā ᾽indaka wa al-Shāmu Shāmuka᾽ idhā al-dahru dhammaka" [India is yours if you have lost most of your possessions and Syria is yours if fate has been unkind to you].[25]

For our purpose, there are at least two ways that a concept of the frontier can be formulated in eighteenth and nineteenth-century Iraq, Arabia, and the Gulf. Basing ourselves on the greater historiography of the region, we can label one approach the agricultural and trade settlements model, and the other the moral-territorial hypothesis. On one level, there is evidence that a full three centuries prior to the emergence of the Wahhābī movement in the mid-eighteenth century, tribal expansion, urban settlement, and intellectual efflorescence paved the way for the rise of the most dynamic revivalist movement in central Arabia.[26] Tribal migration from Najd had an impact on societies in Iraq and the Gulf as well, as "newer" tribal confederations from central Arabia pushed out "older" communities from northern and southern Iraq, at the same time that other tribal sections established principalities in Kuwait and Qatar. In Iraq, tribal expansion was met with fierce government resistance, as Ottoman representatives in Baghdad and Basra attempted to impose imperial order on the wave of tribal migrants and settlers from the south. As a result of this conflict, a secondary clash developed between the tribal frontier, the *dīra,* and the Ottoman political frontier. This clash was endowed with religious symbology in the historical texts of the period, as historians attempted to invest the imperial frontier with "higher" moral properties, and to denigrate the seemingly spurious claims of tribal shaikhs and merchants in the process.

On another level, the polemics of the Wahhābī movement in the mid-eighteenth to early part of the nineteenth centuries gave rise to a subsidiary exchange between historians in the region in which territories were delimited, routes were monopolized and frontiers were defined. As a result of the Wahhābīs' frontal assault on the religious traditions and practices of the region as a whole, and their claim to a higher moral authority embodied in the principles of a more rigorous *Salafī*-inspired Islam, historians of Wahhābī Arabia, Iraq, and the Gulf clashed in print over which polity, the Saʿūdī state or Mamluk Iraq, had jurisdiction over certain frontier districts in the region. Thus, both as a result of the material encroachment of agricultural settlements and trade routes on the Najdī heartland and the migration of Najdī tribes to Iraq, as well as the intellectual currents that swirled in the region both as a result of the imposition of Ottoman control on Iraq and the Wahhābī revival, a "frontierless" region began to take on definition and shape. This frontier-making imperative was directly linked with depictions of "the other," and littered with direct or indirect allusions to the ethnic, religious, and sectarian communities that made up the author's world. Even though most historians tended to disparage the "otherness" of the communities that settled in their space, many of whom practiced distinctive occupations, followed divergent religious interpretations, or belonged to different linguistic minorities, they included them in their narratives all the same. In fact, only through such descriptions can present-day historians begin to even infer the larger complex picture of regional society in Iraq, Arabia, and the Gulf; so it is to the primary literature that we now turn.

TRIBAL MIGRATION, TRIBAL SETTLEMENT, AND THE "GREENING" OF ARABIA c.1400–1800

The pioneering work of Uwaidah al-Juhany on pre-Wahhābī Najd proposes a novel schema whereby nomadic expansion, and the settlement (and resettlement) of towns on trade routes and near oases in turn gave rise to a movement of urbanization that eventually sponsored an unprecedented intellectual efflorescence throughout central Arabia.[27] The most frequent reasons for the migration of tribes from the south-west to the north and east, and their reconfiguration into different confederations were climatological and ecological changes such as droughts, plagues, attacks by locusts, or crop failures.[28] Among the earliest groups to migrate were the important tribal leagues of the ʿAnayza and Zhāfir; these began their northeastern expansion as early as the middle of the fifteenth century.[29] By the seventeenth century, they had been joined by other famous tribal confederations, such as the Shammar, Muṭair, and Banū Khālid.

The constant movement of migration and re-migration of central Arabian tribes to greener pastures was not carried out without a struggle over grazing land and water rights; on the contrary, there was an intense conflict over the most significant pasture lands, setting into motion a movement whereby weaker tribes allied themselves with more powerful ones in order to retain some control of the available resources in Najd. This push to confederate into larger tribal principalities was a natural reflex that drew its strength from the never-ending tribal wars over territory; and one of its unexpected results was that those older nomadic confederations that had been pushed out of their ancestral grazing lands began to make the trek into neighboring Iraq.[30] Among the most important was the Banū Lām, whose journey from Najd to Iraq took close to a century to complete; by the eighteenth century, they had become the successful occupants of the fertile districts of the eastern Tigris, on the borders of Iran.

One of al-Juhany's significant conclusions is that nomadic and semi-nomadic groups were the major force behind the expansion of towns in Najd. By and large, towns were not instituted by sedentary tribesmen because the latter were relatively few in number; in fact, their numbers increased only with the settlement of Najdī pastoralists in the century and a half prior to the birth of the Wahhābī movement. The first reconstituted tribal settlements were established in the districts of al-Washm and Sudair (northern Najd) in or around the sixteenth century;[32] but in that first wave of expansion, other notable towns were instituted, the most important of which were Darʾiyya, later on the chef lieu of the Wahhābī movement, and ʿUyayna. It was only in the seventeenth century, however, that sedentarization really took hold in central and eastern Arabia. In fact, al-Juhany concludes that "by the middle of the twelfth/eighteenth century, the demographic map of Najd became completely different from that which had prevailed before the ninth/fifteenth. century."[33]

While the majority of these settlements eked out a tenuous livelihood from the cultivation of food crops, especially dates, some townlets actually prospered from agriculture, so much so that the leadership of some of the latter towns began to fight over the surplus, meager though it was. Eventually the defeated tribal sections were turned away, which forced them to establish their own settlements elsewhere. For instance, in the year 1300, the al-Wahba of ʾUshayqir locked the gates of the town against the Banū Wāʾil and then expelled them with these words:

> These are your women and this is your property. We have no claims on them; we are only frightened of the consequences that may soon arise between us, so leave this town while we are still friends. Whosoever possesses date plantations, let him appoint an agent to take over their cultivation until the harvest, and whosoever has other property, let him also take on an agent. If any of you would like to come back for trade purposes, you are free to do so. We are only anxious that you might overtake the town, and become the majority.[34]

The Banū Wāʾil left and settled elsewhere, and one of their tribal sections established "the famous town of Hirma" in or around 1386 as an agricultural settlement built around an oasis.[35] Similarly, the town of al-Majmaʾa was built by a Shammarī shaikh in 1417; its population grew very fast, and became very diverse, even attracting sections from the ʿAnayza tribe. Eventually the leadership of the town built a mosque, wells, and plantations; the whole town was later on made into a *waqf* (endowment) for the upkeep of the mosque. In the fifteenth century, other towns such as al-ʾUyayna, al-Ẓarma, al-Mulaybid and al-Ghuṣayba were built in central Najd, to be followed by Buraida(1541), al-Ḥuraymilā (1635), and finally the most significant town of all, Darʾiyya (1726).[36]

Thus, from the fifteenth to the mid-eighteenth centuries, Najdī society witnessed an urban revival. New confederations of nomadic pastoralists elbowed out defeated tribes and established undisputed sway over oases and date plantations, building new settlements over the remains of older ones, and carving out new frontier zones in Najd in the process. These fluctuating frontiers were defended by force against outsiders, and legitimized through the paramount shaikh's patronage of weaker sections and tribes, some of whom settled in the new towns, even though very frequently they had no direct family links to the founding tribe.

THE ESTABLISHMENT OF FREE PORTS IN THE GULF

The migration and settlement of Najdī tribes was also a phenomenon that affected eastern Arabia and southern Iraq. Again, overpopulation, poverty, warfare and starvation pushed Najdī tribes to the coast, where they founded a number of important settlements. In fact, as a result of this in-migration from central Arabia, the region as a whole witnessed the proliferation of many market towns, both large and small, which took their cue from the dramatic upsurge in the building of settlements in pre-Wahhābī Najd itself. Even though climatological adversity was responsible for the creation of many new settlements, a clear pattern emerges of shaikhs-entrepreneurs instituting towns to serve as markets for a large semi-nomadic clientele, founding them on the main routes of trade from Najd to Iraq or Syria.

The growth of urbanization in the Arabian peninsula and the Gulf entailed a number of patterns, chief of which was the phenomenon of tribal "secession,"[37] or the voluntary withdrawal of a substantial part of the population from the paramount shaikh's authority in order to found towns elsewhere. Because certain tribal sections disagreed with the ruling shaikh's actions or pronouncements, migration and resettlement became a realistic option. Although instances of once-disgruntled clans returning to their original abodes are available in the literature, a substantial number of sectional chiefs became independent of their former tribes and went on to build, or resettle "new" towns in Arabia and the Gulf. In this respect, a mid-nineteenth observer's comments underline what could only have been a continuing development in the region:

> It is by no means uncommon for one of the branches of a tribe, to the number sometimes of several hundred individuals, in order to escape excessive taxation and oppression, or with a view to secure to themselves greater immunities and advantages, to secede from the authority and territory of their lawful and acknowledged chief into that of another, or to establish themselves and build a fort on some other spot and assert and maintain independence; nor is it a matter of great moment that the chief they are about to join, or whose friendship and countenance they must in the first place command, is a rival at implacable feud with their own: the advantages attending any numerical increase of subjects ensure them welcome asylum and protection. It will not escape observation, that the facilities thus mutually offered to seceders on the one hand, and the loss of authority and revenue consequent on their secession on the other, act, vice-versa, as a salutary check to the tyranny and oppression of the respective chiefs. . . .[38]

The examples of Kuwait, Zubara (on the borders of present-day Qatar and Bahrain), and Bahrain highlight this development further. A reading of the literature suggests that by the middle of the eighteenth century a number of settlements had made their appearance in the region. From the eastern Arabian coast to the inner reaches of the peninsula, and stretching all the way into Iraq, tribal *sūqs* or markets emerged to take advantage of the carrying trade of the region. The establishment of these centers of trade had come about, in part, as a result of the migration of pastoral tribes to coastal settlements; facing drought and dessication in their traditional *diyār* (communally-owned pasture lands), as well as periodic raids from rival tribes that left them almost denuded of their livestock, tribal sections of one such confederation, the ʾUtūb,[39] migrated to the coastal outposts of Qatar, Kuwait, and Bahrain. Although no exact date can be given for the migration of the ʾUtūb, it is almost certain that by 1750, regional trade in Arabia and the Gulf had received a boost with the settlement of Qatar, Kuwait and Bahrain by ʾUtbi tribesmen. In the space of a generation, these resourceful and enterprising people completed the transition from camel-herders to seafarers and fishermen, building a fleet of merchant vessels that was unparalleled in the Gulf.

The most important aspect of these trading centers was their lack of a customs administration. In fact, they were established as free ports by regional entrepreneurs to service regional loci of trade. As such, the administrations of these market towns allowed regional merchants the freedom of exchanging and trading their goods without the payment of customs tax to the chief merchant, shaikh, or ruler of the town, thus earning their reputation. Unlike the Ottoman port of Basra, which had a regular customs operation supervised by a *gümrükçü* (customs master) with several clerks to help him tabulate the duties on goods exiting Basra by way of the Shaṭṭ al-ʾArab, the free ports of the eighteenth and nineteenth centuries, illustrated by Kuwait, Qatar, and Bahrain, asked nothing from regional merchants other than a small subsidiary payment for the local shaikh.[40] As a result, regional merchants were attracted to these entrepots in droves, and plied their trades freely in the absence of excessive controls.

Other than Kuwait, the most important free port in the region was Zubara. Established by elements of the ʾUtūb, the same tribes that had a hand in redeveloping Kuwait, Zubara soon became a focal point for the regional trade of the Gulf in the early to mid-eighteenth century. Under the able administration of Shaikh ʾAḥmad ibn Muḥammad ibn Ḥusain ibn Rizq, scion of the important al-Rizq merchant dynasty, Zubara soon became a glittering emporium, known for its quasi-monopoly on pearl trading.[41] Again, because there were no taxes levied on merchants or other sectors of the population, the town not only attracted regional merchants but many ʾulamāʿ as well, who benefited greatly from Ibn Rizq's largesse to the migrating scholarly community of the region.

Of course, the emergence of the free ports of Kuwait, Zubara, and Bahrain were not autonomous developments, but were also conditioned by the external influences brought to bear on the region as a whole. While the frequent wars between Wahhābī Arabia and the Banū Khālid tribes was in large part the backdrop for the emergence of Kuwait and Zubara (discussed elsewhere in the chapter), the Persian challenge remained a constant threat to Bahrain. Still, the ups and downs of regional trade allowed the merchants of these free ports considerable leeway in reorienting transit trade to their door. Thus Kuwait, Bahrain, and Qatar were instrumental in furthering the transit trade that circulated from Arabia to India, as well as the internal trade generated by market towns in the Arabian peninsula, southern Iraq, and Arabistan. Pearls, horses, grain, dates, textiles, glass, coffee, copper and Indian teakwood were bought, sold, and exchanged at Kuwait, Zubara, and other regional markets througout the area. Overland merchants, shippers, and livestock agents tied this regional network together and facilitated access to the region by means of a ready supply of revolving credit and a variety of local and international currencies. Because of the vicissitudes of regional supply (which was often tied to the chronic instability of the market, caused by plagues, droughts, and the military adventures of tribal chieftains), economic survival depended on open and easy access to a wide region in which secondary markets made up for traditional trade centers which became inoperative over time.

The proliferation of these regional emporia or market towns in the eighteenth century Gulf still awaits definitive treatment. For while historians can note the appearance of tribal markets from the eastern Arabian coast to the inner reaches of the peninsula, and correlate that phenomenon with the emergence of other free ports in the Gulf, there are still a number of unanswered questions with regard to the dynamics of the intra-regional trade that produced them in the first place. For instance, there is some debate as to whether regional trade experienced a boom in this period, and whether that boom came about as the result of the redirection of trade away from traditional economic centers such as Ottoman Basra, a development that resulted because of the many wars of the period. Thus one line of argument posits the view that since a good number of coastal merchant principalities were established at precisely this juncture, there quite possibly may have beeen a link between the reorientation of trade and the development of free ports.[42] On the other hand, it has been argued that the wars between the Wahhābīs and other regional dynasts may have eclipsed whatever profits the carrying trade may have amassed at this time.[43] Obviously, a little bit of both took place. How much can only be determined by future historians with access to more reliable statistics than we now possess. In any case, it is logical to impute the emergence of free ports to the determination on the part of merchant capitalists to redirect intra-regional trade, for many of these coastal settlements were built on contraband or smuggling, the hallmark of all diverted trade in the Gulf.

Clearly, the key to economic continuity was the internal structure of the market, and the built-in, organic strategies devised by regional merchants, shipping agents, and livestock owners to control, re-route and monopolize trade to their advantage. Undoubtedly, the settlement (and resettlement) of towns itself formed a large part of this regional strategy. The evidence suggests that throughout the eighteenth century free ports were the one method whereby trade survived and prospered in the Indian Ocean. Even though merchants were confronted with a number of natural as well as man-made catastrophes, those merchants that could afford to do so, may have indulged in a traditional regional practice, and seceded from their original tribe or market town in order to establish newer markets elsewhere. Refusing to buckle under, regional merchants continued to reinvest their capital in new urban centers. As a result, the flight of capital usually ended up being re-invested in the region itself, usually by the same merchant families that had holdings elsewhere.

TRIBAL AND IMPERIAL FRONTIERS IN IRAQ FROM THE SEVENTEENTH TO THE EARLY NINETEENTH CENTURIES

The eastward migration of Najdī tribes to central and coastal Arabia, Kuwait, and southern Iraq redrew the frontiers of Najdī society by creating a larger, more populated area in which clans and families, sometimes disassociated from their traditional tribal confederations by force of political or socioeconomic circumstance, found it convenient to re-form themselves under the aegis of different tribal groupings. While this was a process most often identified with Najd, similar conditions occurred in Iraq. Here, too, formerly Najdī-based tribal sections who had either been chased out by stronger tribes, or migrated because of their own free will, regrouped into newer, more powerful confederations in Iraq, and worked out their own bargains with the indigenous tribes of Iraq, as well as the political bureaucracies already in place.

An important reason for the migration of Najdī tribes to Iraq and the Gulf coast was the birth of the Wahhābī revivalist movement in or around 1745. In the late eighteenth century, the Wahhābī movement spread from central and eastern Arabia to the fringes of Iraq, Syria, Kuwait, and the northern Gulf. Military campaigns designed to bring about the submission of townsmen and tribesmen to the Wahhābī *ʿaqīda* (credo) were not confined to Najd alone, but were also waged against the towns, villages, and tribal encampments of neighboring districts, especially Basra, Zubair, Karbalāʾ, and Kuwait. In the turmoil that ensued, the seemingly inexorable expansion of the Wahhābī movement created yet another reason for tribal migration to the south. In fact, many defeated anti-Wahhābī tribes were forced to move out of their traditional pastures, and to head for Iraq in order to regroup their forces and start anew.

The reconfiguration of the tribal map in Najd and Iraq did not fail to make an impression on the historians of the period, as the references in their histories amply demonstrate. For instance, historians noted the reemergence in the seventeenth century of the Muntafiq as one of the powerful tribal confederations in southern Iraq; originally, the latter had been an ancient *ʾimāra* (tribal principality) whose shaikhly house, the Shabīb, had ruled as masters of Basra and al-Ahsa (eastern Arabia) from as early as the thirteenth century, albeit not uninterruptedly.[44] In the seventeenth and eighteenth centuries, the Muntafiq was joined by several "new" tribal sections, the majority of whom had left Najd for Iraq because of drought and dessication. The leadership of the Muntafiq had been traditionally invested in the al-Shabīb family, who were reputed to be Meccan *ʾAshraf* (descendants of the Prophet's family); by the mid-seventeenth century, the Saʾdūn family wrested the paramount leadership away from the Shabīb *riʾāsa* (leadership), and thereafter continued to represent the Muntafiq tribal sections until the twentieth century. Again, tribal recomposition was a constant feature of the tribes of southern Iraq, as it had been in Najd; as a result of which, the main body of the Muntafiq was reconstituted in the seventeenth and eighteenth centuries to allow the fusion of the large tribes of al-ʾAjwād, Banū Mālik and Banū Saʾīd into a powerful confederation. Thus al-ʾAjwād occupied an important stronghold in al-Ahsa (eastern Arabia) before the Ottoman occupation of Iraq, and only allied themselves with the rest of the Muntafiq in the eighteenth century,[45] while ancient tribes such as al-Khafāja (which had been present in Iraq at the time of the Islamic conquests) were completely subsumed into the Muntafiq by the nineteenth century. By 1850, the borders of the Muntafiq *dīra* had taken on their final shape, encompassing important territories between Samawa[47] and Sūq al-Shuyūkh on the Euphrates, and other lands on the Gharraf river.

The Muntafiq was periodically strengthened by fresh tribal recruits from Najd, who had left their traditional pastures either because of overcrowding, dessication, or famine. Again, the impact of the Wahhābī movement provided yet another reason for tribal migration into the Muntafiq dīras. According to a Najdī historian, the Zāfir tribes were defeated in battle by Saʿūdī troops and thereupon took refuge in Iraq in 1688;[48] by the mid-nineteenth century, they were reckoned to be in the vicinity of 30, 000 people, and had settled among the Muntafiq tribes, where they formed a solid phalanx of anti-Wahhābī tribesmen ready to fight the Saᶜūdī state at a moment's notice.[49]

The ᶜAnayza tribe, on the other hand, rallied to the cause of the Saᶜūd 'imāra, all with the exception of the Fidᶜān section which joined the Saᶜūd's inveterate enemies, the Banū Khālid; as a result of which, they "went to live in the lands of the Khawālid."[50] By the latter part of the eighteenth century, tribal sections of the ᶜAnayza had made their appearance in Iraq. Although the sources do not specify why sections of the ᶜAnayza migrated to Iraq, those clans that did settle in south-central Iraq (the Wild ᶜAlī, al-Fidᶜān, al-Rwalla, al-ᵓImārāt and al-Dahāmsha) immediately began to compete for pastureland with the indigenous Iraqī tribes of the region, inevitably antagonizing the Mamluk government of Baghdad in the process, which launched several offensives against them. On one notable occasion, the ᶜAnayza chiefs took refuge among the Qashᶜam tribes, whose leaders refused to hand them over to the Mamluk army that beseiged the Qashᶜam *dīra;* the Iraqī historian who described this incident wrote approvingly that the Qashᶜam had refused to do so "because (doing so) was contrary to Arab tradition."[51] Eventually, however, the ᶜAnayza bought their freedom by presenting 3,000 mules and 50 horses to the Mamluk authorities.[52] By the mid-nineteenth century, Shaikh Ibrāhīm al-Ḥaidarī, one of the most perspicacious historians of the period, noted that the ᶜAnayza (who were now viewed as "belonging to the tribes of Iraq") had become one of the numerically important tribes in the region; according to him, they numbered close to 300,000 people, lived in the Shamiya desert, and were "originally from Najd."[53]

As for the Shammar, they are noted for having been early adherents of the house of Saᶜūd; in fact, a local historian estimates that twenty-thousand Shammarī tribesmen swelled the ranks of the first Saᶜūdī 'imāra.[54] After a conflict of interests soured the alliance between the Shammar and the Saᶜūdī state, sections of the tribe left for Iraq. The first shaikh of the "Iraqī" Shammar to settle in Iraq was Muṭlaq ibn Muḥammad al-Jarbā; he moved to northern Iraq in 1791, and died in 1798 in a battle against his erstwhile ally, Shaikh Saᶜūd ibn ᶜAbdul-Azīz.[56] Repeating a tradition that countless other property-less tribes had initiated before them, the Shammar displaced the ᶜUbaid and Jubūr tribes, took over their pasturelands and soon began to reign supreme in the Jazira district. By the early nineteenth century, they were the undisputed masters of northern Iraq.[56]

As a result of this in-migration, new tribal frontiers (dīras) were established, in which victorious tribes staked out grazing land and agricultural territory. "The tribal term dīra, in keeping with its bedouin origins, conveyed more of the sense of the domain over which the tribe exercized sovereign rights rather than that of exclusive ownership";[58] it was land "that was spoken of in terms of habitual but not exclusive grazing zones." These were the "natural" frontiers par excellence of the Arabian peninsula, the Gulf, and Iraq, and they centered around wells, oases, or date plantations. Dīras were defended by force, and regularly patrolled by the shaikh's militia. The shaikh of the tribe imposed the khuwwa or the "brotherhood" tax on all those unaffiliated with his confederation and who traversed the tribal dīra; he also sent representatives to collect the khuwwa from "protected" tribes and villages within the dīra itself (the khuwwa was normally paid in consumer goods, such as grain, dates, or textiles). Payment of the khuwwa implied recognition of tribal frontiers by all those parties that crossed and recrossed the tribal dīra, be they merchants, pilgrims, or pastoralists in search of water and forage.

When the Ottoman and Safavid empires began expanding into the area early in the sixteenth century, and began fighting over key territories in Iraq, imperial frontiers were established marking out each empire's jurisdiction over terrain won in war, or exchanged in peacetime. These frontiers were ratified by the peace treaties entered into by various Ottoman sultans and Persian shahs, starting with the Treaty of Amasya in 1555. This treaty was adhered to for twenty years, then further wars erupted between the Ottomans and Safavids, ending with the recapture of Baghdad by the Ottoman Sultan Murad IV in 1638. In 1639, Sultan Murad and Shah Safi signed the Peace of Zuhab in which the provinces of Baghdad, Basra, and Shahrizor (including districts in Kurdistan) were placed under Ottoman jurisdiction, while Mehereban and its dependencies were allotted to Iran.[59] In 1746, after yet another war had come to an end between the Ottomans and the Persians, a further treaty was signed by Sultan Mahmoud I and Nadir Shah, reconfirming the territorial provisions of the earlier agreement.[60] However,

> As was customary of border treaties in the region prior to European penetration of the area, the treaty [of Zuhab in 1639] defined the boundaries in accordance with the loyalties of the tribes inhabiting the frontier between the two empires. In essence, control of Iraq was defined by the limits of effective Ottoman administrative control emanating from Baghdad . . . [which] progressively became weaker, and hence more contentious, with geographic and administrative distance. In the peripheral areas, then, the tribes exercized a form of self-determination and considerable autonomy, while the two empires tried to coerce and coax their allegiance. In this way, conflict between the two empires was contained in a frontier zone and was manifested in shifting tribal allegiances, inter-tribal conflicts, and raiding. In the 1639 treaty, the frontier zone was over one hundred miles wide, between the Zagros mountains in the east and the Tigris and Shatt al-Arab rivers in the west. . . .[61]

Even though it has been maintained that the first Ottoman annexation of territory in northern Iraq and Kurdistan in 1516 was accomplished with local support, and that the administrative borders of the Ottoman Empire were fixed once and for all in Mosul and the Kurdish principalities in that same period,[62] the new Ottoman order eventually broke down in the seventeenth and eighteenth centuries. Especially in southern Kurdistan, the resurgence of military campaigns between different Baban ʾamīrs, and between the Baban ʾimāra and other near-autonomous tribal principalities kept the frontier between the Safavid and Ottoman Empires in constant turmoil. Moreover, the Ottoman naval campaigns in southern Iraq and eastern Arabia, while successfully occupying Basra and al-Qatif, failed to completely eradicate Portuguese influence in the Gulf.[63] Significantly, the Ottomans were successful in capturing Aden, Muscat, and Bahrain by 1554; but these were short-lived victories, eventually surpassed by Shah Abbas I's conquest of Hormuz, the most important market in the seventeenth-century Gulf.[64] By the eighteenth century, the Basra-based Ottoman fleet could barely hold its own against the seafaring tribes in the Gulf and Arabian sea, some of which (such as the Ka'ab) retained their mastery of Gulf waters throughout the century. Nor did the Ottoman land campaigns have an appreciable effect on powerful tribal confederations such as the Muntafiq in lower Iraq (see next section). Pitcher echoes Ismael's assessment when he comments that:

> Provincial divisions were fixed during the course of the sixteenth century and thereafter remained fairly constant for two hundred years . . . [but] the boundaries of the empire towards the desert and the Iranian plateau . . . fluctuated greatly, and tended to advance or recoil as the central government grew strong or weak . . . the desert fringe collapsed completely soon after the close of [the seventeenth century] . . . when the Shammar emerged from north Arabia and began to push their way across the Euphrates. . . . [While] the Persian frontier was never defined until the late nineteenth century, it is clear from the number of sancaks on the edge of the Pusht-i-Kuh that Ottoman rule extended farther into Iran than it did two hundred years later. . . .[65]

Despite the fact that the long wars with Iran brought about a parcelling of Iraq into Ottoman and Safavid zones during the sixteenth and seventeenth centuries, the effects were uneven. For one thing, imperial frontiers were never defined in an exact manner; in fact, both the Ottomans and the Persians continued to treat them as buffer zones or strongholds, a no-man's-land defended by tribal armies in the pay of either empire, or sometimes of both.[66] For another, imperial frontiers in Iraq were not only contested by the armies of the Ottoman or Safavid states, but they were also viewed as defensive bulwarks against the paramount leaders of tribal confederations or merchant principalities. Because the priorities of local officeholders and shaikhs had not been taken into consideration with regard to ultimate jurisdiction over the frontier, imperial officers enjoined to uphold the dignity of the Ottoman and Safavid empires were frequently assailed by recurrent raids on "their" sovereign territory by the tribes already inhabiting the region, even though some of these had made prior submission to imperial rule. For the Ottoman or Safavid representatives in Baghdad or Isfahan, imperial priorities of security and defense were the only factors worth considering with regard to the maintenance of the frontier; yet the fact that these same frontiers were superimposed on the local diras of agricultural settlements and tribal pasturelands provided a major point of contention between officers of the empire and provincial notables and shaikhs. That deficiency, inherent in the very structure of imperial conquest and occupation, provoked a number of tribal wars that occupied the Mamluk pashas in Iraq throughout the seventeenth and eighteenth centuries.

An analysis of the Iraqī provinces in the eighteenth century will clarify these issues, and explain why the struggle over tribal frontiers took on such life-and-death proportions. In the eighteenth century, the Vali Hasan Pasha (1704–24), and his son and successor, Ahmad Pasha (1724–47) tried to create a provincial infrastructure that would rationalize and enhance the collection of revenue for the Porte, for which they acted as governmental representatives in Iraq. Both Hasan and Ahmad Pasha attempted to do this through the time-honored practice of instituting state monopolies on items of trade, industries (such as glass making or the manufacture of leather), professions (i.e., the *muḥtasib* or market inspector) and routes of transport. In theory, these monopolies were farmed out to state agents, who collected the revenue in taxes on certain commodities (whether industrial, commercial, or agricultural), or on land or sea passage into certain towns or villages; the taxes were then remitted to the local government according to established fiscal precedent.[67] In practice, however, the system of monopolies was never as water-tight as it seemed, for it was one thing for the government to decree such a policy, and another thing entirely to enforce it. In fact, the evidence shows that nearly all monopolies—whether these were placed on transport routes or on the distribution of important commodities (such as silk, salt, indigo or grain)[68]—were permeable, and prone to abuse. As a result, it was never easy for the local governments of the period to get out the tax, no matter how reliable their agents were. Especially during the eighteenth and mid-nineteenth centuries, tax-farmers—whether these were landholders, urban merchants, or tribal entrepreneurs—seemed to have the upper hand when dealing with the government. Oftentimes richer and more powerful than the governors who were appointed to rule them, they never completely succumbed to the lure of government blandishments, even though, as *mūltezims* (tax-farmers), they were technically responsible for the provisionioning and supply of the provincial administrations of Baghdad, Basra, and Mosul. Disbursing the revenues promised to local governments seemed always to involve long, frequently tortuous negotiations and counter-negotiations, and when these broke down, military campaigns were almost always the response resorted to by frustrated governors.

There were several reasons why the Mamluk pashas of eighteenth and early nineteenth-century Iraq failed to completely monopolize the resources of the region. One involved the on-again, off-again wars with Persia. Since any attempted monopoly of external and internal revenues for the imperial treasury necessitated, at a minimum, that the important trade routes into Ottoman Iraq be secured, it was crucial that Iraq's frontiers with Iran be defended against any outside threat. Thus Ḥasan Pasha and 'Aḥmad Pasha mounted offensive campaigns against Iran in the course of imperial strategy[69] and put up a strong resistance to Persian invasions when these occurred. At first, short-lived successes were achieved against Persia, followed by defeat and then uneasy stalemate. While Ottoman commanders were able to make vast inroads into Persian territory in the early part of the century, capturing key towns such as Kirmanshah and Hamadan, by 1736 the tide had turned. Under Nadir Shah, the Persian armies pushed into Iraq, threatening the walls of Mosul and even Baghdad. Although peace treaties were eventually signed between the Ottoman Empire and Safavid state (and its successors), the frontier between the two powers remained an uneasy no-man's-land, alternately falling under the domination of Ottoman or Safavid/Afshari subjects. Thus as late as 1775, Persian armies began a siege of Basra which eventually resulted in a three-year occupation of the town. A local chronicler records that the first thing that the commander of the Persian forces did upon entering Basra was to take captive the *Mütesellem* (lieutenant governor) of Basra as well as the entire staff of the Basra customs house (undoubtedly along with their trade ledgers), immediately sending them to Karim Khan Zand, the ruler of Persia at the time.[70] Even though Ottoman Basra's trade with Persia had been very important between 1768 and 1777, the town's foreign trade never completely recovered from the calamity of the Persian occupation; in fact, after the rise of the Qajar state in 1794, trade routes to Persia shifted from the south to the north, further exacerbating Basra's commercial woes.[71]

Clearly, the disruptions engendered by military campaigns and foreign invasions were an important reason for the lack of Mamluk success in "sealing" the Iraq-Iran frontier. No attempted monopoly of trade routes, goods, and services could be envisaged under such volatile conditions. Even though wars never brought commerce to a complete standstill (for the contraband trade thrived in such situations), no pre-modern state could completely monopolize commercial traffic to its advantage, least of all in the provinces of Iraq which remained dependent on Persia for such commodities as raw silk,[72] as well as Persian pilgrim traffic to the Shīʿī shrines in Iraq. In fact, the income earned by all sectors of the Iraqī populace from Persian pilgrims may have been one reason why Mamluk administrators were so quick to punish anybody who harmed Persian *ḥajjīs* (pilgrims).[73]

One of the developments that accompanied the war for territory between the two empires was a concurrent war of words between each empire's religious scholars and propagandists concerning which state followed the more righteous Muslim path. In effect, the first frontiers demarcating Ottoman Iraq from the Safavid empire grew out of territorial as well as religious motives, and were legitimized by religious sanction. This is apparent from the focus of two of the most important historians in Mamluk Iraq; both mention the incident of 1722 in which the *shaikh al-Islam,* the highest religious authority in the Ottoman Empire, granted a *fatwa* (religious opinion) to Hasan Pasha, the vali of Baghdad, Basra, and Shahrizor, sanctioning the use of military force against the Persians.[74]

The fatwa made clear that it was permissible to embark on a military campaign against Iran (or, in the terminology employed by the historians of the day, *bilād al-ʿajam)* because those who ruled the country had deviated from the *sharīʿa* (sacred law) and, among other abominations, were following the practice of ritually cursing the first two Caliphs and the *saḥaba* (Companions of the Prophet), including the Prophet's wife, ʿĀ'isha. This fatwa reconfirmed the provisions of an earlier peace treaty between Sultan Murad IV and Shah Safi in 1639 in which the Ottomans had stipulated that, should these same principles be contravened, war might very well ensue.[75] However, notwithstanding the articles of the 1639 treaty, the shaikh al-Islam's fatwa is particularily interesting because it was granted at a time when relations between Ottoman Iraq and Safavid Iran were not especially strained, and may in fact have been on the mend.[76] The literature of the period makes it clear that the real object of the shaikh al-Islam's fatwa was not so much to combat the purported heresies of Safavid rule (which had been going on for too long a time not to have come to the notice of the Sunnī religious establishment in the Ottoman Empire) but, paradoxically, to reclaim Iran from another Sunnī rival, the Afghan mir ʿUwais.[77] Thus, while the ideological motive for the invasion of Iran was couched in the familiar lexicon of Sunnī versus Shiʿa, the real nature of the Ottoman thrust into the country concerned power politics and military expansion. In order to stabilize the eastern frontiers of the Ottoman Empire, it was important to mount a frontal attack on the crumbling Safavid Empire and, in the guise of coming to the assistance of a fellow Sunnī, to wipe out any external threat to Iraq, even if that threat appeared in "orthodox" Sunnī garb. Significantly, religious arguments underpinning the establishment of imperial frontiers in Iraq continued at least until 1746, when Nadir Shah's quixotic attempt to incorporate Jaʿfarī Shīʿism as a fifth Sunnī *madhhab* (school of law) was finally abandoned after it met a solid wall of Ottoman resistance in Istanbul.[78]

While the monopoly of external trade routes and the security of the imperial frontier were central concerns of the first Mamluk governors of Iraq, necessitating the establishment of a large army ready to do battle with Iran, the Mamluks also tried to control the internal frontiers thrown up by tribesmen and shaikhs throughout the Iraqī provinces. Again, religious symbolism was used to make an important distinction between imperial frontiers and those carved out by local dynastic rulers, whether in mountainous Kurdistan or in the southern marshes, an issue that will be discussed in the next section.

The first order of the day for the Mamluk administration in Baghdad was to centralize the administration of internal trade and agricultural revenues by means of the the more efficient collection of provincial taxes. In some cases, this meant the eradication of unjust duties, and the instilling of more orderly processes in the registration of land revenue.[79] The early Mamluks also fortified access roads throughout the Iraqī provinces and built bridges and aqueducts to restore communications.[80] According to a firsthand observer, Hasan Pasha "lifted the ugly cruelties" prevalent in his era by nullifying the gate tax (called the *bāj)* at Baghdad on sheep and other forms of rural produce in 1716.[81] Another tax, called the *tamgha* used to be farmed out by the government to the commander of the Baghdad Citadel; this was imposed on all the *kallakjiya* or owners of local river crafts, and was collected in firewood *(ḥatab)*. Hasan Pasha curtailed that tax as well. Realizing that the first order of business was to alleviate the inordinately heavy burden of taxation borne by Iraq's urban population and resolving to widen the government's net by bringing in rural elements usually considered outside of the government's reach, both valis began a systematic policy of tribal "pacification." Since maximizing revenue for the imperial treasury was the sina qua non of the first Mamluk administration, rural trade had to be brought within the government's orbit, necessitating the disciplining of the tribes. No less important was the control of tribal frontier zones, the tribesman's *espace libre* that functioned as a haven from government intrusion and military pursuit.

Thus the second major threat to the government's internal monopoly of trade and agricultural revenues came about with the emergence of an alternative leadership, embodied in the powerful tribal chieftains that roamed the region, imposing customary law *(ʿurf)* over wide areas of Iraq and collecting rural taxes (khuwwa, or protection money imposed by shaikhs on land and river passage) in the names of these same shaikhs. In order for the Mamluks to secure routes of trade and ports of shipment, important tribes had either to be fought against or placated and concilated. In this, the first Mamluk governors of Iraq faced the limits and constraints of any local power attempting to maximize the sources of revenue of a politically unstable region with fluctuating frontiers.

Ḥasan Pasha's first large tribal campaign was undertaken against the redoubtable Banū Lām, "a *qawm* (tribe) of Arabs living east of the Tigris . . . [who] plundered the Persian [trade] caravans, kidnapped Rūmī [i.e., Ottoman] travellers and made life unsafe for the villages east of Baghdad."[82] Their raids extended from Mandali to Jassan, occasionally threatening Basra. Whenever the government sent troops against them, the Banī Lām retreated to their traditional refuge, Ḥuwaiza, on the eastern bank of Shatt al-ʿArab. In 1705, Ḥasan Pasha massed a formidable army against them. At first, the Banū Lām tribes faded into the southern marshes, but on the second try, the Pasha inflicted a serious defeat on the tribal leadership that left them reeling. Escaping into Persia, the Banū Lām faced another unpleasant surprise: their route was blocked by a Persian army which subsequently defeated them, and captured their women, children and livestock. According to al-Suwaidī, "[as a result], the routes to the East became secure, and less dangerous, and merchants were able to cross them without harm befalling them."[83] Although no mention is made of a formal alliance between the Ottomans and Persians, it does not seem altogether coincidental that two large land armies would come together at the same time in order to rout the Banū Lām, especially since the latter tribe posed a palpable threat to the long-distance trade on which the two empires depended. In the same year, the Khazāʿil chief, Salmān, newly escaped from prison in Baghdad, began to forge wider links with the southern tribes. In the words of a contemporary historian:

> [Salman] began to receive obedience from the majority of the villages surrounding Baghdad . . . and soon this wretch began to [carve out] a *dawla* such as kings have . . . marrying many women [and] becoming so strong that the Shammar tribe were like slaves before him.[84]

Even though Salman al-Khazᶜalī, master of al-Ḥasaka, ("the most productive lands of Iraq"), was to be soundly defeated yet another time by the Pasha, his chastisement did not serve as an example to other tribal leaders. In 1706, a massive governmental offensive was launched against the Muntafiq shaikh, Mughāmis, who was threatening Basra by attacking trade caravans and imposing transport dues on them. It was reported that the town's finances were so depleted by these raids that the local government was unable to pay the salaries of its *lawand* contingent (locally-raised troops).[85] Eventually, Hasan Pasha ran Mughāmis off to Huwaiza. For his troubles, he was awarded the *mutasallimiyya* (lieutenant governorship) of Basra, to assign to whomsoever he wished. Furthermore, the Porte decreed that henceforth the town was to be incorporated to the vilayet (province) of Baghdad. Finally, for his ferocious defense of Basra's mercantile community in the face of Banū Lām raids on trade caravans, Istanbul again crowned Hasan Pasha's efforts by sending him a *khilᶜa* (robe of honor) in 1717.

These examples can be multiplied several times over throughout the rest of the century. Even though the local chroniclers of the eighteenth century imply that all of the tribal campaigns undertaken by Mamluk commanders were resounding successes, the simple fact is that the same offending shaikhs' names crop up over and over again in the sources, sometimes barely a year apart from their last defeat at the hands of the government. Thus the shaikhs of the Banū Lām, Khazāᶜil, and Muntafiq were the three most powerful tribal leaders of southern Iraq, and yet they seemed to be in constant rebellion against the state. One possible inference from this behavior is that even though defeated and denuded of all that they owned, these shaikhs remained uncowed. The reason may have been very simple: these shaikhs' power depended not upon government legitimization, but upon their tribesmen's support. While it is true that there are instances in the literature where tribesmen deserted their elected shaikh, the more common development was for the tribal peasantry to remain at their shaikh's side until he was defeated, deposed, or assassinated. Thus, there was very little that any provincial government could do but keep on legitimizing rebellious chiefs in power, sometimes simply because it had no other realistic option. In order to keep the routes open, and to collect a portion of the *khuwwa* as taxes, provincial governors were forced to accomodate themselves to tribal politics. They sought a comprimise where, in return for government legitimization of a shaikh in power (something, paradoxically, that had already been conferred upon him by the elders of his own tribe), the shaikh would agree to share his monopoly over certain routes with the government. Obviously, one way that the government could make shaikhs comply with this somewhat unrealistic scenario was to threaten recalcitrant chiefs with periodic military campaigns. As Dina Khoury has shown, however, there was a certain point beyond which military offensives were counterproductive, for merchants, the critical factor in long-distance trade, were apt to move to other routes if the latter were constantly being fought over.[87] In fact, fleeing merchants in search of more secure havens appear routinely in the pages of eighteenth and nineteenth-century annals (and will be discussed elsewhere in the book).

In order, therefore, to collect a portion of the annual revenue, both to finance local administration as well as to placate the Porte, Mamluk pashas had to devise methods of power sharing that would accomodate the interests of shaikh-monopolists. For instance, throughout the eighteenth century, the al-Shāwī shaikhs, head of the important Baghdad-based ʿUbaid tribe, buttressed the ruling Mamluk governor of the city with a solid phalanx of tribesmen ready to do his bidding. Granted the honorific of *Bāb al-ʿArab* (literally, "Gate of the Arabs") by the Mamluks, their shaikhs received ample privileges in return for acting as conduits to the greater resources of the rural hinterland. For the most part, these privileges were tied to the control of overland trade routes emanating from Baghdad (which entitled the al-Shāwī shaikhs to a certain percentage of the profits from land duties), but the paramount shaikhs of the ʿUbaid also received title to urban properties. For instance, ʿAbdullāh Beg al-Shāwī (d. 1769), perhaps the greatest shaikh of his line (and justly celebrated by countless poets in his time), is mentioned as having been the holder of a *waqfiyya* (religious endowment deed) in Baghdad.[88] Nevertheless, even as close a government ally as ʿAbdullāh presented problems to the Mamluk Pashas of Baghdad, for he could quickly become an alternative center of power, drawing around him many of the tribes of the district as well as the local Arab aristocracy (ʿulamāʾ and merchants).[89] As a result, ʿAbdullāh, whose immense popularity among the urban as well as the rural sectors of the population was resented by the vali of Baghdad, ʿUmar Pasha (1764–1775), was killed on the orders of the Mamluk administration in Baghdad. His sons immediately commenced an unsuccessful war against the Baghdad pashalik. Eventually, after a period of time, tempers cooled and the rebel shaikhs of the ʿUbaid were granted a government pardon. Remarkably, after all was said and done, one of ʿAbdullāh's sons, Suleimān, even accepted the traditional post of Bāb al-ʿArab from the Mamluks.[90] In other words, even though members of the al-Shāwī family sometimes put up a fight against Mamluk injustices, the majority continued in government office until they were finally replaced (not without considerable resistance) in government favor by the Shammar.[91]

On the other hand, other tribal allies were less willing to toe the official line and even less willing to forgive and forget. In fact, the Muntafiq shaikhs, who trod a delicate balance between outright independence and truculent obeisance to the government, usually made submission to the government only after being defeated in battle. The case of Ḥumūd al-Thāmir, shaikh of the Muntafiq, is instructive.[92] In 1812, a conflict erupted between Saᶜīd Bey, son of the famous Suleimān Pasha the Great, and ᶜAbdullāh Pasha, the ruling Mamluk pasha in Baghdad. Although Saᶜīd was a Mamluk by birth, and scion of perhaps the most important Mamluk household in Baghdad, his path was seemingly blocked by ᶜAbdullāh Pasha's *kāhyā* (deputy), Tahir Agha. Sensing that his life was in danger, Saᶜīd fled to the Muntafiq tribe where yet another erstwhile ally of the Mamluk Pashalik, Jāsim Bey al-Shāwī, had sought refuge. Realizing that Saᶜīd could not be permitted to remain at liberty to foment a dangerous rebellion, ᶜAbdullāh Pasha first wrote to Ḥumūd, ordering his "vassal" to return Saᶜīd to justice. The letter, quoted at length by a firsthand witness to the events, sounded a petulant note: not only had Ḥumūd expropriated the revenues of the territories of Basra but he had refused to pay the government *mīrī* (land tax) for two whole years, and now, to add insult to injury, Ḥumūd was protecting two known felons, Saᶜīd and Jāsim. Knowing full well that there was nothing he could do, ᶜAbdullāh granted Ḥumūd a delay in the disbursement of the mīrī tax but insisted on the return of the two men. Ḥumūd refused categorically, stating that the latter had entered the Muntafiq as *dakhīls* (those asking for protection) and in memory of Suleiman Pasha the Great, Saᶜīd's father, with whom the tribe of the Muntafiq had been on good terms, he would not go back on his word and hand them over. As a result of that categorical refusal, ᶜAbdullāh Pasha assembled a large army of Kurds, Turcomans from Kirkuk and Arbil, ᶜUqaylīs, and a full company of riflemen to do battle with the refractory Muntafiq.

Much to ᶜAbdullāh Pasha's chagrin, the Muntafiq alliance soundly defeated the Pasha of Baghdad's forces; and after Ḥumūd's son, Barghash, died of wounds received in battle, Ḥumūd executed ᶜAbdullāh Pasha and his kāhyā, Ṭāhir Agha. Saᶜīd became pasha of Baghdad, and Shaikh Ḥumūd not only received 30,000 *qurūsh* in cash, as well as a further 30,000 qurūsh in goods, (specifically textiles, sugar, and coffee forcibly expropriated from Basra merchants) but eventually, was given title to Saᶜīd's former *mālikâne* (state lands held in fief with life tenancy) and a vast amount of property in southern Iraq, around the Shaṭṭ al-ᶜArab.[93]

While Ḥumūd's victory signalled the peak of local resurgence to the Mamluk government, and was eventually dissipated by the systematic anti-tribal policies of the powerful Dāwūd Pasha, the two examples referred to above show that governmental control of tribal spheres of operation were fundamental to the monopolization of revenue in Mamluk Iraq. Because direct taxation was not yet a reality in mid-eighteenth century Iraq, pashas relied on tax collectors and monopolists to gain entry to the wealth generated by production and trade. However, as the Ḥumūd-ᶜAbdullāh conflict makes clear, most of the time government-tribal alliances were far from stable, and even with the most durable coalitions, dissension was often a result.

Obviously, the fault did not lie completely with the tribal confederations of southern Iraq. The sina qua non of any successful monopolist was his ability to share power with a number of different socioeconomic groups in any given province, for no government, however much in control of the means of coercion, could govern as a compact, self-contained entity without allies or affiliates. The Mamluks were always in need of strong, stable allies who could deliver key towns or rural districts in dire emergencies, especially in a diverse province such as Iraq. With the exception of successful rulers such as Suleiman Pasha the Great (1780–1802) or Dāwūd Pasha (1817–31), few valis could juggle so many competing interests and always come out ahead. Even though the Mamluks, by and large, became a localized force by the middle of the century, sharing government privileges with other local groups, such as Arab shaikhs, ʿulamāʾ and important merchants, they could not completely operate as indigenous, autonomous elites. The threat of removal was always present; for even though the Porte tried unsuccessfully on at least three occasions to replace Mamluk Pashas with handpicked nominees from Istanbul,[94] the certainty that the Porte would try again was always uppermost in any Mamluk governor's mind.

This is probably why the annual revenue promised to the Porte was promptly dispatched to Istanbul by Baghdad-based pashas. The first Mamluk governor of Iraq, properly speaking, Suleimān Abū Lailā (1748–62), sent little or no revenue to Istanbul throughout his years in government, and refused to accept imperial nominees to office; and Niewenhuis claims that the only other Mamluk to pay little tribute to the Porte was ʿUmar Pasha (1764–75).[95] However, these two pashas were notable exceptions to the rule.[96] Most pashas were circumspect in their accounts with the Porte, and regularly sent the annual revenue, even a governor as immensely popular as Suleiman Pasha the Great.

Perhaps because of these very reasons, the Mamluks used the weapon of religion to justify their position vis-à-vis the tribes of Iraq. Thus, equally significant to the military campaigns waged against local chieftains and tribal merchants was the religious terminology employed by Mamluk pashas—and their state historians—to accentuate the cultural divide between the imperial ideology of the frontier and the seemingly random nature of tribal borders. Thus, the historian ʿAbdul-Raḥmān al-Suwaidī depicts the wars between the Zubaid tribe and the government of Hasan Pasha in 1698 in near- apocalyptic terms. After the pasha's troops beat back the tribal armies, he asserted:

> The party of God *(Ḥizb ʾAllāh)* won while the enemies of religion *(aʿdāʾ al-dīn)* asked for mercy or ran away. . . .[97]

And some time later, the same historian refers to the pasha's army as *junūd ʾAllāh al-ghāliba* (God's victorious troops).[98] In another section of his history, al-Suwaidī even refers to rebellious tribal shaikhs as *zanādiqa* (unbelievers).[99] Finally, the Islamic phraseology employed by Mamluk officials and state-affiliated historians also extended to the *bayʿa,* the oath of allegiance that defeated tribes had to enter into with the governments of Baghdad and Basra, and which reflected their ultimate submission to the Mamluk authorities. Thus, on several occasions, the tribes made peace by pledging to "enter into the Muslim community" and " to live in peace and under Islam."[100]

MUSLIMS OR KUFFĀR? AN ANALYSIS OF FRONTIER-MAKING UNDER THE IMPACT OF THE WAHHĀBĪ REVIVAL

A third form of frontier-making emerged with the rise of the Wahhābī movement. This took place as a result of the "re-Islamization" of the Arabian peninsula under the aegis of the Saʿūdī-Wahhābī alliance. The wars waged by the first Saʿūdī imāra took place in the context of a rapid shift in power relations both in Arabia and in the Gulf, but the balance of military power was not all that was affected by the the Wahhābī campaigns in Najd, eastern Arabia, and the Hijaz. A "new" moral vocabulary based on the religious and juridical precepts of the first generation of exemplary Muslims, *al-salaf al-ṣāliḥ,* was resuscitated to justify the expansion of the first Saʿūdī imāra. This discourse functioned as a legitimator of state conquest; it accompanied the imposition of Saʿūdī military and political institutions on tribal territories and agricultural settlements throughout the Arabian peninsula. Nowhere does this moral-religious discourse become more evident than in the historiography of the period, which is explicit in describing the furious response elicited from the region as a result of the Imām Muḥammad ibn ʿAbdul-Wahhāb's appeal. Of course, the evidence available in the histories of the period must be treated with a certain amount of caution, for it cannot be considered comprehensive by any stretch of the imagination, being neither the expression of the voice of the majority nor the the opinion of a broad sector of the populace (which remain mute in the histories of the region). However, the literature on the Wahhābī movement is significant, if only as a gauge of the movement's effect on the history writing elite of Iraq, Arabia, and the Gulf, and the reaction this produced among their state sponsors.

Simply put, the controversy surrounding the propagation of Wahhābī principles elicited several responses from the region, most of them critical. At the same time that Mamluk historians were trading blows in print with pro-Wahhābī chroniclers on everything from religious dogma to the economic infrastructure of the first Saʿūdī state, another by-product of the debate was the creation of a shifting frontier on the ground, demarcating Wahhābī communities from what they considered to be "polytheistic" or "apostate" states and societies, all of which were Muslim, and some of which were even governed by the representatives of the Ottoman sultan, who was the Servant of the Holy Sanctuaries *(khādim al-ḥaramayn al-sharīfayn),* the Ottoman Sultan. In this respect, one of the epithets used over and over again in the regional historiography, both to distinguish between the "true" Muslims and their enemies, as well as to make appeal to the larger Muslim community in the region, was that of *kāfir* (pl. *kuffār).* The term is originally to be found in the Qur'an and later on, in the *Ḥadīth* where agreement on what it meant differed according to the socio-legal interpretation arrived at by any one of the four established schools of Islamic law.[101] In general, a kāfir is an unbeliever who will be meted out divine punishment on Judgment Day and be consigned to eternal damnation. The controversy in the Ḥadīth over how to define a kāfir is well-documented in the juridical and theological literature; nonetheless, even though medieval jurists held different views on the varieties of *kufr,* and the specific conditions under which a person could be labelled as such, the term gradually took on a more universal meaning because of certain developments in Islamic history. While it had been applied in the main to followers of the Christian and Jewish faiths in certain historical epochs (for instance, during the period of the Crusades), according to other legal interpretations, both Christians and Jews merited more leniency than Muslim renegades because they were the *ahl al-kitāb* (People of the Book, i.e., monotheists). A more important and far-reaching development was the labelling of other Muslims as kuffār, a practice prevalent since the early days of the Islamic empire, which had continued as a result of the various schismatic conflicts that erupted throughout the long span of Islamic history. As a result, by the latter part of the Islamic period, "Kāfir in theological polemics [became] a fairly frequent term for the Muslim protoganist of the opposite view."[102]

It is this meaning of *kufr* (unbelief) that pervades the texts of the eighteenth and nineteenth centuries. The act of *takfīr* (labelling another Muslim a kāfir) was a practice that was regularly employed by pro-Wahhābī historians against the Saʿūdī state's enemies in eastern Arabia, Iraq, Kuwait, and the Gulf; it was also used by anti-Wahhābī historians in Iraq and eastern Arabia to exorciate the Wahhābī movement in scathing terms. Because the labelling of one's enemies as kuffār was tantamount to a declaration of war, (for no relations could ever exist between a true Muslim and a kāfir) kuffār were considered to be legally and morally outside the pale, and fair game for any Muslim army. Even though Shaikh Muḥammad ibn ʿAbdul-Wahhāb labelled as kuffār all Muslims who denied the doctrine of *tawḥīd* (the indivisibility of God), or who resorted to *shirk* (polytheism),[103] in some ways, this was a catch-all statement, leaving considerable leeway for interpretation.

Over and above the label of kāfir, a veritable arsenal of religious terms was used to negate the validity of the other side's claims. For instance, followers of the Wahhābī movement were not only eager to reserve for themselves the privilege of being known as the only true Muslims, and to append the epithet kāfir on their enemies but they also employed other religious terms, such as *mushrikūn* (polytheists) and *munāfiqūn* (hypocrites) to depict those who strayed from the "straight" path *(al-sirāṭ al-mustaqīm)* in a new, more dangerous light. A present-day historian explains the central facets of the Wahhābī *daʿwa* (call) in this manner:

> The social and political dimension of Wahhābīte ideology is the setting of strict limits of exclusivity to a particular *ʿasabiyya* (tribal power group), thus rendering all that is external to this expanding ʿasabiyya social, political, and geographical territory whose plunder and subjugation are legitimate, indeed incumbent upon members of this exclusive group. Kufr . . . is an attribute of others and, in the accentuated Wahhābīte form, of otherness *tout court.* It is an attribute which makes conquest and subjugation incumbent, under the banner of *jihad,* both as the political act of an expanding polity and as a legal-religious obligation. This exterior of kufr comprises not only idolatrous religions nor is it confined to non-Islamic monotheism, but describes non-Wahhabite co-religionists as well.[104]

As a result of the Wahhābī wars, therefore, historical texts began to take on all the appearances of polemical broadsides, and the religious terminology of the period was invested with new ideological meaning that grew out of a specific moral-political climate. This is explicitly seen in the work of Shaikh Ḥusain ibn Ghannām, a Najdī historian who was clearly one of the most zealous proponents of the "new" (or recast) moral discourse that accompanied the extension of Saʿūdī military and political control in central and eastern Arabia and later on in the Hijaz.[105] Ibn Ghannām's book is considered to be the first book written on the intellectual and military history of the Wahhābī movement, as well as being an important eyewitness account of the deeply-entrenched struggle between pro- and anti-Wahhābī forces in Najd, eastern Arabia, the Hijaz, and Iraq. As such, the shaikh uses clear Islamic terminology to describe the "re-Islamization" of the Peninsula, recounting in one instance the defeat of an ally-turned enemy in this manner:

> In 1749, Uthman ibn Muʿammar, governor of al-ʿAyniya, was killed, as a punishment for his deception and concealment (of his true nature); and that is because he increased his evil towards *ahl al-tawḥīd* (the monotheists, usually the term used by pro-Wahhābī historians to denote the Saʿūdī camp), and he began to humiliate them with frequency, and showed his hatred for the Muslims . . . and exposed his loyalties to *ahl al-bāṭil* (the people of falsehood) . . . and his proximity to *al-munāfiqūin* (the hypocrites) . . . and when the shaikh (ʿAbdul-ʿAzīz ibn Saʿūd) investigated ibn Muʿammar's actions and found all the stories to be true, all the people of ʿAyniya district came to ʿAbdul-ʿAzīz and complained to him about their fear of ibn Muʿammar's deception *(ghadr)* and his terrible actions, and the shaikh told all who came to him, "I want the *bayʿa* (oath of allegiance) from you on God's religion and that of his Prophet and loyalty *(walāʾ)* to those who are his deputies (i.e., āl-Saʿūd), and your enmity to those who fight him, even if that be your ʾamīr Uthman," and they concluded a contract of faith with him *(ṣafaqat al-ʾimān)* and gave him the *bayʿa* in droves *(afwājan),* as a result of which Uthman's heart was filled with terror and anxiety, and his hatred and rancor increased, and Satan told him that he would never be victorious in his design so long as he did not destroy or annihilate *ʾahl*

> *al-ʾīmān* (the people of faith, i.e., the Saʿūdī-Wahhābī camp) and expel any Muslim to the ends of the earth . . .[106]

When "the Muslims" realized that Uthman was preparing a new war against them,

> some people from *ahl al-tawḥīd* resolved to relieve the people of Uthman's vindictiveness and his bad deeds . . . so after Friday prayers, these people ran towards him and assassinated him in his own *masjid* . . . and his death relieved the Muslims from further injury (inflicted by Uthman). . . .[107]

The aftermath of the furious debate between pro- and anti-Wahhābī historians affected even those writers who were not particularly touched by the controversies that raged in the region, but who felt it their duty to register an opinion, however minor, of the events surrounding the ideological nature of the Wahhābī movement. Thus a tribal historian of the Bassām family in central Arabia wrote a history of Najdī and Iraqī tribes which, while somewhat sparse and uninformative on the socioeconomic conditions prevalent in the period, nevertheless pronounced a simple formula with regard to the Wahhābī penchant for casting doubts on their co-religionists' faith. Of the Wahhābīs, he said: "Whosoever obeys their ruler is a Muslim; whosoever rebels against him is an unbeliever" (man ʾaṭāʿa malikahum fa huwa Muslimūn wa man ʿaṣāhu fa huwa kāfirun)."[108] This basic principle was understood by nearly everyone in the Arabian peninsula, Iraq, and the Gulf. For example, one of the historians that fulminated most about the Wahhābī movement was the Basra-based ʿālim, Shaikh ʿUthmān ibn Sanad;[109] he may have been deeply influenced by one of his teachers, Shaikh Ibn Fairūz al-ʾAḥsāʾi, one of the most renowned shaikhs in Najd (and a ṣūfī), who had fled to Basra in the wake of the Saʿūdī-Wahhābī occupation of central Arabia in the latter part of the eighteenth century. The latter immediately gathered around him a number of students and adepts, and began preaching the principles of the "true" Islam. Because he was very rich, and was able to fund his students in an ample fashion, he may have been assured of a wide audience in Basra.[110] Al-ʾAḥsāʾī had been invited to meet with the leading Wahhābī ʿulamāʾ of Darʿiyya to discuss matters of theology and politics but refused, quoting parts of the famous Qurʾanic verse: "Qul yā ayyuhā al-kāfirūnạ lā ʾaʿbudu mā taʿbudūna wa lāʾantum ʿābidūna mā ʾaʿbudu" [Say, oh ye unbelievers, I do not worship what you worship, and neither do you worship what I worship] as reply. Because, in effect, he was calling the Saʿūdī-Wahhābī leadership kuffār, he was threatened with death, and was forced to flee to Iraq as a result.[111]

Ibn Sanad was only slightly less critical of the Wahhābīs' claim to divine guidance than his mentor was. Shaikh ʿUthmān ibn Sanad, who is claimed by present-day historians both in Saʿūdī Arabia and Iraq,[112] was an important ʿālim and ṣūfī adept of the Naqshbandī *ṭarīqa* (mystical order). He had ties both to the state (he was Dāwūd Pasha, the last Mamluk governor's favorite historian) and to regional interests in the Gulf and eastern Arabia. Because of Ibn Sanad's abiding concern with state patronage of the religious establishment, and the corresponding role of ʿulamāʾ in state affairs, (issues that are at the forefront of his work), he reacted in some ways as the prototypical ʿālim of the period, anxious to deflect Wahhābī ideas lest they confuse majority opinion, ready to defend state ideology against subversive forces, and intent on uncovering what he considered to be the heretical nature of a "false" Islam. In many ways, then, his arguments echo those of anti-Wahhābī ʿulamāʾ in the Arabian peninsula and Iraq, who continued to wage a covert battle against Shaikh Muḥammad ibn ʿAbdul-Wahhāb's teachings throughout the early part of the Wahhābī campaigns for Najd.

Here is Ibn Sanadʾs description of the Wahhābī dogma:

> And of the beliefs of the Wahhābīs, there is in their *ʿaqīda* (credo) that they can make kuffār of all the Muslims on the earth's surface except those who believe their ʿaqīda . . . they even call themselves *al-salaf* (in reference to the first generation of exemplary Muslims in the Prophet's time) and *al-Muḥammadiyyūn* (i.e., the followers of the Prophet) and they curse all the Sunnī ʿulamāʾ like Abū al-Ḥasan al-ʿAshʿarī and they say they are the only ones who (follow the path of true monotheism). . . .[113]

Ibn Sanad's reaction was typical of the polemical exchange between Shaikh Muḥammad ibn ʿAbdul-Wahhāb and religious leaders in the Arabian peninsula, eastern Arabia, and Iraq, which centered around the validity of the Imām's interpretation of the divine message and the Prophet's role in conveying that message to the world. While it has been suggested that "in the message-oriented call of Muḥammad ibn ʿAbdul-Wahhāb, the summons was simply to return to the Qurʾan and the Sunnah [and] . . . to the model of the unchanging message,"[114] many prayer leaders, shaikhs, and religious scholars either deliberately misrepresented the tenets of the Wahhābī ʿaqīda (because the appeal of Shaikh Muḥammad ibn ʿAbdul-Wahhāb challenged vested interests everywhere in the region), or were genuinely outraged by some of the "innovations" associated with the Wahhābī movement. Even though the Imām's message was not fundamentally revolutionary, but reformist in tone, it raised the hackles of many observers in the region who were, for the most part, adamant that Shaikh Muḥammad ibn ʿAbdul-Wahhāb was an imposter, and his message fraudulent. Accordingly, he was accused of everything from trying to establish a new madhhab (school of law) to creating a new religion altogether.[115]

While the development of the Wahhābī movement engendered a heated religious debate in the regional historiography of the period, pitting pro-Wahhābī historians in Najd against scholars in Iraq and eastern Arabia with sharply different views, it also entailed a reorientation in the political-economic patterns of the region, and a struggle over trade and pilgrimage routes in the Arabian peninsula and Iraq. With the emergence of the Wahhābī movement, the tradition of free trade in Arabia and the Gulf suffered a temporary, but nonetheless serious, setback for a time. This momentous development had grave repercussions on the nature and scope of the regional market's long-distance operations, which was to last for years to come.

In 1745, Shaikh Muḥammad ibn ʿAbdul-Wahhāb, the inspiration for the *muwaḥḥidī* or unitarian revival in Arabia, and Shaikh Muḥammad ibn Saʿūd, warrior, *ḍāmin* (land-holder/tax collector) and trader, sealed their famous pact in Darʿiyya (Najd). This arrangement, by which Shaikh Muḥammad ibn Saʿūd promised to enlist his men and personal fortune to restore the tenets of salafi Islam to the Arabian peninsula, and to resuscitate the fundamentalist message of the first generation of exemplary Muslims was to revolutionize the whole region by setting in motion one of the most successful statist experiments in Gulf and Arabian history. Historians are still somewhat wary of attributing a socioeconomic perspective to the Wahhābī movement, for the religious dynamic that spurred thousands of heretofore "insular" Najdī Arabs to coalesce into a powerful force, threatening the walls of Baghdad and Damascus is too strong an image for most scholars to reject altogether. In some ways, it is a very romantic notion, and one not entirely in keeping with the hard-nosed, practical side of the Saʿūdī statist experiment. For even though there is very little direct reference to Saʿūdī attempts to control the economic resources of Arabia and Iraq in the primary Arabic materials on the Wahhābī movement, there is still a case to be made for the interpretation of the Wahhābī-Saʿūdī alliance from a socioeconomic perspective. It is a case made all the more immediate by the very context of the Wahhābī movement, by the nature of its development in an arid, hard climate where seasonal dessication, drought, pestilence and the rigors of a subsistence existence pushed men to seek their livelihoods outside of their native soil, and where long-distance trade quite simply made all the difference between life and death. If there is no understanding of the social and economic conditions that prevailed in eighteenth century Arabia at the time of the Wahhābī daʿwa, then there is no understanding of why the movement gained momentum and expanded into the fringes of eastern Arabia, Iraq, Kuwait and Syria. Tribal support for the Wahhābī daʿwa, a critical factor in the Wahhābī-Saʿūdī expansion into eastern Arabia and the Gulf coast, was in large part a result of the economic incentives granted to state-sponsored tribal confederations, which provided them with the motivation to back the Saʿūdī state's attempt to monopolize land and sea routes in the region.

In this sense, then, the Saʿūdī state did promote an economic philosophy that aimed at the monopoly of trade and pilgrimage routes into the ʾimāra, and the control of revenue from agriculture and long-distance commercial operations. While more detail will be provided throughout the rest of the chapter, it is noteworthy that even the early leaders of the Wahhābī-Saʿūdī alliance themselves were recorded as possessing a commercial bent that went hand in hand with their religious fervor. For instance, there is some indication both in the anonymous history, *Kitāb lamʿ al-shihāb*[116] and in Ibn Bishr's *ʿUnwān al-majd,*[117] which are on opposite poles of the ideological spectrum, that the Saʿūd family was originally of the landholding merchant class of Najd. The anonymous history claims that Shaikh Muḥammad ibn Saʿūd, who was instrumental in supporting Shaikh Muḥammad ibn ʿAbdul-Wahhāb's call, had a lot of property in and around Darʿiyya, consisting of date-palms, cultivable land, and livestock. He was also a broker, financing the journeys of long-distance merchants.[118] Ibn Bishr, who was zealously pro-Saʿūdī, confirms the fact that Shaikh Muḥammad ibn Saʿūd was a ḍāmin or landholder in Darʿiyya by relating the somewhat apocryphal story of the two conditions that ibn Saʿūd asked the ʾImām to accept, upon agreeing to support him in his mission. One was that the ʾImām would not leave him to seek another patron, once the *jihād fī sabīl Allāh* (striving in the path of God) had been achieved. The second was what to do with his tax-collector status at Darʿiyya, the implication being that now that ibn Saʿūd had undertaken to mount a military campaign to bring all of Najd within the muwaḥḥidī fold, he might not be able to oversee his economic assets as thoroughly as before. The Imām's reply was revealing, telling ibn Saʿūd that, once the Wahhābī movement had achieved its aims, the shaikhs of al-Saʿūd would have a far larger territory from which to collect revenues.[119] While these two accounts provide some evidence to show that the motive for the initial Saʿūdī campaigns may have been started by men from merchant/landholding backgrounds for a combination of material as well as spiritual rewards, other evidence exists to show that the Saʿūdī-Wahhābī alliance was deeply grounded in the economic ideology of the period, which revolved around the control by one, or several parties all at once, of the surplus from trade and agriculture; this was accomplished through raids on neighboring towns or tribal districts. In particular, there are a number of significant examples in the sources that suggest that the Saʿūdī imāra was determined to control all land (and later on, sea) passage into its domains. Because land routes generated revenue in the form of khuwwa, (protection money) which was paid to the important tribal confederations that guarded these routes, the Saʿūdī state made a resolute try to control these passageways and with them, the revenue generated by the pilgrims, merchants and travellers that used them.

Prior to the emergence of the Wahhābī movement, Arabia had been the seat of various localized ʾimāras, each jealously guarding its space and fiercely defending its limited territory (which sometimes did not extend beyond the walls of the town).[120] The two principal powers in the peninsula at the beginning of the eighteenth century were the *sharīfs* of Mecca (in the Hijaz) and the Banū Khālid tribal confederation, the rulers of al-Ahsa (eastern Arabia). At various times, one or two of these competing forces would gain the upper hand over the other, and Najd would come under the suzerainty either of the Hijaz or of eastern Arabia. Neither power directly impinged on Najd's affairs, for both were interested chiefly in plunder and disinclined to spend time, energy, or money on securing trade routes emanating to and from Najd, or on the protection of Najd's townspeoples from tribal parties swooping down to ravage agricultural properties at harvest time. The sharifs of Mecca and the Banū Khālid from al-Ahsa were content to leave Najdīs to their own devices, while they mounted yearly campaigns to collect the district's revenues, fighting each other for control of Najd's meager surplus.[121]

The House of Saᶜūd was different. From its very inception, the first Saᶜūdī ʾimāra paid special heed to the needs of the townspeople for protection, and systematized long-distance trade so that revenue could be appropriated more efficiently. Again, Ibn Bishr and the author of *Kitāb lamᶜ al-shihāb* portray this development clearly, even while writing from different ideological perspectives. Generally speaking, Ibn Bishr's account is full of praise for the new-found security in the districts over which the Saᶜūdi ʾamīrs held sway, constantly reiterating the belief that the Wahhābī hold over central Arabia had displaced an illegitimate order with a moral one. The anonymous author, on the other hand, felt that the Saᶜūdī innovations threatened the old fabric. In fact, the issue of control over trade routes grew out of the determined efforts of various Saᶜūdī ʾamīrs to collect transit revenue more efficiently, and to monopolize the resources of the region for the benefit of the Saᶜūdī state. For example, a Saᶜūdī tradition established by Shaikh Muḥammad ibn Saᶜūd (1725–1765) and carried on by his son ᶜAbdul-ᶜAzīz, the second ruler of the Saᶜūdī ʾimāra (1765–1803) stipulated that all the *ḥujjāj* or pilgrims that passed by way of Darᶜiyya, the Saᶜūdī capital, on their way to perform the pilgrimage at Mecca should be invited to stay as guests of the Saᶜūdī ʾamīr for at least three days. This tradition had been sanctioned by a *fatwa* (religious opinion) from the Imām and it became a Saᶜūdī ritual. Evidence that this ritual became an obligation on all Muslim pilgrims or merchants entering Saᶜūdī-held territories is illustrated by an incident in ᶜAbdul-ᶜAzīz's reign in which a group of unfortunate Persian travellers chose to travel from Kuwait to Mecca, by-passing Darᶜiyya. According to *Kitāb lamᶜ al-shihāb*:

> When ᶜAbdul-ᶜAzīz heard about this, he ordered (his lieutenant) Ẓibyān ibn Rashīd al-Dawsarī to divert them forcefully (back) to Darᶜiyya. The leader of the ḥujjāj told the Saᶜūdī leader that (the pilgrims) could put up a sum of money in order to be allowed to continue on to the *Ḥaramayn* but ᶜAbdul-ᶜAzīz said: We warned you that all who desired to go to Mecca must pass by Darᶜiyya first, as well as contract with us to follow this religion (yuᶜāhidūnā ᶜalā hadhā al-dīn]. . . .[122]

After paying a sum of money, the travellers were allowed to go their own way. Another incident shows that the house of Saᶜūd followed an even more forceful policy with regard to revenues from trade. In 1784, a large caravan setting out from the al-Ahsa district (eastern Arabia) was ambushed by Saᶜūd ᶜAbdul-ᶜAzīz's men at an oasis in al-Kharaj; a fierce battle ensued in which Saᶜūd's troops killed ninety of the three hundred travellers accompanying the caravan, and took as plunder a great amount of money, cloth and camels.[123] In the following year, another caravan on its way to Jabal al-Shammar was attacked; many of the people accompanying the caravan were killed, and the cloth that was destined for the inhabitants of the Jabal seized.[124] These incidents show that the Saᶜūdīs were intent on reversing the laissez-faire attitude of previous administrations; in fact, they put into practice an innovative system by which to control the transit economy of Arabia and the Gulf.

The basis of this new system was simple: the Saᶜūdī ʾamīrs established a brand-new policy whereby the old arbitrary tolls taken by tribal shaikhs on the roads of Najd were stopped, and travellers were forced to pass by way of a narrow corridor controlled by Saᶜūdī allies. Eventually, they ended up at Darᶜiyya where they paid a single toll.[125] In other words, the khuwwa tax imposed by shaikhs on merchants and travellers that crossed "their" territories was disestablished by the Saᶜūdī ʾamīrs, although a direct tax was substituted at Darᶜiyya. In return for giving up this profitable and lucrative impost, the tribes of Najd loyal to al-Saᶜūd (such as the al-Ḥarb, al-ᶜUtaiba, al-Juhaina and al-Hudhail) were allowed to make up the loss by collecting *ghanīma* (literally spoils, in this case wartime revenue), from the districts opposed to the Saᶜūdī forces, for which they had only to disburse the *khums* or the canonically stipulated fifth of the booty to the state.[126] Thus, the khuwwa was replaced with a fixed share of all the revenues accruing to the Saᶜūdī treasury or bait al-māl. Indeed, for all of Ibn Bishr's conviction that the Saᶜūdī ʾimāra was wholly built on the principal of moral renewal inherent in the Wahhābī movement, it is clear that the motive for some tribes' allegiance to the Saᶜūdī state was partly based on material reasons. The Saᶜūdī system, whereby tribes loyal to the state were allowed a free hand in the collection of revenue in wartime, in effect made these tribes shareholders in the state and guaranteed that they would pay lip service to the Wahhābī ᶜaqīda. Although this was not an equal partnership, for the Saᶜūdī's made sure that all the important tribal confederations pledged the bayᶜa to the principles of the faith, and kept the most troublesome tribes in check by assigning control over them to the Saᶜūdī's most zealous lieutenants, it was a partnership that was systematized over several decades, and formed the core of the Saᶜūd's relationship with the tribes. A present-day historian describes it thus:

> For these tribes to be considered as anything but idolators, they had to be incorporated into the political system whose core was (and still is) the Saᶜūdī clan. This entailed these tribes becoming tributaries to the center of power in southern Najd, and this, in turn, entailed not only their subjection to taxation (in kind such as camels), but also their exclusion from the political sphere. The

> centralization in the extraction of surplus and the elimination of the role of these nomadic tribes in the extraction of surplus for their own benefit, as they did from protection fees (khuwwa) paid by agriculturists and by traders passing through tribal territories implied more than the technical reorganization of such extraction in general by relegating this task to a central authority which then redistributed to every group its proper due. It also implied political eradication, that is, the abrogation of tribal rights for the benefit of a political right exclusively excercised by the center. This new political right erected over the debris of tribal rights is itself derived from an eminently tribal concept, that of protection, himaya, excercised by the central authority, in exactly the same way as the nomadic tribes had hitherto offered protection and thus politically neutralized settled and trading groups in return for taxation. . . . In the religious terms of Wahhābīte divines and of the principles of government they imparted to the House of Saʿūd, this reduction of nomads, agriculturists and townspeople equally into subjects of the Saʿūdī polity, this compact of protection and allegiance, was expressed in terms of the canonical tax, the zakat. . . . With the zakat, the criterion of inclusion within the exclusive group is indicated; the group comprises the parties to a compact of unequal power, sharing a common exterior which exists for the purpose of expansion. . . .[127]

The monopoly of transit dues and agricultural taxation was regulated by means of the institution of a cadre of tax officials, the *ʿummāl.* The ʿummāl were the roving inspectors of the Saʿūdī state system, the ones on whom the government depended for the generation of revenue. According to Ibn Bishr, the ʿummāl were divided into various categories: there was an ʾamīr (the leader of the party), a *kātib* and a *hāfiẓ al-daftar* (clerks to list the taxes collected), a *qābiḍ al-darāhim* (a treasurer), and three retainers who took charge of and cared for the animals that came under the collection of zakāt or alms tax.[128] Moreover, there were ʿummāl whose function it was to collect the taxes from the towns while there were others whose specialization was to collect revenues from the rural areas. The extent of the Saʿūdī state's sovereignty over neighboring areas can be measured by the expansion of the tax-collecting area, and the number of pastoral as well as settled tribes that paid duties to the state. Always according to Ibn Bishr, by the end of ʿAbdul-ʿAzīz's rule (1803), government ʿummāls collected taxes amounting to 11,000 *riyāls* per annum from the tribes of the al-Muṭair; while the ʿummāl assigned to the tribal districts bordering Syria collected close to 10,000 riyāls each. Government tax collectors also imposed the zakat on the al-ʿAnayza tribal sections (both those living in Syria and those living in Najd proper) who had to pay 40,000 riyāls and eight pure-bred horses in a good year,[130] al-Ḥuwaiṭāt, al-Shammar, al-Ẓafīr, al-Qaḥṭān, al-Ḥarb, al-ʿUtaiba, al-ʿUjmān, al-Sabīʿ, al-Suhūl, al-Murra as well as the tribes of Yemen and Uman.[131] Furthermore, in Saʿūd ibn ʿAbdul-ʿAzīz's time [1803–14], the zakāt tax was collected on camels and sheep from the Holy Cities, Uman, Yemen (up to 150,000 riyāls from the ports of Yemen alone), Iraq, Syria as well as Najd. Barring exaggeration, this must have been a very large sum indeed.[132] The redistribution of the zakāt tax funded the emergent state structure: one-third went to satisfy the needs of the local government in each district, another third went for the upkeep of the military, as well as to the central government in Darʿiyya and the ʿulamāʾ of ʾĀl al-Shaikh, and the final third was sold for cash to finance state merchants' journeys abroad, where they went to buy essentials for the Saʿūdī ʾimāra. In some years, state revenue was more than ample; Ibn Bishr calculates that in a good year, Darʿiyya's revenues came up to 80,000 *darāhim.*[133]

As important as the internal financial administration of the state were the foreign policies initiated by the Saʿūdīs to monopolize long-distance trade and to render the Saʿūdī ʾimāra one of the most self-sufficient in the region. Part of the Saʿūdī strategy to control transport and trade revenues was to attack significant neighboring districts such as Kuwait, southern Iraq, and Syria. Perhaps the most important focal points in this strategy were the Shīʿī shrine cities of southern Iraq, the Muntafiq districts on the Euphrates and Tigris, Kuwait, and eastern Arabia, especially al-Ahsa. After a number of lightning raids on the fringes of Iraq and Kuwait had taken place, and especially after the Wahhābīs almost destroyed the important Shīʿī shrine city of Karbalāʾ in a fierce offensive in 1801, tribes from Iraq, Kuwait, and eastern Arabia that shared the same trade and pilgrimage routes began a counterattack. Thus, from the 1790s onwards, the Muntafiq tribes of lower Iraq were in the forefront of any planned offensive on Darʿiyya, the Wahhābī capital, and the deposed rulers of al-Ahsa, the Banū Khālid, though nominally subjects of the Saʿūdī ʾimāra after 1796, were not averse to changing sides when it was convenient for them to do so.[134] Moreover, at the same time that the Saʿūdī state formalized a new approach to transit trade in the region by forcing merchants and pilgrims to take the direct route to Darʿiyya, and inducing Saʿūdī-allied tribes to patrol the passageways from the Iraqī, Syrian, and Kuwaitī deserts into central Arabia, the Saʿūdī ʾamīrs tried to destroy the other free ports in the region or, at least, to bring them under control for the greater glory of the Saʿūdī state. Thus the literature records the many instances in which Saʿūdī campaigns against the Arabian coast ended in the defeat of regional merchant dynasties such as ʾĀl al-Rizq in Zubara. The latter town, once the most opulent on the Arabian coast, was completely devastated by a Saʿūdī raid in 1795.[135]

The Saʿūdī state's attempts to destroy the tradition of free trade in the region, and to dominate transit routes by land and by sea was viewed as a calamity by a number of historians of the period,[136] many of whom were divided as to how to treat the Saʿūdī-Wahhābī alliance in the first place. This was not only because the appeal of the Wahhābī daʿwa penetrated the scholarly discourse of anti-establishment ʿulamāʾ in Iraq and the Gulf, and sowed the seeds of religious or ideological resistance to Mamluk governments (in some cases, leading to the espousal of "Wahhābī" ideas in Mamluk Iraq),[137] but also because the expansion of the first Saʿūdī state threatened the westernmost limits of the Iraqī tribes' diyār (communal lands or frontiers), which had been finally determined at the beginning of the eighteenth century as a result of inter-tribal wars. An examination of the Saʿūdī attempt to carve out a wider frontier zone at the expense of the Iraqī and eastern Arabian tribes is therefore very much in order at this point.

THE IRAQĪ CAMPAIGNS IN NAJD

The history of the Iraqī campaigns in late eighteenth and early nineteenth-century Najd is sometimes considered as nothing more than an obscure chapter in the overall relations of Wahhābī Arabia with the outside world. Overshadowed by Muḥammad ʿAlī of Egypt's more successful military expeditions during the period 1811–18, the failed campaigns of one of the ablest Mamluks in the Baghdad administration, ʿAlī al-Kahya (later Pasha), are relegated to a mere footnote in most of the comprehensive accounts of the first Saʿūdī state.[138] And yet a study of these campaigns sheds light on a number of issues related to the formation of the emergent state itself, as well as its expansionist policy with regard to neighboring districts in Iraq, eastern Arabia, and Kuwait. Most of all, an examination of the Iraqī Mamluk campaigns in Arabia reveals the nature of the historiographic, indeed the *polemical* traditions of the region at a crucial point in time. The latter point is fundamental in any study of the Wahhābī movement; for there is ample evidence that the upheavals generated in the region as a result of the emergence of the first Saʿūdī ʾimāra did not go unnoticed by contemporary historians of the period, many of whom described the ascending Wahhābī menace with growing alarm. Oppositional currents in Iraq and eastern Arabia found a receptive climate among many historians of the region, and a literature of resistance emerged that not only tried to interpret the theological and intellectual issues raised by the Imām in the light of realities in the region, but also attempted to draw spheres of political interest around frontier districts in Arabia, Iraq, and the Gulf. At the very same time that the anti-Wahhābī dialectic was being composed in Iraq and eastern Arabia, pro-Saʿūdī chroniclers in Najd were themselves writing histories to rebut the "heresies" of a Ṣūfī-influenced, "liberal" Islam that permeated the districts of Iraq, eastern Arabia, Kuwait and the lower Gulf. The thrust of the pro-Wahhābī histories was that the call of the Imām was just, and would find a ready reception among all true Muslims. The Saʿūdī expansion into eastern Arabia, the Hijaz, Oman and the fringes of Iraq was thus considered to be a necessary function of the Unitarian ʿaqida, for military-political initiatives went hand in hand with a reformist message.

For instance, one of the points of contention between the pro-Wahhābī and pro-Mamluk historians is the casus belli for the Mamluk-Saʿūdī wars in the latter part of the eighteenth century. The case of Shaikh Thuwainī is instructive. Shaikh ʿUthmān Ibn Bishr, the pro-Wahhābī historian, pours scorn on Thuwainī ibn ʿAbdullāh ibn Muḥammad al-Shabīb, head of the Muntafiq tribal confederation in lower Iraq and sometime ally of the Mamluk pashalik in Baghdad, who in 1796 began his Najdī campaign by inexplicably slaying everybody in the small town of al-Tanuma, in the Qasim district. Incensed by the Muntafiq shaikh's actions, Ibn Bishr notes his later assassination with undisguised glee.[139] Because Thuwainī was killed just as his army was poised to do battle with Saʿūd ibn ʿAbdul-ʿAzīz's forces, his demise is seen as divine punishment. In Ibn Bishr's eyes, this punishment is extended to Thuwainī's erstwhile allies, the shaikhs of the Banū Khālid tribe of al-Ahsa for, after the death of Thuwainī, "God put fear in their hearts,"[140] and their troops retreated in disarray, fleeing to Baṣra. Saʿūd ibn ʿAbdul-ʿAzīz's army, referred to as "the victorious Muslims" by Ibn Bishr, then pursued the Banū Khālid and captured their livestock. After Saʿūd had distributed the ghanīma (the spoils of war), he went north into al-Ahsa (and Banū Khālid territory), where its defeated population gave him the bayʿa or swore allegiance to him in the name of "God's religion and that of his Prophet" [*wa bayaʿuhu ʿalā dīn ʾAllāh wa rasūlīhī wa ʿalā al-simʿa wa al-ṭāʿa*].[141]

The Iraqī historians saw it differently: the Saʿūdīs are accused of invading al-Aḥsāʾ and occupying it in the name of the Wahhābī ʿaqīda, in effect shutting down a crucial trade route to Iraq and Kuwait. Thus, the pro-Ottoman bureaucrat-historian al-Kirkuklī inveighs against ʿAbdul-ʿAzīz, the second ʾamīr of the Saʿūdī line, claiming that the latter attacked eastern Arabia with a large force, killing two hundred of its inhabitants; after which he annexed al-Qatif and "gave these districts as iqṭāʿ (land grants) to his fellow tribesmen and followers."[142] Apparently, this so angered Shaikh Thuwainī that he asked permission from the government of Baghdad to recover the district. Al-Kirkuklī's curtly-worded account is corroborated by the more forceful version of another pro-Ottoman historian, Ibn Sanad al-Baṣrī:

> Thuwainī had gone to fight the Wahhābīs in Najd after having sought permission from the wazīr (Suleimān Pasha, vali of Baghdad), for the Wahhābīs had occupied al-Ahsa and taken it from the shaikh of the Banū Khālid, and assimilated it to the rest of the districts they had taken over. And the (Wahhābīs) exhibited their *bidʿa* (religious innovation) in these territories and murdered *ʿulamāʾ* in al-Ahsa, saying they were mushrikūn (polytheists). So Thuwainī attacked them with his soldiers, and many Arab tribes that had pledged their allegiance and obedience to Saʿūd flocked to Thuwainī's army because they were discontented and dissatisfied with the Wahhābīs who forced them to undergo wearisome duties and to undergo many hardships to fight the Muslims (referring, of course, to Thuwainī's men). . . .[143]

More forceful still is Ibn Sanad's description of the climate in the Wahhābī camp after Thuwainī's assassination by a slave called Taʿīs. Always according to him:

> When the followers of Ibn Saʿūd found out that Taʿīs had killed Thuwainī, they praised [Taʿīs] in the most fulsome way, because they believed that Thuwainī was a kāfir, and all of the Muslims on the face of the earth that did not believe what they believed were kuffār as well. In fact, they wrote poetry in praise of the incident and made it sound like one of the many events in the *futūḥāt al-Islāmiyya* (the Islamic conquests). . . .[144]

Another incident is more revealing of Saʿūdī attempts to control the trade and transportation routes of coastal Arabia. The Mamluk ʿAlī al-Kahya's first military campaign against the Saʿūdī state began in 1798–1799, after news filtered into Baghdad of the Muntafiq shaikh's defeat and death at Wahhābī hands. Assembling a large army composed of *Najāda* (tribesmen from Najd settled in Baghdad, and anti-Wahhābī settlers from Zubair), ʿAlī al-Kahya resolved to make straight for al-Ahsa.[145] Assisted by the shaikh of Kuwait, the expedition embarked on boats for al-Ahsa where, finding resistance, ʿAlī al-Kahya's troops fought for twenty days to regain control of the fertile, well-watered district. Because their supply lines were overstretched, and the territory hostile, Ottoman armies faced troubles from the start. Carrying heavy cannons, pack-mules perished in the sand, while expensive equipment and munitions fell in disrepair from the heat; meanwhile, just as the army had been reorganized into a more disciplined fighting force, a huge storm struck the Ottoman encampment and sent men, animals, and equipment flying. Finally, although supplies reached the expedition from Kuwait, they were few and far between. Nevertheless, ʿAlī al-Kahya decided to press on with his military offensive.

At a spot called al-Tāj (or al-Thāj), the Ottoman army met the forces of Saʿūd ibn ʿAbdul-ʿAzīz and a large battle took place, in which numerous members of both armies were killed. According to the Iraqī historian al-Kirkuklī, the Saʿūdī leadership realized they were outmatched so they decided to negotiate. Al-Kirkuklī then cites the full text of a letter sent by Saʿūd ibn ʿAbdul-ʿAzīz to ʿAlī al-Kahya:

> Since we understand under what pretext you came to al-Ahsa [we must explain the following]. The people of al-Ahsa are all treacherous *rafaḍa* [the general Hanbalī term for Shīʿa] and it is we who made them Muslim through the sword. Al-Ahsa is but a village and not part of the Ottoman dominions, and distant from your country and does not produce a thing that is worth your trouble. And even if the whole of al-Ahsa were to pay taxes or revenues [darāhim] to you, the sum would not equal the expenses of your campaign. We have no quarrel with you but with Thuwainī (the shaikh of the Muntafiq who was on the verge of attacking the Saʿūdī *ʾimāra* when he was assassinated) and God has meted out his punishment. So we hope for peace. . . .[146]

Realizing that if he desired the war to continue, he must continue his offensive and, appreciating the fact that his army's morale was very low due to the catastrophes that had befallen his troops, ᶜAlī al-Kahya decided in the end to continue negotiating with the Wahhābīs. To this end, the Mamluk commander sent a letter to Saᶜūd ibn ᶜAbdul-ᶜAzīz informing him of his terms. The Saᶜūdīs were to keep away from al-Ahsa, to return the cannons pillaged from the defeated Shaikh Thuwainī's camp, to stop their attacks on Iraqī ḥujjāj (pilgrims) and to discontinue their *ghazawāt* or raids on Iraqī tribal encampments and villages. Although ᶜAlī al-Kahya's letter merited an immediate reply from the Saᶜūdī ʾamīr, the latter's tone was cagey. Brushing aside the Ottoman condition to withdraw from al-Ahsa, and turning a deaf ear to ᶜAlī al-Kahya's demands for financial compensation for the campaign, Saᶜūd committed himself to one important promise: he would

> pledge on God's covenant that (the Ottomans) would not lose one mule, and that (the Wahhābīs) would not lay a hand on travellers, and they would receive nothing but hospitality and access. . . .[147]

Although al-Kirkuklī's account of ᶜAlī al-Kahya's unsuccessful offensive is by far the most sober, it is not the sole description of the pivotal events of 1798–1799. Ibn Sanad, who nursed grievances both against the Wahhābīs and his fellow historian, the Mamluk bureaucrat, Shaikh Rasūl al-Kirkuklī (referring to him contemptuously at one point as "the Turkish historian" and claiming that he did not even know al-Kirkuklī's name, the title of his history and the town from whence he hailed),[148] gives another version of the Saᶜūd-Alī correspondence. According to Ibn Sanad, Saᶜūd's reply to ᶜAlī al-Kahya's demand to stop attacks on Iraqī merchants and pilgrims was the following:

> And Saᶜūd said: " As for the security of routes, we will continue to fight others to safeguard them, until we make the whole earth God's property, and all Muslims participant in it." [*hattā najᶜalu al-arḍa kullahā lil-lāh wa jamīᶜa al-Muslimīna mushtarikīna fīha* . . .].[149]

Obviously, this was not the statement of a repentant commander. Moreover, Ibn Sanad notes other anomalies in the correspondence between the leadership of the two warring parties. For one thing, Saᶜūd ibn ᶜAbdul-ᶜAzīz addressed ᶜAlī al-Kahya simply by his first name, as if to imply that the Mamluk official had no known father.[150] While this was a grave insult in Arab-Ottoman society, Ibn Sanad was not above condemning ᶜAlī al-Kahya himself, referring to him as "the idiotic katkhuda, who makes conditions even though he is defeated," allowing "the devil Saᶜūd" to escape further punishment.[151] Moreover, Ibn Sanad notes that the assurances that Saᶜūd made to ᶜAlī al-Kahya were nothing but vain promises, for the following year the Saᶜūdīs again raided Iraqī towns and villages, their attacks finally culminating in the ferocious offensive against the Shīᶜī shrine city of Karbalāʾ in 1801.

More significantly, the anonymous author of *Kitāb lamᶜ al-shihāb* (who wrote from the perspective of a disgruntled, anti-Wahhābī opponent) intimated that the Saᶜūdī campaign to attack border villages and towns in the last years of the eighteenth century was the most systematic attempt yet seen to control the transit routes into the Arabian peninsula. This attempt had a firm socioeconomic basis. Thus the anonymous author believed that:

> Al-Ahsa was a district that was full of benefits, and many resources, trees, and rivers. It has rice that is sufficient for the whole of the Arabian peninsula, as well as dates. And that is why the ʾĀl al-Saᶜūd could not rest until they had conquered it, and whosoever of the Saᶜūdī-allied tribes that approached near-scarcity conditions was told to go to al-Ahsa to replenish its supplies. . . .[152]

At the same time that Iraq and Kuwait were coming under Wahhābī attack, the Saᶜūdī ʾamīrs were beginning a large offensive against the free ports of the region (such as Zubara); they also targeted al-Ahsa and especially Uman, the chief power in the Gulf. The account of Zubara's fall is instructive. As early as 1786, the Saᶜūdī ʾamīrs began to covet the town and sent an advance army under one of Ibn Saᶜūd's ablest generals to lay siege to the trade emporium. Because Zubara's merchants and leading townspeople had no independent sources of fuel or water, but instead relied on eastern Arabia for their supplies, the Saᶜūdī army was able to close in on Zubara and seal it off from its land routes. As a result, the town fell and its merchants dispersed to Bahrain.[153]

Eventually, the attacks on al-Ahsa spilled over into forays against Uman and the Gulf principalities as well. In the latter invasions, the Saᶜūdīs were assisted by a formidable ally, the Qawāsim of Rās al-Khaima. According to the author of *Kitāb lamᶜ al-shihāb,* the Qawāsim were enjoined to become Saᶜūdī allies, in return for which they and their supporters in the Gulf would receive twenty laden *baghlas* and *dhows* (sea-going vessels) from the Saᶜūdīs, a third of which would come directly under Qawāsim control.[154] At first, the Qawāsim refused, earning a stiff rebuke from the Saᶜūdīs who told them, in no uncertain terms, that the time had passed when they could take to the seas and fight whomever they pleased. Although the latter continued their raids on Gulf shipping a full three years before renegotiating an agreement with the Saᶜūdīs, they eventually pledged to assist the Saᶜūdīs in their seaborne campaigns, and so became their staunchest allies in the Gulf. In fact, by the last part of the eighteenth century, the Saᶜūdīs had developed an ironclad association with many of the coastal tribes that inhabited the strip of Gulf shore owing allegiance to the Qāsimī shaikhs. According to al-Rashīd, the Qawāsim joined the Wahhābī movement because they were Sunnī and Ḥanbalī, and jihād "appealed to their warlike instincts," and also because the Saᶜūdīs were asking them to raid their traditional enemy, the ruler of Masqaṭ.[156] Whatever the true reason for the Qawāsim's espousal of the Wahhābī daᶜwa, they proved to be most adept at fighting and defeating numerous enemies of the faith, including the Umanīs, the Ottomans, and the Egyptians.

However, apart from sporadic attacks on British vessels in 1797–98, the Qawāsim dared not interfere with British shipping in Gulf waters in the last quarter of the eighteenth century, although they continued to carry out raids against local merchant fleets throughout the period. In 1804, however, partly because their centers of power had been conquered by the ʾamīrs of ʾĀl al-Saʿūd, leaving them with no resort but to comply with the latter's wishes, the Qawāsim's alliance with the Wahhābīs was transformed into a compact by which the tribes of Rās al-Khaima embarked on naval warfare for the greater glory of the Saʿūdī state. According to a British observer, the compact stipulated that the Qawāsim would

> cruise in the service of the Wahabee[sic] Shaikh against all vessels appearing in the Gulf, without exception, reserving one-fifth as his share of the pirated property, the remainder being divided among the captors.[156]

Regardless of contemporary British assertions that the Saʿūdīs instigated anti-British "piratical" attacks on the part of the Qawāsim, there is no conclusive proof that the latter were persuaded to raid British shipping as part of an overall Wahhābī master plan.[157] Still, anti-Wahhābī suspicions abounded among British officials, and did much to cloud the issue. For instance, in that same year, the Qawāsim captured two vessels, the *Shannon* and the *Trimmer,* belonging to the British Resident in Basra. When British officials remonstrated with the Qāwāsim, the ships were returned, but only after having been completely stripped of all that they carried. A truce was then signed between the ruling Qāsimī shaikh and the British, leaving the former free to continue their attacks on local shipping, but binding the shaikh and his followers to respect the peace with the British. As a result of that hotly-contested action (for which the Qāsimī shaikh suffered a permanent loss of credibility among his follwers), the tribes from Rās al-Khaima turned their attentions to the western coast of India; and by 1808, their depradations were so successful that in that year alone, it was estimated that the Qawāsim fleet captured twenty "country" [local] boats.[158]

Naturally, the Qawāsim's naval successes invited a sharp response, both from local ʾamīrs (Saʿīd ibn Sulṭān of Masqat) and the British East India Company. On 12 November 1809, Rās al-Khaima and other Qāsimī towns were bombarded, and the Qawāsim were driven into the interior of the country. Many of the inhabitants were killed and upwards of fifty vessels docked in port were destroyed, including the British ship, the *Minerva,* which was burned.[159] Nevertheless, the combined British-Umanī expedition achieved little, for many ships in the Qāsimī fleet escaped damage, having been kept out of harm's way by their owners, while the Qawāsim retreated to their refuge, totally unrepentant. In fact, they continued their attacks on local shipping until the demise of the first Saʿūdī state. With the invasion of the Saʿūdī-Wahhābī capital, Darʿiyya, by Ottoman-Egyptian troops and the collapse of the first Saʿūdī state in 1818, the Qawāsim were forced to come to terms with the changed conditions in the Gulf and eastern Arabia, eventually laying down their arms and signing a peace treaty with the British.

CONCLUSION

By 1811, the Arabian peninsula was unified under the banner of the Saʿūdī state. While pockets of resistance remained, they were marginalized; the majority of anti-Wahhābī tribesmen, townsmen, merchants, and scholars had either submitted, been killed, or had fled to Iraq and the Gulf. The frontiers of the Saʿūdī state were not only hammered out through military expansion but through religious instruction and moral example derived from the Qurʾan and Ḥadīth. Thus, one of the symbolic ways in which the Saʿūdīs extracted submission from the tribes and towns of the peninsula was to oblige the defeated parties to make the bayʿa, an oath of loyalty and obedience to the ruler which was usually contracted in public, and sealed with monetary or other forms of material compensation. In the Wahhābī case, the bayʿa was usually entered upon after tribal shaikhs or leaders of towns pledged to obey "God's religion and that of his Prophet" [*wa bāyaʿahum ʿalā dīn ʾAllāh wa rasūlihi wa al-simʿa wa al-ṭāʿa*].[160] The bayʿa was followed by the collection of ghanīma (war booty), in the form of livestock, crops or money, from which the Saʿūdīs extracted the canonically stipulated taxes for the support of the state. The whole operation terminated in a peace pact or *ʿaḥd* which transformed the moral climate of the vanquished districts; by entering into a peace treaty with the Saʿūdī ʾimāra, "unbelievers" were transposed from the age of *jāhiliyya* (ignorance) to one of submission to God's revelation.

On another, perhaps more fundamental level, the Saʿūdī statist experiment threw into relief two antithetical, yet important features of frontier societies in Iraq, Arabia, and the Gulf. On the one hand, the tradition of free trade continued to thrive and prosper in Kuwait and Bahrain, even though the Wahhābī invasion of Zubāra terminated it once and for all in that town. Although statistics on eighteenth century Gulf trade are still largely lacking, information culled from secondary sources provides some theoretical backing for the thesis that Gulf trade evinced a certain prosperity at the turn of the eighteenth century. For instance, Jacqueline Ismael points out that one of the clues for the transformation of Kuwait's leadership from the pastoralist mode to one based on a mixed sector (overland trade as well as fishing and pearling) may have resided in the renewed "imperialist competition between the expansive mercantile powers of western Europe"[161] in the seventeenth century. This, in turn, led to a renaissance in trade that indirectly contributed to the resurgence of tribal settlements in Arabia and the Gulf. As a result

> Some of the powerful bedouin families were already shifting their attention from the pastures of the desert to the trade routes and urban centers of trade that were emerging in the area, precipitating inter and intra-tribal conflicts as expropriation from trade became a real alternative to appropriation from camel pastoralism. . . .[162]

Another, more frequently cited, reason for the unhampered establishment of regional ports of trade was the emergence of the first Saʿūdī state, and the wars that erupted throughout the peninsula as a consequence of the extension of Saʿūdī leadership on the tribes of Najd and eastern Arabia. From 1785 to 1793–95, the Banū Khālid tribes of eastern Arabia entered into a life- and-death struggle with the ʾamīrs of the Saʿūdī house, freeing tribal clans and sections formerly under Khālidī tutelage to govern themselves. As a result, the latter, most of whom came from ʿUtbī tribal sections, were able to establish their own states in Kuwait, Bahrain, and Qatar.

The establishment of these coastal settlements serves to underscore the point that by the latter part of the eighteenth century, regional networks of trade, for which these free ports performed a necessary function, may have started to coalesce into a regional system. This system was dependent upon the institution of market towns to link Gulf merchants with sources of capital, an ample supply of goods, and mechanisms for the distribution of regional commodities. Thus a regional market was created in which the establishment of these towns played a critical role. In order for the regional market to survive and to expand, secondary commercial centers had to be built to replace traditional ports of trade that had either been subjugated by military leaders, had fallen prey to all too frequent epidemics, or had been damaged by fire or flood. Kuwait, Zubāra, and Bahrain thus took on the functions of alternate depots for the regional market.

The second characteristic of the regional economy of Iraq, Arabia, and the Gulf, on the other hand, was the near monopoly of routes and resources by religious-commercial entities such as the first Saʿūdī state and Mamluk Iraq. The increased attention paid to economic factors by the first Saʿūdī ʾimāra (1745–1818) resulted in the first attempts by that peninsular power to put controls on the free flow of regional goods and services from within the region itself, a development totally inimical to the free trade traditions of the period. While neither the Saʿūdī ʾimāra nor the Mamluk administrations of Iraq were completely successful in rerouting the transit economy to their door, both made a determined effort to subvert the commercial conventions on which regional trade depended, bringing about severe, albeit temporary disruptions in the regional economy.

There is a tendency in the secondary literature on the Wahhābī movement to shy away from attributing *any* economic motives to the Saʿūdī state. Still, some historians are beginning to stake out a middle ground on the subject; thus Michael Cook believes that the one significant difference between the Saʿūdīs and their opponents was that the Saᶜūdīs relied on faith, which "tipped the balance in [their] favor."[163] However, he does concede that trade was not unimportant in the overall picture. Cook notes that:

> More modest commercial links between Najd and the international trade of the Persian Gulf undoubtedly existed, and the Najdī population at the end of the first Saᶜūdī state is described as a highly mercantile one. An increase in the volume of such trade, although trivial by the standards of the outside world, could well have been crucial in Najd. What can we say of the hypothesis that such an increase lies behind the formation of the Saᶜūdī state?[164]

The distribution of revenues from trade may indeed have played a part in the attachment of Najdīs from all walks of life to the emerging Saᶜūdī state. As recounted above, an important obligation of tribesmen and townsmen allied to the state was the disbursement of the zakāt tax to the state treasury on all booty obtained in war, as well as that accruing from agricultural or trade revenue. Moreover, even though the *khuwwa*(or " protection"tax) was reformed under Saᶜūdī auspices, it was not entirely disestablished. In fact, it became the solid core for a state-wide monopoly of land routes and resources which was redistributed in turn as state patronage. In addition, trade revenues (whether amassed from attacks on trade caravans or from stopping commercial craft at sea) also became systematized for a time. Besides the attempts at the control of land routes, the Wahhābīs also tried to control access to sea routes by means of their tactical alliance with the Qawāsim tribes. At its height, the Wahhābī-Qawāsim alliance was so powerful that it alarmed not only the local emirates of the Gulf but also the British, Ottoman, and Persian navies. Vincenzo Maurizi (a.k.a. Shaikh Manṣūr, an Italian physician who, through an incredible twist of fate, became the Sultan of Masqat's "Commander against the Geovasseom and Wahabee Pirates") was reportedly told by a Wahhābī emissary to Uman at the beginning of the nineteenth century that

> the expense of foreign expeditions is not entirely defrayed from the internal revenue of [Saᶜūdī] dominions [for] the great treasure taken from the tomb of Ali [at Karbalāʾ, during the attack of 1801] is not yet exhausted, besides which all of [the Saᶜūdī] neighbors endeavour to avert hostilities by the payment of regular tribute. . . .[165]

At its peak, the first Saᶜūdī state became extremely prosperous. Again, Ibn Bishr provides us with a gauge of Saᶜūdī success by commenting on Darᶜiyya's wealth prior to its destruction by the troops of the Egyptian general ʾIbrāhīm Pasha in the early nineteenth century. According to him, Darᶜiyya's power radiated far and wide, "in a way that is indescribable . . . for if I were to try to describe the people . . . of wealth that entered the town, from all over the region, and those that settled there . . . then this book would be insufficient, and you would hear wondrous things."[166]

Finally, whatever the merits of the present-day debate on the socioeconomic background of the first Saᶜūdī ᵓimāra, it is obvious that contemporaries of the Wahhābī movement were fully aware of its impact on the material and strategic contours of the region as a whole. By the early nineteenth century, a Christian merchant from Basra, reflecting on the misfortune of living in a city where the governor could impose extralegal taxes on the mercantile community almost at will, made the following wistful remarks in his personal diary:

> In 1801, the Wahhābī (ᶜAbdul-ᶜAzīz ibn Saᶜūd) . . . conquered Bahrain and tried to conquer Muscat. . . . The Arabs of the ᵓUtūb tribe followed the Wahhābī because they desired the justice of his administration. Because he did not take the gumruk (duty) in all of his districts but (confined himself to) the *ᶜushr* (the legally stipulated tenth) from all his subjects, which he spent on necessary things such as feeding strangers who passed by his districts, (everybody) ate as well or as frugally as he and the indigent in his district did. . . . As for his government, in all of the districts under his rule, all swear the *yamīn* (an oath) on God . . . and there are no divisions between the tribes or the people, (for) everybody obeys the law (of ᶜAbdul-ᶜAzīz ibn Saᶜūd). And that is why the country is at peace. As for ᶜAbdul-ᶜAzīz, who is head of this tribe, he behaves as if he was one of them, and he does not countenance distinctions between his followers, nor in his manner of dress. He does not wear a glorified *ḥijāb* like the Ottoman governors or take on titles such as Agha or Effendi or anything of the sort. For if a poor man were to walk into his chambers, in order to explain to him his problems, his speech would begin, "O, ᶜAbdul-ᶜAzīz, my problem is such-and-such," and the Wahhābī would listen with attention. This type of just and fair government therefore does not countenance the existence of any aggressor or thief, and there is no fear nor insecurity on the roads, and in all these diyar the livestock roam freely, for there is no enemy that would disrupt their existence. . . .[167]

-Two-

The Structure of the Regional Market of Iraq, Arabia, and the Gulf

This chapter is concerned with the development of a trading region that encompassed the desert settlements of Najd, the agricultural belt of lower Iraq, the seafaring coast of Kuwait, and the riverine port of Muḥammara. It seeks to delineate the inner rationale of this vast economic region by describing the production and trade of each locality as well as the economic practices and traditions of the region as a whole prior to the full impact of Ottoman centralization and British economic designs. By the last quarter of the eighteenth century, the regional market that had grown up around the Gulf, Arabia, and Iraq had evolved certain characteristics that were peculiar to it. These characteristics, and the structure that predetermined them, will form the substance of this chapter.

A REGION IN FORMATION

Ever since the sixteenth century, when the governor of Basra, Rāshid ibn Mughāmis ibn Ṣaqr ibn Muḥammad al-Faḍl, later anointed *Sulṭān al-Sharq* by Ahsaʾī historians, was called upon to rescue al-Ahsa from the clutches of the Portuguese,[1] Arabia has had strong links with southern Iraq. Although this connection waxed and waned depending upon the socioeconomic and political circumstances of the moment, the inhabitants of the two regions felt sufficiently contiguous in a cultural as well as geographic sense to influence each others' destinies for close to four hundred years. Even before the irruption of the Wahhābī movement, prominent town leaders at the helm of important Najdī settlements were already fanning out to develop strong commercial and intellectual ties with eastern Arabia and lower Iraq. Thus, the ʾamīr ʿAbdullāh ibn Muḥammad ibn Muʿammar (1685–1725) of ʿUyayna, probably the most significant town in seventeenth and eighteenth-century Najd, encouraged trade with Basra, and especially al-Ahsa "to such a degree that they became interdependent."[2] Regular migration of Najdī ʿulamāʾ and merchants to eastern Arabia and lower Iraq was complemented by ease of settlement in these two districts, "[and] it was not unusual for a Najdī family to have relatives in Iraq, Kuwait, or al-Ahsa."[3]

Moreover, after the Wahhābī movement consolidated its hold over the Arabian peninsula and expanded up to the fringes of Iraq, Syria, and Kuwait, contact increased by leaps and bounds as fierce battles between the Wahhābīs and their enemies spilled over into Iraqī and Kuwaitī frontier-towns such as Zubair (in southern Iraq) and Jahra (in Kuwait). Disruptions increased as pastoral migration and flight from Arabia created new demographic realities: in lower Iraq, the vehemently anti-Wahhābī tribe of the Ẓāfir settled in the Muntafiq districts and joined the latter confederation in its sporadic wars against the Saʿūdī state while sections of the Muṭair took refuge in Kuwait. As a result of all this in-migration, the once-sleepy hamlet of Zubair, a few miles away from Basra, was reinvigorated by the settlement of a number of different clans and families from central Arabia.[4] And while demographic and economic trends coalesced to create a larger terrain for regional interaction, intellectual developments proceeded apace. In the last quarter of the eighteenth century, the ʾImām Muḥammad ibn ʿAbdul-Wahhāb began circulating missives to the ʿulamāʾ of Iraq and eastern Arabia in which he explained the reformist message of the Wahhābī daʿwa; and while he seems to have been partly successful in gaining followers in those two districts,[5] the whole exchange led to a heated debate between the religious leadership of Iraq, Arabia, and the Gulf that paradoxically cemented regional propensities regarding the development of a more salafī-inspired Islam. By the last quarter of the nineteenth century, the message of influential Sunnī ʿulamāʾ in Iraq such as Shaikh ʾIbrāhīm al-Ḥaidarī promoted a strict orthodoxy in all religious matters, the disassociation of Sunnī Islam with the "rejectionist" elements of Shīʿa philosophy, and a reawakened interest in the activities of the much-diminished, yet still significant, Saʿūdī state.[6] In the early twentieth century, the articulation of such ideas gave rise to a pronounced salafī slant among such distinguished Sunnī scholars of Baghdad as Shaikh Maḥmoud Shukrī al-ʾAlūsī, whose many works included a sympathetic history of central Arabia appropriately entitled *Tārīkh Najd.*[7]

At the same time that socioeconomic and cultural relations were being cemented between eastern and central Arabia, Kuwait, and Iraq, an expanding regional economy was projecting its influence over the district of Arabistan, in what is now southwest Iran. Ties between Basra and Ḥuwaiza, across the Shaṭṭ al-ʿArab, had long been in existence;[8] and were it not for the dessication of Ḥuwaiza's main river channel at the beginning of the nineteenth century, they probably would have continued. After the decline of Ḥuwaiza, the new town of Muḥammara took its place, earning a place for itself in the regional historiography of the period by coming under the turbulent rule of the Kaʿab tribe. Although the history of Kaʿab rule in Muḥammara will be discussed elsewhere, here it is important to reiterate that nineteenth-century historians of Basra, Kuwait and Najd also wrote about Muḥammara as a matter of course,[9] linking Arabistan to Iraq, Arabia, and the Gulf in manifold and complex ways.

If we attempt to redraw the contours of the region by focusing on the course of an ordīnāry journey undertaken by a travelling merchant in the late eighteenth or nineteenth centuries, and assume that he would proceed on a south to north axis, the logical starting point would be Najd (see map, p. 12). Leaving Najd, our traveller would arrive in the prosperous and well-watered region of al-Ahsa, or eastern Arabia. After boarding a sailing ship from the Ahsa'ī port of ʿUqair, the traveller would either land in Basra or in Kuwait, both of which had coastal access through the Shaṭṭ al-ʿArab which in turn abutted on the Gulf. He might make a last trading foray into Arabistan, and visit any one of the busy ports on the eastern side of the Shaṭṭ. Finally, he might book passage on a merchant vessel to India. However, in order to understand what commodities our traveller would be trading in and what form of payment he would accept for the exchange, it is essential to retrace his journey from where he first began, placing special emphasis to the place of production.

CENTRAL ARABIA

Until very recently, any history of pre-modern Arabia necessarily began with a short description of the Wahhābī movement, as if the Wahhābī daʿwa had sprung full-blown from the arid ground of Najd. In recent years, unpublished evidence points to the gradual settlement of central Arabia by migrating pastoralist tribes who founded towns, turned to agriculture and eventually sponsored a movement of intellectual revival that sowed the seeds for the Wahhābī movement a full three centuries before its birth.[10] Two of the most important towns discussed in the local sources are Buraida and ʿUnaiza, in the Qāsim district. At the beginning of the nineteenth century, they functioned as the centers of the livestock trade, where camels and horses were sold.[11] While important for its livestock, the Qāsim also depended upon a wider area for items of trade. Supplied with horses by the Muṭair tribesmen, the towns of Qāsim also sold stallions and mares that had been reared further inland, such as in Jabal Shammar and ᶜAridh. By the mid-nineteenth century, travellers were able to relate that the Rashīd ᵓamīrs in central Arabia possessed magnificent horse farms and traded in colts and yearlings as far afield as India.[12] As with all other parts of Najd, the district of al-Qāsim was tied into long-distance trade by caravans which brought essential foodstuffs such as rice and grain from Iraq and dates from al-Ahsa. In 1852, it was estimated that one of the imports into Najd by way of al-Ahsa and Yemen were European and Ottoman gold coins which were exchanged "at a considerable profit" with resident merchants for *shāmīs* (local currency) so that the latter could buy *ᶜabās* (woolen cloaks) and shirtings from lower Iraq.[13]

In 1862–63, the British traveller W. G. Palgrave visited ᶜUnaiza and made the following remarks:

> This large town had been for centuries the capital of the province . . . of what we may call the northwestern center (of Najd). Its commerce with Mecca and Medina and with central Arabia, nay even with Damascus and Baghdad . . . had gathered in its warehouses stores of traffic unknown to any other locality of inner Arabia, and its hardy merchants were met with on the shores of the Red Sea and the Persian Gulf, and occasionally on the more distant banks of the Euphrates or by the waters of Damascus. . . .[14]

Although European travellers who visited the district of al-ᶜAridh and especially its "capital," Riyāḍ, in the same period invariably considered the town's trade to have been monopolized by "foreigners" (i. e., merchants from al-Ahsa, Uman, the Hijaz and Yemen), local merchants saw no barriers to trading with resident traders, and often went into partnerships with them in order to make hefty profits. In fact, according to al-ᵓAlūsī, the author of *Tārīkh Najd,* by the early twentieth century the town numbered around 20,000 people, and they were "all Wahhābīs."[15]

EASTERN ARABIA

While no one region in Najd was more historically distinctive than another (except perhaps al-Yamāma, a large and amorphous region that in certain historical periods may have included all or parts of Najd),[16] eastern Arabia was most often identified with its large and prosperous coastal district, al-Ahsa. In the last quarter of the eighteenth century, al-Ahsa had been the domain of the powerful Banū Khālid tribes, an ᵓimāra that possessed superior facilities for sea as well as land transport. By 1792–95, however, the Banū Khālid had been defeated and forced to make the *bayᶜa* or oath of allegiance to the first Saᶜūdī state. Although the Wahhābīs paid special heed to reforming the "irredentist" practice of the Ahsaīs (who were, for the most part, Shīʿa),[17] the Saʿūdī ʾamīrs could not afford to alienate completely the inhabitants of al-Ahsa and the districts beyond it, if only because the commercial acumen and technical expertise of the people on the coast was essential to the successful outcome of the Saʿūdī-Wahhābī seaborne campaigns of the early nineteenth century.[18] However, even before the Saʿūdīs had begun to use al-Ahsa as a springboard for their naval assaults on Uman and the northern Gulf shaikhdoms, the district functioned as the oasis of Najd. It was the frequent meeting place of pastoralists from central Arabia as well as traders of the towns. Al-Ahsa was therefore an important center for regional trade, and carried with it a prestige and a prominence that far exceeded its territorial confines.

If traders were to specialize in the agricultural and pastoral products that their districts produced, they needed to settle in these districts either for a short or a long time. In so doing, many became resident merchants for "foreign" firms operated by kinsmen or people from their home towns. A significant literature concerning cross-cultural trade has sprung up with regard to other similar commercial regions in Africa and Asia, and the term "trade diasporas"[19] has come to signify the institution, over time, of regional merchant communities in areas distant from the merchants' point of origin. The same practice held in Arabia, the Gulf, and Iraq, and both the local and foreign sources are replete with information concerning these resident traders. With respect to al-Ahsa, observers noted that the towns and oases of the district sheltered a significant community of Iraqī, Bahrainī, and Indian merchants who traded and frequently settled there, using the port of ʿUqair to warehouse their goods in anticipation of the sailing ships that would eventually transport them to India.[20] According to an anonymous history written in or around 1803 (whose author may have been a Najdī merchant),[21] seasonal tribal markets were organized in al-Ahsa, whose sites bore the names of the various days on which they were held (such as *sūq al-thulāthāʾ* or the Tuesday market). Al-Ahsa's hot springs were so famous that they merited detailed mention in the latter's history.

> Al-Ahsa is a great country, and full of palm-trees. It is distant three days from the sea by camel . . . and it has thirty-six springs of water. It has a spring called the hot one, whose water is hotter than bath-water that has been placed on the fire. . . .[22]

Prior to 1818, al-ʿUqair, the port of al-Ahsa, was considered to be the chief seaport; it possessed a customs house, which handled all overland goods coming from al-Ahsa and central Najd. Merchants paid a tax of ten percent on all goods other than dates and agricultural produce, on which custom duties of twenty percent were levied.23 After the demise of the first Saʿūdī state, however, al-

ʿUqair was scaled down to a half-functional customs house and a small fort; nevertheless, because it was still considered to be the most direct route to the interior of central Arabia, overland merchants and camel caravans still preferred setting out inland from ʿUqair.24 Finally, in 1833, a French observer noted that the district's biggest exports were dates, along with gums, aloes, spices, myrrh, incense, and indigo.25 By 1852, al-Ahsa's rice (shileb) and dates were considered among the best in the region; it also produced ghi (clarified butter) and possessed a small but growing ʿabā (woolen cloaks) industry.

Kuwait

In Kuwait, as also in southern Iraq, the most important regional traders were of Najdī or Persian origin. Kuwait itself had been built in the mid-eighteenth century by migrating tribal peoples from the Arabian peninsula, the Banū ʿAtāba or the ʿUtūb, and until the 1920s still functioned as a market town for Najdī pastoralists.[27] In fact, many of the Kuwaitī traders who carried on long-distance commercial activities with Indian ports in the nineteenth century were themselves of Najdī origin.[28] Situated at the mouth of the Gulf, Kuwait relied on its stock and trade, fishing and pearl-diving. Easily the best sailors in the region, the Kuwaitīs depended upon the regional network to provide them with a fresh water supply, energy in the form of wood, and sail-cloth for their ships.[29] In 1852 it was estimated that Kuwait also imported Iraqī wool, up to "one hundred thousand fleeces, " each fleece weighing about two and-a-half pounds.[30] The wool was paid for with dates, itself an import either from Iraq or al-Ahsa.

Kuwait's tax-free status continued up till the late nineteenth century, much to the annoyance of the Ottoman authorities in Iraq, who hovered surreptitiously around Kuwait's ruling shaikhs in the hopes that one would accept to enter into a long-term alliance with the Porte.[31] In 1854, a British observer noted that

> The members of the ruling family [of Kuwait] are thrifty and inoffensive, and engage themselves principally in trade, and in the navigation of their vessels. The political condition of Kuwait varies from that of the other Maritime States, in that the inhabitants acknowledge the sovereignity of the Ottoman Porte, and use the Turkish flag, although their allegiance to the Sultan is merely nominal. Their Shaikh, on the contrary, receives an annual allowance of dates, stated at 200 *karrahs* (small), value about 4,000 crowns, from the Pasha of Bussora, as the condition of protecting that port from foreign aggression whenever his aid may be required. Koweit possesses a safe and capacious harbour. The number of men capable of bearing arms is said to amount to 6,000; the population of the town to 22,000. The estimated gross annual revenue amounts to 22,000 crowns, derived from contributions, and a small tax levied at the gate on goods carried into the country, or brought into town.[32]

SOUTHERN IRAQ

With the exception of Basra, the shrine-cities of Najaf and Karbala, as well as a few provincial centers such as those congregated around the Hilla-Diwaniya axis, southern Iraq was a patchwork of tribal market towns.

Basra

In 1840 a French consular agent wrote that Basra was nothing but a mass of ruins; due to the chronic epidemics that had visited the town, its population had been reduced to 5, 000 people, of which "one-third" were African slaves imported from Muscat and Zanzibar.[33] In 1860, this impression was confirmed by a *Qāḍī* (religious judge) of the place, who added that alongside the regular appearance of plagues, the inhabitants of Basra also suffered at the hands of extortionate mutasallims (deputy governors) and rapacious tribes.[34] While the latter historian held many personal grievances against the administration of Basra that may have influenced his perspective,[35] there is a good deal of truth in his account. Quite simply, Basra was no longer the thriving city it had once been at the turn of the century, when it could be said that

> by the late 1760s . . . Basra's trade was booming [and] a spectacular increase in English shipping and the rise of the Masqat fleet acted as the backbone of this boom. . . .[36]

But the picture was not completely one of gloom. Obviously, whatever profits regional merchants made in buying and selling commodities over a large area did not trickle down equally across the region. Some market towns achieved a temporary prosperity while others faded into obscurity; in an era where economic and political instability conspired to render the lives of ordinary people totally hostage to fortune, it could not have been otherwise. Nevertheless, one of the principal facets of regional trade operations in Iraq, Arabia, and the Gulf is that Basra still commanded a dominant role among overland traders by the middle of the nineteenth century. A trade report compiled in 1852 by the British agent in Basra admits as much; for while the latter could not be completely precise about the figures and statistics he was reporting on, he was more definite about where the trade was going, and who was consuming most of it.[37] Apparently, Basra was the fulcrum of regional activities. During the date season alone (September through October) it attracted Najdī traders, resident merchants from Basra, as well as representatives of Kuwaitī merchant houses, tribal cultivators from the riverine districts ready to sell their produce, shaikhs from the big agricultural tribes bordering the Shaṭṭ al-ʿArab, and Arab, Persian, Umanī, Indian, and British shipping firms. Small wonder, then, that up to the early twentieth century, Basra retained a certain privileged position among the traders of the interior; for alongside other large cities such as Baghdad and Bombay, it had the reputation of being a source of great bounties among Arabs from Najd and Kuwait.[38]

Because Basra and its tribal periphery were host to a large resident merchant community, an ʿālim-historian from Baghdad complained that he had never seen "a town more dominated by foreigners" in the mid to latter part of the nineteenth century.[39] Basra was settled by Najdī and Persian merchant communities of long standing.[40] In the nineteenth century, Persian traders formed an important commercial network for the distribution of goods coming up the Shaṭṭ al-ʿArab to Basra and Baghdad, and from there to Persian border towns, and thus competed with Iraqī traders for control of the major routes for goods entering Iran.[41] The Persian merchant community probably grew from the yearly influx of pilgrims intent on performing the *ziyāra* (pilgrimage) at the Shīʿī shrine cities in Iraq (Najaf, Karbala, Kazimayn, and Samarra); in fact, many of the pilgrims were merchants who made the journey to trade in local goods. In 1852 their economic significance to the provincial treasury of Baghdad had grown to such a degree that a temporary standstill of their commercial activities (brought on by the on-again, off-again Ottoman-Qajar relationship, which held trade hostage to foreign policy) moved the *defterdār* (provincial treasurer) of that city to complain that "he could not realise one-tenth of the revenue for the year."[42]

In 1880, a French major anxious to establish a line of steamers to Marseille temporarily set up shop in Basra. He began his account by describing the social hierarchy of the town. At the top of the social ladder was the *Naqīb* of Basra who, although head of the Sunnī religious hierarchy, was also a wealthy landholder. He came, mounted on a superb white horse, to pay Major de Rivoyre a visit, while a parasol-carrying servant preceded him. Next to the *Naqīb* in importance was the Qapudan Pasha, the commander of the Basra navy, whose fleet was in much need of repairs and renovation. Finally, there was the Persian consul and various members of the "Persian" community in Basra (by which the Major may have also meant Arabic and Persian-speaking Shīʿī merchants, of Arab and Persian origin). According to the Frenchman, this was the largest, richest, and most distinguished community in Basra; they lived in magnificent houses on the banks of the ʿAshar canal, and they dressed in cashmere and silks, the quality of which "might render Parisian women mad with jealousy."[43] Finally, de Rivoyre commented that, "[Even though Persian merchants] were settled on foreign soil, they had nothing to fear [from the local government]."[44]

De Rivoyre's comments were obviously those of a casual observer who had barely skimmed the surface of Basra's social structure; perceptive though he was, he had failed to include the important Najdī merchant community in his *tour d'horizon* of the city. Although merchants of Najdī origin assimilated easily into Basran society, sometimes so imperceptibly that they barely left a trace, their presence attracted the attention of biographers and historians all the same. For instance, al-Ḥaidarī's survey of regional merchant houses did not fail to include those merchants from central Arabia who had settled in Basra, Kuwait, or Muḥammara; and in one of the categorical statements for which he was later to become famous, he asserted that, in the mid-nineteenth century, "most of Basra's merchants are Najdīs. " (A fuller survey of Najdī merchant houses will be attempted below.)

The ʿAshar canal, so important that it was often mistaken for a river, not only housed the Persian merchant community but also the *saray* (government offices), the mansions of other influential notables, and the larger markets of Basra.[46] In fact, the town was intricately laid out across interconnected creeks and canals, most of them lined with a growth of palm-trees that grew Basra's most famous product, dates. As a result, not only did Basra function as the main port of shipment for goods destined to and from India, serving as a conduit for the products of Najd, Kuwait, Baghdad, and Arabistan, but it was also the *débouché* for surrounding districts, such as the agriculturally fertile districts of the Shaṭṭ al-ʿArab.[47] The districts that grew dates stretched from Abū al-Khaṣīb in the south to al-Haritha in the north. Basra's outlying districts also produced barley, broad beans, rice, and a host of other vegetables and legumes.[48]

At mid-century, it was estimated that Basra harbor was capable of admitting cargo boats of medium tonnage, which could unload at the door of the customs house. Larger ships (up to six hundred tons) were stationed at some distance outside the town, and were serviced by *mashḥūfs* (lighters) which unloaded the cargo in mid-river and transported it to the quay. During the date season in September and October, the dates were packed, sold, and immediately shipped to India; and it was only a month later that the first riverboats, laden with produce from Bengal, made their way upriver to Baghdad.

Zubair

A few hours away from Basra, Zubair was a developing center of trade and agriculture, dependent on the overland trade routes from Najd. Its main products were fruit, vegetables, and cooking-oil.[49] Zubair was, in many ways, the last "gate" before the open desert, and due to its strategic location on the overland routes from central Arabia, functioned as the fort that protected Basra from the west. However, its relations with Basra were frequently patchy. In 1852, it was calculated to possess four or five thousand inhabitants, and to be only nominally subject to Ottoman Basra.[50] Although Zubair was in large part free of "the constant miasma and its attendant diseases, which render Basra nearly always fatal in those seasons to an European,"[51] during the winter months when heavy rains caused the Euphrates to flood, parts of the town were transformed into an enormous lake up to four feet deep, leaving travellers no other option but to reach the town by boat. The town's main inhabitants were influential merchant-capitalists of Najdī origin who had made most of their fortunes in the long-distance trade with India; some of this capital was either reinvested in date plantations or in goods for sale to the large, and transient Bedouin population that made Zubair their chief market town. Zubair imported grain, rice, and ghi from Basra, nearly all of which was consumed by the local population, as well as manufactured linen cloth from India and England, and large quantities of coffee, dates, and sugar that were exchanged with neighboring districts.[52] Finally, Zubair was also a market for horses, from central Arabia as well as Iraq.

Sūq al-Shuyūkh

Further north was Sūq al-Shuyūkh, an important tribal market in the mid-Euphrates district and seat of the Muntafiq *riʾāsa* (leadership). The Muntafiq territories began on the Hai river, stretched up to Qurna (at the juncture of the Tigris and Euphrates) and included large territories on both banks of the Shaṭṭ al-ʿArab. In 1852, it was estimated that the territory of the Muntafiq, including, of course, Sūq al-Shuyūkh, was "an immense and wealthy district studded with date groves on the banks of the river [which was] in a high state of cultivation. . . ."[53] Sūq al-Shuyūkh was peopled with resident traders from Najd, and the town itself depended on the transit trade from Najd and Basra. In return for ʿabās and shirts from Najd, merchants circulated such products as barley, rice, and ghi to central Arabia, and cereals, buffalo skins, ghi and wool to Baghdad and Basra.[54] Sūq al-Shuyūkh was an expanding agricultural center in the nineteenth century, but it also had its own textile industry; for like eastern Arabia, it too produced woolen cloaks, the ʿabās that formed the everyday attire of tribesmen. It also had its complement of muleteers and camel drivers to carry out internal trade with other market towns and neighboring regions. For instance, the Sūq merchants derived considerable profit from hiring camels to pilgrims for the Holy cities of Mecca and Medina by way of their intermediaries in Najd. Finally, the horses bred and sold at Sūq al-Shuyūkh were reputed to be among the best in Iraq.[55]

ARABISTAN

Across from Basra, in ʿArabistan, the northern trading center of Ḥuwaiza was fast making way for the new development of Muḥammara (now Khorramshahr). Ḥuwaiza had long been the seat of Arab tribes, especially the Muntafiq ʾimāra in the sixteenth century,[56] and in the 1880s its population was still considered to be wholly Arab in ethnic origin and traditions.[57] As a result of the dessication of its main tributary, the town withered away, and by 1852 it was considered to be almost depopulated and completely at the mercy of Muḥammara and Basra for its supplies of dates and grain.[58]

Muḥammara

Originally built as a peripheral addition to the extended domains of the Kaᶜab tribes, Muḥammara (situated at the confluence of the Karun river and the Shaṭṭ al-ᶜArab) had nevertheless began to outstrip the older Kaᶜab capital of Fallaḥīyya. By mid-century, some observers even felt that it had the potential of posing a serious future threat to Basra's supremacy.[59] Although the last development was not to materialize, the new town did rapidly set about attracting an important clientele. In part, this was due to its excellent and capacious natural harbour which could accommodate vessels of up to six hundred tons. Thronged with merchants of every nationality, it became a center for resident trading communities, including those from southern Iraq and Kuwait.[60] These merchants supplied the Persian hinterland with goods that Iranian merchants themselves could not obtain nor transport in an efficient manner, beset as they were by the numerous obstacles relating to transportation and to costs of passage that formed the backdrop to all trade with central Iran before the 1890s. This was largely because, prior to the opening of the Karun river to steam traffic in the latter part of the century, routes from southern Persia to the center were nearly inaccessible.[61] For instance, as late as 1908, a British intelligence officer complained that all European imports had to arrive in Muḥammara, then be transported by river steamer to Ahwaz, after which they were transshipped by tramway to a point on the upper Karun river, there to be carried by mule or cart to the interior of Persia.[62] Moreover, tribal feuds made commercial traffic difficult, for goods destined for central Persia were forced to pass either by way of the Bakhtiyari road to Isfahan or via Baghdad and Kermanshah.[63]

Muḥammara, situated as it was at the mouth of the Karun river and able to oversee all traffic passing up and down the Shaṭṭ al-ᶜArab, "was the major transshipment point for the foreign trade of the province."[64] It was also the granary of southwest Persia, as well as its main producer of dates, rice, and opium. Persian horses were a staple of the province, and boat building was a major industry. In 1850, Muḥammara imported Indian goods from Bushire (Abu Shahr) in boats; included were items such as sugar, tea, ginger, pepper, nutmeg root, indigo, and textiles from Gujerat and Benares. It also imported English manufactures, cotton shirtings, chintz, guns, pistols, flints, gunpowder, lead, iron, tin, china and glassware.[65]

A STATISTICAL DESCRIPTION OF REGIONAL TRADE

The description of the regional market of Iraq and the Gulf would be incomplete without statistics, however incomplete.[66] The fullest data available on the transit trade of the region before the phenomenal rise of seaborne exports in the late nineteenth century was compiled by Consul Rawlinson in Baghdad in the

1840s, and especially by the British agent in Basra, J. Taylor in 1852. The latter report is especially detailed, and worthy of study.[67] Furthermore, it is unusual for the period because it attempts to give an idea of the trade passing by land as well as by sea. Most significant of all, the author of the report estimates the trade of each locality, as well as the general volume of the region in local currencies, such as the *shāmī* and the *kerān,* noting that traders in the Muntafiq districts refused payment in all other currencies, including the British-Indian rupee or the more official Constantinople piaster. Clearly, the fact that rural areas only accepted payment in the shami is an indicator, however small, of the continuing autonomy of regional economic networks, and the still significant place of the local market in transit trade.

The report begins by enumerating the exports of Sūq al-Shuyūkh (woolen ʿabās, woolen shirts, wheat, barley rice, and *ghī*) to Basra, which totalled 523, 000 shāmīs (approx. £114, 014). It then proceeds to calculate Baghdad's imports (British manufactures, Indian textiles, cashmere shawls, indigo, iron from England, sugar, spices, drugs, and tea from Singapore) from Basra which stood at 1, 186, 932 shāmīs (approx. £258, 751, 3 shillings and 7 pence). Basra's imports from India (indigo, Surat piece-goods and Indian produce) by way of the annual ship from Calcutta, which were then circulated to Baghdad, amounted to 625, 000 shāmīs (approx. £136, 250). Its total imports from the various countries with which it had commercial connections (i. e., India, Persia, Yemen, Muscat, Bahrain, and Batavia) rose to 2, 891, 724 shāmīs (approx. £630, 395, 16s. 7d.); from Sūq al-Shuyūkh and Baghdad, the sum was 861, 160 shāmīs (approx. £187, 732, 17s. 7 d.). Riverine tolls and duties collected by tribal shaikhs as well as other government agents came up to 437 shāmīs (approx. £95, 5s. 4d.). Baghdad's trade with Persia was negligible, the whole amount not exceeding 40, 000 kerāns (approx. £1, 832, 6s. 10d.), of which 30, 000 kerāns' worth consisted of tobacco from Shiraz (approx. £1, 374 and 5s.). Interestingly, dues from *iltizāms* (revenue farms) were calculated to amount to 213, 115 shāmīs (approx. £46, 459) for the Basra vilayet alone. Finally, Baghdad's manufactures (headcloths such as *ʿigāls* and *tangībs,* as well as slippers) and its wheat added up to 265, 000 shāmīs (approx. £57, 770). The rest of the consular report deals with the itemization of regional products and an indication of their origin. Thus goat-hair for tents came from Persia, as did tobacco from Shiraz, grain from Bushire, madder and henna from Bandar Abbas, coffee from Yemen, olive-oil soap from Damascus, pearls from Bahrain, and cloth from Switzerland. The important regional products, horses and dates, still topped the list, although in 1852 the export of horses to India was suffering because of a temporary lull in the market.

As can be seen, Iraq's import trade with India and with Persia far exceeded its exports; this was to be the case until 1869, when the opening of the Suez Canal led to a dramatic increase in Iraqī exports of grain and dates, and a large increase in Basra's trade.[69] Furthermore, over and above the large amount of specie that was drained away from the Iraqī provinces to pay for these imports, an additional burden of remitting the annual revenue to Istanbul fell upon the shoulders of the Ottoman authorities in Baghdad and Basra. Thus the latter were constantly being forced to juggle their figures around to make up for a palpable deficit in their annual budgets that even the large expenditures of Persian pilgrims into Iraq could not completely turn around. Nevertheless, the report makes a very interesting case for the survival of some sections of the regional economy, showing that while some districts had indeed been impoverished by the flight of capital and the almost total dependence on British-Indian imports, others actually showed a profit. For instance, upon deducting Sūq al-Shuyūkh's imports from its exports, a healthy balance of 3 *lacs* of shāmīs (approx. £65, 400) remained.[70] And yet

> a traveller passing through their district will find the capital of their principality a heap of mud hovels, the *reaya* and the fellāḥs (cultivators) the poorest and most oppressed of this portion of Iraq, the government miri share of the revenue more than two years in arrears and their wealthiest merchants refugees. But the Montefik rule is notorious for its severity, oppression and exaction; the government officials must be privately influenced and the numerous shaikhs conciliated, and the burden falls upon the hard-working agriculturists, traders and laborers. . . .[71]

In another part of the report, the Muntafiq is labelled a "wealthy district." Of course, this assessment may have held true only in the period immediately prior to the first Ottoman attempts at the dismemberment of the Muntafiq *mashyakha* (shaikhdom); for after 1852, and the imposition of gradual, but effective Ottoman rule on the district, each annual auction of Muntafiq lands detached more and more territories from the overall territories of the tribe, drastically reducing the Muntafiq shaikhs' incomes as a result.[72] Moreover, the free ports of Zubair and Kuwait are also given their due. The one was termed "an opulent town" inhabited by "men of large fortunes, " the other an impartially-governed shaikhdom settled by "large ship owners" and "wealthy traders. " Was this pure hyperbole on the British consul's part? Even though the usual picture of mid-nineteenth century local markets continues to be one of general retreat in the face of advancing British trade,[73] and even while there seem to be no independent statistics either to confirm or to deny the report's assertions, it is entirely possible that as late as 1852, certain inland markets were still experiencing a mild prosperity. For instance, in 1845, the Assistant Resident at Bushire thought that Kuwait

> presents a singular instance of commercial prosperity. Its population consists of nearly 25, 000 inhabitants, who possess 31 Buggalows (*baghlas*, an ocean-going vessel), from a hundred and fifty to three hundred tons burthen, which trade constantly with India; 50 smaller boats are employed in the coasting commerce of the Gulf, and about 350 boats are engaged in fishing on the pearl banks. . . .[74]

Obviously, the fact that Kuwait was a free port, devoid of a customs administration and unhampered by the constant surveillance of tax-hungry officials, was a point in its favor. Although an overland market, Zubair possessed the same characteristics: both Kuwait and Zubair functioned without excessive controls, and so attracted a stream of regional clients eager to do business in a free economic climate.

An additional and related, question concerns smuggling, which was widely practiced throughout the region, not only in unsupervised free ports but wherever there was a watchful and overzealous customs administration (see the chapter on the horse trade). In fact, even while British officials were self-righteously calling attention to the existence of contraband in the Gulf, British merchants in Iraq were indulging in it themselves. For instance, in 1815–16, due to highly favorable relations with the then Mamluk governments of Baghdad and Basra, East India Company agents won the right to discharge their goods in Agency warehouses, without having these commodities inspected by customs officials; naturally, "this gave British traders the opportunity to avoid the payment of duty on all their merchandise by smuggling parts of it."[75] Again, in 1849–50, in conjunction with Ottoman efforts to put an end to the "illegal" navigation of British steamers on the Euphrates, the deputy governor of Basra wrote the Porte that there was ample evidence of British smuggling goods on their steamboats; however, due to a number of different circumstances, Istanbul let that pass too.[76] Generally speaking, smuggling was a systematic endeavor in Iraq, Arabia, and the Gulf; it was not episodic, haphazard, or unusual. While a more detailed analysis of smuggling costs will be attempted elsewhere, here it is enough to indicate that while statistics on the contraband trade are few and far between, such activity must have been the principle raison d'etre of free ports throughout the region, and possibly one of the chief reasons that they survived at all in a highly competitive climate.

CASH, CREDIT, AND BARTER

It has already been remarked in a previous chapter that the inception of the regional market was due in no small part to the rise and development of a number of significantly-placed market and port towns which integrated trade on a regional scale. These markets functioned as tax havens, shielding regional merchants from oppressive governmental taxation, while guaranteeing access to scarce commodities. Although their initial establishment may have coincided with the rise of certain lucrative routes, they were nonetheless abandoned when the same routes declined. Thus, one of the strategies of this trading region seemed to be the institution of secondary market towns to take advantage of new routes and commercial opportunities, as well as the creation of alternative venues for regional merchants to fall back on in the event their traditional markets became obstructed, a subject that will be dealt with separately in chapter 7.

The flexibility of these commercial centers and the rerouting of regional trade was built on the entrepreneurial instincts of regional traders, as well as on common trading practices such as partnerships and contractual obligations between different sectors, cash transactions and exchange or barter. While details on these questions will be discussed later, it is useful to point out here that the economy we are describing operated on several different levels, as befits any sophisticated economic system. Embedded within it were aspects of simple exchange, but it was also characterized by the sophistication of its credit operations and the variety of its currencies. Moreover, as befits a regional economy, commercial practices and usages applied to town as well as to countryside, to urban *effendīs* as well as to rural *tujjār*. Thus tribal merchants formed commercial arrangements with merchants from the city, bespeaking profitable alliances between town and countryside. Trading corporations emerged to take advantage of important monopolies for land and sea transport and the dues attached to them. Finally, occupational specialization existed throughout the regional market, tying livestock supplier to transport agent, and both of them to the resident trader in Bombay. Since all of these features of the regional economy will be dealt with at length elsewhere in the book, this section will be mainly concerned with the proliferation of family firms over the extended region, and the ways in which cash, credit and barter tied the regional market together.

MERCHANT HOUSES AND FAMILY FIRMS

The Bassām Family

In the local annals of merchant firms, there is probably no family that has received as much attention as the ʾĀl al-Bassām. The Bassāms traced their lineage back to Shaikh ʾAḥmad ibn Muḥammad ibn ʿAbdullāh ibn Bassām, the paterfamilias of the ʾĀl al-Bassām from ʿUnayza. In 1601, he was a qāḍī first in ʿUshayqir, then in ʿUyayna, where he died in 1630. The Bassāms were from the very important Banū Tamīn tribe in Najd.[77] In the mid-nineteenth century, members of the Bassām family in ʿUnayza are mentioned as being engaged in long-distance trade, money-lending, and landholding. For instance in the 1860s, the intrepid traveller Charles Doughty made the acquaintance of ʿAbdullāh al-Bassām, "a merchant of Jidda and chief of the house of Bassām at Aneyza." ʿAbdullāh's father, ʿAbdul-Raḥmān al-Bassām had been a horse trader who died early, leaving his son to fend for himself. The latter went to Baghdad, where he began to dabble in trade, eventually becoming a slave trader with Zanzibar. Afterwards, he traded slaves for Mauritius sugar, sold rice to Bombay and the Arab ports on the Gulf, and finally established himself in agricultural pursuits in Basra where he told Doughty that "he had corn lying in his granary to the value of £5000!"[79] When Doughty met him in 1861, ʿAbdullāh al-Bassām had invested £120 of his earnings in land; he was growing corn, "for corn was always dear in poor Arabia."[80]

More importantly, ʿAbdullāh's eldest son, ʿAbdul-Raḥmān, had been sent to India on business by his father while another son resided in Basra, and yet a third (Suleimān) made Jidda his home.[81] While there is no information on what the Bassām family members traded in, the importance given this resident merchant house by travellers as well as local chroniclers points to their significant trans-national interests which, as late as 1904, was earning them the sobriquet of "large traders" by British officials.[82] In 1917–1918, H. St. John Philby met with a number of family members while in ʿUnayza, and recounted that, while most of the Bassām family had remained loyal to the ʾamīr Ibn Rashīd, formerly the reigning power in Najd but now on the verge of being dispossessed of all his properties by ʿAbdul-ʿAzīz Ibn Saʿūd, one or two Bassām cousins chose Ibn Saʿūd's side. Moreover, while Philby was in ʿUnayza, he learned that, true to his merchant origins, yet another cousin by the name of ʿAbdul-ʿAzīz al-Bassām had been caught trying to break the British blockade of the Ottoman army in Iraq by attempting to smuggle goods from Kuwait to Ottoman Iraq by way of Haʾil (northern Najd).[84]

The Al-Rashīd Shaikhs of Jabal Shammar

In 1862–1863, the British traveller W. G. Palgrave noted that the shaikh of Jabal Shammar, Ṭallāl ibn Rashīd, not only built the requisite palace in Ḥaʾil, but "a long row of warehouses . . . [and] a marketplace consisting of about eighty shops destined for public commerce and trade."[85] The ʾamīr Ṭallāl was known for his business acumen and commercial interests; for alongside the new marketplace at Ḥāʾil, he also instituted a policy of inviting merchants from Basra, Karbala, Wasit (in Iraq), Medina, and even Yemen to set up shop in his refurbished "capital. " There he made "lucrative" commercial contracts with long-distance traders, and went into partnership with the best of them.

> Many of these traders belonged to the Shīʿā sect, hated by all good Sunnīs and doubly hated by the Wahhābīs. But Tallal affected not to perceive their religious discrepancies, and silenced all murmurs by marks of special favor towards these very same dissenters, and also by the advantages which their presence was not long in procuring for the town. The desired impulse was given, and Ḥaʾil became a center of trade and industry, and many of its inhabitants followed the example of the foreigners thus settled among them, and rivalled their diligence and wealth. . . .[86]

Throughout the nineteenth century, Jabal Shammar was reputed to be the heartland of the Arabian horse. Quite naturally, the Rashīd ʾamīrs had corralled the very best of the breed, and by the middle of the nineteenth century were considered to be the largest horse-breeders and dealers in northern Arabia. In 1864 the ʾamīr Tallal was estimated to possess a stud of six hundred mares alone.[87] He and his descendants sold horses yearly to India; and in 1877–1878, the British traveller, Lady Anne Blunt, was told that horses from Ibn Rashīd's stud fetched as high as £100 a piece in Bombay.[88]

The Zuhair Family

Like the Bassāms, the Zuhair family was associated with one town—in the Zuhair's case, Zubair—but had fanned out all over the region so that, by the 1840s, they had family representation in Aleppo, Basra, and Baghdad. A local historian described them as *bait majd wa tijāra* (a house of nobility and trade).[90] The Zuhair family led a tribal coalition in the defence of Basra in 1831, after the Kaʿab tribes of Arabistan had launched a preemptive strike against the city and its environs in the confused period after the decline of the Mamluk pashalik, and in the few months prior to the restoration of Ottoman power in Basra. In 1834 the Zuhair merchant house was nearly eradicated after most of its leadership was decimated in the Muntafiq-Zubair struggle (see Chapter Seven); in 1884, however, a member of the Zuhair family, Qāsim Pasha, having returned to Basra from his birthplace, Aleppo, became a member of the Ottoman parliament for Basra, after having briefly occupied a position on the commerce court (al-maḥkama al-tijāriyya).[91]

The Naqīb (or Rifāʿī) Family

The Naqībs (sometimes called the Rifāʿīs because of their links with the Rifāʿī ṭarīqa) were the foremost merchant-ʿulamāʾ family in Basra. Their prosperity arose through waqfs, date properties, and mercantile activities with India.[92] According to a family historian, a branch of the Naqībs had lived in Basra since the beginning of the Islamic conquests, and claimed descent from the Prophet.[93] While part of the family remained in Kuwait, another branch continued to reside in Basra, where the most famous member of the family, Sayyid Ṭālib, first entered politics at the turn of the century.[93] By the 1870s, as a result of their wealth and the strength of their regional alliances, the Naqīb family had become the de facto rulers of Basra.

In 1872, a series of robberies occurred in Basra which the authorities seemed unable or unwilling to stop. The British Vice-Consul intimated that, were they so inclined, some of the most influential men in the city—amongst them Shaikh Suleimān Zuhair and the Naqīb of Basra and his brother, Sayyid Muḥammad Saʿīd—could have put a stop to them but they allowed them to continue with their tacit approval, if not their encouragement, in order to embarass the deputy governor of Basra, Saʿīd Effendi, with whom they were on bad terms.[95] What is interesting in this connection is that a French traveller in 1880 mentions that, among Basra's many guilds, there was a corporation for robbers whose members openly offered their services to any city "boss" who wanted to hire them, functioning in much the same way as the medieval *ʿayyārūn,* or the "mafia" of nineteenth century Karbala.[96] Did large merchants cum city bosses use the services of the robbers' guild? There is indeed evidence that some merchants and notables of late nineteenth century Basra funded political assassinations in the city, and in tandem with a few government officials, may have been behind the "random" murders of two important notables, i.e., the shaikh of Zubair, Khālid Pasha al-ʿAwn and the head of the Salmān family in Basra, al-Ḥaj Manṣūr Chalabī al-Salmān.[97] For instance, Suleimān Faidhī, a distinguished lawyer in Basra, recounts in his memoirs that as a result of this breakdown in law and order, Fakhrī Pasha, temporarily the vali of Basra in 1904, entered *ḥārat al-luṣuṣ* (the robbers' quarter) one day and indiscriminately opened fire, killing six people and wounding five. He then made an appeal to the people of Basra to turn in the known thieves, who were then thrown in prison, although some fled to Muḥammara. Most of the latter were sent back in manacles, and twenty-one were executed and thrown in the Shaṭṭ al-ʿArab in sacks. After Fakhrī Pasha's departure, Wahbī Beg became the deputy governor of Basra, and finding out there was open collusion *(talāʿub)* between notables, merchants, and government officials, he immediately prosecuted the most guilty, "paralyzing the city courts whose cases were backlogged" by this action.[98] Finally Mukhliṣ Pasha became vali in 1905 (only after the British ambassador in Istanbul blocked Sayyid Ṭālib's candidature),[99] and set about reforming the civil administration by building police posts in the city and its environs, army barracks in the district of al-Ashar, plus a vast network of roads and guardhouses in the main quarters of Basra. He ended his "reformist" governership by killing Sayyid ʾAḥmad Pasha al-Naqīb's famous black Mamluk, ʿAmir, who was widely believed to be the brawn, if not the brains, behind the extortion and racketeering in the city.[100]

Before 1908, the Naqībs had established strong commercial links with the shaikh of Muḥammara and the shaikh of Kuwait, and were able to play off the rival ʾamīrs, ibn Saʿūd and ibn Rashīd, against each other. Their influence was paramount in southern Iraq, for even though the energetic Sayyid Ṭālib had made powerful enemies, amongst whom were the Zuhair merchant family in Zubair, the Muntafiq shaikhs and various Ottoman valis, the family was able to surmount these problems and to retain its hold of Basra's merchant-landholding establishment for a very long time. For instance, in 1903–04, the Naqīb of Basra antagonized the British as well as local date merchants in Basra by putting pressure on the vali of the moment, Nuri Pasha, to discontinue date shipments to Europe, America, and India, so that the Naqīb could receive a better price for his date crop.[101] Although the matter was eventually resolved to the Naqīb's satisfaction, individual members of the family continued to browbeat the Ottoman government of Basra, British merchants and shippers, and the local opposition until the beginning of the First World War.

The ʿAbbūd Family

According to commercial papers and personal diaries left by a family historian, in the early part of the nineteenth century the ʿAbbūd merchant house had family representation in cities as diverse as Basra, Aleppo, Baghdad, Izmir and Calcutta.[102] The ʿAbbūds were Catholic merchants, one of whose members, Mikhāʾīl ibn al-Maqdisī Yūsuf ibn Dīmitrī al-Khūrī ʿAbbūd, was a firsthand witness to Basra's economic turmoil in the wake of the epic rebellion mounted by Ḥumūd, the Muntafiq shaikh, against the Mamluk government in 1812–13. Mikhāʾīl ʿAbbūd's diaries are valuable for the light they shed on currency fluctuations, the local government's relations with resident merchants, and trade patterns in turn-of-the-century Basra. However, although there is a fair amount of information on the commodities exchanged in the city (and a graphic description of the ruinous effects of the coffee glut on local merchants), there is little or no material on what the ʿAbbūds were trading in, and what routes they favored.

The Asfar Family

According to the diaries of Yaʿqūb ibn Niʿmatullah ibn Maqsud, a cousin of the ʿAbbūd merchant family in Basra and Baghdad, Khwāja Jabra Aṣfar was one of the largest Christian merchants in Basra in 1812. He was one of the four prominent merchants called upon in that year to pay the extraordinary dues demanded of the Basra deputy governor by the newly installed Mamluk pasha, Saʿīd.[103] He is mentioned as being the only important merchant in Basra who stood his ground and refused to leave in the wake of the Basra government's policy of forced loans; "and had he not been under British protection, the government would have taken everything from him."[104]

Later on in the century, Gabriel ʾAṣfar is mentioned as being the deputy of the French Vice-Consul in Basra; according to Major de Rivoyre who visited the town in 1881, Mr. ʾAṣfar was a "native" Christian who dressed *à la Française* and lived in the aristocratic quarter, conveniently close to the bazaar. Contradicting the earlier reference that made of the ʾAṣfars British-protected merchants, the family claimed to have been French protégés "for generations."[105] As staunch members of the Christian community in Basra, the ʾAṣfars contributed to their church, which was being renovated in the latter part of the nineteenth century, perhaps as a symbol of increasing Christian mercantile influence in the city.[106] In 1912, one Gabriel ʾAṣfar, who went by the French title of *comte,* is mentioned as having become involved in land speculation and sale in Baghdad. He reportedly bought land in the *maḥalla* (quarter) of Sayyid Sulṭān ʿAlī in 1906. Six years later, with the advent of German construction firms involved in the Baghdad-Berlin railway scheme, and the rise of land prices in Baghdad, Comte Gabrial ʾAṣfar was able to ask seven times the price for his plot.[107] While there is no evidence that he received it, the development is interesting in itself; for the transition from mercantile interests to landowning was a significant historic trend in Iraq, evident from at least the eighteenth century onwards.

The Al-Mandīl Family

According to al-Ḥaidarī, in the mid–1860s, ʾIbrāhīm al-Mandīl was a cunning and crafty merchant who traded extensively with India; he had a house in Basra and another in Zubair.[109] The al-Mandīl family was reportedly from the Banū Khālid tribe. In the early part of the twentieth century, Philby reported that Ibn Saʿūd had married a woman of the al-Mandīl clan (who had given him a son and heir, Turkī);[110] possibly as a result of that connection, ʿAbdul-Laṭīf Pasha al-Mandīl was named honorary Ambassador for Ibn Saʿūd in Baghdad and Basra in the 1930s.[111]

The Al-Badr Family

In the mid-nineteenth century, Sālim al-Badr al-Kuwaitī is mentioned as having many mercantile connections with India, Bahrain, east Africa, Muscat, and Persia. According to al-Ḥaidarī, "his house was open to all seafarers." Sālim is mentioned as having a brother called Suleimān who also traded with a number of ports and market towns. Although the al-Badr family had settled in Kuwait, they were originally from the ʿAnayza tribe in Najd;[112] possibly because of this tribal connection, they fielded some of the best horses in the Bombay market in the latter part of the nineteenth century. In the period between 1885–1891, for example, Ḥasān al-Badr developed the reputation for transporting first-class race horses to India; two of his imports, renamed Euclid and Lanercost, won major races in Bombay while still colts.[113]

The Muḥaisin Shaikhs of Muḥammara (Arabistan)

The shaikhs of Muḥammara (Jābir, Mizʿal, and especially Khazʿal) had become the near-independent rulers of Arabistan in the latter part of the nineteenth century. They financed their government chiefly through trade revenues, including the trade in horses. George Curzon, the future Viceroy of India, travelled in Persia in that period and stated that Shaikh Mizʿal, governor of Muḥammara in 1881, was "reported to be very rich, having made a large fortune by the horse trade with Bombay."[114] As late as April 1891, Shaikh Mizʿal continued to view the British as his archenemies with regard to the regional trade of the province. A British official explained it as

> commercial hostility, [for] he competes by every means in his power, fair or otherwise, even to ordering his people not to sell to the Agents of Messrs. Lynch and Company . . .[115]

Shaikh Mizᶜal forbade his subjects from selling wheat or wool to the British firm, reserving the wheat solely to himself. He was reported to possess three steamers on the Karun River; and while seemingly undeterred by the fact that only one was of much use, he continued to charge one-third more for transporting grain than the Lynch shipping firm. Predictably, his steamers ran at a loss.[116] After Mizᶜal's assassination (under mysterious circumstances), his younger brother, Khazᶜal took over. Almost at once, the anti-British stance evaporated, and Shaikh Khazᶜal became a chief ally of British trading houses in Arabistan.

Finally, there are a number of merchant houses on which there is little or no information, but which deserve notice all the same. For instance, the ᶜAbdul-Razzāq family hailed originally from Basra but had largely become extinct in that city by the middle of the nineteenth century; however, branches of the family continued to prosper in India and Kuwait.[117] The al-Jamāl family, originally from Basra, had deserted the city (for reasons unknown) and settled in Muscat; and the family of ᶜAbdul-Azīz al-Ṣāliḥ al-Najdī lived in Majmaᶜa in Najd while another branch lived in Kuwait; both branches carried on an active trade with India.[118] It is also known that the ᶜAbdul-Waḥīd family were large proprietors in Abū al-Khaṣīb and Basra; they too traded with India. Finally, Shaikh Muḥammad ibn al-Ḥaj Niᶜma traded with Bombay and was considered to be very rich; interestingly, he is the only merchant mentioned by al-Ḥaidarī that was a member of the Kaᶜab tribe.[119]

PARTNERSHIPS, BARTER, CREDIT, AND CASH

In 1812, some resident merchant houses established on the Gulf coast were involved in such commercial enterprises as date cultivation and pearl fishing. According to a British source, the sale of their annual produce netted them a hefty profit, of which one-tenth was customarily paid to the central government of either coast, whether Ottoman or Persian.[120] Their fleets consisted of a number of large ocean-going vessels, such as the dhow or baghla, as well as the smaller river boats that traversed the many canals, creeks, and inlets of the region. The former sailed to India, Yemen, Africa, and Oman, manned by a local crew of thirteen to twenty-five people, and received payment in the form of shares, which were calculated in terms of the distance and importance of the sea voyage. For instance, the voyage to India netted the sailor from 50 to 60 rupees, to Yemen, 80 rupees, to Africa, 40 rupees, to Muscat, 12 rupees, while the voyage to Basra netted the seaman nothing, presumably because it was but a short distance from either coast of the Shaṭṭ al-ᶜArab. The medium-sized boats traded with

Bahrain and al-Qatif, for which each sailor received a share of 4 to 6 rupees; and they transported grain from Basra to Rās al-Khaima, for which each sailor was paid 10 rupees.

The famous pearl banks of Bahrain attracted many trading vessels, somewhere close to the vicinity of four hundred ships of large or medium tonnage. Two hundred were large boats (carrying a crew of one *nakhoda* or captain, twelve divers, and twelve assistants) while one hundred boats of intermediate size transported one captain, six divers and six assistants. In 1812, the annual sale of pearls was estimated to be close to 40, 000 *tumans*. As was the custom, one-fourth was reserved for the boat-owner, while three shares went to the captain, two shares were allotted for the diver, and the assistant was entitled to only one share. According to Alan Villiers, an observer of the pearl trade in the early years of the twentieth century, risks were a built-in clause in partnership contracts, although they were not shared equally, for merchants financed nakhodas, but the latter, being the weaker parties to the contract, shouldered the loss of seaborne commerce.[121] Because nakhodas could not otherwise acquire a big sailing ship, they were at the merchants' mercy. As a result, seaborne trade "was built on a structure of debt . . . [in which] the merchants owned the ships . . . and owned the nakhodas as well as the ships, for the nakhodas could scarcely ever expect to be free of debt." However, there was a system in place to give borrowers time to repay their debts; for in unfavorable seasons, merchant capitalists usually deferred their claims until the third year when they either expropriated the boats of debtors or worked out an arrangement with the latter that would allow the debt to be paid off in degrees.[123] Obviously, risks were part of any commercial partnership, and even though the responsibility was unevenly distributed, profits were the key. A good trading season might allow the nakhoda to pay off his debts, and if he was lucky, to even clear a little profit for himself, while the merchant parlayed his greater share into more diversified merchandise and increased earnings.

There is no question that regional ships were functional, seaworthy vessels that remained in operation long after British steamships had supposedly carried the day with their faster and more novel technology. In the 1930s, Arab dhows were still maneuvering their way down the East African coast, and still sailing to India, laden with dates and various local commodities produced in Iraq and Kuwait.[124] Obviously, this long maritime tradition did not succumb all at once to the technical superiority of Western steamships. The British agent in Basra in 1852 mused that the import trade with India was so far superior in volume to the export trade from Baghdad and Basra that

> at first glance, the supposition [might be warranted] that an extra number of British ships employed in the traffic might prove a desirable speculation, but from the low freights charged by the owners of native crafts . . . and the fact that the consignments and the consignees consist entirely of native Houses who engross the entire Indian trade in connection with these parts, and who but

> rarely care to effect insurances upon their goods, this branch of trade would be anything but a profitable one for British shipowners [and] the expenses attendant upon the running and maintenance of the native craft are also as nothing when compared to that incurred by a British vessel of the same tonnage. . . .[125]

Not only were freight charges low and ships uninsured, but the economic and technological dynamic behind local sailing ships was entirely different from European vessels. Whether it was a deep-sea, oceangoing *boom* or the smaller riverine variety, such as the *guffa,* the Arab sailing ship was designed to be economical, multifunctional, and easy to use.[126] The captain and the crew not only built it, but manned it and traded in it. The ordinary sailor doubled as a carpenter, sail-maker, dockworker, surveyor, and small merchant. The ship itself was "a floating bazaar,"[127] to use Braudel's apt phrase(although he used it in a different context), in which, in order to cut down on costs and turn a little profit, practically every deckhand traded in his own merchandise while transporting the merchandise of others. The ship was frequently a floating warehouse as well, which cut down on the sometimes exorbitant costs of on-land storage, while the expenses of maintenance were lessened by crew members who knew how to handle the necessary repairs. Sometimes, in order to turn a fast profit, the ship's carpenter would even construct a smaller vessel on board and sell it upon reaching port. Finally, older ships were frequently dismantled after reaching their final destinations, and the sailors would disperse to other sailing ships for the return journey home, for ships always travelled in convoys.

Because regional sailing ships had the advantage of economy, which the European steamships were unequipped to match, the British agent concluded that

> the disadvantages a British ship would have to encounter in a competition with native craft, and in the absence of any European Houses here, would be too overwhelming to allow a supposition even of probable ultimate success.[128]

Of course, partnership contracts and the extension of credit operated in land trade as well. The various arrangements undertaken to finance long-distance trade were usually carried out from the chief ports of the trading region, although in the more remote areas, tribal market towns served just as well. Traditionally, the most frequented port in the Gulf was Basra, closely followed by Muḥammara in the late nineteenth century, where the busiest trading season as a rule occurred right after the date harvest in October. In these two port towns, the date season functioned as the largest occasion for the assembly of date producers, middlemen, and shipping agents in the area, so much so that the period following the date harvest was considered to be the most momentous occasion of the trading season in the northern Gulf. The season began with regional merchants bidding for the date crop and trying to outmaneuver competitors to get the best price from the proprietor of the date groves. This usually lasted about two months, during which time other goods were also bought and sold, currency exchanged and distributed, and prospects of future sales ascertained. In some ways, then, the date season functioned as a prototype of the great rural fairs Braudel discusses in his economic history.[129]

The date season began with the packing of the *ḥillawee* variety of dates (usually, the first to ripen and therefore the first harvested) in chardāghs, or temporary woven reed huts put up especially for the occasion. Each date proprietor or merchant had his own chardāgh in which he employed tribal labor (especially women and children) to pack the fruit. The packed dates were then bought by merchants and shipped on Arab baghlas, Indian and Persian dhows, and later on, British steamers to India and Batavia (Java); inland merchants from Kuwait, Zubair, Sūq al-Shuyūkh and Najd bought the remainder, and distributed them in the interior markets of the region.

Most regional goods, including dates, were financed through long-term credit. The usual method for date proprietors was to arrange to reserve their future crop for specific merchants, in return for which they were paid an advance about six to seven months beforehand. Interest on the loan usually was compounded at three or four percent a month of the original loan. Sometimes the terms of the loan were prolonged for two or three years; because dates always found a ready sale, however, the money-lender/merchant could rest assured that "his" tract of land was a sure investment.

Although evidence exists for direct negotiations between the date proprietor and the date merchant, it was more usual for a middleman (who was usually trusted by both sides) to intercede between buyer and seller. In the 1890s, the middleman had to hold title of at least one *jarib* of date palms (the area taken up by one hundred palm trees), which served as a guarantee for the monetary advance which the trader entrusted to him.[131] The middleman then disbursed the sum to the proprietor when the crop was harvested. After the dates came to term, the general method followed throughout most of the region was for the seller or supplier to pay the middleman's fee. In Basra, however, the buyer or the merchant paid the date agent's fee.[132] General usage allowed for the middleman or agent to be present at each such transaction between supplier and trader, whether to record the contract of sale (called *sulfa)* or the final negotiation.

In Muḥammara, as in Basra, goods were bought on credit. Transactions in Muḥammara and its environs were usually carried out on a face-to-face basis, with the exchange of contract notes sometimes the only record of purchase, and much like Basra, crops were sold to be paid in installments after the date harvest in October. Thus

> the transaction between the importer and the *bunakdar* (wholesaler) was really . . . an open account and was generally paid off in installments. The bunakdar sold to the inland trader, or to the retail trader on similar conditions. The re-

> tail trader sold usually for cash, occasionally on book accounts with customers. Negotiable bills were not made for any of these transactions and the *sarrafs* advanced to traders on current account. The retail trader advanced goods on credit to pedlars who worked the neighboring districts, often taking produce in exchange for goods which were in turn brought back to urban centers and sold for cash . . . the inland trader who forwarded his goods to a correspondent or agent in another town drew real bills which could be negotiated by the sarrafs and foreign bankers.[133]

One of the problems associated with long-term credit in the literature is that its widespread use is often seen as antithetical to the money economy. For instance, Shahnavaz claims that the prevalence of long-term credit indicated the poverty of the consuming class in the region,[134] for lack of ready cash is sometimes taken as proof of the non-integration of certain societies into the market economy.[135] While it is undeniable that one of the problems of the region was shortage of specie, this was not reason enough for the dependence on credit. Credit coexisted with cash transactions in the regional economy because it *facilitated* long-distance trade. In fact, it was instrumental to the integration of the regional economy, and indicated, among other things, that merchants and their clientele could always depend upon reliable and steady payments for goods received. In effect, banking (ṣirāfa) and credit operations freed merchants to conduct their business over great distances. It also allowed them to diversify, buying any number of commodities in order to spread their risks over the long term. No wonder, then, that as early as 1750, the agents of the Dutch East India Company complained to their superiors in Batavia that because the company did not allow its staff to make barter agreements or grant long-term credit, it was being edged out of the Gulf region by the British, who did.[136]

Nevertheless, some aspects of regional trade were highly monetized. The date trade itself was permeated with the cash nexus. Dates were bought on credit in Iraq and Arabistan by regional traders but sold strictly for cash to merchants in India.[137] In fact, it was estimated that

> with the departure of the first [date-laden] boat to India and until the whole produce has been sold, the resident merchants [of the Gulf region] are profitably employed in exchange operations.[138]

In some respects, currency exchange was one of the most lucrative and profitable aspects of regional trade; in fact, it formed a trade by itself. In 1852, for example, it was calculated that the nakhodas and merchants from Kuwait, the Persian coast, Muscat, Yemen, and India imported a "large" amount of specie for the payment of their date cargoes, which they then shipped by dhows and baghlas to their home ports. The amount was estimated to be about nine lacs and 25, 000 gurūsh, ʿayn or shāmīs (£201, 650).[139] Obviously, the flooding of regional markets with a variety of coins in the date season brought about a money glut that gave date importers ample scope to manipulate the value of various currencies by means of money exchange operations. In 1852, for example, only 500 horses were shipped to Bombay, a truly dismal figure compared to years past. To make up for the losses incurred in the horse trade, regional merchants quickly switched to exchange operations, thereby making small fortunes as a result of currency fluctuations.[140]

Cash, like credit, assumed diverse forms: as has been indicated, one of the most characteristic features of the regional economy was the widespread use of competing currencies in the marketplace. The more varied the goods and the more distant their provenance, the more there were traders specializing in the exchange and distribution of local and international currencies. No regional market town worth its salt traded in a single, standardized medium; in fact, the strength of a particular market depended upon its ability to absorb a host of gold and silver coins of different weights, measures, and denominations, for only by doing so could it attract and satisfy an ever-fluctuating regional clientele. A hallmark of this trading region was its adherence to local currencies, even in the face of governmental pressure.[141] For instance, in 1884, the Ottoman policy of introducing a standardized currency in the Baghdad marketplace came to naught when faced with wholesale resistance from merchants, indicating that this principle of regional economic practice would not be done away with, regardless of government pressure. In this instance, reliance on local coins such as the shāmī to the virtual exclusion of the Ottoman *majīdī* rendered the latter coin all but useless as legal tender in the marketplace. However, it is significant that at the same time as the majīdī was facing an uphill battle to gain acceptance as the coin of choice in Baghdad, the British-Indian rupee was making headway in the markets of the capital.[142]

One reason for the continuing diversity of regional currency may have been its physical scarcity. Ottoman officials, regional merchants, and European shippers all had reason to complain of the chronic money supply; local governments in particular needed hard currency to offset their trade deficits with India and Europe, a problem of major dimensions for Ottoman valis in Iraq.[143] Currency shortages led to the reinforcement of local coins in the economy simply because there may not have been that many coins to go around. Thus, other than the stubborn adherence of one sector of the population to a certain currency because of its familiarity in the countryside, another reason why the majīdī was forced to coexist with the Persian *kerān* and the Indian rupee in the markets of late nineteenth century Iraq may have had to do with its very paucity as a circulating medium.

Barter was the third medium of transacting business in the regional economy. It was on the decline in most areas, but was strengthened in others (such as the tribal countryside) for practical reasons. In some cases, as in the horse trade, a cash shortage made it imperative to "buy" horses with camels.[144] We hear of a tribesman of the Muntafiq in the 1860s selling thirty camels for the price of one horse in southern Iraq. In the same period, the Italian horse agent, Guarmani, mentions buying three horses with one hundred camels, noting in a rather insouciant manner: "A hundred camels is the price of one stallion, if really well-bred."[145] While it is true that traditionally only inferior breeds of camels were bartered for other livestock, the question is an important issue. Throughout this period, in southern Iraq, an ongoing process of tribal settlement and sedentarization was taking place, instigating a fair number of camel-herding tribes to invest in agriculture.[146] Sedentarization is a complex process involving a whole range of factors, an examination of which is beyond the scope of this study. Suffice it to say that at present the point is to examine the effect of tribal settlement on the position of camels in the pastoral economy. Camel herds, the mainstay of pastoral tribes, assumed a less significant place than before, although they continued to fulfill the basic needs of the riverine or settled tribes, as they had for "pure" pastoralists.[147] Theoretically, the value of herds decreased in proportion to the level of sedentarization, and it is quite conceivable that the price of camels fell as a result. Even in a barter economy, items of trade fluctuated according to the importance placed upon them; thus undervalued camels could be exchanged for horses which commanded good prices on the Indian market.[148] Thus while British traders paid for horses in currency, Arab merchants preferred to gauge a horse's value in camels. Economic logic was the paramount reason for them doing so.

CONCLUSION

Production, trade, and transport in nineteenth-century Iraq, Arabia, and the Gulf operated on internal, and purely practical lines. A rationale based on the pursuit of elusive profits tied diverse economic areas together and integrated regions into one market. While the trading region under discussion suffered adverse blows from within as well as from without (for instance, the attempts of the late eighteenth century Saʿūdī state to control trade routes into the Arabian peninsula, or the Persian occupation of Basra in 1775–77), the internal dynamic and overall unity in the region was not totally impaired. After these temporary setbacks were overcome, goods continued to flow to market towns and ports *of the region,* albeit at a reduced rate.[149] Trade continued to operate within its fluctuating but traditional regional boundaries; it was neither permanently diverted to other routes nor completely transferred to other hands. While it is true that by the beginning of the nineteenth century, British-Indian merchants had made inroads into the maritime trade to India, they were not able to control totally the river trade of Iraq nor the land trade from Arabia. That development would have to await the last quarter of the nineteenth century. Regional merchants of Iraq, Arabia, and the Gulf continued to dominate the routes and markets of a significant portion of the internal market, although their control everywhere was being challenged by European merchants and their protégés.

In the mid-nineteenth century, however, combined British and Ottoman efforts to control regional trade once and for all were set into motion. Although Ottoman efforts to resist British encroachment largely hinged on the effectiveness of their regional alliances with merchants in Iraq and the Gulf, by the beginning of the 1860s, the alliance between the two began to fray. As a result of increased British competition, and superior technology, local merchants faced reverses in the control of riverine trade and land-borne commerce. Denuded of their once-powerful regional connections, Ottoman pashas and bureaucrats were forced to come to terms with the reality of the British presence in the region. Thus while British and Ottoman aims largely diverged throughout the period in question, at mid-century, they became reluctant allies, determined to work together to control regional resources, albeit for different purposes. The socioeconomic and political strategies designed to maximize these aims took three broad avenues. One was to establish a dominant position in the riverine areas of Iraq, thus gaining control of both land and river routes. The second was the attempt to infiltrate the food supply of the provinces of Iraq—the largest regional producer of grain in the nineteenth century—and the livestock trade of Arabia and the Gulf (especially the commerce in horses). The third was to obtain an influential position in the market towns of Iraq and the Gulf so as to divert the supply of goods to British or Ottoman venues. These three interrelated developments shaped the historical context for the struggle for control of regional trade in Iraq, Arabia, and the Gulf throughout the nineteenth century. They will form the substance of the following chapters.

-Three-

Regional Trade, Ottoman Centralization, and the British Economic Challenge: The Background to Economic Conflict in the Nineteenth Century

Although the previous chapters have delved into the internal history and development of the regional market of Iraq, Arabia, and the Gulf to the virtual exclusion of outside factors, an attempt must now be made to draw in the two largest external powers in the area, and to describe their significance with regard to the regional market in the nineteenth century. On the one hand, the Ottoman Sulṭān, ruler of a broad section of humanity from the fringes of the Caucasus to the highlands of Yemen, governed the provinces of Iraq through his appointed representatives, the valis (governors of Baghdad), mutasallims (governors of Basra, replaced by valis in the latter part of the nineteenth century) and kahyās (deputy governors) that meted out judgment in the government saray (palace complex), mounted punishing campaigns against "lawless" tribal confederations, and ensured the collection—and disbursement—of the annual revenue to the Porte. On the other hand, the rising commercial and industrial challenge of Britain manifested itself in the increasingly intrusive presence of British consuls and shippers in the provinces of Iraq, the Arabian littoral, and the Gulf. Eventually, the profits of seaborne trade (and, to a lesser extent, of overland commerce) touched off a struggle for the resources of the region involving Ottoman governors in Iraq, regional merchants, and British trading firms. Chapters Four to Seven explain the dynamics of the struggle in detail. The purpose of this chapter is to delineate and analyze the rationale for the Ottoman policy of provincial centralization in the eighteenth and nineteenth centuries, especially with regard to the provinces of Iraq, and the Porte's subsequent attempt to replicate, where possible, its policies in Iraq within the overall strategy of military-commercial expansion in eastern Arabia and the Gulf. A second, and interrelated theme of this chapter, is the slow but steady encroachment of British commercial designs on Iraq and the Gulf, and the various methods adopted by British merchants and consuls to achieve control of the trade of the region. Central to this strategy was the tariff policy articulated by the makers of the Anglo-Turkish Convention of 1838 (otherwise known as the Balta Liman Treaty), the way that the Convention was applied to Iraq, and the ineffectuality of the policy in the face of regional opposition, all of which will be detailed below.

OTTOMAN POLICIES OF REASSERTION AND CONTROL WITH REGARD TO IRAQ, ARABIA, AND THE GULF

From about 1534 onwards, when the formerly Safavid-administered province of Baghdad was conquered and occupied by the Ottomans, the Porte attempted to safeguard the trade routes of the region by knitting together trading centers in a wider economic zone under Ottoman influence. This continued to be the trend throughout the sixteenth century even as the continued presence of the Portuguese in the Gulf brought about a partial, and temporary diversion of trade routes away from embryonic Ottoman markets in the region such as Basra, and towards Portuguese colonies in India.[1] Although the Ottomans reinforced Basra with an important naval fleet, and fought two significant sea battles in 1553 and 1581 with the Portuguese and the Persians for mastery of the Basra-Red Sea route, their struggle was not completely crowned with success. Even though the southern Iraqī port town remained under Ottoman control, and the Porte was able to secure the overland trade route to Syria, the lower Gulf continued under Portuguese influence throughout the sixteenth century. However, what is significant for the incipient development of the regional market is that even while the Portuguese, Persians, and Ottomans were fighting over the Gulf-India route, and making and breaking local alliances in the process, none of them were able to control completely the regional trade with southern Persia and, of course, central Arabia.[2] Those markets remained under local domination throughout this period. Perhaps in tacit recognition of this development, the first Ottoman administration of sixteenth century Basra levied two general categories of duties: one on goods in transit such as broadcloth and spices, and the other on "Arab" (i.e., tribal) produce, which was paid for with one gold *dīnār.*[3]

The point is that, despite Ottoman domination, goods continued to be traded *within* the region. They were not completely supplanted by international, "rich" trades,[4] such as silks or spices, nor were they totally absorbed by the large demand from Istanbul. This is implicitly shown in the Ottoman reorganization of the province of Basra, for which two qānūnnames (imperial law codes regulating the tax structure of a given province) exist, issued by the Porte in 1551 and 1576, respectively.[5] These documents explain in detail what commodities transited the port, what was produced inside and outside the province, and what taxes were levied on goods circulating in Basra. Many regional products jostled each other for supremacy in the Basra market. Regional products arriving by sea and by overland caravan (indigo, cotton cloth, iron, wool, and carpets from India, Damascus, and Aleppo), as well as items of trade from Persia and the riverine districts adjoining Basra (horses, soap, ʿabās or woolen cloaks, wheat, and dates) balanced out internationally sought-out commodities such as spices, silks, and textiles. To the early Ottomans, Basra province appeared to be the hub of a large economic region extending from al-Ahwaz (Arabistan) to eastern Arabia. Situated at the mouth of Shaṭṭ al-ʿArab, the port of Basra occupied an enviable position that made it a strategic location for the transshipment of regional commodities, and one of the chief bases for a highly developed regional network that bought, sold, and exchanged goods by land and by sea. Because of its proximity to the Indian subcontinent, it was well-placed to be a key player in Asian trade. If it is indeed true that early sixteenth century Ottoman strategy aimed at nothing less than the capture of trade routes to India,[6] then Basra was an excellent place from which to contemplate an invasion strategy of the Asian mainland.

However, inspite of the fiscal reorganization of Basra's trade under the Porte's directives, and the extension of Ottoman protection to regional traders, the sociopolitical situation in Basra and its environs did not immediately improve. The Ottomans were forced to rely on the traditional leadership of the province, the shaikhs of the Muntafiq tribe, who continued to regard the former as interlopers. Shaikh Rashīd al-Mughāmis even went so far as to enter into commercial relations with the Portuguese, selling them wheat and horses.[7] This invited a response from the Ottomans, who sent a military force under Iyas Pasha to Basra to dislodge the shaikh. However, even after the direct occupation of the town in 1546, the Porte could not introduce new elements from Istanbul into the province, and had to continue working with members of the older elite of tribal shaikhs and Arab notables.

In fact, the new Ottoman-affiliated elite that emerged in the wake of the occupation of the Iraqī provinces (and later on, in eastern Arabia) may have been neither Ottoman nor new. After Basra was occupied by Ottoman troops in 1546, a cadastral survey was carried out, and most of Basra's agricultural lands were reclassified as *ʿushr,* following Islamic usage. While the prevailing interpretation finds that the *timār* system (land granted to provincial officers in lieu of salary), never made an appearance in Basra province, even though it flourished almost everywhere else throughout the newly-integrated Ottoman provinces, it is probably more correct to say that, on the basis of several *tapu defters* found by researchers in the Ottoman archives, timārs and *ziamets* were not as widespread as in other Ottoman provinces.[8] For instance, a quick survey shows that, with the exception of some timārs granted to Ottoman bureaucrats such as the *qapudan Pasha* (Admiral of the Fleet) or the governor (most of these timārs being in the *khāṣṣ* category), the majority of landholders endowed by this method seemed to be Arab shaikhs or local notables.[9] That the foremost military institution of the Ottoman Empire failed to make headway in Basra province calls into question the whole nature of Ottoman authority in Basra, and the bases on which it was built. While the evidence can only be conjectural at this stage, it does seem plausible to infer from the meager evidence published on this question that the Ottomans were not able to impose a cadre of imperial administrators brought in from Istanbul or other "core" provinces of the empire on Basra, at least not initially, and therefore had to be satisfied with local candidates instead.

In fact, it was the rare official who could govern uninterruptedly for a long stretch of time without meeting local resistance; most governors remained the prey of urban factionalism in Basra and rural insurgencies in the countryside. Early Ottoman administrators dispatched from Baghdad, or farther afield to Basra, were often forced to come to terms with the reality that the submission of a province to Istanbul only came about through making expedient alliances with local forces, some of whom (such as the shaikhs of the Muntafiq) felt that they had the right to rule by virtue of having been there first. Longrigg echoes this point by claiming that

> Although the Basrah Pasha lived, in the clearer intervals, in pomp based on the sure and copious revenues of his Customs House, his rule scarcely extended beyond the town ditch; many river-side forts were needed to protect shipping from the Huwaizah robbers; and the marshmen of the lower Tigris and Euphrates showed little signs of coming permanently to terms [with Ottoman rule]. . . .[10]

The Ottoman occupation of eastern Arabia faced similar problems. In 1552, or possibly even earlier, an Ottoman force occupied al-Ahsa (eastern Arabia) and installed one Muḥammad Pasha as governor of the newly-formed *sanjaq* (administrative district), which was administered as a district of Basra.[11] One of the first things that the new Ottoman administration did was to build mosques-masjids and bring in scholar-preachers to revive the teachings of Islamic theology and jurisprudence in the region.[12] The Ottomans also carried out a land survey of the villages of al-Ahsa and, in conformity with established practice, began granting out lands to high Ottoman officials as timārs, ziamets and later on, as *iltizāms* (tax farms). While most land grants were registered in the regular manner, there were some confiscations of local property by the Ottoman forces during the initial occupation; however, these were reversed in later periods.

For the Ottomans, al-Ahsa functioned as a "defensive outpost" against the Portuguese, then commanding a dominant position in the Gulf.[13] Besides controlling the eastern approaches to the peninsula, and forming a second line of defense (after Basra) against Portuguese attacks carried out on Gulf waters, al-Ahsa's rulers were also enjoined to ensure the safety of trading vessels plying the Indian ocean. However, they were forbidden to initiate any military action against the Portuguese base at Hormuz; the functions of the Ottoman garrison were solely confined to the defense of the eastern Arabian seabord.[14] In fact, the one notable offensive undertaken by the governor of al-Ahsa against the island of Bahrain in 1559 resulted in complete and total failure for the Ottomans, and the capture of the al-Ahsa garrison in Bahrain.

Whatever the reason was for the Ottoman desire to occupy al-Ahsa in the first place, economics may have played an indirect role, for the Portuguese grip on the Gulf and the Indian Ocean threatened to cut off vital trade routes to other Ottoman bases in the region, and access to important commodities. It may not entirely have been coincidental that the Ottoman occupation of al-Ahsa occurred when it did. Thus, the pearl trade was an ongoing regional operation that attracted numerous clients from within the region; and the pearl banks of Bahrain may have been a coveted prize for the Ottoman rulers of al-Ahsa. That is perhaps why, after the failed Ottoman offensive in Bahrain, and the capture of the Ottoman garrison in al-Ahsa in 1559, the ransom demand for their release consisted, for the most part, of 176 pearls belonging to the late governor of al-Ahsa, Mustafa Pasha, which were kept in the district treasury. Whether these formed part of his profits from trade is left to conjecture.[15]

While the published Ottoman archival material on sixteenth and seventeenth century al-Ahsa allows researchers a clearer picture of the events of the period, the documentation on the tribes is fragmentary.[16] It is obvious that the Ottoman garrison at al-Ahsa never completely overawed the tribes of the region, least of all the Banū Khālid, the most powerful confederation in the area. While their shaikhs were given administrative titles, land grants, and salaries to boot, the Banū Khālid failed to submit totally to Ottoman jurisdiction. The Banū Khālid counteroffensive, led by their renowned shaikh Saʿdūn, began in earnest in 1558 and continued intermittently until 1669–1670 when the paramount shaikhs of the tribe saw their chance to get rid of the Ottoman occupation force altogether. Under the leadership of Barrāk ibn Ghurayr ibn ʿUthmān, the ʾĀl-Ḥumaid section of the Banū Khālid tribe was finally able to defeat the Ottoman garrison in battle, leaving the administration no option but to withdraw peacefully from al-Ahsa.[17]

One is forced to conclude that, despite the existence of Ottoman *mühimme* documents purporting to regulate everything in al-Ahsa from land grants to the recruitment of volunteers for the the Ottoman army, from the very beginning the Ottomans were forced to rely on local manpower. Thus, in 1575, Shaikh Saᶜdūn of the Banū Khālid was prevailed upon to return to al-Ahsa, his traditional pasture grounds, not only to collect the salary from certain lands allotted to him by the Ottoman district governor but also to keep his side of the bargain and to restore peace among the tribes. While the Ottomans were understaffed with regard to the provision of law and order in the desert districts, they were equally lacking in manpower when it came to the core of their army. Due chiefly to the lack of funds in the Al-Ahsa treasury, imperial recruits into the Janissary regiments fell off drastically from the 1560s to the 1570s, and locals took their place.[18] While the localization of power was a phenomenon observable all over the Empire, in al-Ahsa it must have only served to underline the vulnerability of the Ottoman presence in the region, and its untenability over the long-term. This was further exacerbated by the fact that most of the Ottoman army's basic requirements, as well as all their military supplies, were sent by sea from southern Iraq to al-Ahsa. While Mandaville believes that the logistics of supplying al-Ahsa from Basra was "an extraordinarily viable system, functioning smoothly even through the war with the Safavids into the seventeenth century, funneling goods and men from Anatolia, Aleppo, Diyarbekir, and Amid down the Euphrates and Tigris to the Gulf," he concedes that it was precisely this operation "that kept Lahsa (al-Ahsa) alive as an Ottoman province."[19] In other words, were it not for major resupply operations from Ottoman Basra, Ottoman al-Ahsa would not have been able to function on its own.

From the very beginning of the Ottoman domination of Iraq and the Gulf, then, the principle of active cooperation with regional elites was both accepted and encouraged. What this meant in reality was that the politics of Ottoman rule in the region was more of an interplay between local and imperial interests than a straightforward colonization on the French Algerian model. Because the struggle for regional trade was never completely resolved in the Porte's favor, and Ottoman sociopolitical imperatives kept meeting strong resistance in Iraq, Arabia, and the Gulf in the sixteenth and seventeenth centuries, the Ottoman governments of Baghdad and Basra were forced to work out a modus vivendi with regional merchants and notables in order to collect a fraction of the rents that the imperial center felt was its due.

NINETEENTH-CENTURY CONTINUITIES

Thus, as early as the middle of the sixteenth century, Ottoman bureaucrats were forced to make expedient local alliances, and to rely on local intermediaries in both Iraq and the Gulf so as to achieve a modicum of political and economic control of the region. Fundamentally the same development took place from the mid-eighteenth to nineteenth centuries. Far from acting as omniscient and all-powerful agents of the imperial government, most Ottoman governors hedged their bets by ingratiating themselves with local merchants and office-holders in order to collect a fraction of the provincial revenue owed to the imperial center. This is not to deny that in certain periods, the central government was strong enough to compel the acquiescence of the tax-paying members of society; in general, however, power-sharing between the provincial government and local elites was a recurrent feature of Iraqī/Gulf history throughout the mid to latter part of the Ottoman period, even as the making and unmaking of local alliances was a constant source of disquiet or tension.

Viewed from this perspective, then, the history of nineteenth-century Iraq and the Gulf is but a continuation of earlier traditions that manifested themselves throughout the long span of Ottoman history. Far from it revolving around the imposition of the Tanzimat edicts on a supine Iraq (the usual thesis advocated by "Modernization" theorists and Arabic secondary sources),[20] the history of Iraq and the Gulf from 1830 to 1900 is one of a series of attempts at the installation of a more efficient state machinery for the collection of state revenue, as well as the creation of a new "Ottomanized" elite to mediate between the provincial administration and local revenue-farmers and merchants. Both elements, let us repeat, lay at the core of Mamluk ideas of governance (see Chapter One). It is also a history of adaptation and change, without which any understanding of "centralization" cannot be attempted. Contrary to the standard interpretation, governmental centralization was neither the outcome of one governor's brief tenure in office, nor was it a foregone conclusion the minute the full array of the Tanzimat edicts became law. Rather, it was a complicated, interactive process in which regional merchants from Basra and the tribal districts of southern Iraq, Kuwait, and eastern Arabia, none of whom were completely immune to the growing influence of provincial governments, played out the full range of possibilities open to them in the face of mounting challenges from the center. Thus, centralizing, "reformist" governments felt compelled to draw upon all the resources available to them to maintain power, including coercion; while regional merchants worked to see that trade was carried out in an atmosphere free of excessive controls, all the while maintaining a discreet profile so as to escape governmental confiscations of their property. At the same time, the central government in Istanbul needed revenue at all costs, and did what it could to affect the outcome of negotiations between merchants, landholders, and Ottoman bureaucrats in the provinces. Therefore, this chapter will detail the flexibility of systems of regional trade, and not the artificial periodization of Iraqī/Gulf history into "reformed" or unreconstructed decades, for the history of of the region is properly that of the complex of structural relations that developed as a result of provincial reattachment to the center, with all of the manifold levels of intricacy and difficulty that this entailed.

A revealing example is that of the deposition of Dāwūd Pasha, marking the end of Mamluk power in Iraq in 1830–31. The war for Baghdad that pitted the last Mamluks against the invading Ottoman army is a prime illustration of the limits of political centralization in the context of the continually fluid situation that obtained in early nineteenth century Baghdad. A dual catastrophe, that of a flood and the plague, plus the threat of a well-equipped Ottoman army at Baghdad's gates finally forced Dāwūd Pasha to plan his personal surrender to the Ottoman commander, ʿAlī Riḍā Pasha al-Lāz. Just as negotiations for his surrender began, a gathering of Baghdādī notables and Mamluk officials decided to fight on. The final battle for the capital is described in epic prose by Suleimān Fāʾiq Bey, the historian-bureaucrat of Mamluk Iraq.[21] Not only does the conflict serve to underline continuing local support for the Mamluks but it focuses attention on the manner in which the Ottomans reoccupied, and eventually governed Iraq. For one thing, the coalition of Mamluks and local notables in Baghdad was not defeated in open battle, but surrendered only after its demands were met by the Porte.[22] For another, the new Ottoman governor, ʿAlī Rizā Pasha al-Lāz was forced to come to terms with the still-pervasive Mamluk presence in Baghdad even after the last Mamluk pasha had been deposed. Even while a policy of torture and executions of remaining officials (and their wives) was being carried out with the thoroughness of a pogrom,[23] another apparent tendency was to allow ex-officials of Mamluk households to infiltrate government posts and to staff the Ottoman administration.[24] In fact, up till the late forties,[25] most of the administrative personnel of note in Baghdad were drawn from former Mamluk households, or comprised a cross-section of the notable class in Mamluk times. The new governor of Iraq set an even more significant precedent by marrying the daughter of a former Mamluk governor, Suleimān Pasha the Little (1807–10).[26]

In addition, it is not clear whether the agents of the new government regarded the local and regional economy in a light different from past Mamluk administrations, for they proceeded in the time-honored tradition of coolly pocketing most of the revenue from Mamluk-held urban properties or villages.[27] On one occasion, the defterdār (provincial treasurer) presented the charred remnants of tax defters (tax rolls) to an Ottoman inspector sent from Istanbul to assess the value of the tirka (estate) of individual Mamluks; whether these defters had been put to the torch by fleeing Mamluks or somehow burned by a negligent Ottoman bureaucracy is left up to conjecture in the literature.[28] Nevertheless, if the Porte had to delay its averred policy of provincial centralization on several occasions, and then negotiate its way out of a less than successful siege of Baghdad with lavish guarantees of peace for the defeated Mamluks,[29] then the limitations of direct political authority are clear. Moreover, the insinuation of defeated Mamluk cadres into a centralising Ottoman government may have had a practical purpose. For instance, contemporary sources point to the deep contacts between some of the Mamluks and local notables of the Iraqī provinces, eventually precipitating such extraordinary alliances as those between Saʿīd Effendi (later Pasha) and Ḥumūd al-Thāmir, shaikh of the Muntafiq, which bypassed traditional military forces such as the Janissaries, irregular Ottoman troops, and other Mamluk contingents. A reliance on local armies and administrators, and a blurring of ethnic and professional lines allowed the Mamluks access to local sources of revenue such as waqfs (endowments) or iltizāms (tax-farms)[30] (which may have bought them local support in the first place); in such a case, then, the reincorporation of individual Mamluks into the early Ottoman administration of Iraq must have facilitated and encouraged the Ottoman bureaucracy's relations with a broader-based elite, even while allowing Mamluk households further leverage with the new government.

In any case, the early Ottoman administration of Iraq continued a number of other practices prevalent under previous Mamluk administrations, the most important of which was the collection by state agents of provincial revenue by means of state monopolies on trade, industries and agriculture. Monopolies on such staples as salt and tobacco, as well as on luxuries such as silk, had been in existence from the mid-sixteenth century throughout the provinces of Iraq.[31] By the nineteenth century, the chief monopolies of Baghdad were classed as follows: the supply of oil, the manufacture of soap, the trade in bitumen, the dying and printing of textiles, tanning, the cleaning of raw cotton, the refining of spirits, and the storing of grain.[32] Theoretically, monopolies were commercial privileges granted by the central Treasury as iltizāms either to the vali of the province, or to another tax farmer. Clearly, they were meant to defray a vali's expenses in office, and to bring revenue into the treasury. Even though the British-engineered Anglo-Turkish Convention abolished all monopolies in the provinces of the Ottoman Empire after 1838 (a subject discussed in the next section), these commercial privileges continued to be upheld by Ottoman officials and state-affiliated merchants in Iraq until the early 1860s. In fact, the struggle of governors and merchants to retain control of the regional economy in the face of exterior pressures remained an important dynamic in nineteenth century Iraqī history, only subsiding with developments at the turn of the century.

For monopolies to exist, certain fiscal arrangements had to be entered into with the central government. By custom, provincial governors had to pay a certain sum to the central Treasury in Istanbul prior to taking up the reins of provincial government. This sum, the badal, was the equivalent of a monetary bid for the privileges of office, and was usually disbursed in specie.[33] The badal amount was usually high enough to warrant immediate recompensation once the governor was installed in office, the more so because of the brevity of his tenure; and the weapon of choice was the monopoly of certain food items or industrial products by the new governor, which indemnified the provincial governor for his prior payment to the Porte.

It is important to note that the "sale" of office, the imposition of extraordinary taxation, the institution of personal monopolies on certain items of trade and the reordering of provincial revenue to suit a governor's fiscal priorities were all considered to be legitimate means by which non-salaried officials maintained themselves in power. Thus, monopolies were not unique to the provinces of Iraq but formed the main feature of provincial governments "from the Bosphorous to the Himalayas."[34] In fact, they were part and parcel of a governmental system that saw no distinction between the private or public sphere. To put it in Rifaʾāt Abou-el-Haj's words:

> The Ottoman ruling class made no distinction between personal patrimony and property on the one hand, and the public treasury on the other. Those members of the ruling class who were in power appropriated whatever wealth they could, without any sense of corruption or greed, but rather out of a sense of entitlement. The most often quoted expression of that sanction is found in the "divinely" inspired formula: "Verily He created you into (separate) orders." The notion that these Ottoman practices are an indication of corruption stems from the modern assumption that the public interest is separate from the individual interest of the dominant members of the ruling class.[35]

Precisely because it did function as a system, the badal could be negotiated or re-negotiated as the situation warranted or as provincial appointees saw fit. For instance, in 1851, sources note that one governor of Baghdad contracted for a better bargain with Istanbul in the following manner:

> The roads in every direction continue unsafe, trade and commerce seriously impeded, and the dimunition of the revenues from the depreciation of the value of district farms (i e., iltizāms) remains constant. The extraordinary inactivity of (the Vali) Wejhi Pasha under such circumstances has confirmed the conjecture, long since formed, of a design on his part (which is) by maintaining the existing confusion, to reduce the Ottoman Ministry to the necessity eventually of giving him the Province in farm on the same terms and conditions as it was held by the late Najīb Pasha (governor of Baghdad in 1842–1849). . . .[36]

However, while the Ottoman system decreed that all forms of revenue extraction (monopolies on articles of food or clothing, rural tax-farms, and transit dues) were necessary to the survival of the class in power, it was apparent that decrees alone were insufficient to bring this about. Thus, even though taxes, monopolies, and different forms of landholding were the financial emoluments underpinning the ruling class, the system did not provide for automatic control of the sources of revenue. It allowed the governor or the multazim (tax farmer) to buy the right to tax the inhabitants of Baghdad and Basra (by means of the badal), and theoretically it empowered them to monopolize certain food items. But the evidence shows that these economic prerogatives were almost always met with resistance on the provincial level. Thus, the collection of provincial revenue entailed a constant and recurring struggle during each vali's tenure, for payment of the badal guaranteed the office-holder only the *theoretical* right to collect taxes: the practical test of a governor's power came about only as a result of his control of the resources within the province.

As a result, Ottoman governors had to build a local base from which to fight for their economic "rights." The struggle for the control of resources was the key to the provincial politics of the nineteenth century, as was the alliance between the bureaucracy and the landholders-merchants who powered the struggle. In fact, Ottoman governors would not have been so successful had it not been for their alliance with local traders, in the countryside as well as the town. Indeed, the most striking manifestation of this alliance was the cooperation between state merchants and the governors of Baghdad and Basra in vital aspects of the regional economy, such as the grain trade (see chapter 5), and the control of riverine routes (see chapter 4).

However, a note of caution must be injected at this juncture. While a class of state merchants did emerge as a result of government-sponsored access to sources of revenue in the countryside as well as the towns, not all merchants were fortunate enough to be included. An untold number of regional merchants were squeezed out of their former routes and markets precisely because of the success of this new alliance. It must be recalled that merchants formed one of the most heavily taxed sectors of the population in the nineteenth century, for alongside duties on goods brought into market, and subject to a number of gate taxes and shop dues, were those exported or imported into the provincial ports of the Gulf which normally paid heavy transit fees. Besides the more traditional taxes established from as early as the mid-sixteenth century (such as the duties on land and sea transport, collectively called bāj or, in the wider Iraqī context, *gamārik),*[37] other governmental imposts weighed heavily on the merchant. In 1846, these imposts consisted of:

> transit duties levied under a hundred different names, by land and by water, tolls at ferries, bridges or even at the passage of rivers where ferries or bridges once existed, duties on carriage, monopolies of farming rafts for the conveyance of produce, and a whole host of minor fees levied at the Customs House, at the gates and the market-place at Baghdad. . . .[38]

While regional traders frequently evaded these taxes by shifting trade venues or indulging in contraband (issues discussed elsewhere in the book), many merchants were undoubtedly ruined by this new development. For instance, the twelve-year rule of the new "centralizing" Ottoman vali, ʿAlī Rizā Pasha al-Lāz (1830–42) witnessed the concentration of power among a triad of officials, the most important of whom was ʿAbdul-Qādir bin Ziyāda al-Mosulī, the *nāẓir* (superintendant) of the customs.[39] As head of the gümrük or customs of Baghdad, the latter became a powerful monopolist, and acted in effect as the chief merchant of the city. He developed his own supply and distribution network, posting hand-picked agents in Syria and elsewhere to inform him of the needs of a specific market at any given time, and he traded in regional commodities purely on his own account. Furthermore, he forbade competition from other Baghdādī or regional merchants, and cultivated his own coterie of long-distance merchants.[40] The merchants who could afford to bribe their way into his favor were allowed special dispensation to carry on with their business, while the others were left to their lot, often facing forced loans and impoundments of their properties. In addition, the nomination of multazims and tribal ʾamīrs passed through al-Mosulī's office, thus allowing him responsibility for virtually all of the important internal appointments in the provinces of Iraq, and giving him influence beyond measure over these provincial appointees.

Although the sources paint a one-dimensional picture of the concentration of power in one individual's hands, it is quite possible that al-Mosulī relied on local merchants as much as they did on him. In particular, questions concerning the ultimate control and monopoly of regional production and trade must have grown out of the corporate interests of merchants in and out of government and did not depend on the totalitarian diktat of one man, powerful though he was. The sources do not elaborate on the measures al-Mosulī used to thwart his competitors, but the alliances that the Customs master of Baghdad forged with tribal shaikhs in the riverine districts of lower Iraq granted him (and his goods) free passage on the Tigris, even while disallowing other regional merchants, and even British shippers, from plying the same routes (see chapter 4). This commercial privilege continued long after this particular Customs master's departure,[41] indicating that, insofar as commercial monopolies were concerned, government officials were not the prime movers in the control of regional commodities or trade routes but were part of an on-going commercial tradition that accentuated the involvement of state-affiliated merchants. The latter were clearly more important in the overall tenor and direction of regional trade, for they continued to control the production, trade, and transport of certain commodities even though government officials changed, or were transferred to other provinces. That these commercial alliances continued inspite of the signing of the Anglo-Turkish Convention in 1838 (which banned Ottoman monopolies) is clearly manifest in the sources, and will be discussed elsewhere in the book.

The nineteenth century also saw the reinvigoration of British commercial interests in Iraq and the Gulf, which inevitably led to fierce economic rivalry between them and the alliance of Ottoman bureaucrats and regional merchants. In order to understand the basis of the confrontation between British shippers (and consuls) and Ottoman-affiliated merchants, a deeper investigation of British motives must be attempted.

THE BRITISH ROLE

As early as 1798, British officials of the East India Company, in conjunction with the Government of Bombay and "His Majesty's Ministers" in London, were attempting to establish a permanent foothold in the provinces of Iraq. The appointment letter of the first British Resident to Baghdad stipulated that:

> it having been judged advisable by the Secret Committee [of the East India Company], with the consent and approbation of His Majesty's Ministers, [that] under the present state of affairs and the rumors which have prevailed, the French might endeavour to penetrate to India either by the Red Sea or the Persian Gulph, [that therefore] a Resident should be established at the Court of the Pashaw of Bagdad, [and] you have been selected for that purpose. . . .[42]

Harford Jones (later Sir Harford Jones Brydges), the Resident in question, was given a detailed list of things to do. He was to proceed first to Vienna where he was to chase down every stray bit of information on the destination and progress of the French fleet in the Mediterranean. Then he was to hasten to Istanbul where he was to meet with the British Ambassador in that city, and collect all the pertinent information offered by that gentleman, after which he was to depart for Baghdad. On his arrival, he was immediately to forward that information by cipher either to Aden or Mocha, where Commodore Blankett of His Majesty's Navy was patrolling the sea routes all the way from the Straits of Bāb al-Mandab (Yemen) to the Gulf, "and obstructing the Progress of the French should they attempt to penetrate to India by either of these Routes." Once settled in Baghdad, the Resident was to notify the vali of his arrival and to arrange an introductory meeting (during which the Resident was to present the vali "with such presents as may be usual"). According to the scenario envisaged by the Court of Directors of the East India Company, the meeting was to consist of stern warnings delivered by the Resident to the vali, informing the latter that:

> you [i.e., the Resident] have been deputed by the East India Company to strengthen the friendship that has always existed between him and the Company; and, should the appearance of affairs render it necessary, you will point out to him the fatal Consequences which must ensue to his Dominions and the Turkish Empire in general, should the French be permitted to enter or pass through any part of the Turks Dominions or be suffered to obtain a footing there, or in Egypt. You will endeavour to prejudice him against such attempt on the part of France, and also to engage him to oppose it by all the Means of which he is possessed, either by his own Resources or his Influence with the Beys of Egypt and the Wandering Tribes of the Desert.[43]

Finally, the Resident was enjoined to collect information on the population, armed forces, resources, and commerce of the Iraqī provinces, as well as those of the Persian and Egyptian governments, "or of any Independent Princes inhabiting Arabia, or of any of the Parts through which an inroad might be made into India, either by the Inhabitants or strangers." While this was a tall order,

Jones seems to have fulfilled it admirably. In fact, because of its close scrutiny of the habits, customs, and manners of local communities from Basra to Najd, Harford Jones' mission became the model for future diplomatic exchanges between the East India Company (and its successor, the Government of India) and the Ottoman vilayets of Iraq throughout the last quarter of the eighteenth century.

Nevertheless, the British concern with the affairs of the province of Iraq was short-lived, a development that must be seen in the context of the Napoleonic wars in Europe. From the last quarter of the eighteenth century onwards, the British role in Iraq and the northern Gulf had grown steadily to include commercial as well as political privileges. According to a recent dissertation, in the 1790s the English agent in Basra was considered to be one of the most important personalities in the city; in part because of the East India Company's growing control of the freight trade with India (which made Britain an important commercial rival to regional shipping), as well as the British navy's ready assistance to the Ottoman governors of Baghdad and Basra to help put down local invasions. More importantly, "British influence over the Porte was generally growing during this period, and reflected itself, though in a limited way, in their dealings with the Basra government."[44] This assessment is all the more remarkable when an analysis of the British political and commercial presence in nineteenth century Iraq is attempted. As noted above, the first British Resident to Baghdad was appointed in the wake of heightened tensions in the Mediterranean, principally as a result of Napoleon Bonaparte's invasion of Egypt in 1798. As a consequence of the French occupation of Egypt, a significant, though nominally loyal Ọttoman province, Iraq took on important geo-strategic ramifications in the overall British desire to control the route to India. That importance dwindled after the French defeat. In 1806, there were even attempts on the part of the East India Company to shut down the Residencies at Baghdad and Basra, eventually leading to the closure of the Baghdad Residency in 1821, and the scaling down of the Basra agent's position to Assistant Resident. It was only during the early 1830s that Iraq took on renewed interest for the British, in part because of awakened apprehensions about "the Russian threat," and the anxieties aroused by Muḥammad ʿAlī's expansionist policies with regard to the overall integrity of the Ottoman Empire.[45] Even then, British interests were slow to materialize. For instance, although an investigation of the suitability for steam navigation of the Euphrates river was undertaken under the command of Francis Rawdon Chesney in 1835–37, it failed to produce any tangible results other than the grant of an imperial *firmān* to Chesney's successor, Henry Blosse Lynch, to continue his survey work of the Tigris and Euphrates. And while the Lynch family was later to branch out into shipping (founding the Euphrates and Tigris Steam Navigation Company) which eventually captured most of the freight trade by the latter part of the nineteenth century,[46] in the period between 1837 and 1861 (the date when the Lynch firm was granted permission by the Ottoman authorities to operate two steamers), British interests continued to face an uphill struggle to pry open the river trade of Iraq.

Prevailing academic opinion views Great Britain's economic policies, quite rightly, as emanating from different, and conflicting spheres of operation. Arguing that the period between 1780 and 1830 must be seen as a continuum in the development of British colonial policies in India, southeast Asia, Africa, and parts of the Ottoman Empire, C. A. Bayly believes that European attempts to penetrate regional trade in Asia and Africa was not the primary motive in colonial expansion, at least not before the third decade of the nineteenth century. While it is true that the theme of free trade was propounded by many sectors of the British economy, and provided a ready pretext for overseas expansion, in the case of India, it was "territorial revenues, not trade [that] remained the chief economic prize for the British in the East."[47] In fact, Bayly believes that British exports to India in this period were unimportant, and the expansion of British trade worldwide between 1790 and 1830 greatly exaggerated.[48] Although a reappraisal of the full impact of the "Second British empire" is just beginning, with several historians amplifying on Bayly's themes, there is already some disagreement with the latter's conclusions, at least with regard to British trade with the Ottoman Empire. While agreeing that the period between 1770 and 1810 should be viewed as a continuum, historians of the Ottoman state in particular are adamant that foreign imports into the Ottoman Empire not only rose sharply in the mid-eighteenth century but peaked at an all-time high by the its end. Although there was massive disruption as a result of the Napoleonic wars, "imports exploded during the 1820s and early 1830s, surpassing previous nineteenth century levels."[49] In fact, Şevket Pamuk has shown that from the 1830s onwards, total Ottoman exports increased more than five times, from £4.7 million to £28.4 million, while imports expanded six and a half times, from £5.2 million to £39.4 million.[50]

With regard to Iraq, the situation was somewhat similar. Overall trade figures from the 1830s onwards indicate a large import surplus with India, bringing with it a large trade deficit which remained the general trend throughout the early to mid-nineteenth century. In April 1846, however, it was calculated that the aggregate imports from India, Persia, and Arabia to Basra only amounted to 30, 54, 667 kerāns or £138,848, far less than in previous years. This excited some comment from the British Consul at Baghdad who reported that in 1805, the imports from Bombay and Madras alone had equalled £275,087. Concluding that "in the last forty years, the trade of the port has been reduced to less than one-half of its former extent,"[51] the consul put the blame for the situation on the reorientation of routes of trade away from the Gulf to the Black Sea and Mediterranean. By 1851–55, however, the Gulf route had regained some of its importance; as a result, imports from India again rose drastically, reaching a combined average of £129,000, while in the same period exports climbed to £73,000. In general, imports consisted of European manufactures, Indian spices, and Persian grain, while exports centered on livestock (horses and mules) and dates. While commerce with India and Europe continued to improve throughout the mid to latter part of the nineteenth century, the foreign trade of Iraq only took off with the opening of the Suez Canal, which

> gained immensely from the fact that its sea route to Western Europe was reduced from 14,000 miles to under 10,000, putting it within reach of the steamers of the time. Its sea trade multiplied several fold, and its agriculture was profoundly affected by the expanding demand for its produce. . . .[52]

Traditionally, the argument has been posited that the Anglo-Turkish Convention of 1838 was in large measure the key to the unprecedented growth of the Ottoman economy in this period. This argument has recently come under attack from revisionist historians of the Ottoman Empire. The Free Trade Treaty, which opened up the provinces of the Ottoman Empire to world market forces by abolishing state monopolies and internal duties, and imposing revised import and export tariffs, is now considered only to have accentuated certain trends already prevalent in the Ottoman economy, and to have underlined internally-generated changes that made the Porte receptive to the introduction of the new British-sponsored tariffs policy.[53] Of these internal changes, the most important were the emergence of the *aʿyan* or local notable families in the eighteenth century Balkans and Anatolia, the development of provincial autonomy throughout the empire and the concomitant decentralization of government. The rise of provincial landholding dynasts who could make their own commercial agreements with foreign merchants and commercial firms ultimately posed a danger to the integrity of the empire, the fragmentation of which seemed to be an actual possibility at the beginning of the nineteenth century. In the end, the Porte's perception of Muḥammad ʿAlī of Egypt as a very real threat to its Syrian provinces proved to be the final spur that goaded the Ottoman Sulṭān to action; partly because of Palmerston's assurances to help defend the empire against external enemies, Sulṭān Mahmud II signed the document on 16 August 1838.[54]

However, while it is obvious that the effects of the Convention on the empire's trade depended on the socioeconomic structure of each province, and its direct relation to the nature and impact of foreign trade, it is probably fair to say that the Convention alone never had the sufficient power to transform the empire's trade in any radical fashion. This is clear from the repeated complaints of British and Ottoman officials alike, nearly all of whom wanted the treaty revised almost as soon as it was ratified. The original draft stipulated that, besides the abolition of monopolies, British merchants were to be allowed to buy goods anywhere in the Ottoman Empire, and imposed duties of five percent on imports, twelve percent on exports, and three percent on goods in transit. Some present-day observers have concluded that because the Ottoman Empire soon realized that the rates were injurious to Ottoman producers, and detracted from the growth of revenue, the Porte began to petition for a reduction in rates soon after.[56] In 1861–62, therefore, new treaties were signed, raising import duties to eight percent and gradually reducing export duties to one percent. However, it is quite possible that, as a result of the non-effects of the treaty on such out-of-the way provinces as Iraq, the British, as well as the Ottomans, realized that a modification of the earlier convention was urgently needed. In fact, the treaty provided numerous loopholes for local merchants willing to circumvent the clauses of the Convention, allowing them the immense satisfaction of turning economic liabilities into clear advantages. Thus even though some regional merchants acknowledged the obvious advantages of shipping their produce and livestock on British steamships, it is by no means certain that they faithfully adhered to British commercial regulations at their home ports. In fact, the articles of the Balta Liman Treaty were cheerfully transgressed almost as a matter of course by merchants of all persuasions, including Ottoman bureaucrats and officials.

THE NON-EFFECTS OF THE ANGLO-TURKISH CONVENTION ON IRAQ

One of the more immediate problems of the Anglo-Turkish Convention was that even those responsible for interpreting the chief clauses of the treaty were not completely certain of what they meant, or what they applied to. This included Ottoman grand viziers, Ottoman governors, and foreign consuls alike. For example, in 1844 Henry Rawlinson, the British consul in Baghdad, explained to his superiors that no less than the grand vizier himself and the French ambassador at Constantinople had written to the governor of Baghdad, Najīb Pasha, wanting to be officially notified as to the exact nature of the duties called the tamgha (stamp tax on cotton goods in transit) and the *iḥtisāb* (octroi duty), for fear that they were being levied on European merchants in violation of the articles of the Treaty.[56] When both were reassured that the taxes in question applied only to the empire's internal trade, and had nothing to do with the import or export of merchandise, they must have been greatly relieved. One wonders, however, if even at the time, this sort of query could have been passed off as an ordinary misapprehension on the part of the central authorities in Istanbul and the representative of a Great Power, or whether it was viewed as a major blunder.

Certainly, more misunderstandings of this nature were to surface in British-Ottoman relations. In 1845 Rawlinson complained that the Baghdad authorities had petitioned him with regard to the nonpayment of certain taxes by British-protected merchants.[57] Even though Rawlinson was certain that British merchants and their protégés were exempt from these taxes because of past precedent, he insisted on procuring a vizirial letter from the British ambassador at Constantinople to the authorities at Baghdad, allowing British merchants immunity from payment. The most significant duty, in this respect, was that of the *qālibiyya,* originally levied at Baghdad on river craft

> in order to supply funds for the repair of the bridge [at Baghdad] . . . [but] the tax becoming productive, [it] was shortly afterwards diverted from its original purpose and incorporated in the established sources of Crown revenue, the exemption of British subjects from its operation being at the same time tacitly conceded.[58]

Now the Ottoman authorities wanted to abrogate this exemption. Rawlinson explained to the Foreign Office that, according to his understanding, the qālibiyya had first been introduced as an irregular duty on local craft, and applied in different proportions on each trip the boat made up or downriver. In the main, the duty was imposed on the cargo rather than the vessel. Since the Anglo-Turkish Convention was notoriously equivocal on internal taxation, he therefore proposed a comprimise. While local craft were obliged to pay the tax because their cargo was intended for internal consumption, British boats would be exempt if they loaded their boats with local goods for export, or British manufactures. Rawlinson's comprimise clearly stemmed from a close reading of the text of the Treaty; for as he further commented to his superiors at the Foreign Office, "many" years ago, the Porte, worried because so many of its subjects were becoming European-protected merchants, granted berāts (imperial patents) to several important Muslim merchants in Iraq, conferring, among other privileges, exemption from the qālibiyya duty.[59] So long as these berāts remained in force at Baghdad, British merchants could refuse to pay the qālibiyya tax, citing the third article of the treaty, which entitled British traders to the same privileges as "the most favored class of Turkish subjects." Thus, there were at least two ways in which British merchants could escape payment of the tax in question, both stemming from a liberal interpretation of the treaty. Nevertheless, Rawlinson's comprimise seems not to have been completely accepted, for the qālibiyya remained an onerous duty of which British merchants repeatedly complained until 1869. In that year, the governor, Midḥat Pasha, abolished it along with the iḥtisāb and a number of other "irregular" duties.[60] In fact, duties on river transport continued to plague the British throughout the century, even though major breakthroughs on the issue were repeatedly announced over the years by successive British consuls in Iraq (see Chapter Four for more details).

In fact, the nebulous nature of the convention continued to elude the understanding of officials on all sides. On 5 August 1846, for example, the British consul in Baghdad wrote to the Foreign Office to explain that because of the disparity between the English draft and the Turkish translation on the matter of the first Article, he was encountering difficulties in its application.[61]

Article one basically reconfirmed all rights, privileges, and immunities conferred on the subjects and ships of Great Britain previously granted by the Capitulations, as well as granted British subjects and ships all rights, privileges, and immunities granted by the Ottoman Empire to any other foreign subjects.[62] Rawlinson conceded that the clause, while ostensibly having been drafted to "combine a general protection of British goods and consequent extension of British commerce, with the acquisition of a special privilege for English merchants" in enabling them to import foreign goods on the same terms as goods from Great Britain, was vague enough to allow Ottoman merchants to claim the same privilege.[63] In fact, the latter wasted no time in pressing their case, arguing that the clause granted immunity to Indian goods transported in British ships, regardless of whether their proprietors were British or Ottoman subjects. Of course, this distinction ran counter to Rawlinson's interpretation of the Treaty, not only because it placed Ottoman merchants on par with British traders (and theoretically gave them equal protection under the convention), but also because it actually legitimized the Ottoman merchants' financial edge. The latter (mostly "Arab and Jewish merchants, all subjects of the Porte") were instrumental in importing close to £100,000 worth of Indian goods (and transmitting a further £20,000 worth of such "colonial" commodities to Persia), while British merchants were only able to control one-tenth of the Indian import trade into Basra. As a result of this and other questions, which seem not to have been solved to anyone's satisfaction for quite a long while, Rawlinson informed the Foreign Office that a revision of the first article was long overdue.[64]

In fact, by August 1846 Rawlinson was forced to admit that because of these and other problems

> throughout the whole period of seven years during which the Convention of Balta Liman has been in force, the Tariff in this part of the Turkish empire has, as far as exports are concerned, been almost inoperative. . . .[65]

In large part, this was because regional merchants could evade taxes with impunity. Rawlinson drew attention to the fact that the Ottoman policy of farming out the customs of each provincial district institutionalized competition in the gümrük (customs). There were three custom houses "in active competition with one another" at Mosul, Baghdad, and Basra. By allowing each customs master to lower export duties at will, and to make his own bargains with regional merchants, tax farmers could outbid their competitors and draw merchants away from their rivals. But the issuance of counterfreit certificates of export, falsifying the rates which merchants paid to clear their goods, drew the ire of the British consul who could not understand how an open display of such certification was allowed to pass official eyes. When confronted by Rawlinson, several regional merchants bluntly explained that "only under such an arrangement could they export at remunerative prices," and that the fault lay not with them but with the "vicious" system of tax farming that pervaded the whole empire. Even were export rates to be reduced, Rawlinson wrote resignedly, merchants would still not

> contemplate an abrogation of their right to make their own bargain with the Customs Masters. By suggesting that they be allowed the option of paying at the first Customs House they pass, they aim indeed at a legislation of the system of competition, and if export duties were reduced from 12% to 8%, they would still expect to clear out at 6%. . . .[66]

As late as 1879, a British official at Baghdad claimed that tax evasion was routinely practiced at the customs house, and continued:

> Although the rate demanded by the Tariff is supposed to be nominally paid, yet in point of fact it is generally believed that payment of a great deal of it, as much as 20%, is often evaded through the low moral tone of the merchants, and the connivance of the Turkish officials who give false denominations of goods to ensure lower taxation, thus colluding to defraud their own government. For instance, indigo, which is an expensive article and taxed ad valorem, is often passed under another denomination of goods. Another point complained of in the Customs House is a well-organized system of private extortion excercised by the officials. . . . It may easily be imagined that if obstruction be offered and delays made in the delivery of goods that owners will pay to get them passed quickly, and those who do not pay the Customs House subordinates will meet with obstacles or detention.[67]

DEFICIT AND DEBT

The Ottoman administration in the provinces of Iraq had to grapple with two other intractable fiscal problems in the nineteenth century: the continuing outflow of specie to pay for imports from India and Europe, and the Ottoman public debt, which began with the Porte signing its first foreign loan agreement in 1854 and culminated in 1876, when:

> Turkey joined the long list of nations . . . which, some time or other during the nineteenth century, had been unable to meet their commitment to their foreign creditors. . . .[68]

Throughout the nineteenth century, specie was being continuously exported from Iraq to India to pay for foreign imports. For instance, according to the diary of the Basra-based Christian merchant, Mikhāʾīl Yūsuf ʿAbbūd, on 13 August 1812:

> two boats, the *Eliza* and *Safinat al-Rusul* sailed to Bengal, with horses of the East India Company on board. They were going to Mangalore (west coast of India). Along with the horses, the ships carried hundreds of rupees because the cargo was small, and the merchants had nothing else to carry on board. . . .[69]

Because money was becoming physically scarce, all sorts of gold and silver coins were at a premium, including the Marie Therèse Thaler (dollar), which was widely used in the Arabian peninsula, the *ghāzī* in gold, and the kerān and ʿayn piastre in silver. By 1846 British officials were intimating that, unless something drastic were done, the shortage of specie would result in a chronic deficit in Baghdad's balance of trade with India and Europe. According to Rawlinson, the quantity of specie exported to pay for imports from Europe, Syria, Anatolia, India, Bahrain, and Persia amounted to at least forty lacs of kerāns, or £200,000.[70] Another £50,000 went to pay the annual revenues to the Porte. Only the expenditure of Persian pilgrims on their way to the shrine cities of Iraq provided "a perceptible return" in cash; however, this too was prone to dislocations brought on by periodic hostility between Ottoman Iraq and Qajar Iran. Unquestionably, money was fast diminishing each year, and something had to be done about it. Rawlinson's suggestion was to encourage the production of cash crops in the provinces of Iraq, so as to offer some means of marketable exchange for British-Indian imports. This was an idea that formed a current of the economic philosophy of the day, and which was already being tried in neighboring Persia with some success.[71]

However, in order for the production and export of raw materials to become a fact, they had, at the very least, to turn a profit for both the producer and the exporter. This was clearly impossible in the 1840s, in view of the fact that both the fourth and seventh articles of the Anglo-Turkish Convention stressed that duties of twelve percent were to be fixed on rural produce at the port of shipment, and not the place of production. Since land transport was expensive in Iraq, by virtue of the sometimes enormous distance between place of provenance and place of shipment, the lack of passable roads and bridges providing access to the nearest market, and the very heavy internal duties placed on goods in transit throughout the province (amounting, in some cases, to seventeen and three-fourths percent), merchants usually paid a great amount more once they reached their destination.[72] Because it was unprofitable to send produce to market, British ships sometimes left Basra in ballast, for want of cargo, causing European merchants a good deal of anxiety and frustration.[73] Rawlison envisaged that in the future revision of the Treaty, provision should be made for paying duty at the place of production (or, as he put it, "on the spot") rather than at the port of shipment.

Although the two issues—i.e., the export of specie to India and Europe, and the growing Ottoman debt—were to sap the strength of the provincial economy to the point of near-atrophy, the local literature treated them as if they were one and the same issue, brought about for the same reasons. Not only did local historians compound the problem by failing to differentiate between the two questions, they frequently laid the responsibility at the wrong door. For instance, Suleimān Fāʾiq, a Mamluk historian-bureaucrat who had served as head of the Military Accounting department in the Baghdad-based government of ʿAlī Rizā Pasha al-Lāz in 1849, penned a memoir of his early years in service in which he roundly criticized the "profligate" administration of Najīb Pasha. According to Fāʾiq, it was the latter's greed and excessive corruption that brought the province of Baghdad to rack and ruin. However, nowhere in Fāʾiq's history is there mention of economic factors outside the control of the Baghdad administration, such as the constant outflow of cash to pay for textiles and other goods from India, or the constant increase, as the century wore on, in "irregular" taxation to pay for the Porte's bad loans. Instead, according to Fāʾiq:

> in Najīb Pasha's time, even though the state Treasury received 20,000 *bedras* in funds, it lost 500,000 bedras (or thirty-two years of revenue in livestock). About 60,000 of the population ran away to the tribes to get away from oppressive and unjust exactions of the state. These runaways chose to live among the bedu rather than suffer exactions. The country was denuded from everything. . . . From the years 66 to 78h (i.e., 1849 to 1861), the imperial Treasury paid out 120,000 bedras so that the Baghdad-Basra governments could pay troop salaries, buy equipment and uniforms; and in conjunction with other supplies and equipment (donated by the Porte), the price went up to 150,000 bedras. . . .[74]

In 1853, Rawlinson echoed Fāʾiq's calculations, estimating that

> [The vilayet of] Baghdad yields at present, inclusive of Suleimāniya and Kirkuk, an annual revenue of about £350,000 . . . this amount being raised from customs, land tax, and Arab tribute. The present income does not nearly equal the expenditure, £250,000 being expended on the troops alone and the aggregate expenses of civil government, collection, religious establishments, public works, pensions and accounting to at least £150,000 more, so that £50,000 requires annually to be remitted from Anatolia. But a deficit is quite a financial novelty at Baghdad, and is merely owing to the recent augmentation of the military force. For many years, the entire military force of the Pashalik did not exceed 5,000 men and a surplus of £50,000 was then annually remitted to the Porte. . . .[75]

In Fāʾiq's account, the chief culprits for the mismanagement and waste in the Baghdad pashalik were governors such as Najīb Pasha. He failed to distinguish between the forces of an increasingly aggressive world market which used all the tools at its disposal—among them tariffs on trade and gunboats on the

Tigris and Euphrates—to wrench an opening for itself in the regional markets of Iraq, Arabia, and the Gulf. Rawlinson, on the other hand, pinned the blame for Iraq's budget problems on a host of other reasons, most of them centering around the "underdeveloped" nature of the Ottoman administration of Baghdad and Basra, and its lack of investment in, and promotion of, commercial agriculture. In the early 1840s, he opined to his superiors that the deficit was caused by a currency shortage brought about by an import surplus in Baghdad's trade with India; in 1851, he added that Baghdad's financial problems continued to deepen, as the local administration attempted to follow the Porte's orders by establishing and reorganizing the niẓām army, which was at the heart of Istanbul's reformist agenda. Prior to mid-century, Baghdad had actually operated a surplus with Istanbul; by 1851, the frenetic restructuring of the Sixth Army Corps *(al-failaq al-sādis)* had brought about a massive deficit, with nothing much to show for all of the efforts expended on the military.

FIRST CONCLUSIONS

By the middle of the nineteenth century, a number of economic and administrative measures had created disturbing new developments that directly or indirectly impacted regional networks of trade in Iraq. While the Anglo-Turkish Convention of 1838 failed to affect any visible transformation in merchants' livelihoods—at least not until the second half of the nineteenth century, the continuing administration of monopolies and the imposition of extraordinary taxes by an elite of merchants and governors created disarray in regional networks of trade. Although local chronicles blamed the worsening economic situation on the rapacity of governors and their deputies, it has been shown that the increasing trade deficit, and the borrowing by Istanbul from provincial governments to offset the imperial debt were two reasons why mid-nineteenth century administrations in Iraq were forced to impose punitive new duties on their subjects. As a result of these burdensome taxes, and fiscal obligations, there was a sizeable transfer of merchant capital to more receptive ports of trade.[76] Many fleeing merchants were rich property owners with established positions in Baghdad, Basra, and Zubair. Their livelihoods depended upon the transit trade to India, and they were familiar with all the elements necessary to conduct long-distance commercial transactions. Consequently, punitive measures undertaken against them by the governors of Baghdad and Basra—in the form of forced loans, sequestration of properties, and the imposition of monopolies on crucial food items of regional significance—ultimately destroyed the fortunes of the merchants who specialized in the sale and distribution of transit goods. With the exception of those traders allied with the government, the remainder saw their livelihoods ruined, a factor which no doubt was instrumental in forcing the most beleaguered to leave their home ports and migrate elsewhere.

In 1850, Maʿshūq Pasha, the mutasallim of Basra, wrote a detailed report to the Porte, discussing the situation of regional trade in Iraq and the Gulf.[77] In response to Istanbul's direct orders to do the utmost to attract back regional merchants that had left Basra for other ports of trade, he bluntly confirmed the fact that governmental oppression was the chief reason for their departure. Another reason was that the government had been unable to save townspeople from tribal depradations, such as raids at the close of the date harvest. Moreover, Basra had been severely ravaged by the plague both in 1830 and in 1846; these recurrent epidemics plus Basra's unhealthy climate, as well as the town's overall unsanitary conditions, forced merchants to put down roots elsewhere. However, Maʿshūq Pasha's report also underlined the competition of alternative ports of trade; admitting that the existence of free and independent administrations in Kuwait and Muḥammara (Arabistan) was attracting people away from Basra.

Maʿshūq Pasha's many conversations with regional merchants alerted him to the fact that Kuwait in particular had become a sizeable settlement of 6,000 souls, in part because it functioned as a haven for those merchants fleeing Basra's governmental oppression.[78] Nobody paid taxes of any kind, except a duty of two riyāls on each bundle of goods coming by sea. Because duties were so low, most merchants preferred to off-load their goods in Kuwait, and then send them by land to Iraq, Najd, al-Hijaz and eastern Arabia. In a good year, Kuwait's annual revenue actually came up to 100,000 riyāls, an astounding figure for Basra's mutasallim. Another point that Maʿshūq drew the Porte's attention to was the shaikh of Kuwait's compensation for coming to the aid of Ottoman authorities whenever necessary—such as in attempts to end the Kaʿab siege of Basra in the eighteenth century—for which he received 140 kara(s) of dates annually from the government of Basra.[79] The mutasallim of Basra made the following suggestions: if Kuwait or eastern Arabia (some of whose merchants had expressed a willingness to come under Ottoman sovereignty) were to be tied more firmly to the Ottoman administration in Basra, then an annual economic stipend of dates was not enough. Ultimately, nothing but the strengthening of the fleet at Basra would do. A strong navy could outmaneuver Kuwait's fleet and force obedience to Basra, while a corps of niẓām troops could garrison Kuwait (and presumably eastern Arabia) with the same purpose in mind. Although the people of Kuwait appeared to be loyal to Basra, the simple fact was that Kuwait's resources and revenues ultimately ended up in the shaikh of Kuwait's coffers; as a result of which, the latter felt no need to ask for assistance from the government of Basra for anything at all. If there was a genuine desire on the part of the central Ottoman government to incorporate Kuwait, al-Ahsa, and Bahrain into the Ottoman Empire on a more formal level, even though there already was a strong relationship in existence between these ʾimāras and the Baghdad and Basra administrations, then only a strong navy could force the issue. Moreover, an efficient, well-equipped and well-manned navy was essential, because only then could the Ottoman Empire challenge Great Britain's creeping influence, and defend Ottoman interests.[80]

While the suggestions of the mutasallim of Basra were heard in Istanbul, ultimately they were not acted upon, in part because ready funds were lacking to reestablish a strong navy, and the Porte's financial priorities were tied to other concerns. Nevertheless, uneven attempts to rescue the Porte's position in the Gulf were still being launched in the middle of the nineteenth century. Thus, in March 1847 Rawlinson drew attention to what was developing into a major political irritant for British consuls and merchants. Rāghib Bey, one of the senior officials in Istanbul, had gone on record as saying that the Porte was determined to have war steamers on the Euphrates and a "respectable naval force at the mouth of the river."[81] Echoing that sentiment, the vali Najīb Pasha told the British consul that detaching a part of the imperial fleet and stationing it in the Gulf made sense as a defensive move, just in case the ongoing Erzerum negotiations between Iran and the Ottoman Empire over the future shape of their respective territorial boundaries broke down, and Iran might try to occupy neighboring Muhammara by force. The latter town had been a source of Ottoman-Persian contention for decades, and a continuous source of dispute at the Conference. Five years later, the question resurfaced. Two iron steamers, whose construction at Liverpool had been financed by the Porte, were about to leave England to Basra, where they were to be reassembled to patrol the Tigris and Euphrates. The British consul remarked that these ships had been built with the obvious intention of thwarting Persian desires to annex Muhammara and added:

> And if that cession [of Muhammara] should be forced upon (the Ottomans) by the mediating European Powers, (the Ottomans would most likely) attempt to cripple the commerce of the place by a system of vexatious intimidation. . . . If it has been found difficult to keep the Turks within due bounds in regard to the Chaab country (i.e., Muhammara) with their present contemptible naval means on the Lower Euphrates, Your Excellency may understand that with two efficient war-steamers at their disposal [they would be unmanageable]. . . .[82]

Furthermore, the British consul sounded a note of caution with regard to the assistance the Ottomans might request from the Indian navy. Complaining that "the Turks" could never assemble the steamers in Basra on their own, nor organize a steam establishment independent of British-Indian supervision, he wondered whether it was in Britain's interest to allow this cooperation to continue. Although Rawlinson was quick to see the benefits for British trade in this venture in increased riverine security, he finally came down hard against the project, stating that:

> I think it would be highly desirable at present to impede rather than to encourage the Turks in their design for establishing steamers on the rivers of

> Mesopotamia and I would not recommend the entertainment of their application for assistance from India . . . unless they were determined at all points to carry out their enterprise, and are prepared in the event of our refusal to aid them, to employ the officers of other European Powers. . . .[83]

Attempts to reform the dilapidated Basra fleet continued to preoccupy the central administration in Istanbul; by the middle of the nineteenth century, these discussions seem to have reached a new and more promising threshhold. Darwīsh Pasha, one of the Ottoman representatives on the border commission to demarcate the frontier with Iran, wrote a report to the Porte, date 6 March 1850, in which he described in detail the lamentable state of the Basra fleet, and proposed solutions to help save it.[84] He began by pointing out the importance of Basra's strategic position. It was significant because of its large periphery of villages and *muqāṭaʿāt* (agricultural districts) and its tribal hinterland, plus its proximity to Iran and the rebellious tribes of the Gulf and Iraq such as the Kaʿab, the Muntafiq, and the Banū Lām. Because of the constant flare-ups on the troubled frontier between Iran and Iraq, in which the tribes of the region frequently took part, Basra needed a continuous defense. Although the port town only possessed seventy or eighty soldiers who could man cannons, and 250 infantry, many of the cannons were in disrepair and the soldiers incapacitated by ill health and disease. The Basra fleet consisted of six ships, but these ships were falling apart from disuse and bad maintenance. They all needed massive repairs. Because they were posted at strategic locations on the Shaṭṭ al-ʿArab, their sole function seemed to be to act as floating custom houses, regulating commercial traffic on the river.[85]

Darwīsh Pasha's memo to the Porte suggested that in order to strengthen Basra's naval presence, it was necessary to assemble a fleet of four large warships, one additional ship for the merchant fleet and two river tugboats on the Tigris and Euphrates to sail from Basra to Baghdad, and vice-versa. It was also necessary to repair and expand Basra's old port. Only with such a naval presence could the Ottomans even begin to think of reincorporating al-Ahsa and al-Qatif (eastern Arabia) into Basra province. Moreover, it was obvious from correspondence between the Porte and Oman that the latter needed a strong counterweight to the British presence in the Gulf, and might be willing—if the terms were right—"to come under the protection of a powerful Islamic state."[86] Furthermore, Darwīsh Pasha suggested that once the ships had been built in Bombay, a commander of the fleet should be appointed (along with a complement of technically-trained officers) to teach the arts of naval warfare to those under his command. He also thought it imperative—and in the imperial interest—to reinforce the garrison at Basra with two extra companies of men. Nevertheless, while the naval committee in Istanbul agreed in substance with these suggestions, the Porte's lack of finances, the effects of the Crimean War, and the cost of subduing internal insurgencies throughout the empire all combined to render the project null and void. By the end of the nineteenth century, Basra's fleet was still in need of rejuvenation and repair.

Meanwhile, the British were entertaining precisely the same idea. Even as they put pressure on the Ottomans to disestablish their project for placing steamships on the rivers of Iraq, the British surreptitiously went ahead with their own. As a result, the focus of British-Ottoman contention switched from Muhammara to Miᶜqal. One of the large rivers that flows into the Shaṭṭ al-ᶜArab, the Miᶜqal lay on the west bank of the Shaṭṭ, between the villages of al-Haritha and al-Ribat, a distance of five kilometers from Basra. In the late eighteenth century, the Lynch firm bought the lands lying at the mouth of the river from a former East India Company agent and British consul of Basra, who had himself bought it from the Saᶜdūn shaikhs of the Muntafiq tribe, and converted it into steamship depot to repair river steamers.[87] From that moment on, the river Miᶜqal was called Kūt al-Faranjī (Foreigner's Village), its earlier name forgotten until the British occupied Iraq in the early twentieth century had transformed the steam depot into an out-and-out naval base, whereupon its original name was restored.[88]

According to a present-day Iraqī historian, a reading of Ottoman archival materials confirms that Miᶜqal/ Kūt al-Faranjī was never simply a coal depot or a warehouse for British naval supplies, but a secret military base for British warships.[89] Even at the time, however, this was an unknown fact. In fact, in 1849–50, news that British men-of-war were stopping periodically at Basra came as a revelation to the Porte, which hastened to find out by communication with the governor of Baghdad, Nādir Pasha, whether permission to use the base for military warships had in fact been granted to the British by local subordinates, independent of Istanbul's orders. The ṣadr al-ʾaᶜẓam's letter to the vali of Baghdad explained that information had been relayed to the Porte to the effect that a British military ship had arrived in Basra with two hundred Indian troops on board, had stayed in Basra for four days, and then had gone on to Bushire. Istanbul wanted to know if any of these troops had left ship, and whether anything had been said about their mission. Nādir's secret memorandum to the Porte on 12 September 1849 stated that the British frigate *Alveston* had arrived in Basra from Bushire four months ago in order to be repaired, and to swap worn spare parts for new. Twenty days later, the *Alveston* set sail for India, after having made contact with one of the British steamboats that plied the Tigris on its usual journey downriver. The governor added that, in fact, some of the British gunboats that belonged to the East India Company made journeys to Basra two to three times a year. Seemingly unperturbed by the development, Nādir Pasha repeated the statement that the *Alveston*'s mission was nothing less than the exchange of used spare parts for new. Nevertheless, nearly seventy years after the sale of Miᶜqal to the British, and forty years after the erection of harbor facilities on the site, Istanbul decided finally to investigate the base.

Initially, the governor of Baghdad and the mutaṣarrif of Basra thought that nothing untoward was taking place in Miᶜqal/Kūt al-Faranjī; in fact, in his communications to the Porte, Nādir Pasha stressed that the area was nothing more than a plantation *(bustān)* and summer resort for the British Resident in Basra and his family. And he went on:

> Today, boats coming from India loaded with goods dock at al-Anbar (the Arabic term for the depot) and in summertime, the (East India Company) Agent goes there for his holidays. (The base) is open to the public; and there is no sign of any war-related activities. . . .[90]

Similarly, the mutaṣarrif of Basra, Maᶜshūq Pasha, reported that for all intents and purposes, there was nothing suspicious going on at Miᶜqal/Kūt al-Faranjī. All that could be construed to be war-related matériel were some old machines and tools that lay rusting on the shore. It was basically a *jubbakhane,* a depot for old and used military spares, and there was nothing sinister about it at all. Alarmed, rather than appeased, by the contradictory evidence from its men on the spot, the Porte decided to solve the predicament it faced by ordering Maᶜshūq Pasha to prevent the British from expanding and enlarging their base; to observe and inspect all the materials entering and leaving the base; to bring anything suspicious to the notice of the Porte; and finally, and if at all possible, to buy back the base from the British. Although Maᶜshūq was actually able to wrest a promise from one of the representatives of the Lynch firm to buy back the base, evidence exists that the latter were able to countermand that proposal through pressure exerted on the Porte by the British ambassador in Constantinople. Always ready to serve British interests until the very last, the ambassador was able to paralyze the Porte's intentions to restore Miᶜqal/Kūt al-Faranjī to Ottoman control most probably by pointing out that in view of the Porte's well-known financial straits, there were better ways to spend the imperial treasure. As a result, despite the pleas and comments of Maᶜshūq Pasha, the subject was closed forever.[91]

THE INVASION OF EASTERN ARABIA

By far the most ambitious attempt to recapture Ottoman initiative in Gulf affairs, however, occurred in May 1871. In that month, Midḥat Pasha, governor of Iraq, sent a force by sea to invade and occupy eastern Arabia, after the Porte's nominee for the leadership of the house of Saᶜūd, ᶜAbdullāh ibn Saᶜūd, appealed for Istanbul's help in the battle against his brother and rival claimant to the throne, Saᶜūd. According to Midḥat Pasha, the Ottomans felt that it was incumbent upon them to intervene, since ᶜAbdullāh had been appointed *qāʾim-maqām* (deputy governor of a *qaḍāʾ*) by the Porte,[92] and the Porte still retained administrative-legal rights by virtue of the sixteenth century occupation of al-Ahsa by Ottoman troops. Nevertheless, there were a number of other reasons for the military expedition as well. One of them may have been that the Ottomans "had for some time been considering regaining their former provinces in the peninsula to compensate for their territorial losses in Europe."[93] Another reason hinged on the control of long-distance trade routes. Even though Ottoman influence was never to extend into central Arabia, but remained confined to the littoral, the occupation marked an important turning point in the Ottoman expansionist policy towards the Gulf as a whole, indicating that nothing short of an overt, physical occupation of the land routes emanating from Iraq to Najd would suffice at that juncture. In fact, Midḥat Pasha's actions confirmed that the regional market that spanned Najd, southern Iraq, Kuwait, and Arabistan was a power to be reckoned with. The rural/tribal merchants of these territories had long held informal sway over the domestic and transit trade of the region, working in cooperation with urban merchants to maximize their profits, while paying as little as possible by way of state taxes. The expedition therefore had an economic motive: to capture the transit trade flowing through the land routes to Iraq. Thus

> the subsequent history of Najd was greatly influenced by the Turkish annexation of Hasa, which brought the shortest of all the routes from the sea to the Wahhābī country under Ottoman control; indeed, all practicable lines of access to central Arabia, except that from Kuwait, ran after this throughout Turkish territory, and a powerful hold was thus obtained by the Porte. . . .[94]

Although the occupation and annexation of al-Ahsa was to take many convoluted twists and turns, the fate of the expedition need not detain us here; what is important is the alliance of interests that coalesced in support of it. From the very beginning, Shaikh ʿAbdullāh al-Ṣabāḥ of Kuwait, who was later to accept the title of qāʾimmaqām himself from the Porte,[95] acted as intermediary between Shaikh ʿAbdullāh ibn al-Saʿūd and the Baghdad government; later on, he also offered material support in the form of transport ships and soldiers. The main army setting off from Baghdad consisted of niẓām regiments, complemented by tribal irregulars from the south of Iraq, principally the Muntafiq, Ẓāfir, ʿAnayza, and Shammar. The assistance provided by the shaikh of the Muntafiq, Nāṣir al-Saʿdūn did not stop with the successful annexation of eastern Arabia; for he was again enlisted to put down a local uprising in al-Ahsa soon after, and appointed Shaikh Bazīgh al-ʾArʿar of the Banū Khālid tribes as Ottoman governor of the district. When in 1874, another rebellion brought about the latter's dismissal, al-ʾArʿar was replaced as *mutaṣarrif* (governor of a *liwa'* or *sanjaq)* by Mizyad al-Saʿdūn, Shaikh Nāṣir's son. In 1884, when Mizyad was still mutaṣarrif, the Wilayet of Basra was reconstituted, incorporating Najd and al-Ahsa as administrative sub-districts of Basra, and Nāṣir Pasha al-Saʿdūn became its first governor.[96] In conjunction with the al-Ṣabāḥ family and the Muntafiq shaikhs, the Ottoman expansion into central Arabia also enrolled the talents of prominent Basran and Moslī families. Chief amongst them was the Naqib family, whose most famous member, Sayyid Ṭālib, became mutaṣarrif of Najd in 1902–03; while ʿIzzat al-ʿUmarī, a celebrated poet from Mosul, became mutaṣarrif earlier on in the century.[97]

However economically viable al-Ahsa may have seemed at the beginning, the Ottomans were not completely successful in their strategy to control and keep trade routes under their domination. For one thing, the sanjaq (province) of Najd, as eastern Arabia was now labelled, was composed of three qaḍās (administrative sub-districts): Najd, Qatar, and al-Qatif which only fielded 1,200 soldiers of the Sixth Army Corps, too few to maintain law and order and to check refractory tribesmen. This became all too obvious as the decade wore on. In the second year of the occupation, the *muftī* of the Ottoman army, Sayyid Dāwūd al-Saʿdī, led over one hundred pilgrims and merchants from Iraq to Mecca and Madina; they chose the land route because it was supposedly safer, having come under the more regular administration of the Ottoman authorities of Baghdad. On their way to Mecca from Riyāḍ, however, they encountered a raiding party from the ʿUtaiba tribe, who forced the pilgrims to pay 144 riyāls for "safe" conduct. Because the authorities intervened in Mecca, the pilgrims were recompensed for the money lost by the shaikh of the ʿUtaiba himself, while the muftī received an jewel-encrusted silver sword. The shaikh of the ʿUtaiba, Ḥusain ibn Jāmiʿ, was later imprisoned. However, on their way back to Iraq, the pilgrims were again robbed enroute, this time by unknown parties.[98]

In fact, the Ottomans were unable to completely secure trade and pilgrimage routes in eastern Arabia throughout their long occupation of the territory. Realizing that the little amount of resources at their disposal could never completely pacify the district, the Ottoman government in al-Ahsa decided to concentrate its energies in order to safeguard trade routes to al-ʿUqair (al-Ahsa's chief seaport) for at least one day. Monday was picked as the day in which caravans were to proceed under paid tribal escort to the coast. Even then, problems arose. In 1902, for instance, the shaikhs of the al-Murra and Banū Hājar tribes asked for an increase in the salaries paid them to patrol the trade routes; when they did not receive it, they attacked a trade caravan and killed over fifty men at al-Qaḥdiyya, a spot near ʿUqair. As a result, the mutaṣarrif of Najd was dismissed and Basra's strong man, Sayyid Ṭālib al-Naqīb, replaced him. The latter was able to restore order but it was a temporary peace; for in 1907, the al-ʿUjmān tribe again attacked al-Ahsa.[99]

Moreover, unlike other Arab provinces within their hold, the Ottoman authorities granted major concessions to the population of Najd. Its inhabitants were not conscripted into the niẓām army, nor were they forced to conform to civil law. In fact, an imperial *ʾirāda* (command) proclaimed that, contrary to other parts of the empire, the sharīʿa alone sufficed in Najd. Thus, the only notable Ottoman "reform" to be imposed on Najd was the institution of the Vilayet Council.[100] In other words, the Ottoman authorities had always to tread carefully in eastern Arabia; for whatever administrative arrangements were put in place were never wholly a reflection of the reality of Ottoman control. In fact, as in all other provinces under Ottoman control, power was a reflection of the balance worked out between local shaikhs and Ottoman bureaucrats. The inhabitants of al-Ahsa, for instance, may have accepted to pay taxes to the Ottoman garrisson when the latter were supreme; but after the regiment's withdrawal in the early twentieth century, the Ahsaīs went back to their own devices.

In fact, true control always depended on a number of factors, chief of which was the way that respective ʾamīrs in the district viewed their interests with regard to the Ottoman state, British officials and other local shaikhs in the region. This interplay between social forces continued up till the last days of the Ottoman government in al-Ahsa, even extending to the Ottomans' trusted allies in central Arabia, the al-Rashīd ʾamīrs of northern Arabia. For instance, in 1901, the British consul in Basra reported that an emissary from Ibn Rashīd, the shaikh of Jabal Shammar, relayed a message to him from his overlord in which he complained of Ottoman exactions, and wished to be taken under British protection, "in the same manner as the sheikh of Koweit."[101] The emissary, Fahad Pasha, even proposed a scheme by which Shaikh Mubārak of Kuwait would be deposed and one of his nephews appointed in his stead, a plan that would give Ibn Rashīd great leverage over Kuwait, which was a vital conduit of arms and ammunition to Jabal Shammar. Even though the British consul suspected that Ibn Rashīd's offer was not completely genuine, and stemmed from his mounting grievances with the Ottoman authorities on the one hand and the shaikh of Kuwait on the other, the British official felt that he could not reject it out of hand because the Russians were waiting in the wings, anxious to forge links with the rulers of central Arabia and Kuwait in the event that the British gave up on the latter. Although the ʾamīrs of Jabal Shammar made several overtures to British officials throughout the early part of the twentieth century, they seemed to have remained firmly wedded to the Ottoman line until the First World War. In fact, barely a year after Fahad Pasha's offer, Consul W. S. Richards in Damascus wrote his superior in Istanbul to tell him that a certain Nāṣir Pasha al-Ghushmān, Ibn Rashīd's envoy, passed by Damascus on his way back to Najd from Istanbul, where he had been sent with presents from Ibn Rashīd to the Sulṭān. According to the consul, "by this action, [the Porte] showed what a keen interest in the affairs of Najd is now felt, in the highest quarters at Constantinople, rather more so, perhaps than in the past."[102] It also showed how adept the ruler of Jabal Shammar was at playing his cards, and how keen he was to preserve his independence in the face of a number of contending forces in the region. Playing off the British against the Ottomans, he managed to retain his supremacy in the district until the turn of the century, when Shaikh ʿAbdul-Azīz ibn Saʿūd finally managed to regain control over northern Najd.

CONCLUSION

By the last quarter of the nineteenth century, the strategic-commercial alliance between the Ottoman authorities of Basra and Baghdad and select regional merchants and shaikhs was theoretically still strong, even though it was beginning to come under pressure from internal as well as external sources. While British consuls and merchants continued to chip away at the fiscal privileges that buttressed this class in power by complaining continuously to Istanbul with regard to the non-application of the Anglo-Turkish Convention in Iraq (and eventually gaining some redress later on in the century), some state-affiliated merchants began to abandon their Ottoman partners in favor of European firms (see subsequent chapters). While the transformation from Ottoman-affiliated to British-allied merchants was slow, it gathered momentum with the upsurge in British trade by the 1880s. Thus, the Ottoman invasion of eastern Arabia in 1871 may have been the last hurrah of the old alliance, for it grouped together for perhaps the last time loyal Ottoman clients such as ᶜAbdullāh, the shaikh of Kuwait, recently converted clients such as Nāṣir al-Saᶜdūn, shaikh of the Muntafiq of southern Iraq, and fledgling "Ottomanized" elite families such as the al-Naqīb of Basra and the al-ᶜUmarī from Mosul. By the 1890s, however, the circumstances that had propelled the alliance of Ottoman governors and state-affiliated merchants was no more. Shaikh Mubārak of Kuwait reversed the century-old alliance between the al-Ṣabāḥ family and the Basra government by coming to a secret but binding agreement with Great Britiain not to cede, sell, or lease any property in Kuwait without British permission; Shaikh Nāṣir's once-formidable power had sharply eroded among the Muntafiq tribesmen that were once his followers with his total acceptance of Ottoman jurisdiction in his once-independent tribal district; and Sayyid Ṭālib al-Naqīb, while continuing to portray himself as an Ottoman loyalist until the turn of the century, eventually joined the first British-sponsored government in independent Iraq. The following chapters will chart this socioeconomic transformation in more detail.

-Four-

River Routes

At the turn of the century, the fight for dominance over trade routes became an important factor in the struggle to control the available resources of Iraq, Arabia, and the Gulf. Because trade routes were the lifeline of the regional market, any hostile takeover usually resulted in the disruption of trade in some districts while creating a temporary prosperity in others. Shaikhs and merchants who had been denied access to their traditional routes either fought to regain control over them or tried to divert trade by creating new commercial channels.

The attempt to control the passage of transit trade must be seen in the context of constantly fluctuating borders. Shaikhs in Kuwait, Iraq, and central Arabia who managed to gain control of an important district invariably tried to extend this same control to other neighboring areas. By carving out new spheres of influence, merchants and tribal entrepreneurs were able to create economic regions by means of the monopoly of trade routes. In this respect, the Saᶜūdī ʾimāra was significant because it was possibly the first attempt by local rulers to fully centralize the economic resources of the region, and to control all trade routes emanating into the peninsula. In fact, the Saᶜūdī statist experiment, comprising within it an important commercial component, threw into relief economic practices and traditions that later on became the stock and trade of regional merchants from al-Ahsa to Bombay. Inevitably, one of these "new" traditions was the attempted monopoly of trade routes.[1] Henceforth, any regional economic initiative designed to maximize profits from long-distance trade strove to incorporate monopolies within its overall strategy; and free trade, the leitmotiv of early eighteenth-century ports and emporia, was supplanted in the latter part of the century by a deadly struggle to control all available commercial channels into the region by one party, whether that was a tribal confederation, a state-affiliated merchant, or a British shipping firm. While the first chapter discussed this development, and the transformations it brought about in the regional market, this chapter takes as its starting point the changes wrought in the mid to latter part of the nineteenth century, when the second Saᶜūdī state faltered, then failed altogether, and the control of land routes passed into other hands.

With the invasion of ʾIbrāhīm Pasha's troops and the subsequent occupation of Najd and the Hijaz by an Egyptian force sent deliberately to destroy the Saᶜūdī-Wahhābī state, the Saᶜūdī attempt to carve out a wider socioeconomic zone incorporating land and to some extent, sea routes was shattered. After the dissolution of the first Saᶜūdī dynasty in the early nineteenth century and the turmoil that ensued in the wake of the Egyptian occupation of Najd, the struggle for trade routes into Najd gradually abated, for the Saᶜūdī rulers who came to power after 1820 were themselves beset by internal problems and no longer interested in the expansion of their socio-economic hold on neighboring districts. Facing internal dissension at home and threats to their power from within their own ranks, the House of Saᶜūd became yet another local shaikhly family intent upon restoring its hard-won political and commercial privileges.[2] Furthermore, the struggle for the local control of land and sea routes, while still extremely important to the overall dynamics of regional trade, began imperceptibly to give way to other challenges. These stemmed chiefly from foreign penetration of riverine commerce and the presence of European ships on local waters.

THE COMPETITION OVER RIVERINE ROUTES AND THE BEGINNING OF FOREIGN CONTROL OF THE PASSAGE OF TRADE

It is useful at this point to recall that the introduction of steam transport to the Gulf region has been viewed by some historians as a near-cataclysmic event and, over and above everything else, as the major force for change in the area. Economic historians of the modernization school have long asserted that the placing of British steamers on the rivers of Iraq marks a watershed in Iraq's history because, among other things, it provided one of the primary incentives for the commercialization of agriculture, the sedentarization of pastoral tribes, and the growth of new administrative towns, ultimately ushering in the phenomenal growth of foreign trade in the Iraqī provinces.[3] However, while it is true that British steamships were instrumental in the more efficient and rapid transfer of regional goods to foreign markets, they were by no means wholly responsible for the intensification of commercial agriculture in southern Iraq, the growth of a cash economy, or the spread of towns. Many of these economic features already existed throughout the region; they did not originate from outside. Thus, regional merchants in Iraq, Arabia, and the Gulf could count on a cash economy, long-term credit, ports of trade, and efficient systems of transport before the coming of the British. In fact, the great expansion of foreign trade in the last quarter of the nineteenth century was, in part, built on the so-called "traditional" economic practices and institutions of the region. Nevertheless, it was one thing to enter into partnerships with local merchants and another thing entirely to make inroads in local trade. And here we come to the crux of the problem: totally absent from the work of economic historians of the modernization school, at least until very recently, is any attempt to study local resistance to Western economic and technological intrusion in the Arab provinces of the Ottoman Empire.[4] For resistance there was. While there is a certain truth to the statement that foreign shipping soon began to intrude upon, and compete with, local sailing ships to the detriment of the latter,[5] the process was by no means an easy one. As shaikhs and merchants in Najd, Kuwait, and Muḥammara continued to fight for supremacy over vital routes linking economic centers within the broader framework of the regional market, another struggle for the monopoly over shipping lanes within Iraq proper began to unfold. As in the fight over land communications, however, the struggle to capture riverine routes was by no means an easy undertaking. For whereas up till the 1840s, all control excercised over regional trade was generated by internal conditions and followed an internal dynamic, after the mid-nineteenth century, new factors came to trouble the relative peace of regional merchants. By far the most important was the establishment of British steam power on the twin rivers of Iraq, the most important shipping routes of the region. The intrusion of foreign traders in the riverine areas upset the delicate balance of economic alliances in the districts of lower Iraq, and destroyed the monopolies on riverine trade upheld by regional merchants in conjunction with government officials. In turn, economic disruption generated resistance and area-wide oppositional movements.

THE KHUWWA AND OTHER "PROTECTION" DUES

Riverine routes functioned as adjuncts of the land passage from Najd and Kuwait to Basra; they were also significant to the transit trade of southwest Iran, which used the tributaries and channels of the Tigris to reroute goods into the central part of the country. As a result of their economic potential, therefore, eighteenth and nineteenth century shaikhs in the area of lower Iraq soon began to gain control of the waterways and to demand transit fees from travellers and merchants. These "protection" dues were often subsumed into the larger expense of long-distance trade and formed an important item of revenue for the tribal districts.[6] For example, in the last quarter of the eighteenth century, the shaikhs of the Muntafiq confederation in southern Iraq regularly levied a duty on all riverine craft passing through their tribal "borders." In 1785, Shaikh Thuwainī, the most important of the Muntafiq leaders, stopped an official convoy of Indian diplomats and merchants passing by way of Basra and demanded customs duties on articles they had brought from Mysore as presents for the Mamluk pasha, Suleimān Agha.[7] The Khazāʿil also levied tolls on the Euphrates, and strategically placed their "tollbooths" on the most common lanes of trade between Baghdad and Basra.[8] Other significant duties were those imposed by the Shammar on the routes of trade between Baghdad and Mosul, and those between Mosul and Bilād al-Shām (in which tolls were paid at Tikrīt); khuwwa or *ʾatāwi* taxes imposed by the Zubaid on the river routes between Baghdad and Basra (which were paid at a small village north of Kūt); similar duties extracted by the ʿAnayza on the desert road west of the Euphrates (which were collected at Aqra);[9] and those that the Banū Lām tribes imposed on both banks of the Tigris and Euphrates.[10]

The function of transit fees in the tribal economy has often been misconstrued as an illegal taxation imposed by stronger tribes on weaker ones, sometimes entailing exorbitant sums of money which consular officials were in the habit of calling "blackmail."[11] Transit fees fell into several different categories. Not the least significant was the aforementioned khuwwa tax, a fee usually paid to shaikhs of militarily important tribes by smaller tribes, villagers, and regional merchants in order to cross districts over which the shaikhs claimed jurisdiction. Although the khuwwa was levied by tribes living on the fringes of urban settlements as well as those inhabiting the open desert, it also existed in agricultural settlements and in riverine areas in which tribal parties held sway, such as in or around the mid-Euphrates. And while it was usually paid either in cash or in kind,[12] at least one historian continues to claim that the khuwwa was not so much an economic compact between strong tribes and those requiring protection as an indispensable aspect of social relations that tied the tribesman to the townsman through *ḥilf* (alliance).[13] Nonetheless, the khuwwa (in a sense, the generic name for a whole compendia of transit fees imposed by nineteenth century shaikhs in Arabia, Iraq, and the Gulf) was sometimes very lucrative indeed.

The khuwwa was the symbol of military and political power, legitimizing a tribe's hold over certain territories and serving notice of its military and political sovereignity.[14] It was also a practical method by which shaikhs gained access to a share of the transit trade that flowed across their borders. Thus, certain river districts in the Muntafiq territory (such as an obscure village thirty miles above Qurna) were designated as places where customs taxes were collected on boats sailing down the Euphrates. However, these taxes did not completely enter the paramount shaikh's coffers; but formed part of the revenue which shaikhs of the Muntafiq and other powerful tribes farmed for the governments of Baghdad and

Basra. It is important to note that at no time were these various taxes (going by such names as the *zakiyya* or *tesyāriyya* duties) considered illegal in the tribal mode of operations; indeed, the practice of collecting tolls in desert areas or in river districts was sanctioned by usage and tribal tradition. Moreover, granting the right to collect transit fees to shaikhs as part of their iltizām or tax-farm meant not only that the government was legitimizing these commercial duties but that it derived a profit from their collection as well.

The Ottoman governments of Baghdad, Basra, and Mosul also imposed taxes on river transport, and had done so from the sixteenth century onwards. The best known tax seems to have been the *bāj-i-sefineh* (boat-tax),[15] which was still being levied in the nineteenth century, much to the consternation of the British consul in Mosul who insisted (with no foundation whatsoever) that it was "illegal."[16] In the province of Mosul in the sixteenth century, the bāj tax was levied on the crew as well as the cargo. Other taxes relating to river transport are mentioned in the sixteenth-century *kanunnameler* (law codes) of Mosul, as well as those of Basra.[17] The significant thing here is that all of these taxes were the responsibility of the shaikh-multazim of a given tribe, who was charged with collecting this large revenue. Therefore, as exorbitant as these taxes may sometimes have been (for shaikhs frequently raised river duties whenever they thought they could get away with it),[18] they were part of a systematic policy of collecting revenue in land and river trade. In the river areas in particular, the stopping of boats at fixed points in order to collect transit fees became a regular part of riparian operations, and the object of every shaikh's tenure in power. As has been mentioned, nineteenth-century consuls seem to have misconstrued the nature of these river duties by making an artificial division between "illegal" and "legal" taxes. Because of the British perception that the tribes were inherently lawless, the first category naturally applied to tolls and duties exacted in tribal districts,[19] and the other to government dues. As has been pointed out, however, there was no fundamental differences between the two sectors, and shaikhs and government officials were frequently partners in the collection of revenue in riverine districts. In fact, as the following examples show, the association was so profitable that orders relayed to Baghdad from Istanbul to curtail the imposition of these taxes fell on deaf ears, much to the chagrin of British merchants, who were forced to pay transit dues which Ottoman officials evaded as a matter of course.

COMMERCIAL ALLIANCES BETWEEN OTTOMAN GOVERNORS AND TRIBAL SHAIKHS

Thus in July 1846, British merchants reported that that there were large duties levied upon loaded boats on their passage from Baghdad to Basra and vice-versa; that these duties were sanctioned by the local government at Baghdad and Basra, and that they were levied directly on the cargoes and not the boats. In other words, empty boats passed free. In an accompanying letter, consul Rawlinson in Baghdad estimated that the duties levied on a cargo-laden boat on her passage from Basra to Baghdad amounted to close to 4,155 Constantinople piasters, equivalent to £38; he also listed the various duties that a merchant would have to pay on the trip up or downriver. These included imposts levied by Arab tribes such as the Banū Lām, the Zubaid, and the Shammar, as well as government taxes such as the qālibiyya, the zakiyya and the different gamārik duties, and finally, the tolls taken at Basra, Qurna, and Baghdad. In other words, the problem for British merchants lay as much with the price exacted for each river journey as with the bewildering array of duties they had to pay at each stage of the journey.

Moreover, part of the problem was that the Arab tribes on the banks of the Euphrates, who were more than likely in alliance with the Ottoman governors of Baghdad and Basra, remitted a large tribute in money to these same authorities, "so that the duties charged in the above manner (were) actually an increase by the Turkish government on those sanctioned by the [Balta Liman] Treaty."[20] As a result, British merchants had been trying to recover some of the "illegal" payments they had been forced to make to Arab tribes on a large quantity of British manufactures for the past four years, but to no avail. Perhaps most distressing of all, however, was the fact that riverine tribes had forced European merchants to pay a large sum of money so that they could send their goods downstream even though this tax was not applied to all merchants using the river routes, as the following extract makes clear:

> We stated to [the British Ambassador to Constantinople] that the charges in question were only partially levied, and trading vessels of persons connected with the government of Abdul-Qadir Agha, the late *Gumrugchee* (customs master) of Baghdad, paid nothing. . . . Again, we think it proper to remark that in June 1846, a large trading boat belonging to some person connected with the present government came up from Bussorah laden with a cargo of merchandise, the *Nakhoda* (captain) of which was furnished with letters from the government to the authorities on the river which exempted her entirely from the payment of any of these duties, while other boats in company with her were obliged to pay. If any doubt, therefore, remained on the subject, this would prove that the duties in question are taken with the concurrence and sanction of the government.[21]

Two years later, it was the British consul's turn to complain. He wrote to the Foreign Office that the governor in Baghdad, Najīb Pasha, was not fulfilling his part of the bargain with Istanbul to put a stop to all "illegal" river dues, even though the consul had positive proof that instructions to that effect had been delivered to Baghdad by the Porte's emissaries.[22] The consul's despatch intimated that a monopoly on riverine trade had been established by the three most powerful tribes on the Tigris and Euphrates, namely the Muntafiq, the Shammar, and the Zubaid, and that the shaikhs of these confederations had:

> driven away the outlying band of marauders that formerly infested the banks and levied blackmail on river-craft, and in their general accounts with the Baghdad government actually allow credit to the Pasha for the proceeds of the taxes in question. The exactions have now become so systematised and so much under the control of government that a boat furnished with a free passage under the hand of the Pasha is usually allowed to pursue its voyage up and down the river unmolested, and if therefore, H. E. [Najīb Pasha] should still decline to bring the orders of the Porte into operation, it can only be from a disinclination to lose a productive source of revenue. . . .[23]

Obviously, the alliance between the government and the paramount shaikhs of the Tigris and mid-Euphrates was not one that had been imposed by the government on tribal chiefs, for even had they wanted to, the governments of Baghdad and Basra were hardly in a position to assert their claims by force. Local governors could not even quell local uprisings closer to home, let alone mount successful campaigns against the independent-minded inhabitants of the rivers and marshes of southern Iraq. Rather, it seems obvious from the sources that the alliance was between two enterprising sectors of the economy, which had joined forces in order to maximize and to profit from the revenue potential of the districts of lower Iraq, a development European traders viewed with considerable disquiet. In fact, the alliance between riverine shaikhs and Ottoman officials went from strength to strength in the period from 1820 to 1850 for, contrary to European expectations, a few months after Rawlinson's despatch, British merchants suffered yet another setback. The Porte relayed instructions to its governors at Mosul, Baghdad, and Basra, defining the rules of operation for British steamboats navigating the Euphrates and Tigris. If a seagoing vessel arriving from a foreign port were to continue its journey to Baghdad, without stopping at Basra, it could forego any river dues; if, however, the vessel's regular route was solely between Baghdad and Basra, it had to pay the same fees to the Arab shaikhs on the river that local craft paid.[24] This agreement had been arrived at between the Porte's representatives and the British Ambassador in Istanbul, possibly signifying that up at least through November 1846, the British government was still biding its time with respect to the perceived insubordination of the Porte's representatives in Baghdad, Mosul, and Basra. The reluctance of British officials to press the point home and to put pressure on the Porte to discontinue river duties perceived by British merchants and consuls to be "illegal" can perhaps best be explained by a brief analysis of the surrounding context of British-Ottoman relations.

It has been argued in a previous chapter that British commercial as well as political privileges suffered a temporary setback in the period between

1840–1860. Whereas in the last quarter of the eighteenth century, the English agent in Basra was considered to be a significant player in the city's politics;[25] partly because of the East India Company's growing control of the freight trade with India, by the nineteenth century Britain's role took on less importance in the wake of Napoleon's invasion of Egypt. Because of the French defeat in the Mediterranean, Iraq's geo-strategic position seemed no longer as significant as before, and the Baghdad route suffered as a result. Only during the early 1830s did Iraq take on renewed interest for the British, and that was largely as a consequence of Russia's growing political and military importance, and Muḥammad ʿAlī's threat to the unity of the Ottoman Empire.[26] Even then, British interests continued to face an uphill struggle to pry open the river trade of Iraq. Thus the period between 1840–1860 was crucial for the British, in which attempts to infiltrate the regional markets of lower Iraq and the northern Gulf were met with repeated failure. Whether it was their lack of success in applying the provisions of the Balta Limanı Treaty (see chapter three), or the ongoing struggle to place river steamers on the Tigris,[27] British merchants faced obstacles at every turn.

As far as the latter were concerned, the situation on the rivers of Iraq could not be allowed to continue. As regional resistance to British trade was manifested more openly, British pressures to curtail the local power of shaikhs-merchants and government officials mounted. As before, the official pretext given for the British insistence on the discontinuation of illegal river duties was that the Balta Limanı Treaty forbade any tax higher than twelve percent on British exports, and that if any of these riverine duties were added to the total taxes paid by British merchants to export goods from Basra, they would contravene the amount stipulated in the treaty. Alongside their insistence that the articles of the treaty had to be enforced, the British began using gunboats to patrol the rivers of Iraq, a continuation, perhaps, of their centuries-old reliance on the policy of "armed trading" in the Gulf and Indian Ocean.[28] In fact, were it not for the presence of a man-of-war on Iraqī waters in the 1830s and 1840s, British merchants might well have lost whatever commercial edge that they had managed to gain in regional trade.

In 1842, Rawlinson, still in residence as the British consul-general in Iraq, had expressed these same sentiments in a despatch to the Foreign Office. Citing the protection of merchants as the most immediate reason for the presence of armed steamers on the rivers of Iraq, he stated unequivocally that the use of British military power was largely responsible for the extension of the British presence in riverine trade. He went on to say:

> The insecurity of the river and the rapacity of the Arabs who live on its banks presented in former times serious obstacles to the introduction of our manufactures into the Pashalik of Baghdad, but these evils have now almost disappeared. . . .[29]

Four years later, British merchants echoed his sentiments. Writing collectively to thank the consul-general in Baghdad for his efforts at stemming local duties on transit trade, they added:

> Since the British government in the year 1836 established war-steamers on the rivers of Mesopotamia, we gratefully acknowledge the assistance and support that we have derived from them. We have had reason, it is true, to complain of the exorbitant dues levied by the Arab chiefs with the sanction of the Baghdad government, in excess of the import and export duty fixed by the Treaty. We have indeed sustained pecuniary loss from the outrage of marauding bands, but we are bound to admit that the general navigation of the river has been rendered far less dangerous and expensive than formerly by the presence of a protecting power . . . the best proof of the increased security of the river is to be found in the extension of British trade during late years in this part of the Turkish Empire. Where a British trader rarely ventured to penetrate, we have now become established in extensive business . . . as we attribute the comparative impunity from outrage which we have hitherto enjoyed to the wholesome dread of the power of the British government which has been inspired among the Arabs by the presence of war-steamers constantly running between Baghdad and Bussorah, so are we persuaded that the total disappearance of our flag from the river will be followed by renewed disorders and acts of piracy against which we shall in vain protest. . . .[30]

These optimistic hopes were soon dashed, for on February 2, 1852, the British commander of the sloop *Nitocris* at Basra wrote to Rawlinson in Baghdad to complain that British merchants had again suffered losses because of the continuing insecurity in riverine trade. A boat belonging to the Lynch firm was stopped, and some "British Indian subjects of respectability"[131] who had been on the ziyāra to the shrines in Baghdad were insulted, while the Arab captain and crew were stripped of their clothes and property. On another occasion, the laissez-passer granted to the captain was spat upon and stamped on; the ship's passengers were left unmolested, but warned that if they valued their lives, they should obtain a firmān from one of the local shaikhs the next time they ventured out to do business. Obviously the presence of armed steamers on the Tigris had failed to quell all resistance, for in the same year, the region witnessed a resurgence of tribal power that did much to curtail European commercial efforts in the lower Euphrates and Tigris districts.

THE CIVIL WAR IN THE MUNTAFIQ AND THE EMERGENCE OF THE ʾALBŪMUḤAMMAD TRIBE

The renewed threats to these efforts arose in the context of the struggle for the Muntafiq *mashyakha* (the usual term for the tribal leadership; because of governmental centralization efforts in the 1850s, it came to signify an administrative subdistrict) that spanned the years 1851 to 1855. In that same period, a bitter civil war erupted between several contenders for the title of *shaikh al-mashāyikh* (paramount shaikh) of the Muntafiq, and ravaged the districts where this tribal confederation held sway. The struggle for leadership of these tribes is discussed at length in chapter 7; here it is important to point out that one of the byproducts of this fight for power was the even closer union between Manṣūr, a contender for the Muntafiq leadership, and Wadīʿ, the shaikh of the Zubaid tribes. The Zubaid tribe had formed part of the same monopolistic coalition which had levied transit fees on travellers and merchants in the riverine districts earlier in the century. The increasingly close association between their shaikh and Manṣūr, temporarily the victor in the Muntafiq struggle,[32] meant that a growing power now controlled important resources in the districts of lower Iraq. Much to the consternation of local historians, this alliance, short-lived though it was, not only disrupted riverine trade by levying new taxes and confiscating the merchandise of rival merchants, but even began to threaten the gates of Baghdad.[33]

It is interesting to note that in all of these instances, the governor of Baghdad, Namīq Pasha, undertook no immediate reprisals; and while there is no proof that he secretly backed the alliance or condoned its excesses, there is evidence that he tried to divert attention from the Muntafiq-Zubaid raids by imprisoning less threatening shaikhs and sending them to Istanbul as a gesture of appeasement to the Porte.[34] Suleimān Fāʾiq, an Ottoman bureaucrat whose family was affiliated with the last Mamluk Pasha, Dāwūd, saw it differently: according to him, Namīq Pasha initially made haste to pardon Shaikh Manṣūr, and welcomed him to Baghdad so that the latter could air his grievances. When the governor's offer of clemency was rejected, Namīq Pasha had no other recourse but to dismiss Manṣūr, and install another contender in office.[35] Eventually, Namīq Pasha himself was dismissed from government and recalled to Istanbul; and while the primary sources, both local and foreign, are silent on the reasons for such a move on the part of the Porte, there is speculation in the literature that as a result of the growing depradations of the Muntafiq-Zubaid coalition, and because of the lackadaisical attempts to check their power, Namīq Pasha was forced to forfeit his position.[36]

The turning point came at midcentury. This time, the joint efforts of the Porte and the British Ambassador in Istanbul were successful, and seem to have coincided in the imposition of severe pressure on the governors of Baghdad to curtail the so-called "illegal" dues. In the meantime, internal developments were working against the freedom of action of riverine shaikhs. Thus, at the same time that the Muntafiq-Zubaid alliance reached its greatest heights, it sowed the seeds for its eventual dissolution. By the mid-1850s, the rise of another tribal coalition, the ʾAlbū Muḥammad, had wrested control of the river banks from the once-powerful Muntafiq confederation, upsetting the carefully laid plans of British consuls and merchants alike. Indeed, just as the British had finally managed to arrive at some form of accommodation with the shaikhs of the principal tribes monopolizing riverine trade (thereby, the British hoped, bringing to an end the on-again, off-again rivalry with British merchants), another monopolist group arose in their place, this time with far-reaching consequences.

The rise to power of one tribal group and the weakening of another, formerly the strongest military and economic confederation in the south of Iraq, requires detailed explanation. From 1850 to 1855, the lower Euphrates was in turmoil. The war that pitted rival members of the Muntafiq mashyakha against each other brought an end to the iron-fisted control this tribal confederation had excercised in the riverine districts. The war also brought about a prolonged insecurity along the trade routes crisscrossing the vast territories of the Muntafiq. Because of the numerous military campaigns that took place in these districts, trade routes were badly patrolled and security was poor. As a result, Persian pilgrims were deterred from entering Iraq to visit the Shīʿī sanctuaries and to trade in sorely-needed goods, thus curtailing a major source of revenue for the Baghdad government.[37] Additionally, because of the lack of security in tribal districts, harvests were not gathered. In fact, rival Muntafiq armies seemed to have been spending most of their time pillaging their enemies' headquarters and occupying themselves with military matters at the expense of trade and agrarian pursuits. As a result of all the turmoil, another riverine tribe, the ʾAlbū Muḥammad, made a grab for power and eventually ended up as master of the trade routes. Levying new duties on the riverbanks and stopping boats at will,[38] they defied Muntafiq hegemony on the river, and a scant four years later managed to bring British and local trade almost to a standstill.

An incident in 1856, involving a raid on a ship chartered by a British merchant firm, led to redoubled British efforts to stem the "illegal" trade. Briefly, the ship carrying merchandise belonging to Alex Hector and Bros., a Baghdad-based British firm, was proceeding to Kūt on the Hai river when it was "completely plundered" by tribesmen, even though it was but an hour's distance from the ruling Muntafiq shaikh's camp. Although the boat was ostensibly under the protection of the Muntafiq, two of the tribesmen acting as guards for the ship and its crew were assaulted, as were the nakhoda (ship's captain) and the local trackers (one of whose functions was that of pulling the boat upstream when it got mired in mud, or in the shallows of the river). At the same time the ʾAlbū Muḥammad continued to impose duties of their own, so much so that the British believed that:

> were this system to continue in force, in consequence of lax government, . . . it promises soon to take the place of a tax in the same manner as other dues, recognized by governments, levied by the different tribes on the two rivers. . . .[39]

And the list of grievances went on. Another incident occurred in the same month when Persian pilgrims who refused to pay the sums demanded of them by the ʾAlbū Muḥammad were reportedly fired upon, and four were killed on the spot. Even so, regardless of the opprobium meted out to the ʾAlbū Muḥammad in consular sources, British officials seemed to imply that these were no ordinary robbers but discriminating wholesalers; for alongside cash, tribesmen were in the practice of demanding silk dresses *(ʾizārs),* gold-worked *ʿabās,* coffee, and loaf sugar, which were just the sort of commodities that sold well at tribal markets.

By 1857, the situation had become so critical that the British and the Ottomans, exhibiting a rare concord, began to apply pressure on the Muntafiq shaikhs to stop these "irregular" practices.[40] Unable to control the ʾAlbū Muḥammad tribes, the Ottoman and British authorities tried to enlist the Muntafiq shaikhs to do the job for them, an irony that even the British must have appreciated. Thus by an unlikely twist of fate, the same shaikhs whom the British had accused of illegally imposing riverine duties in the early part of the century were now called in to restore the status quo ante. However, since all parties realized that the Muntafiq shaikhs possessed certain military limitations in successfully waging war against the ʾAlbū Muḥammad,[41] a solution was worked out which, while predictably falling short of Muntafiq expectations, only underlined the impotence of outside authorities in dealing with the internal affairs of the tribal districts. Thus, on August 19, 1857, a "compromise" was reached: Bandar, shaikh of the Muntafiq, was asked to terminate the river duties that shaikhs of the ruling family had farmed for a century or more (the gamārik taxes which the Muntafiq paid to the provincial treasury in Baghdad, as well as the tesyārriya and/or zakiyya duties taken on the banks of the Tigris and at Sūq al-Shuyūkh, the Muntafiq capital). In return, he would receive "a remission of tribute [i.e., the badal tax] in lieu of compensation, or the assignment of freehold lands yielding a corresponding income."[42] In other words, to placate British merchants who had suffered reverses at the hands of the ʾAlbū Muḥammad tribes, riverine dues historically considered to be the appanage of the Muntafiq shaikhs were done away with, while "illegal" taxation levied by tribes over which the government had no control remained in force. To add insult to injury, the governor in Baghdad, Muḥammad Rashīd Pasha *(al-guzlakhi,* because he was considered to have been the first governor to wear eyeglasses in Iraq) made various noises about embarking upon a military expedition to coerce the ʾAlbū Muḥammad into submission but in the end, balked at sending additional military reinforcements to quell the tribe in question because of the real fear that the niẓām troops might be defeated. As a result, the ʾAlbū Muḥammad, whose shaikh, Faiṣal, had just received legitimization by the Ottomans, was left to roam the river banks in total impunity while the dues that British merchants claimed had been imposed on them unjustly were never returned.[43]

What made Bandar, the Muntafiq shaikh, succumb to such a patently unfair arrangement? Obviously, the sharp downturn in the Muntafiq leader's fortunes, brought about by the swift rise of the ʾAlbū Muḥammad tribes, was one reason. The fact that the revenue-producing areas on the river, which had formerly been under Muntafiq control, had been taken away by force of arms was a shock, certainly; however, even more disturbing was the realization on the part of the Muntafiq leadership that, even had the territory on the river reverted to Muntafiq control, the latter would no longer be its undisputed masters. For as a result of the civil war in the mashyakha, peasants of the Muntafiq were no longer paying taxes to the shaikhs and no longer manning their militias in times of war, leading to the absurd situation in which the paramount shaikhs of the Muntafiq tribe had to resort to the inducement of petty shaikhs of other tribes to fight the Muntafiq leaders' battles against their own tribal cultivators.[44]

A more important reason for Shaikh Bandar's acceptance of the British-Ottoman terms was the general disturbed state of the Muntafiq mashyakha. The Muntafiq was the largest and most powerful ʾimāra in the south of Iraq, almost a nation unto itself. Throughout the eighteenth and nineteenth centuries, the Mamluk and Ottoman pashas in Baghdad and Basra made sure to enlist the Muntafiq on their side, for otherwise they made implacable enemies. In the period between 1830–50, a new Ottoman tribal policy was formulated, and was slowly put into effect. Briefly, this envisaged the settlement of the pastoralist tribes living on the fringes of the great Syrian and Arabian deserts, such as the Muntafiq, the Shammar, and the ʿAnayza. As early as 1842, an Ottoman strategy to dismember the Muntafiq mashyakha had been on the books; due, however, to the weakness of the Ottoman presence in Iraq, the time was not yet deemed propitious for striking a blow at the powerful Muntafiq ʾimāra. In 1851, however, Muḥammad Rashīd Pasha became both the vali and the mushīr (General) of Iraq and the Hijaz. As a military man, his main task was to apply the right mix of force and persuasion to bring about a dissolution of the ʾimāra. As it was considered still too costly (in men and money) to establish control of the Muntafiq all at once, a partial weakening of the shaikh's resources was considered to be the next most feasible step. The idea was formulated that the lands of the Muntafiq given as *iqṭāʿ* (tax-farms) to the Muntafiq shaikhs would be redistributed at each yearly auction, thus bringing about a gradual dimunition of the ruling shaikh's hold over the vast territories under his control. Eventually, as discussed elsewhere, an Ottoman-controlled *mutaṣarrifiyya* (administrative district) was indeed carved out of the greatly diminished Muntafiq dīra in the 1870s, and the Saʿdūn shaikhs not only had to contend with a military garrison but with an Ottoman customs house as well.[45]

Thus the repeal of the Muntafiq's riverine tax privileges must be seen in context. Anglo-Ottoman pressure, applied in concert, as well as internal problems in the Muntafiq mashyakha itself brought about the first curtailment of the Saʿdūn leadership's economic potential, and must have brought about a retrenchment of sorts among the bitterly divided ruling family. Because the paramount shaikh-multazims of the Saʿdūn, that is, Bandar, as well as Manṣūr, and much later on, Nāṣir, must have felt their influence slipping away, they reluctantly acquiesced to a notably unfavorable agreement in order to make the best out of their reduced options.

Nonetheless, resistance to British trade continued in this period. The ʾAlbū Muḥammad continued to wage war against foreign and Ottoman concerns on the two rivers. As a result, the latter part of the nineteenth century witnessed a violent response to British trade in particular in which European pressures on local commerce backfired as tribal shaikhs set their sights on British targets. Thus from the 1860s onwards, it is possible to discern the onset of a period of armed resistance to British trading vessels on the Tigris and Euphrates. Indeed, the opening shots had been fired as early as 1839, when the first steamers to appear on Iraqī rivers attracted random fire from various tribes on the banks of the Euphrates. By the last part of the nineteenth century, however, the attacks had grown in gravity in terms of human and material loss, so much so that in 1855, the British naval commander of the *Nitocris,* stationed at the mouth of Basra harbor, was prompted to remark that "a new feature"[46] had developed in the habits of riverine tribes. This was the wholesale attack and plunder of British steamships, which formerly had been inviolable. Perhaps the worst incident took place in the 1870s, when the British steamer *Cashmere* was stopped, its crew assaulted, and several deckhands killed. The attackers, suspected to be members of the ʾAlbū Muḥammad tribes, made off with 48,000 rupees. They were later apprehended, and because of intense British pressure, nine of them were hanged by the Ottoman authorities in Baghdad.[47]

The frequency and regularity of these attacks leads us to believe that they were not random assaults, but part of a deliberāte strategy on the part of the tribes inhabiting the banks of the river. There is a sharp division between the earlier period (1830–60) in which British steamships were afforded relatively safe passage on the rivers of Iraq, and the later period (1860–90) in which assaults on British ships were becoming almost commonplace. It is tempting to relate the later development to the growing frustration of the river Arabs and to their weakness in the face of the mounting British economic challenge, for the intensification of attacks on British establishments occurred in the latter part of the nineteenth century at approximately the same time that European—and especially British—trade began its ascendancy.[48] A further distinction must be drawn between the two periods. In 1880–90, there were several incidents in which tribal leaders stopped boats and demanded transit dues;[49] however, unlike the earlier period, their actions were not truly confrontational. They were undertaken principally to underline a grievance against another tribe, or a government official; once the grievance was rectified, the forced stoppage of boats disappeared. Thus the economic and political situation on the rivers had shifted so dramatically by the latter part of the nineteenth century that no single tribe, or even coalition of tribes, could ever again muster the support for a continuous trade war against British shipping houses.

However, the whole development of local resistance on the rivers of Iraq gives one pause. Perhaps the powerlessness of the riverine tribes led to violent confrontations because, in the words of Eric Hobsbawm, violence was "the active response to defeat," and bold attacks against British vessels were but "the afterglow" of a fire that had already been extinguished.[50] Whatever the reason, figures for the tonnage of European ships entering Basra make it all too clear that by the 1880s, the attacks created barely a ripple in the volume of British trade, which had become the preponderant force in the region.

THE DECLINE OF LAND ROUTES

Overland trade passed through the same cycle of disruption and decline. By 1869–70, the civil war pitting Saᶜūd against ᶜAbdullāh for control of Riyāḍ and the adjoining districts had begun to tear apart the fragile unity of the second Saᶜūdī state. The culmination of the battle for leadership of the Saᶜūdī ʾimāra was that Ottoman troops occupied eastern Arabia at the behest of the weaker party, ᶜAbdullāh, marking only the second time in the Ottomans' four hundred years of rule that the peninsula had come under direct Ottoman sovereignity. While the occupation of al-Ahsa was never as effective as the Porte's generals would have liked it to be, it did have one important effect. Ottoman control of coastal Arabia blocked access to al-Ahsa, Najd's window to the east, and curtailed the flow of regional trade from Iraq and Kuwait. Moreover, it allowed for the consolidation of firmer Ottoman ties with once-independent regional actors, such as the shaikh of the Muntafiq and the ʾamīr of Kuwait; for the latter actively participated in the invasion of Najd's eastern seaboard and shared in the spoils.[51]

Events in northern Najd compounded the problems faced by the weakened Saᶜūdī ʾimāra. The rise to power of Muḥammad ibn Rashīd, ʾamīr of Jabal Shammar, added to the House of Saᶜūd's woes. After defeating Saᶜūdī forces and their allies in the northern districts in 1887, the shaikh finally entered Riyāḍ. As Winder put it, "almost without firing a shot, Muḥammad ibn Rasheed had conquered the Wahhābī state."[52] This blow was the last of several Wahhābī defeats in the central and northern parts of Arabia, effectively curtailing the power of the once-powerful Saᶜūdī ʾimāra until the turn of the century, when the young ᶜAbdul-Azīz ibn Saᶜūd was able to restore Saᶜūdī fortunes once more.

Significantly, Ibn Rashīd's meteoric rise was limited to Najd. Unlike the eighteenth century Saᶜūdī rulers who had depended on the monopoly of trade routes into central Arabia, Ibn Rashīd could no more monopolize the passage of goods into Najdī districts than any other local shaikh or merchant in the region. For the regional market which had depended on the rerouting of products over long distances and on the establishment of strategic market towns to control the passage of trade had been fractured by the ascent of European trade. Local trade networks were irretrievably shattered, and regional merchants now followed a dynamic other than their own. Ibn Rashīd serves as the best example of this process. In 1884, the British resident in Baghdad noted the trend in this manner:

> Muḥammad ibn Rasheed, the well-known shaikh of the Jabal Shammar [northern Najd], recently appeared with a large force in the neighborhood of Kobeysah, distant about four days' journey to the west of Baghdad, and made a successful raid upon three sections of the ʿAnayzah and upon the Deleim Arabs [in the Shāmiyya district of lower Iraq], carrying off their tents, 16,000 sheep, 500 camels and 28 valuable mares and horses. The money which he is paid for escorting pilgrims to and from Mecca by the land road from Najd and the various exactions which he levies upon them form a main source of Ibn Rasheed's income. Latterly, however, and especially last year, there has been a great falling-off in the number of pilgrims by the land route, owing not only to the special difficulties and dangers it presents, *but also to the increased facilities which year by year are being offered by steamers from Basrah, Bushire, Bombay, and other ports* [emphasis mine].[53]

By the last quarter of the nineteenth century, the supremacy of British seaborne trade had sealed the fate of the land passage from central Arabia into Iraq, Kuwait, and southwest Iran. It also destroyed the fortunes of those merchants and transport agents who had depended upon it. Muḥammad ibn Rashīd, ʾamīr of Jabal al-Shammar, and in the absence of a serious candidate from the House of Saʿūd possibly the most significant local power in the 1880s, was forced to undertake massive armed campaigns in order to capture revenues lost because of the rerouting of trade channels. No longer able to rely on the khuwwa and other transit fees for their livelihoods, he and other shaikhs were forced to resort to desperate measures in order to gain access to diverted resources.

-Five-

The Grain Trade

After describing the characteristics of the regional market of lower Iraq and the northern Gulf in the nineteenth century and giving an indication of the external forces that were brought to bear on the market's operations throughout this period, an important feature of the regional network needs to be examined. This is the ongoing struggle for control of the food supply between local forces (regional merchants and their Ottoman allies) and British shippers. From about 1830 to 1862, the control of the grain trade in lower Iraq was in Ottoman hands; after that period, and continuing into the twentieth century, British shippers managed to dominate the trade in wheat and barley. In order to understand the background to this transformation, the tensions produced by the economic rivalry between state-affiliated merchants, government officials, and British shippers will be examined, especially with regard to the period between 1830 and 1860.

COMPETING PERSPECTIVES IN THE GRAIN TRADE

Regional merchants exchanged basic foodstuffs and animal products for textiles, wood, sugar, and tea from British India, and pearls, silk, cotton, and rice from the Gulf.[1] Grain was the primary food item of the regional economy and, in addition to dates, was the mainstay of the daily diet for peasant and townsman alike. Wheat and barley formed the cardinal exports of Kurdistan to Baghdad and Basra, in part because the latter districts could not supply enough grain for their own consumption;[2] although there was also some cultivation in the mid-Euphrates, eastern Arabia, and Arabistan. Overland caravans setting out from Baghdad usually carried a plentiful supply for market towns of the interior, such as Buraida and ʿUnaiza in Najd. Later on in the nineteenth century, Iraq's expanded output of cereals went to feed ḥajj pilgrims in the port towns of the Hijaz, as well as Ottoman armies at the front.[3] Because grain was such an important food item, it became the object of state monopolies and a valuable commodity which eventually excited considerable competition among local and foreign merchants. To reiterate a point made in a previous chapter, the most striking characteristic of this competition was the emergence of commercial alliances between Ottoman bureaucrats and state-affiliated merchants; indeed, the cooperation between the two interest groups in the development of the grain trade eventually posed a direct threat to growing British economic influence in the region.

British interest in the region's food supply arose out of several factors. In the early part of the nineteenth century, partly because of the Napoleonic wars, Britain had been locked out of European and American markets, and was therefore anxious to secure wheat overseas.[4] The principles of free trade were in the process of becoming governmental policy, as was the concomitant fight to abolish all restrictions on grain imports.[5] Nevertheless, the struggle to open markets for British goods and to secure a reliable supply of raw materials was no easy task. In 1838, trade with the Ottoman Empire, a large grain producer, was not sufficiently impressive to warrant a relaxation of British fears of economic competition. The "Russian threat" loomed large in British plans to secure a most favored nation status in Turkey, and British attempts to check Russian economic influence in the Ottoman Empire led her to seek preferential tariffs in her trade with the Porte.[6] No less serious were the expansionist policies of Muhammad ʿAlī of Egypt, whose material base afforded him the capital and the military power to overtake other provinces in search of raw materials for his factories, and whose ambitious plans posed a grave threat to Ottoman hegemony. As a result of these interrelated factors, British ministers such as Palmerston and consuls such as Bulwer were able to play on Ottoman fears of imperial dismemberment and collapse, and to extract major economic concessions for Britain in return for vague assurances of military aid against Muhammad ʿAlī. And so the Anglo-Turkish Convention was signed by the Porte, as has been explained in a previous chapter.

One of the important points in the treaty was the preemption of Ottoman produce. According to consular officials stationed in the empire, a major consequence of this clause was the prohibition of "Turkish governmental interference with the export of grain from Turkish provinces."[7] According to the treaty, henceforth "Turkey had no right to pre-empt her own grain if it were desired by foreigners who had the money to pay the current market price for it,"[8] a major and ultimately very damaging concession awarded to British traders by the Porte. Nevertheless, to understand how little the Anglo-Turkish Convention affected the trade of grain from the province of Iraq, a closer look must be taken at the problems of the sale and distribution of the commodity in Baghdad, Basra, and the districts in-between.

THE EMERGENCE OF A STATE-ALLIED MERCHANT CLASS IN IRAQ

British consular officials usually portrayed the Ottoman governors of Mosul, Baghdad, and Basra in less than favorable terms. They had a particular loathing for Muḥammad Najīb Pasha, vali of Baghdad from 1842 to 1849. According to Rawlinson, the British Consul-General in Baghdad at the time and the man who was thought to know him best, Najīb Pasha was despotic, greedy, vengeful and massively, irredeemably corrupt. He was criticized for everything from attempting to extract revenue "illegally" from the Baghdad Pashalik to the cold-blooded murder of an important shaikh of the Shammar tribe, and even of plotting against members of his own government. When all is said and done, however, it is obvious that British officials had significant reasons for vilifying Najīb Pasha: he was, after all, one of the chief obstacles to European trade on the rivers of Iraq (see chapter 4), and an important competitor in the supply, distribution, and sale of grain throughout the country. Nonetheless, despite the personalized tone of the despatches sent to the Foreign Office, it was obvious that the vali in question was incapable of fighting European firms for a dominant share of the grain market all by himself; in fact, it quickly became apparent as the decade wore on that he had made associates of certain local merchants and with their help, had managed to control almost entirely the exchange and distribution of wheat and barley in the province of Baghdad.

The first object of British concern was the issue of state monopolies, now considered "illegal" by the terms of the Anglo-Turkish Convention. While the apparent purpose of monopolies was to allow the government to provide a more regular supply of food for the major cities of Iraq, it has already been related how monopolies were sometimes taken over for the benefit of the vali and state-affiliated merchants, much to the detriment of the population at large. The abuse of monopolies made life extremely difficult for all segments of the population. In 1847, for instance, the British consul in Baghdad complained about the dearness of grain in the city and made the following remark:

> these high rates are in some slight degree to be ascribed to the partial and arbitrary interference of the local government in forcibly throwing open the

> granaries of the minor corn dealers and in compelling the sale of their contents with the view thereby of lessening the competition and giving the command of the market immediately into the hands of a few of the principal wholesale merchants with whom some of its influential members are known to be closely connected in mercantile speculation (particularly the brothers Saleh, Salman and Reuben, who are believed to be the possessors of 1,500 *tghars* of grain . . .).[9]

To judge by further estimates provided by the consul, the brothers in question were large traders in grain, for the total supply of the commodity in private hands was calculated to stand at 3,000 tghars ("being the produce of the year, and the surplus of the past"),[10A] with an additional 5,000 tghars stored in private granaries in and around Baghdad. For one family to possess so much grain, therefore, implied state patronage at the very highest level.

Again, in August 1848, the British consul commented upon the extraordinary interdictions enforced by the vali of Baghdad, Najīb Pasha, on the sale of grain by cultivators outside of Baghdad, which had the effect of preventing rural merchants from disposing of their surplus. Concluding that these interdictions were occasioned by the vali's desire that "nothing should interfere with [his] monopoly of the corn market,"[10B] the consul added that legally cultivators could sell their grain only to certain state-affiliated merchants, who just happened to be associates of the vali's son, ʾAḥmad Beg. The big traders made life difficult even for British shippers and agents by forcing them to travel extraordinary distances to buy wheat for their own accounts, even though there was "a plethora of grain in the districts [above Baghdad]."[11] The consul estimated that by these actions, designed to drive out all but the merchants with whom the vali was allied, "at the lowest calculation" Najīb Pasha had made a net profit of £100,000.[12]

Meanwhile, famine prices ruled in the corn market in Baghdad, and starvation seemed imminent. The government hypocritically railed at the monopolists and the hoarders of grain while working hand in glove with these same profiteers, to the point where the vali stubbornly refused to distribute grain from the government's ample stores, even though the population of Baghdad and its environs clamored for food.[13] As a result of these actions, many grain merchants were ruined and the market became dominated by government-allied merchants. Furthermore, many landholders, forced to pay their rents in grain but unable to do so because of the exceedingly poor harvest of 1847, saw their farms taken over by government agents.[14] The sources paint a bleak picture of a province caught in the throes of abject tyranny:

> By restricting to a limit of five tghars the quantity of grain to be purchased by any one single individual, by arbitrarily prohibiting the amassing of corn by any one of the parties engaged in the trade and by holding the threat of a com-

> pulsory sale, [the vali, Najīb Pasha] can only aim . . . at driving the few remaining independent corn-dealers out of the market and thus retain in his own hands the entire supply of the city, the prices being kept at the same time far above their natural rates by his permitting no more corn to be brought in than will suffice for current consumption, or possibly by suspending occasionally all importation. . . .[15]

Barely nine years later, local sources described the rise to power of the new merchant class buttressed by government favors. Thus the alliance between the big traders and the valis of Baghdad continued to thrive and to prosper, even while restrictions on the sale of grain to British shippers and local competitors were still in effect. As an example, the al-Dānyāl, an important Jewish merchant family, reportedly became "the favorites" of Vali Muḥammad Rashīd Pasha al-Gōzlakhi, one of Najīb Pasha's successors.[16] They became *ḍāmin(s)* (tax farmers) of several rich agricultural properties in the mid-Euphrates, instituting monopolies on grain and rice, and manipulating the production and sale of sought-after commodities. By controlling both the distribution of seeds and animals to peasants, as well as the final sale of grain, state-allied merchants were able to indulge in large-scale speculation that completely destroyed their rivals. Three years later, in 1859, corruption in the sale of government leases had become so rampant that it was described as "positively gambling" and grain became the object of hoarding once more.[17] By 1860, a combination of poor harvests, governmental manipulation of grain supplies, and widespread chicanery among state-affiliated merchants had brought about such misery among the populace that foreign consular intervention reportedly was interjected in the economic affairs of the Baghdad Vilayet and, partly as a result of this representation, government stores were open to all and bread prices fell almost immediately.[18]

By the 1860s, then, a number of things had occurred with regard to the production, and especially the trade of grain. Monopolies on food crops and manufactured items, while not new in the Ottoman system, nonetheless, seem to have been enforced with a good deal of zeal. It seems clear from the facts described above that in the period 1830–60, monopolies on grain imposed terrible burdens on the producing class as well as undermined independent merchants. This is all the more surprising when we note that the Balta Liman Treaty had expressly forbidden the imposition of commercial monopolies throughout the Ottoman Empire. Clearly, the alliance between officials and state-affiliated merchants openly flouted the articles of the convention.

Monopolies also signalled the rise of a different group of regional merchants, the *mallāks,* to economic power. These mallāks were so called because they were able to disburse sufficient cash to buy mīrī or state lands from a financially-strapped government. The developments that brought about the rise of a state-allied merchant class to landholding status warrants further examination, for it is this aspect of provincial affairs that brings into focus the whole question of the struggle of resources, and the alienation of mīrī lands in the countryside, which was of considerable import to later developments in regional trade.

LANDHOLDING MERCHANTS AND THE TRADE IN GRAIN

The most important facet of Iraqī agriculture in the period between 1840–66 was that

> it had a . . . great area of unused but easily cultivable land, (and) that water transport made it much cheaper to carry heavy produce to the coast, even though right up to the end of the period, expensive transport prevented the extension of cultivation in many areas. . . .[19]

However, the extension of agriculture depended not only on improved transport but on a number of factors, all of which were not readily available in early nineteenth century Iraq. To prevent chronic flooding of cultivable land, it would have been necessary to dam the Euphrates and the Tigris; but throughout the nineteenth century, although various projects for dams and irrigation channels were initiated (see below), by 1866 little change had taken place.[20] Secondly, the mode of cultivation in tribal districts discouraged intensive agriculture; because the fellāḥ could shift away from salinated or exhausted land, neither the acreage of cultivable land nor the volume of crops increased. Moreover, cultivated land was scattered, chiefly centering around the big towns and lanes of trade as well as around river tributaries, and access was contingent upon tribal acquiescence in the maintenance of trade routes. From the above account, therefore, it is clear that agriculture remained at a subsistence level, for the grain-producing districts of Iraq barely supplied enough wheat and barley to feed the province itself.[21] Thus in order to derive profit from their investments, the new landholders could either concentrate on extending the agricultural acreage of the districts that came under their control (which, for reasons discussed above, did not come to pass until the 1870s) or intensively exploit the resources at hand. Needless to say, they chose the latter route. Again, the period of Najīb Pasha furnishes us with ample examples.

Despite his much-publicized shortcomings, Najīb Pasha was considered as something of an innovator. For instance, on 8 January 1845, the British Consul-General in Baghdad, Henry Rawlinson, wrote his superiors to inform them that, in conformity with the ordnance issued by the Porte on September, 1844, which stipulated that agriculture in Iraq was to be encouraged by all possible means, Najīb Pasha had opened up a new canal from the Euphrates near Karbala, laying down the groundwork for what he hoped would be a new irrigation system across the country.[22] Because private capital was unavailable for the desilting, clearing, and construction of canals in the southern portion of the province (either because landholders and merchants were unable or unwilling to part with the necessary cash), Najīb Pasha's undertaking was considered an auspicious beginning. Nevertheless, even with official encouragement, the "ordnance in question [was] totally inoperative in the Pashalik of Baghdad,"[23] principally because the local administrations of Baghdad, Basra, and Mosul refused to follow Najīb Pasha's example, and put up additional monies for other projects. Even so, Istanbul continued to put pressure on Najīb Pasha (and later administrations) to do something with regard to enhancing the agricultural system, and with it the revenues of the provinces of Iraq.

In April 1846, Rawlinson again wrote the Foreign Office, stating that:

> The Kahyā [deputy governor in Baghdad], Rashīd Bey, has left for Constantinople and . . . the object of his deputation, I am informed, has a principle reference to the improvement of the revenues of this Pashalik, both by curtailing the expenditure, and by developing the productive capabilities of the lands. . . . The suggestions which he will lay before the Porte for the improvement of agriculture, are based upon the acknowledged principle of the necessity of supplying fresh means of irrigation. . . . [Thus] it is proposed to grant to any capitalists who will engage in this speculation, leases for a certain number of years (not less than five or more than ten) of such lands as they may lay under cultivation. . . .[24]

A novel system was being proposed to end the insecurity of land tenure in Iraq, which entailed the grant of "blank orders" with the Sulṭān's signature on them, to be filled up in Baghdad according to the financial agreement reached between the future lessee and agents of the imperial government. The merit of the proposal lay in strengthening the relationship between the future landholder and the Porte. From then on, it was hoped, lessees would be less likely to have their property confiscated by local administrators. Insofar as the financial agreement between the Porte and the future lessees was concerned, there was speculation that the agreement might include everything from a remission of earlier revenue for the first three years to the distribution of new land to potential landholders willing to pay a share of the produce to the government in return for being assigned a tenth of the crop in perpetuity. Naturally, Rawlinson could not help but remark that

> Under such circumstances, indeed I have reason to believe that several British merchants would like experimental farms, and by the introduction of machinery and scientific husbandry would prepare the way for a general improvement of the agricultural system of this part of the Eastern world.[25]

The British were not the only ones who wanted in on this lucrative scheme, for a number of other parties were also avid to exploit the agricultural resources of the Iraqī provinces. However, Najīb Pasha and his merchant allies had already beaten them to the draw by bidding for the choicest properties. In 1847, for example, the Baghdad administration announced that it would lease out heretofore unproductive lands in order to encourage the production of grain. It was reported that Najīb Pasha was taking special interest in the clearing out of the ruined irrigation canals that formed the core of the government's project, and that his officers were employed in collecting laborers to assist in completing the work. According to the British consul, orders had been transmitted from Constantinople authorizing the lease of these heretofore unproductive farms for a term of two to even five years. However, even before the bidding season commenced, these lands were withdrawn by the Baghdad administration. In fact, the vali and his associates immediately monopolized the choicest properties, Najīb Pasha rejecting certain offers to rent for two years the canals of the Riḍwāniyya and Iskandariyya on the Euphrates, on the grounds that he was reserving them for the benefit of the government. Again, according to the consul, this peremptory refusal "led to a very general belief that [the vali] proposes retaining these farms as well as those of Abū Ghrayyeb and Maḥmūdiyya [outside of Baghdad] in his own hands as a private speculation."[26] This was obviously a good investment, for it was estimated that, under production, the latter properties would yield the considerable yield of 5 to 7,000 tghars of grain annually.

Again, because a vali's tenure in power usually entailed a year in office, and sometimes even less, and above all, because the system of badl obliged governors, no less than other provincial officers in the vilayet, to recoup their investments rapidly and before their tenure in government was up, the primary object of the alliance between bureaucrats and mallāks were quick profits. By the 1840s, these profits may have been on the rise in the mid-Euphrates because of the noticeable export of grain,[27] even though wheat and barley were still crippled by heavy imposts throughout the rest of the Iraqī provinces.[28] In fact, since there was no incentive to produce it in exportable quantities, every time a famine occurred in Iraq, the government had to rush in imported wheat at exorbitant prices.

THE REGIONAL RESPONSE: RURAL REVOLTS AND THE FLIGHT OF REGIONAL CAPITAL

While internal monopolies undeniably contributed towards the misery of regional merchants, they did not leave them without alternatives. The establishment of food monopolies in scarcity-prone societies, where supply was uneven and floods and droughts precipitated periodic shortages, initially may have had disastrous consequences for the maintenance of regional trade. But it is also possible to theorize that monopolies may have been instrumental in bringing about the movements of rural resistance which erupted throughout the mid-nineteenth century, a sure indicator that, regardless of commercial exactions, regional trade had not been completely destroyed. One response to these government-wrought disruptions was the outbreak of recurrent rural rebellions throughout the period under discussion. In the rice and grain-producing districts of the lower Euphrates, governmental efforts to put pressure on the landholding shaikhly stratum in order to meet Ottoman economic demands aggravated an already festering situation. In 1848, for example, Najīb Pasha tried to increase the government's annual revenue from the Hindiya district (lower Euphrates) by pressuring the shaikh-multazim of the Zubaid tribes to forcibly extract produce from peasants so that Shaikh Wadīʿ could meet his badal payment on time. This effort, designed to squeeze more yield out of the mainly rice and grain-producing region, backfired, and the Hindiya district remained in a state of open rebellion for two years, with government troops able only to control district towns such as Karbala, Najaf, and Hilla.

In sum, the Ottoman policy of farming out the district to Wadīʿ, shaikh of the Zubaid, ran into trouble when Najīb Pasha, avid for more money, raised Wadīʿ's badal payment from 3,500 kīs (purses) to 10,000, thereby forcing the shaikh to extract from the peasants more revenue, in cash as well as in kind. In a rich grain-producing area such as the Hindiya, more often than not peasants paid their taxes in barley, wheat, and corn; thus in order to pay the extraordinary tax imposed by government officials intent upon controlling the production and trade of grain, the peasants had to strain their already overextended resources. To make matters worse, the government's insensitivity to the peasants' lot was equalled, if not surpassed, by Wadīʿ's behavior. In the space of several months, he managed to collect the fantastic sum of 21,000 kīs from the tribal peasantry in his districts, a tax so staggering that, in the words of the British consul in Baghdad, it totaled "in excess of the sum for which credit had been given to the Porte."[29] The vali had attempted to recuperate his badal by pressuring the Zubaid shaikh to collect an inflated tax, while the multazim in question had burdened the fellāḥs in his district with extortionate demands in order to collect an even larger share for himself.

The Ottoman policy of supporting extortionate shaikh-multazims in the Hindiya area led to widespread peasant resistance. Among the first actions undertaken by tribal insurgents in 1848 was the plunder of government storehouses and public granaries in the region,[30] graphically illustrating the harm inflicted by grain monopolies on small producers and traders. Equally important was the development of the conflict within the Baghdad government itself as a result of the Hindiya uprising. The sense of injustice faced by peasants in the Hindiya was echoed by shaikhs and fellaheen in other areas; a month after the rebellion had taken hold, a coalition of disaffected tribal leaders made common cause with the serasker (highest military official in the province), ʿAbdī Pasha, who was engaged in a struggle for power with Najīb Pasha, and petitioned the Porte for redress against the vali's financial exactions. Although they received some relief from the exorbitant demands placed upon them by Shaikh Wadīᶜ of the Hindiya region, the system of falsifying returns in order to maximize personal gain went unchecked. Thus

> The Serasker . . . resolved to proceed to the Hindiya in order to endeavour by personal communications with the Arab chiefs and by a series of conciliatory measures, to prevent any further complications of the pending question, or any default occurring in the legitimate revenues of the state. Najīb Pasha, of course, sought to throw every possible difficulty in the way of the General and even sent emissaries amongst the tribes, repudiating by anticipation all the arrangements which might be made. . . . Several of the chiefs, who were previously in revolt, attended at once to the invitation of the Serasker, professing the utmost loyalty, and even devotion to the Sulṭān, and declaring that they had taken up arms as the only means left of protecting themselves against the tyranny of Najīb Pasha and his minion, shaikh Wadee. These parties which included the Afaj and Khazail tribes and the local chiefs of the Hindiya, received accordingly their robes of investiture from the serasker and entered into sureties for the payment of revenue, considerably above the amounts entered against them in the Government registers but of course far under the assessment demanded by shaikh Wadee. . . .[31]

Partly as a result of this confrontation, Najīb Pasha was recalled to Istanbul, and the serasker, ᶜAbdī Pasha, appointed in his place. Nevertheless, this was not the end of the monopoly system in Iraq. Grain monopolies were not restricted to Najīb Pasha's era, but continued to plague the ordīnāry fellah and townsman up till about 1865, when new developments completely reoriented the grain trade. In 1859, however, disguised monopolies were still the order of the day. On 28 September of that year, the British consul in Baghdad complained that the local government was erecting great obstacles to the purchase of grain by British merchants, even while colluding openly with "favored Capitalists . . . in overestimating the returns of the harvest with the view of magnifying the tithes and of introducing or reviving oppressive taxes."[32] Meanwhile, even though the price of grain continued "exorbitant," government stores of grain remained closed, accentuating the distress of the people of Baghdad. Four months after a ban on the export of grain had been put into effect, and orders had been received to open up government—as well as private merchants'—granaries, the price of grain was still high. Famine threatened to become a reality in the city. Finally, after several boat-loads of wheat arrived from Basra (whether this was government wheat or that of private agents, the sources do not say), and merchants realized that they could no longer play with the price of the commodity, grain-stores were reluctantly thrown open, and the misery of Baghdādīs was assuaged by the appearance of bread in the markets.[33]

A second reaction to the imposition of monopolies of grain and other commodities on the consuming public was the removal of merchant capital to more receptive ports of trade. While the flight of capital has been commented on in previous chapters, here it is important to enter the mind-set of people of the period, and to understand why this was a problem of major import for historians of Baghdad and Basra. For the most part, local chroniclers were describing economies which depended on the constant rerouting and supply of regional commodities to feed towns and villages. Since regional traders specialized in provisioning these societies with necessary goods over long distances, merchants were critically important to the consuming public, perhaps even more significant than provincial administrators or religious judges. Scarcity, droughts, plagues, and governmental interference in mercantile operations, not only damaged the fortunes of regional merchants but also inflicted hardship on the societies they supplied with necessities. Historians, then, viewed the plight of the merchant in life-and-death terms precisely because it affected the fundamentals of existence for the majority of people. For the problem was not wholly economic; it involved, most of all, the survival of people and the supply of necessary goods to keep them alive. Commercial monopolies exacerbated the already tenuous supply of products upon which the regional market depended, and an overextended trading network had to scramble to find different outlets where the provisioning of staple items was more plentiful and more competitively priced. And if at the same time the government refused to provision people with grain in the face of famine, and hoarded corn in order to keep prices artificially high, ruining merchants who traditionally supplied the cities, then the populace was left with few prospects for obtaining food. Small wonder, then, that historians lamented the migration of regional merchants and mourned their passing,[34] for regardless of their often unsavory tactics,[35] at least they provided the people of Iraq with ready access to basic commodities, even if only to make a profit.

Unlike the peasants and the petty traders who were left no alternative but to starve, regional merchants who were forced to leave Baghdad and Basra for the most part fared well. In fact, a number of them, not all who traded in grain obviously, used their regional contacts to set up shop elsewhere. For instance, a member of the influential Faddāgh family had to disburse a great sum of money to the mutasallim of early nineteenth century Basra or risk the consequences; fearing the worst, he fled with his family to Kuwait and resumed operations there.[36] Others followed, all prominent merchants of Basra, such as Shaikh Salīm ibn ʿAbdul-Razzāq and Shaikh ʾAḥmad ibn Marzūq.[37] Another merchant, al-Ḥaj ʿAbdullāh Jammāl, fled to Muscat in the wake of an abortive uprising against the Basra government, and Muḥammad ʿAbdul-Razzāq, who had stood his ground in the face of several catastrophes (including the devastating plague of 1831), finally left for Bombay in the late 1830s. A local chronicler noted in 1884 that "he [ʿAbdul-Razzāq] is now the most important Arab merchant there."[38] The same chronicler, writing in the last quarter of the nineteenth century, deplored the wholesale departure of merchants in this manner:

> Because all the big *tujjar* fled Basra, and because the *fitnas* (civil wars and uprisings) and the plague had decimated the population, houses began to crumble and they are crumbling to this very day, until a governor appears to rebuild the city, and to bring back the big merchants from all the countries [they had fled to]. . . . Because governors do not remain long in power, and because they [have no interest] in helping the *reaya* [subjects], things do not happen as they should. Because merchants receive no support from the government, and the government is influenced by evil-doers, Iraq cannot attract back [men of fortunes]. . . .[39]

The problem was the same in nineteenth century Baghdad. In the 1840s, when grain monopolies were wreaking havoc on the fortunes of independent merchants, a usually reliable witness estimated that about 60,000 Iraqīs had to leave the province and take refuge among the bedu.[40] The number may be overstated, but the symptoms are not. Not all of the fleeing Iraqīs were merchants, of course, and not all of the merchants traded in grain, but the mercantile segment of the population was among the most affected; in the words of Suleimān Fāʾiq, a chronicler of the period, they were left without even one *fils aḥmar* (red cent).[41]

The phenomenon of the dispersal of regional merchants to other, possibly more hospitable, economic zones was a significant development in the history of the region. It was mentioned that Kuwait, Muscat, and Bombay were but three of the many venues of trade that attracted regional merchants from lower Iraq. In the case of Baghdādīs, the *rīf* or countryside was another alternative. In either case, the existence of secondary economic centers, which provided sanctuary to regional merchants and a chance to start all over again, can only be attributed to the strong inter- and intra-regional links that tied districts as remote from one another as Najd and western India. Among the factors that led to the systematization of regional trade were the existence of resident merchant houses in India (representing trading families as diverse as the Bassams of Najd and the ʿAbbūds of Basra), the strong commercial links connecting distant regions (such as bills of exchange, varieties of currencies, and maritime contracts), and the growth of market towns which accommodated the constant influx of merchants in search of new routes. Systematization led to the creation of merchant communities where standardization in commercial behavior and practice was the rule, and where expatriate merchants, providing they had the requisite know-how in long-distance trade, could easily pick up where they had left off. Conceivably, a merchant just off the boat from a Gulf port, with little or no funds, could fall back on loans and credit afforded him by an expatriate family member, or perhaps join in an ongoing venture by virtue of being from the same town or district as his other partners. As long as he was familiar with the rules governing the transactions of long-distance commerce and could play on the exchange rates of different currencies or finagle long-term credit from any one of a number of merchant bankers, then he was using a common language, understood by merchants from the Gulf to the Indian Ocean. He could become part of a regional merchant community that used standardized methods of sale, exchange, and distribution in order to conduct business. If luck was on his side, the exiled long-distance trader might even, in the long run, recoup some of his lost fortunes.

Nevertheless, this scenario was not wholly true for many merchants in the middle to lower income brackets, for grain monopolies were particularily harsh on the small trader. Thus, in the period 1830 to 1862, grain monopolies in Iraq had several devastating consequences. First, they inflicted hardships on the the producing classes, instigated rural rebellions, and accelerated the prospect of famine in the bigger cities such as Baghdad. Second, they spurred the rise of government-allied merchants to power and brought about the near-collapse of an unaffiliated, independent class of regional merchants. Third, monopolies, together with other economic measures directed against transit trade, forced the majority of merchants to flee to other ports of trade, thus bringing about a considerable transfer of capital and expertise to other regional centers.

In the 1860s, however, a new factor—British shipping firms—intruded on the scene and forced the Ottoman authorities of Baghdad and Basra to rethink their basic strategy with regard to the control of food items such as grain. The period between 1840 to 1860 entailed years of crisis for the Ottomans as well as for the British. The Baghdad and Basra administrations had their hard-won privileges—principally their commercial alliances with local merchants and landholders—put to the test as British traders attempted to control the local economies of Iraq and the Gulf. But in those crucial twenty years, neither side had yet gotten the upper hand, and a sustained struggle for the resources of the region ensued, which focused on the making of strong alliances with the local merchant class in order to gain entry to regional trade. The following section will treat this question in more detail.

GRAIN EMBARGOES, LOCAL INSURGENCIES, AND THE ECONOMICS OF REGIONAL INTEGRATION

The first indication of a new commercial policy aimed at the disruption of the British supply of grain in Iraq came about in the mid-1870s. Bans against the export of regional goods passing into Iraq included such items as ghee, horses, and of course, barley and wheat.[42] By the 1870s, a firmer resolve by the Baghdad government led to the beginnig of a set policy of economic bans that caught British merchants by surprise.

In September 1877, the consul-general of Baghdad, Colonel Nixon, sent an urgent telegram to the Foreign Office informing the secretary of state that the Baghdad authorities had clamped down on the export of grain, and issued instructions that henceforth an interdiction prohibiting all grain shipments from either Baghdad or Basra would be the rule.[43] The reasons for such an order were straightforward enough: because the peasants who usually cultivated the crops had been conscripted into the army to fight the Russo-Turkish war, and earlier harvests had been of poor quality, the usual distribution of grain on the market was inadequate. Another reason may have had to do with the sharp competition by local and foreign merchants for a commodity in very short supply on both the Baghdad and Basra markets, which caused inflated prices and the ensuing threat of famine. Thus while despatches from the mutasallim of Baghdad tried to reassure consular officials and British merchants alike by stressing the temporary nature of these interdictions, steps were taken to implement them.[44] For instance, British contracts for the sale and shipment of grain were revoked, even though they had seemed valid enough at first, and local merchants allied with British commercial houses were made to feel the wrath of an exasperated Ottoman administration. As an example, grain belonging to the London firm of David Sassoon and Company was deemed to be unsupported by a proper contract of export; consequently, the Sassoon firm's local agents in Baghdad were reprimanded for having the temerity to think that their shipment was an exception to the rule, and would go through as usual.[46] While the bans did temporarily bring down the price of grain (from eight shillings the *wazna* to five), their real objective seemed to have been the dislocation of British grain shipments. And in fact two months after the bans were instituted, representatives of the British shipping firm of Gray, Mackenzie and Company complained bitterly to the vice-consul at Basra that, failing to find a return cargo to India, their ships were forced to leave Basra in ballast, stating that the embargo on grain had "paralysed trade" in Iraq.[47] Hyperbole aside, the bans probably did affect a temporary setback in British trade, but the sources do not show a drastic decrease in the level or volume of British commercial activity. Quite to the contrary, this period marks the beginning of the phenomenal rise of grain and wool exports to India and Europe.[48]

In any event, some British firms (and their local agents) continued to ship grain out under cover of darkness, and a few of the more cynical British shippers nonchalantly bought wheat and corn despite the standing edict against the sale and export of these food items. Consequently, they bore the brunt of universal condemnation when food riots exploded in Baghdad on 1 December 1877. On 3 December, the consul in Baghdad severely reproved the important firm of Stephen Lynch and Company for willfully contravening the Ottoman ban and laid the responsibility for the riots at their door.[49] A detailed report was sent to the Foreign Office in which Colonel Nixon, the British Resident, stated the case as he understood it:

> There seems to have been a very serious organization of the populace and the Turkish authorities were powerless in the matter. It appears that on the morn-

> ing of the first of December, a large number of people went to the Serai and had an interview with the Pasha of Baghdad and demanded that the exportation of grain should be stopped. This interview was not satisfactory and immediately the work of plunder commenced, and in a very few minutes, seven vessels loaded with grain belonging to ʾIbrāhīm Zeebuck, Ezra George of David Sassoon, ʿAbdullāh Uda [and] Haji ʾAḥmad Tikriti were plundered.[50]

Nevertheless, British shippers were not so easily impressed by popular grievances or consular displeasure, for barely two months later, when grain prices had fallen as a result of the bans on export, a lone European merchant, acting in complicity with Stephen Lynch and Company, began to buy up all of the available grain on the market and to load it on the British steamer, the *Blosse Lynch*. An observant traveller, Grattan Geary, picks up the story:

> When the treason became known, the populace rose in fury. A number of men set out for Ctesiphon [Mada'in] to intercept and to destroy the buggalows [*baghlas,* river craft]. They only found vessels, however, which contained no grain, and they let them go. In Baghdad, the Customs-house, off which the "Blosse Lynch" was lying, was beseiged. The gates were fortunately shut in time, and the rioters could not gain ready admittance, but they declared that if the grain was not re-landed from the "Blosse Lynch," they would break the vessel up. There was no adequate force at hand to coerce them, so an order was given, with the approval of Colonel Nixon [the British Resident] to re-land the grain. For a time, the general plunder of the grain stores belonging to export merchants seemed imminent but the crisis was passed, and there was no renewal of the rioting.[51]

The popular disturbances in Baghdad and the lack of effective governmental measures to stop covert British designs for exporting grain from Iraq were sufficiently alarming to the Porte that they resulted in the immediate recall of the vali, ʿĀkif Pasha, to Istanbul, and the installation of a new governor, Qadrī Pasha, in his place. Nevertheless, the incidents involving prohibitions on grain in the nineteenth century were not confined to Basra and Baghdad. The period between 1890 and 1893 witnessed similar developments, this time on a regional scale involving parts of Arabistan. For example, in Shustar and Ahwaz (northern Arabistan), anti-European riots took place in 1893 and 1895 in which specific targets were British grain merchants.[52] A mob of angry Shustarīs, led by ʿulamāʾ, first attacked a caravan of goods belonging to the firm of Stephen Lynch, then switched its attention to the warehouses of the Hotz company, Dutch merchants engaged in the grain trade. The reason for the attacks had to do with the same disregard for local demands that had sparked the Baghdad disturbances. Notwithstanding the fact that the region was undergoing a period of scarcity and approaching a crisis stage in the supply and distribution of food grains, European merchants had continued to export barley and wheat. As a consequence of the flagrant conduct of foreign shippers, European concerns in Shustar incurred the wrath of local insurgents who attacked the depots and warehouses belonging to European merchants. Eventually, this first anti-European demonstration developed into a major insurrection, and the governor-general ordered Shustar to be shelled in order to quell the protest.[53]

By the 1890s, the trade of local merchants in Iraq as well as Arabistan had begun to suffer as a result of the British domination of regional commerce, and whether in overt or covert form, resistance to foreign penetration of the grain trade became an ongoing process in the late nineteenth century. While such opposition never managed to disrupt European incursions into the grain trade, its *potential* for trouble remained a factor to be reckoned with. Thus, Ottoman valis continuously referred to past precedent in their memoranda to British shippers by stressing the inherent danger of exporting grain in periods of scarcity. For instance, when prohibitions against the export of grain from Iraq were put into effect in the 1890s, the reasons put forward for doing so echoed those of 1877.[54] Chief among them was the menace of further popular disturbances breaking out.

Local merchants were not the only ones taking part in insurrections and popular demonstrations. Throughout the latter part of the nineteenth century, the Ottoman bureaucracy in Baghdad and Basra also tried to undermine British trade. In this respect, there were certain key concepts the Ottoman bureaucracy used in the battle against British firms, one of which was the recurrent term, "famine." The latter concept was invariably applied whenever British shippers traded a heavy volume of goods,[55] or managed to manipulate the local competition in order to ship grain that may have been destined for Hijazī ports.[56] While it is true that the organization and transport of grain within the provinces of Iraq did leave a lot to be desired, and blocked routes and uneven supply did lead to scarcity, the continued reaffirmation by Ottoman bureaucrats of the specter of famine may have been as much an ideological tool used to combat British inroads in to the grain trade, as a valid reflection of the food situation in the provinces of Iraq. Because the Balta Liman Treaty expressly prohibited internal monopolies on certain commodities, including grain, the eventual result was the termination of the flourishing tradition of such monopolies in the latter part of the nineteenth century.[57] As a result, Ottoman valis and government-affiliated merchants had to find other strategems to compete with British grain merchants. It is quite possible that the new policy of commercial bans on the export of specific food items was just such a strategy, for it must be borne in mind that the concept of famine played a critical role in the formulation of this policy.

There are glimmers of information in the sources indicating that Ottoman grain embargoes and the recurrent theme of famine in official proclamations evidenced a far more subtle and complex policy than European consuls had been led to believe. In particular, the suddeness of the measures designed to curtail the export of grain, the unusual severity of their enforcement and the belated release of government stores in years of alleged scarcity are phenomena which cannot be ignored, and which can be translated as signs that, on an informal level at least, the Ottomans were doing their best to halt further British encroachment in the grain trade. Moreover, the selective nature of the embargoes and the fact that they were applied to British traders (to the exclusion of local merchants) indicates that Ottoman bureaucrats and state-affiliated merchants had declared an official trade war on British shippers.

When the first embargo on grain was announced, its immediate enforcement caught British traders by surprise. In some cases, the lack of any warning stopped short shipments of grain that British traders had bought and paid for as much as three months before.[58] British merchants complained, with some justification, that had conditions of scarcity truly obtained in the provinces of Baghdad and Basra, Ottoman measures to curtail the export of grain would have gone hand in hand with the immediate release of government grain to the local populace. Actually, the latter seldom occurred, and government reserves continued to be withheld, even in periods of impending "famine."[59] As a result, the price of grain remained high in the markets of Baghdad and Basra even though, by all calculations, it should have dropped since a greater supply was made available in the sūqs because of the imposition of the bans on export.[60] In reality, the release of British-held grain stores to local markets as a result of the bans on export did not force the price of wheat or corn down as radically as it might have, leading one British shipper to comment: "[this development] proves that there is no scarcity of grain in the province."[61]

"Famine," then, was a term that could be used to browbeat the opposition; in fact, the Ottoman bureaucracy in Baghdad and Basra used the word to prevent the sale and shipment of British grain to India and Europe, even while attempting to fix prices on local markets by withholding grain, thus keeping the price artificially high. In this respect, as further evidence that Ottoman valis and state-affiliated merchants colluded to prevent British shippers from exporting grain, it is significant that in September 1878 indirect grain export was taking place from centers such as Hilla, which was well-connected with river transport and which may have been preferred to Baghdad, where grain riots were still a possibility. Were these shippers local merchants working in tandem with the Ottoman government to export grain surreptitiously in spite of the ban, as the British consul intimated? Or were they independents, similar to the large community of Jewish merchants in Baghdad who "combined to place direct steamers on the line to carry their own goods,"[62] thus competing with both British shippers and Ottoman-affiliated merchants? Unfortunately, the sources do not clarify these essential connections. What is clear from the limited evidence in our possession is that Ottoman valis may have in fact applied economic policies in a selective fashion, maintaining a strict enforcement of such policies with regard to British trade while allowing state-affiliated merchants to export grain at will.

Resistance to foreign trade was but one factor that characterized regional markets. Another equally significant factor was regional integration. The regional bond that tied Muhammara and its surrounding countryside to Basra and its adjacent districts meant that adverse conditions affecting either market could be alleviated by regional interdependence. When one economic center languished for lack of food, an alternative market existed to provide it with the necessary crops. In fact, chronic food shortages must have afforded the merchants of Basra and Muhammara the potential for a fast profit and for indulging in unlimited commercial speculation, all the more so because shipping grain across the Shaṭṭ and marketing it in either port entailed minimal transport costs. In the 1870s and 1890s, this aspect of regional interdependence allowed the local population on either side of the Shaṭṭ al-ʿArab to counteract the devastating consequences of famines, food shortages, governmental manipulation of wheat reserves, and British domination of the grain trade.

In years of impending scarcity, then, valis and merchants alike relied on Muhammara, or even India,[63] to offset grain shortages. Even when export bans were imposed on Muhammara's own grain reserves,[64] barley and wheat were shipped covertly to lower Iraq in order to forestall possible famines. Embargoes notwithstanding, grain was usually available for delivery to wherever the price was right, and wherever it commanded the best sale. Furthermore, even though agricultural expansion in lower Iraq could not keep up with exterior demand,[65] thus inhibiting grain production for both the domestic and the export markets, secondary economic centers existed to reinforce the areas that fell short of the expected yield.

CONCLUSION

In spite of regional resistance and economic interdependence, British efforts to capture a sizable part of the regional trade in grain finally succeeded in the latter part of the nineteenth century. This development can be dated to the middle of the 1860s. Free trade in grain, a British theme throughout the nineteenth century, was now discussed with increasing frequency in consular reports emanating from Iraq. Novel means of transport—British steamships—carried goods more rapidly and efficiently to India, making them more profitable for local traders. British agents and shippers paid regular market prices for local commodities, even inflated prices where Iraqī and Gulf merchants could get away with it;[66] this was a definite improvement over the forcible seizure of goods carried out by Ottoman armies. More importantly, in the period 1865–1914, a large amount of land was put to the plow in Iraq.[67] As a number of pastoral tribes settled on the land and took up agriculture, more grain was exported, and local merchants now found it profitable to trade in the commodity as British agents. By 1905, Britain had gained unquestioned supremacy in the foreign trade of the provinces of Iraq. Consular sources calculated that the value of imports by sea to Basra, approximately £511,000 in 1887, rose to £1,387,000 in 1905, "an increase of nearly one million sterling in eighteen years."[68] Meanwhile, the value of exports during the same period increased from £947,000 to £1,515,000, or about half a million sterling.[69] To further underscore the significance of these statistics, we can note that in terms of the composition of articles of trade, grain (chiefly wheat and barley) made up one of three major export items of the province, the other two being wool and dates. Figures for the tonnage of ships entering Basra make the same point. A consular official reported that

> of 102 steamers cleared at the port of Basra in 1888, 101 were British with an aggregate tonnage of 103,296 tons. Of 169 cleared in 1905, 163 were British with an aggregate tonnage of 182, 180 tons. Thus British commercial interests in Turkish Arabia [Iraq] predominate over those of every European country. . . .[70]

It was estimated, then, that between 1900 and 1913, British (and British-Indian) commercial interests were responsible for nearly two-thirds of Iraq's imports and nearly one-half of its exports,[71] edging out not only local competition but Western challengers as well, including German, Belgian, and Austrian interests. As a result of the greater impact of the world market on Iraq after the 1860s, grain prices in Basra and Baghdad fell under the influence of the London market, so much so that the occurrence of world-wide depressions began to influence the cultivation of grain in remote Iraqī agricultural districts.[72] As a consequence of these changes, shaikhs eager to plant lands with barley or wheat no longer considered local conditions but relied instead on foreign demand to stimulate production.

Table 5-1. Exports (in British Pounds)

Year	Wheat	Barley
1864	—	—
1866	2,108	158
1868	15,475	2,911
1875	9,467	2,654
1887	—	—
1889	91,341	25,123
1890	183,530	65,522
1892	160,000	123,751
1893	45,000	78,025
1894	79,561	51,198
1895	181,169	94,872
1897	4,200	17,857
1898	5,055	11,390
1899	169,500	181,055
1900	35,379	38,212
1901	31,683	244,262
1902	8,299	79,786
1903	29,775	255,738
1904	40,638	217,719
1905	76,162	226,062
1906	106,675	192,737
1907	208,647	426,079
1908	241,093	370,977
1909	11,531	82,788
1910	66,907	220,904
1911	195,329	772,025
1912	243,054	1,118,490
1913	10,009	362,690

Source: Ḥusain Muḥammad al-Qahawātī, *Dawr al-Baṣra al-tijārī fil-khalījalīj al-ᶜArabī 1869–1914* (Baghdād: ʾIrshād Press, 1980), 449

-Six-

The Horse Trade

The control of the food supply in lower Iraq and the Gulf became the object of an intensified struggle in the period from 1877 to 1898, and food grains continued to increase in value as the twentieth century unfolded. In the same period, however, the export of livestock declined sharply.[1] Southern Iraq and the Gulf had been the major distribution points for the export of live animals—particularly horses—to the Arab provinces and India throughout the eighteenth and nineteenth centuries International rivalry over the trade in horses grew during the 1870s and 1880s but declined at the turn of the century. One reason may have been that while the struggle over supply developed into a major source of conflict between Ottoman and British/Indian armies in the nineteenth century, after World War I the advent of mechanized vehicles shifted the focus of the trade, and the conflict subsided. Arabian mares and stallions became the fancy of sportsmen and breeders, and were no longer transported in great numbers to India.

Horse breeders and traders formed an indissoluble part of the regional economy; they were not immune to market constraints or to economic pressures. However unevenly understood over remote distances, the forces of supply and demand did play an active role in the trade and shipment of horses to India, especially in the nineteenth century. While horses perished on the way to overland markets and ships carrying an equine cargo sometimes foundered on the open sea, the argument can nonetheless be forwarded that it was not the difficulties of transport that were the determining factor in the volume of horses shipped in a certain year but the number of customers who would buy Arabian colts in Bombay that spurred the shipment in the first place. For even though information on potential customers could only have been rudimentary at best, most of the evidence (at least from the mid-nineteenth century onwards) points to the fact that in Bombay, or other Indian horse markets, few horses were left unsold after a particular shipment. That is to say that horses falling under certain set criteria (usually those of the British army in India) became the norm. Gone was the indiscriminate selection of Baghdad hacks or racially questionable yearlings. By the last quarter of the nineteenth century, horse trading had become a fully rational economic venture in which regional specialists were enlisted to ship a specified number of "pure" Arabians to select customers in Bombay.[2] Even so, throughout the eighteenth and nineteenth centuries horse traders may have functioned as the original "versatile tribesmen,"[3] not confining themselves solely to the sale of one commodity, but spreading their risks evenly in the event that demand in India might be low and the sale and shipment of horses might suffer a downturn as a consequence.[4]

Horse trading has had a long history in Iraq, Arabia, and the Gulf. As early as the sixth century, horses from the region—Persians, Arabians, and mixed strains—were supplying the markets of Ceylon, and by the twelfth century India was absorbing most of the exports from Iraq, Persia, Syria, Hadramawt, Yemen and Bahrain. When the Portuguese historian Duarte Barbosa wrote his economic history in the early part of the sixteenth century, he focused on the strategic importance of the island of Hormuz in the central Gulf. Among the varied and diverse products that were transshipped by way of Hormuz, horses formed a singularly prized commodity. Indeed, as the century wore on, they became the most valuable export from the island, and a large number were regularly sent to southern India as luxury items.[5]

While the Indian market continued to exert a strong pull on the internal supply of Gulf horses throughout the sixteenth, seventeenth and early part of the eighteenth are centuries,[6] no statistics seem to be available on the number of horses exported to Bombay throughout the Ottoman period. However, some time after the provinces of Iraq had been absorbed into the Ottoman Empire, serious attempts by Ottoman officials must have been made to cut into this lucrative trade, for by the beginning of the eighteenth century references begin to crop up in the literature to Ottoman officials riding Gulf horses.[7] By the nineteenth century, Ottoman officers and pashas—indeed the flower of the Ottoman cavalry, were relying on Arabian horses to the exclusion of other, possibly hardier strains. The pure-bred Arabian thus came to occupy a central position in the military as well as civilian needs of the Ottoman infrastructure in Iraq.

In addition to being purchased for Ottoman armies, Arabian horses soon began to interest supply officers from other land armies, chiefly the British in India. Possibly influenced by Indian reliance on these horses, British experts and travellers had considered supplying the Indian army with Arabian horses as early as 1817, but the reputed fragility of the pure-bred Arabian and the fact that it was untested in battle were seen as chief obstacles to European use.[8] By the 1860s, however, it was recognized that Arabian horses could outstrip any contender on the racetrack and could carry a cavalry officer of average weight into war. Moreover, a steady supply of horses had become necessary for all British armies in the field, partly as a result of the Crimean conflict in 1856 and the importance placed on light cavalry in British military operations. Fleet, indefatigable Arabian stallions, capable of carrying "fifteen stone [210 lbs.] or more with apparent ease,"[9] became the favorites of the British cavalry in India. By the late nineteenth century, competition from Australian ("Walers") and South African horses had begun to cut into the supply of Arabian horses intended primarily for the army, but by that time the preference for the pure-bred Arabian had begun to confound all expectations, growing into a British preoccupation that had somewhat less to do with the animal's practical purpose than with its fabled beauty, lineage and power. Indeed, a certain aesthetic of the Arabian horse became de rigeur among those who professed an expertise in horses in general, and may even have been one of the chief reasons for the pure-bred Arabian's continuing popularity in the latter part of the nineteenth century.[10] Whatever the reason, the pure-bred Arabian stallion, mare or yearling grew to be an important addition to the Bombay horse market in the period between 1860–1900, and soon developed into a bone of contention between British and Ottoman officials.

But the struggle over the horse trade cannot be understood without an appreciation of the socio-economic context within which this important commodity was bartered or sold. The local exigencies of a regional trade predicated on the supply, transport, and sale of livestock overseas have been imperfectly pieced together in the past; in this section, I propose to place the background and development of the horse trade squarely within the emergence of a regional network of suppliers, transport agents, shippers and merchants in the eighteenth and first part of the nineteenth centuries. Quite simply, one would have been impossible with out the other, and so it is to the local roots of the regional market that I now turn.

A HISTORY OF THE HORSE TRADE, 1750–1890

The most significant facet of the breeding, exchange, or sale of horses in the mid-eighteenth to nineteenth century was that it sprang from the dynamic of long-distance trade. It was therefore a regional undertaking, in which formal borders, such as there were, mattered little, if at all. In Najd, the breeding of horses for sale was carried out by the great pastoral confederation of the ʿAnayza (who, up till the last quarter of the nineteenth century, maintained their reputation for pure-bred (ʾaṣīl) Arabian mares). Horse-breeding for sale was also undertaken by the Mutayr and Ẓāfir tribes in central Arabia and among the al-ʿAmāyir in al-Ahsa. In Iraq sections of the former Najdī-based tribe, the ʿAnayza continued to raise horses in the Shāmiyya desert, while in the northern Jazira the Shammar, also originally from central Arabia, bartered or sold their horses to townsmen, sometimes at great profit. On the lower Euphrates sections of the sprawling, powerful Muntafiq bred distinctive horses while smaller clans and subsections of the Banū Lām and the Khazāʾil on the eastern Tigris, as well as the Dulaim, ʿUbaid, and Jubūr in central Iraq, either raised their own horses or brought them from larger, camel-breeding tribes.[11]

The clue to the constant mobility of pastoral tribes and horse-breeders—from Iraq or Syria to central Najd in the winter, and from the Arabian desert to the fringes of Iraqī and Syrian towns in the spring—can be explained as much by the pastoral imperative (the constant search by livestock breeders for water and grazing land) as by a continuing Najdī association, cultivated assiduously by tribal shaykhs long after they had come to be considered "Iraqī" in everything but lineage. For instance, all during the eighteenth and nineteenth centuries, the "Iraqī" section of the ʿAnayza retained a certain freedom of access to the market towns and wells of eastern and central Arabia, even as the Shammar, who had acquired communal pasturelands within Iraq proper and who had evolved into a local power vis-à-vis the Mamluk and, later, Ottoman bureaucrats in Baghdad and Mosul, continued to play an important role in the politics of Jabal Shammar (Najd).[12] Economic necessity cemented the ties of patrilineal descent and ran counter to the concept of territorial or "national" frontiers espoused by statist-minded pashas in the nineteenth century. Indeed, for pastoral tribes, survival decreed a regional network of diyar (communal grazing lands) and market towns that had little to do with official patronage.

Regional ties made an overall difference in the pursuit of the horse trade, as they affected practically every commercial undertaking in the area. The mechanisms by which horses were bought, sold, and transported overseas evolved out of the historical conditions shaping the region in the eighteenth and nineteenth century, and specifically out of the ties between the Gulf and India. From 1750 till around 1860, the supply, marketing, and shipment of horses to India was the regional monopoly of Gulf merchants who pursued the trade inspite of governmental restrictions (high taxation imposed on camel and horse-breeding tribes, monopolies on livestock or blockades on shipment), economic constraints (dearth and famine affecting herds) or market factors (a glut of horses in India). That the regional market faced up to all of these catastrophes, and survived is testimony to the flexibility and innate stability of the regional network itself. How this market operated in practice is the subject of the next section.

SUPPLY

The supply of Arabian mares or stallions was contingent upon several factors, most of which revolved around the manifold and complex functions of horses in Gulf societies. Mention has already been made of their military uses, for they were eagerly sought after as army horses by local Arab shaykhs, Mamluk pashas and later, Ottoman governors. But throughout the mid-eighteenth to early nineteenth centuries, horses were also used as a form of currency, either offered as gifts as symbols of state patronage, or to legitimize rulers in power, (for sometimes their exchange solidified the newly sovereign authority of ascendant Gulf shaykhs) or finally, to curry favor with a governor. A discussion of this phenomenon is warranted at this point.

From 1702 to 1831, a class of Georgian Mamluks established themselves as rulers of Iraq; their chief mission was to restore order in Iraq, to guard the frontier with Persia, and to send a yearly revenue to the imperial capital. From 1702 to 1747, Ḥasan Pasha and his son, ʾAḥmad, were able to counter the weight of the pastoral and semi-settled tribes of Iraq through a combination of military campaigns and political guile. One of the results of these repeated military offensives was that, once the battle was over, the Mamluk commanders were usually left with the defeated party's property, which sometimes consisted of the enemy's wives and children, but more often took the form of camels, sheep and, of course, horses.[13] Up until 1747, which is the date of ʾAḥmad Pasha's demise, scrupulous care was taken to liquidate the property of defeated enemies and to send the revenue to Istanbul, for this was one way by which Mamluk commanders could ascertain that they would receive the title of Pasha and be presented with a khilʿa, or robe of honor, from the Sultan at their accession.[14] In later years, the evidence seems to indicate that the yearly revenue, still less the traditional presents sent to the Sultan and his coterie, were not delivered with the same alacrity to the Porte. For with the accession of Suleimān Abu Lailā (1750–62), provincial revenue may have been collected but not as swiftly remitted to Istanbul, and in some years, no annual revenue was sent at all.[15] While this never became regular practice, the development was far-reaching. It may be surmised that it grew out of internal constraints which had much to do with the consolidation of Mamluk power within Iraq. It may be that in some years, under exceptionally strong Mamluk pashas, capital earmarked for the imperial government was being amassed by local governments for purely local coffers. Defying the imperial government, some Mamluk administrators were joining with local forces to finance a home-grown constituency, using revenues from tax-farms, monopolies, transport dues, and the sale of captured livestock in this effort.

An analysis of how horses supported this effort is incumbent at this point. In 1762, the Mamluk ʿAlī Pasha became governor of Baghdad. One of the first things he did was to enter Baghdad and imprison the then governor, ʿUthmān

Effendi al-ʿUmarī, immediately "taking over his property and horses."[16] Two years earlier, the governor of Mosul, ʾAmīn Pasha al-Jalīlī, sent his son Suleimān Pasha to fight "the people of Jabal Sinjar" (i.e., the Yazīdī tribes). After their defeat, the Yazīdīs sent their wives and some of the elder notables to ask for pardon, which was granted on the condition that the Yazīdīs would send the vali "1,000 head of sheep, and three head ot horses,"[17] which condition was accepted. As a result, the Yazīdīs were allowed to return to Jabal Sinjar in peace. On yet another occasion, Suleimān Pasha al-Shāwī, the leader of the famous ʿUbaid tribe, went to war against the Millī Kurds in 1791; as a result of the Kurds' defeat their chief, al-Jaḥjaḥ, was thrown in prison. However, a deal was later struck between the two tribal shaikhs. In order to receive al-Jaḥjaḥ with honors, and to sweeten a contract already made between Suleimān Pasha and al-Jaḥjaḥ, in which the latter promised to kill his chief ally, Timur Pasha, Suleimān Pasha promised the Kurdish chieftain a fine Arab horse as recompense. As it turned out, Suleimān Pasha was the one who defeated Timur; and in order to buy back his freedom, Timur Pasha sent the governor of Baghdad (Suleimān Pasha al-Shāwī's overlord) sixty camels, ten Arab steeds, and the Kurdish shaikh's own tent.[18]

These examples illustrate the manifold ways in which horses were used in the eighteenth century. They were seen primarily as loot from military campaigns and *ghazūs* (tribal raids), but as the case of the Yazīdīs of Jabal Sinjar suggests, horses were also viewed as currency with which to pay off war reparations. In addition, the examples related to the contract between Suleimān Pasha al-Shāwī and both al-Jaḥjaḥ and Timur Pasha illustrate the way in which horses were used to seal agreements relating to war as well as to peace. Finally, it is interesting that the evidence, selective though it may be, indicates that the governor of Mosul sometimes sent most of the captured livestock to Baghdad, clearly indicating that for at least part of the century, the governors of Mosul saw themselves as subordinate to that city.

A further example merits attention. Dāwūd Pasha (1817–31), the last Mamluk governor of Iraq, inherited a bankrupt administration and set out to restore the government's finances by forced loans, bribery, and plunder. Among other practices, he was known to suddenly descend upon tribes and denude them of their flock. This seems to have been the practice of a number of Mamluk pashas, as well as Ottoman governors, later on in the century; Dāwūd was certainly not the first governor to mount preemptive strikes, designed to break the power of unwary tribes before they had time to regroup. Nevertheless, Dāwūd Pasha seemed to be the one governor who honed the practice into an art. As a result of his various military campaigns, and his alliances with some of the important horse-breeding tribes of Iraq, such as the Muntafiq, he amassed a "great treasury"[19] which was looted by the Baghdad mob in the last days of his rule. Among this treasury were several Arabian horses. Moreover, the historian Suleimān Fāʾiq relates that even before the civil war erupted in Baghdad, eventually bringing about the end of Dāwūd Pasha's administration, one of the governor's diversionary tactics was to send a number of fine Arab horses to the Porte in order to buy time so as to regroup his forces, and stave off an Ottoman invasion in the process. Incredibly, the tactic worked for a while, but in the end, Istanbul decided to regain the upper hand and send an army to recapture Baghdad from the Mamluks.[20]

Thus while the evidence is fragmentary at best, and with regard to the supply of horses in Iraq, altogether elusive, it nonetheless points to a certain development. From 1704 till 1747, captured horses may have been sold to meet the necessities of provincial revenue, while a number may have remained in the pasha of Baghdad's hands, and those of his allies. Certainly the pasha's lieutenants must have gotten their share of the booty, for evidence points to the fact that, in the earliest stages of the Muntafiq tribal confederation's composition, two sections that had been part of the Rabīᶜa confederation (the ᶜAbbūda and Banū Rikāb) not only joined the Muntafiq but began to pay the ḥaṣṣān tax, appropriately paid in horses by the Muntafiq shaikhs to the Baghdad administration.[21] In the latter part of the eighteenth century, as Mamluk governors became more confident, and began to derive their sources of support from the local *ʾaᶜyān* and important tribal commanders, provincial revenue was not as promptly dispatched to Istanbul, and the pasha of Baghdad was able to disburse it with more freedom in Baghdad. We can speculate, therefore, that the supply of horses was diverted to the internal market, or at least, to the pasha's coterie. While we have no firm knowledge as to whether Mamluk pashas established horse-farms or studs, (as Ottoman governors did later on),[22] it is clear that they must have had a ready supply of horses at hand to distribute as gifts, bribes, or material compensation whenever the occasion warranted.

A parallel development took place in Arabia and the Gulf. As discussed in the first chapter, the first Saᶜūdī state was established in Arabia through the combined efforts of the amirs of the Saᶜūd family and the descendants of the reformist shaykh, Muḥammad ibn ʾAbdul-Wahhāb in the mid-eighteenth century. The first wave of Saᶜūdī-Wahhābī successes centered around Najd proper, and later on in al-Ahsa, where one tribal district after another succumbed to the Saᶜūdīs. Invariably, the defeated party was obliged to sue for peace by making the bayᶜa, the swearing of an oath of allegiance to the conquerors. For instance, in 1792 an epic battle took place between Saᶜūd ibn ᶜAbdul-ᶜAzīz, second ʾamīr of the Saᶜūdī line and Barrak ibn ᶜAbdul-Muḥsin, newly-installed ruler of the Banū Khālid tribe of al-Ahsa, and a sworn enemy of the Saᶜūdī-Wahhābī alliance. Barrāk's forces were taken by surprise, the former escaping with his life to the Muntafiq district in southern Iraq, while his army was dispersed and his tents pillaged by the Saᶜūdī armies. This was an event so traumatic that a local source claims that after this battle "the Banū Khālid had no more importance."[23] After accepting the bayᶜa from the remnants of the Khālidī forces, Saᶜūd busied himself with appropriate compensation, taking over the property of the defeated shaykh and dividing it. A fifth went to him, while two "shares" *(sahmān)* went to the horsemen in his army and one "share" was awarded to the ordinary foot-soldier. Significantly, among the property to be divided were two hundred horses.[24] In this context, it is significant that horses were viewed as a valuable exchange, donated by a defeated party in lieu of monetary compensation to appease a victorious commander, and thus frequently used to cement peace treaties in the field.

While other evidence corroborates the fact that Saᶜūdī commanders began to expect the bayᶜa as their due,[25] sometimes military raids, in which horses were one of the chief objects, were carried out without resort to any ideological appeals whatsoever. For instance, in the latter part of the eighteenth century, the Muntafiq shaykhs of southern Iraq, powerful overlords of a diverse confederation of tribes, sometimes embarked on punitive campaigns against other tribes, and on notable occasions against the Saᶜūdī state itself, for the sole purpose of gain. Even though a distinction may be drawn between Saᶜūdī campaigns and Muntafiq-led offensives on the basis that the former were mounted for ideological-religious reasons while the latter were pursued for profit, this distinction is largely overdrawn. It may have arisen as a result of the terminology used by the Wahhābīs and rival tribes. For the most part, pro-Wahhābī historians used the phrase *"wa bāyaᶜūhum ᶜalā dīn ᵓAllāh wa rasūlihi"* [and they (i.e., the defeated party) pledged the oath (to the Saᶜūdī ᵓamīrs) on the religion of God and his Prophet] while Iraqī historians, in reference to the Muntafiq and other non-Wahhābī tribes, usually used the expression *wa bāyaᶜūhum* (or *wa ṣālaḥūhum) ᶜalā māl* [and they pledged the oath on material property, whether that was cash, livestock, or crops].[26] However, whereas the Saᶜūdī campaigns may have been undertaken to seal tribal allegiance to state ideology, they were also carried out for economic reasons. That is, Saᶜūdī military offensives were designed to cut into, and possibly control the transit trade of the Peninsula, and later, of the Gulf region in general. Thus both Saᶜūdī and Muntafiq-led military campaigns essentially followed the same form, the only difference being that the Wahhābīs invoked the bayᶜa to legitimize their religious-ideological mission (and collected zakāt in sheep, horses, and camels at the same time) while the Muntafiq blatantly demanded—and received—livestock and crops as spoils of war without the mention of any religious obligation.

Finally, a word must be inserted about the changes brought about by internal market conditions. Other than government raids on horse-breeders, which constituted a form of external interference in the local supply of horses, sedentarization also brought about the decline of herds. For instance, a history written in or around 1818 by a tribal ᶜālim from Najd purports to assess the number of horses owned by important tribal sections in al-Hasa Najd and southern Iraq. In general, the camel-breeding tribes possessed the most horses—such as the ᶜAnayza, Muṭaīr, Zāfir, Shammar, Muntafiq and Khazāᶜil[27]—but as the century progressed, sedentarization wrought a subtle change in the ratio of camels to horses among the nomadic population, a subject that has been discussed in another part of the book. Suffice it to say that by 1877-78, a number of horse-breeders had sold or exchanged their stock and settled down as farmers, and former pastoralists whose reputations had depended on the purity and blood-lines of their horse stock, were no more. Only the ʿAnayza continued to command the purest breed of Arabian mare or stallion [for reasons which have yet to be elucidated, the ʿAnayza in Iraq seemed to be the least willing to adapt to the agricultural policies of the latter nineteenth century].[28]

PARTNERSHIP

Even though supply was sometimes predicated on the regularity of tribal campaigns where horses often appeared as ill-gotten booty, other suppliers—professional horse-dealers, for instance—still had to work within set rules and regulations concerning ownership, sale, or barter of livestock. The overland merchant had long been an indispensable factor in the regional network, and his transformation into a horse trader was a simple step in the same direction. Overland merchants sold horses, camels, grain, dates and cooking-oil (ghi) to trading towns such as Buraida and ʿUnaiza (Najd) or Zubair (lower Iraq). More often than not, they worked in partnership with important shaykhs, or indeed, entire tribal units.[29] Sometimes, in order to spread the risk, they only bought one or two horses from a tribal section, for a peculiar feature of the horse trade was the corporate nature of horse ownership. Arabian horses were seldom the property of a single individual, and the better the breed the more people were likely to own shares and divide profits. In 1880, for instance, a British major who had been sent to Najd to buy horses for the Indian army made the following comment:

> I assure my readers that among the genuine bedu of the Arabian desert, we found no prejudice against parting with or selling a mare. Difficulty there certainly is to induce such people as the ʿAnayza to sell either horses or mares for they do not traffic in horses, but . . . there is another difficulty, however . . . A mare may often belong to two, three or more persons and all of their interests have to be consulted and arranged; whereas a stallion is generally or often the sole property of one person . . . For the purchase of a mare, you may have the difficulty of arranging with the several part-owners. In buying a horse, if a good one is promising, you may have to overcome the general dissent of the whole tribe, for in the sale of a good horse to a stranger, of course the whole tribe is interested. It is a loss to the entire tribe. . . .[30]

Ownership took a variety of forms: one tribesman might "own" the fore-leg of a particular horse, while another might lay claim to his hind-leg; there are even instances in which ownership was established before a foal was born.[31]

Usually, however, only the influential shaikhs could afford to own an entire horse (for frequently their horse farms held a substantial number of valuable colts and mares);[32] nevertheless, sometimes even they went into partnership with a horse trader in order to defray transportation and other costs. Thus in order to share costs of passage, feeding, and stabling once in Bombay, the more common practice was that of multiple ownership. Finally, a *sāyis* (groom) was sometimes sent to sail with the horse, but more often than not, the same merchant who had bought the horse from the tribes doubled as a groom to protect his investment.

SALE

Although horses were usually either bought by means of barter or cash, there were certain proprieties that had to be observed. Among desert Arabs, horses were often bought with camels, for "a beautiful dromedary exercises an extraordinary power over the hearts of the Bedouin."[33] The Kuwaitī horse dealers were known to prefer this method of payment over cash.[34] Moreover, when it came down to currency, "[the horse agent] must carry the requisite cash, in gold if he go towards Damascus, or in [Maria Therese] dollars [or Thalers] in Arabia proper, for the wandering Arabs laugh at paper money."[35] Even where coin currencies were used, there was a graduated scale of prices, according to the age of the animal, his place of origin (whether he had been reared in the desert or in a tribal village), and most importantly, his lineage. In the 1880s, a thoroughbred commanded as high a price as £300, while £50 to £70 seemed a fair price for an "ordinary" horse.[36] By 1906, the average price of a horse had fallen to £50 or even £10,[37] and during the interwar period, the market for horses reputedly came to a complete standstill, leaving many horse dealers high and dry.[38]

TRANSPORT

Long-distance merchants were almost always resident traders who formed part of the production unit of a tribal section, and comprised in some cases town traders who had come to some form of agreement with the shaikhs to exchange protection for profit. For the most part Baghdādī Jews, Christians, or *mashāhīda* (Shīʿī traders from any one of the four shrine cities of Iraq),[39] they had contracted with the shaikh to distribute and sell regional commodities, perhaps on a commission basis.[40] Because the resident trader's position owed to the long-distance commercial transactions from which he himself benefited, as well as members of the particular tribal section to which he was offering his services at the time, in some cases he was not compelled to take part in ghazū(s) or tribal supply operations in which horses figured prominently.[41] So there may well have been a compartmentalization of functions in the horse trade, in which the resident trader's obligations were primarily those of the transport agent, that is, the overland specialist whose responsibility it was to get the goods safely to market.

Thus it is not surprising that transport agents frequently came together in a like-minded organization, in effect as a rudimentary "corporation." Most indicative of this trend were the ʿUqaylīs (or ʿUqaylat). Originally from Najd but settled in their own quarter in Baghdad from the eighteenth century onwards, the ʿUqaylīs were horse and camel traders, as well as caravan rafīq(s) (guides) who escorted merchants and pilgrims across the Syrian, Iraqī and Najdī deserts, both in official (governmental) capacities and in unofficial or private ventures.[42] As late as 1935, a European traveller noted that the ʿUqail bartered rice, coffee, sugar, arms, and gold for horses from pastoralist tribes, to whose shaikhs they paid a small sum for the privilege of pursuing their business.[43] More significantly, because the ʿUqaylīs virtually monopolized overland trade operations and systematized transport activities to an unparalleled degree of sophistication in the eighteenth and nineteenth centuries, their name was soon applied to all types of overland traders, whether they were from the original ʿUqaylī tribes or not. In other words, the trend toward the efficient rationalization of transport activities had become so important, in the countryside as well as in the towns, that the name ʿUqaylī took on a generic quality and soon was applied liberally to all overland traders.[44]

In conjunction with resident traders among the various horse-breeding tribes were to be found other itenerant merchants of various social backgrounds, who travelled towards the tribal domains to buy horses, either independently or in partnership with town merchants. The sources are somewhat vague as to the social composition of this mobile merchant class but glimmers of information provide some clues. Sometimes men of rural origin—for instance, the Qassāb family from Iraq—traded in horses.[45] Often city merchants from Baghdad and Basra sent thelir own agents to scour the countryside; such may have been the case of the Khuḍairīs of Baghdad and the famous Jewish family of the same city, the Sassoons.[46] In addition, the paramount shaikhs of tribal confederations had their own representatives; for instance, agents such as one ʿAlī al-ʿĀyid sold Ibn Rashīd's horses in the 1870s, when the latter was the richest shaikh in northern Najd. Other important merchant families were the Bassāms of central Arabia, and the shaikhs of Muhammara, who were reputed to have made their fortunes in the horse trade. Finally, the largest and perhaps most successful horse traders in the region were from Kuwait, chief of whom were the Badr family.

Whether tied to a multitude of partners or allied to one, the overland merchant drove his horses either to Basra or Muhammara, the two chief ports in the region for the shipment of horses in the nineteenth century. Since this was indeed a regional activity, collection points for the sale and transport of horses were organized and distributed over a wide geographical area. The towns of Buraida and ᶜUnaiza in Najd were the main centers for the horse trade in central Arabia. In Iraq and Syria, horses from the north were driven to such distribution centers as Dair al-Zūr, Tadmur (Palmyra), and ᶜAmīd, while horses from the southern tribes appeared in Baghdad, Ḥilla, Sūq al-Shuyūkh, Zubair, and Basra. As discussed above, Basra and Muhammara were the scene of seasonal horse shipments to Basra. The European steamships that transported horses to India never shipped horses in rough weather, but waited for the seas to calm before setting forth with their equine cargo. Sometimes new or refitted horse-boxes or cribs were used on board, in which horses were housed and fed, and let out for excercise on deck when the groom saw fit. At other times, horses were ranged by each other on the upper deck of the ship, covered with protective covering, and left out in the open under the watchful eyes of their owners or agents.

The last link in the chain of regional trade had to do with the sale of horses in India. Once in Bombay, horses were subject to the vagaries of international demand, for Indian markets were the hub of all trade. As former British Consul-General Tweedie put it in 1894:

> We lately wintered in Bombay. In five or six months, about three thousand horses were received from the ports of the Persian Gulf. Out of that number, stud-horses were selected for the whole of India, and for Queensland (Australia), Germany, the United States, and other countries. Every day witnessed the sale of horses and when the season closed, the unsold residue was inconsiderable. . . .[47]

Horses were assembled for sale at fairs designed specifically for that purpose. The Bombay horse fair was the largest of its kind in India and was noted, more often than not, for its virtual monopoly on the sale of horses by Gulf merchants and dealers. Gulf merchants dominated most of the Bombay stables as well, even though ownership was nominally in Indian hands.[48] In fact, Doughty mentions that one of the more important stables in the late nineteenth century was controlled almost exclusively by a Najdī merchant from the district of Washm.[49] The Arab dealers were a distinct group, all wearing "long cloaks and particoloured head-dresses." Each dealer was responsible for the horses under his supervision until they were sold. He kept his stallions or mares in stables run by one or more commission agents, who divided the business among themselves. According to Tweedie, this highly profitable business consisted of nothing more than owning or preferably, leasing a plot of ground on which to put up a few sheds, and engaging a bookkeeper for the accounts. "At every deal, a fixed fee from the purchaser, and an equal sum from the vendor pass into the stable-keeper's pocket, by way of rent, commission, and all other charges."[50] Finally, it is obvious from the preceding accounts that foreign demand was predicated on Gulf expertise, for European buyers often did not buy directly from the Bombay stables but relied on Arab brokers for their selections. This practice may have led some important merchants, such as the Qurṭās family from Najd and Basra, to settle quasi-permanently in India.[51]

The horse trade was a commercial activity that derived its support from a network of local suppliers, dealers, and merchants. In fact, up till the late 1840s, the logistics of supply, overland transportation, and sale were still dominated to a large extent by regional merchants. In order to understand how this important trade became the focal point of Ottoman strategies of centralization on the one hand, and of British economic designs on the other, we now turn to the international dimensions of this regional activity.

ANGLO-OTTOMAN RIVALRY IN THE HORSE TRADE

An earlier chapter noted the Ottoman attempts to expand their centralizing mission and the British countermeasures taken to thwart their designs. Grain was one commodity over which both Ottoman valis and British shippers fought tooth and nail, and horses, which figured prominently in Ottoman efforts to recapture regional trade, soon became another bone of contention between the two parties. Thus, in 1845, the British Consul-General in Baghdad, Henry Rawlinson, alerted the Foreign Office to the fact that, contrary to the stipulations laid down in the Balta Limani Treaty, horses were escaping the twelve percent duty applied to "all native produce." And he continued:

> Horses, it appears to me, bred upon the banks of the Tigris or in the Mesopotamian desert, can hardly be excluded from the category of native produce yet, strange to say, the provisions of the Treaty of Balta Liman in this part of the Turkish Empire have never been applied to them. A small fixed liability of 150 piastres at Bussorah and about 20 piastres at Baghdad alone have been imposed on them, and the Arab merchants in this trade have thus exported cattle to India at an average duty of 5%. Among the British residents of Baghdad and Bussorah, the exportation of horses has been hitherto limited to the execution of commissions for their friends in India, and the duty has been in general . . . remitted. On the present occasion, however, the Defterdar claims the same amount from Messrs. Lynch that a native merchant would pay on sending horses from Baghdad, and Messrs. Lynch object to the payment on the ground that an export duty is alone leviable at the last port of shipment, namely Bussorah. The results of this difference between the Defterdar and Messrs. Lynch will be, I imagine, that an attempt will be made to establish a duty of 12% ad valorem at Bussorah on all horses exported by British subjects while the native merchant will continue to pay a fixed duty. . . . I forsee in this distinction a perpetual source of misunderstanding and a real injury to British merchants engaging in the horse trade.[52]

Here, then, was the crux of the British dilemma with regard to the transshipment of horses to India. Because regional merchants were not paying export duty, they could still compete; in fact, they dominated the trade. British merchants were only irregularly sending horses to India and had not yet entered the competition for horses in any systematic fashion. It was only when the defterdār (provincial treasurer) attempted to impose a duty, however small, on British shippers that complaints of unjust commercial exactions began to filter into Rawlinson's embassy. Unmistakable signs of an imminent trade war soon became apparent. In the following year Rawlinson, in his famous memorandum to the Foreign Office, indirectly counseled for a stricter application of the articles of the Anglo-Turkish Convention. He warned that horses needed to be included as "native" produce and to be taxed according to the stipulations laid down in the Balta Liman Treaty, lest a serious imbalance result in the Ottoman state's balance of trade. Horses exported the previous year (1844) had netted regional merchants £60,000, and were bound to increase in importance, thus providing the Ottoman government with steadily accruing income. Nonetheless, Rawlinson seemed less interested in the shape of Ottoman Turkey's finances than in the paramountcy of British trade in the region. His concern for the pursuit of British commercial initiative in lower Iraq and the Gulf was expressed in urgent tones, and he stated his views in his usual forthright manner:

> Hitherto, the traffic has been entirely in the hands of Arab dealers established in Bombay and Calcutta but British merchants are now turning their attention to it, which renders it particularily desirable that in order to avoid misunderstanding, horses should be declared under authority to be subject to the same rate of export duty as other articles of native produce. If it be considered a gratuitous act, thus to anticipate an increased liability, I would observe that of the parties for whom horses are exported to India they are the best able to pay an increased price in order to secure the Turkish government their full and legitimate dues that the principle of an ad valorem tax on the exportation of horses and mules had already been recognized and acted on in Persia; and that the voluntary concession to the Turks of their right to raise the duty on this class of exports might be conveniently set off against a remission of the oppressive rates of produce required for the home market. . . .[53]

The position of Rawlinson, and that of the majority of British merchants in Iraq, was transparent enough. The most urgent priority was to bring the horse trade within the commercial orbit of British traders. However, this would not be easy because, as late as the 1840s, the trade was still firmly monopolized by local merchants. As a result, a stricter application of the articles of the Balta Liman Treaty became the rallying cry of British merchants everywhere, for the latter naturally set great store by the complaint that Arab merchants were "contravening" the treaty by not paying the ad valorem tax on this article of trade. In order to become truly competitive, British merchants had to see to it that their commercial rivals were encumbered with an extraordinary tax that would debilitate all but the richest of them.

While the Balta Liman Treaty was partly responsible for destroying the local export trade in the region, the transformation was slow and did not really take effect until the mid-1860s. Moreover, evidence for the trade war involving the export of horses is detailed enough for the early part of the century, but somewhat sketchy for the latter period. There are certain clues in the literature, however, that impart some information and provide a point of departure for further questions regarding the acceleration of Anglo-Ottoman competition over the horse trade. One way of gauging British domination in the horse trade is to note the corresponding shift in Ottoman policy after 1862. In the latter part of the nineteenth century, the Ottoman government launched an economic counteroffensive to recapture lost ground and to restore Ottoman control over regional trade. This renewed Ottoman thrust can be inferred from the government's economic behavior in the 1860s, for bans on the export of many items, including horses from every corner of the Empire[54] were first introduced in this period. Moreover, obstructions placed against British trade became more noticeable in this period, whether these were Ottoman attempts to prevent British steamers from plying the Tigris[55] or incidents in which Ottoman inspectors were accused of "willfully" causing grievious delays at the Baghdad Customs House.[56]

This having been said, however, certain caveats are in order. However tenacious a place it holds in the consular literature, Anglo-Ottoman rivalry is not the real issue here, even though historians have tended to view it as such in the past. The real issue concerns the reasons for the imposition of export bans in the first place, and these ultimately have to do with the changes occurring in regional trade. For the vigor with which the bans on export were pursued indicates that it was not simply a case of the Ottoman bureaucracy wishing to obstruct British trade that was at the root of the problem—although as the Gulf slowly went "British," it must have been a thorny issue indeed—but that the bans were supposed to prevent the wholesale migration of regional traders into the British camp. For regional merchants to continue to export livestock or grain to British India in British boats and for British firms, especially when the Ottoman administration was sorely in need of such items in Iraq proper, must have been quite galling.[57] Thus throughout the latter part of the nineteenth century, the Ottomans had to mount a double strategy, one against the by now preponderant British presence in Iraq and the Gulf, and the other against regional merchants who continued to ply their trade in the face of repeated obstacles thrown their way by the central administration of Baghdad and Basra. The horse trade is a case in point.

OTTOMAN EFFORTS TO REORIENT THE HORSE TRADE AND THE CONSOLIDATION OF REGIONAL RESISTANCE

Insofar as horses were concerned, then, the Ottomans tried to apply bans on their export from Iraq in 1864, 1875, and 1882. On the 5th of September 1866, the political agent in Iraq wrote to the Secretary of the Government of Bombay to state that after two years of reiterating the British point of view with regard to the free export of horses from the Iraqī vilayets, the governor Namīq Pasha was ready to listen, and even to approve a limited export of stallions to India if the Porte authorized it, but that the general provisos of the export ban would remain in force, regardless of the consequences. Plainly, the British argument that state-affiliated merchants should follow the play of free trade and enter into competition with Indian traders in the export of horses to the Indian subcontinent fell on deaf ears; far more significant for the Ottomans was that immediate measures should be instituted to stop the loss of stallions and brood mares, whose numbers were decreasing rapidly in Iraq as well as Syria[58]. Moreover, the brisk export of horses had brought about the creation of a caste of horse-traders attuned to the vagaries of the British-Indian market and its supply requirements; some of the best cavalry horses were being shipped to Bombay. Thus it may be possible to surmise that the export bans were also aimed at regional merchants who had forsaken local markets to ship their horses directly to India. British officials indicated as much by pointing out that a sharp decrease in overseas demand would lead to cheaper prices on the home market, and that by curtailing the shipment of horses the Ottomans would be in a position both to dictate prices and to profit from the pick of the litter.[59] One effect of these export bans was that in 1866 frustrated British officials began to make overtures to the Sultan of Oman to establish an export trade in horses there, although the project never seems to have gotten off the ground.[60]

From 1862 onwards, a flurry of correspondence concerning the Ottoman interdictions on export took place between agencies and departments of the British Empire which set the tone for Anglo-Ottoman relations, finally forcing an aggrieved Ottoman administration to succumb to British pressure, and to rescind the bans. That the bans were lifted in the end was attributed to British skill and ingenuity, but it is worth noting that regional incentives within Iraq, and the Gulf as a whole, were no less important in the abolition of these measures. As always, the most important aspect of this question is not to probe in greater detail the rising tensions between British shippers and Ottoman bureaucrats, but to examine how these bans were themselves undermined by the very regional network they were supposed to destroy.

The ineffectiveness of Ottoman commercial policies in this instance was due, in part, to the growth of smuggling and contraband, the hallmark of all diverted trade in the Gulf from the eighteenth century onwards. The emergence of the contraband trade made a shambles of Ottoman commercial policy and allowed British consular officials to note, with a certain satisfaction, that notwithstanding the bans on exports, the number of horses sent annually to India remained at the same level as in previous years; in some instances, the number even went up (see table 6-1). Al-Qahawātī, using British sources, estimated that in 1887 (a year in which the ban was in operation), the number of horses smuggled to India rose to 2,500, twenty-five percent more than in the preceding year,[61] while Lorimer shows that in 1900 and 1901, years in which the bans were still on the books, the number of horses actually increased over the preceding years.[62] While it is true that in some years, decreased demand in India disallowed any profits from trade, legal or otherwise, steep upturns in the export of horses seemed to be the general trend, as more goods reached their destination than ever before.

Table 6-1. Horses Exported to India by British Shipping Firms

Year	Number	Amount *(in British Pounds)*
1887	2,500	62,500
1888*	2,206	51,150
1889	2,815	61,930
1890	3,193	63,860
1891	3,149	73,230
1892	2,268	37,504
1893	3,432	50,480
1894	3,218	48,270
1895	4,581	68,715
1896	1,704	25,560
1897	1,311	19,665
1898	1,936	29,040
1900*	2,279	45,580
1901*	2,455	49,100
1902	945	5,670
1903	3,845	46,140
1904	2,682	53,640
1905	2,262	49,764
1906	1,741	43,525

* *In these years horses were smuggled to Muḥammara in defiance of the bans on export.*

Source: J. G. Lorimer, *Gazeteer of the Persian Gulf, Oman, and Central Arabia,* vol. I: Historical (Calcutta: Government Press, 1908), 2337–38, and the Parliamentary Papers, vol. 77, 1890; vol. 88, 1894; vol. 94, 1897; vol. 99, 1898; and vol. 103, 1899.

Of course, several factors should be taken into consideration to explain these extraordinary trends. Besides the qualitative improvements in navigation techniques, the larger, more reliable holds of British steamships, and the better care taken of livestock on board ships, all of which allowed more horses to be exported to India, it is also worth noting that British figures were at times overinflated, having been computed from suspect sources.[63] Nevertheless, when all is said and done, another set of reasons must be forwarded to explain the increased volume of trade in a period when every official sanction was taken to impede it. This leads us to the existence of a regional network whose raison d'être was to channel commodities towards other outlets when traditional venues had been obstructed, for any number of reasons.

As early as 1866, a British consular official warned that "horses of the superior class, though in diminished number, continue to find their way to India through Persia and the Arabian ports"[64] and in 1876 the Consul General of Baghdad, referring to the fact that he needed a special firmān from Istanbul that would allow him to export fifteen stallions from Iraq, remarked that:

> the Turkish government is losing vast sums of money by not permitting the export trade to go on, and the Persian government, or rather the shaykhs of Arabistan and Faylieh are reaping the profits as horses pass out of Arabia via Persian territory. . . .[65]

By the 1880s, the thin stream of horses smuggled out of Iraqī ports had become a flood. Among regional horse-traders, the practice grew of circumventing Basra altogether (where the Ottoman Customs House was located) and driving their horses to Muhammara or to Kuwait, there to board them either on British steamers or more often than not, on ordinary dhows or sailing-boats for a passage to India. Arabian horses were now trumpeted as "Persian" articles of trade,[66] so that by a simple expedient arising out of commercial necessity a hasty new equine configuration was created. What is most significant is that a commercial transaction such as the switching of trade outlets from Basra to Kuwait depended on the active cooperation of Kuwaitī or Persian merchants, chief of whom were the ruling families of both shaykhdoms. British consular officials duly noted the trend in their despatches. For instance, in June 1883, Consul-General Tweedie in Baghdad sent the following memo:

> From information collected during the last few weeks, there seems more and more reason to believe what is said by Persians and others here, that when his Excellency Namīq Pasha, during his government of the Baghdad Wilayat, instituted vigorous measures for the stoppage of the horse trade, the Irak breeders, finding their outlets for colts closed, disposed of large numbers of mares to landholders in Persian territory. . . .[67]

The landholders in question were none other than shaykhs Mizʿal and Khazʿal of the Muḥaisin tribes, the by now hereditary rulers of Muhammara and its back country. After Khazʿal succeeded his assassinated brother in government, he reinforced the family policy of buttressing the position of Muhammara as a free port by granting every incentive to horse traders to ship their colts from that port, allowing merchants to bypass both the Ottoman bans on export and the crippling fines levied on horse suppliers. In return for a small fee, traders were welcome to send as many horses as they wanted to Bombay. The Vice-Consul in Basra developed on the theme in his despatch of June 1883:

> On horses exported from Bussorah, the practically prohibitive duty of five Turkish Liras per animal is levied by the Turkish authorities, with the result, I am told, of swelling the revenues of the shaykh of Muhammara, into whose territory the majority of horses now exported are smuggled by dealers.[66]

Interestingly, there is evidence to show that Ottoman pashas also colluded in smuggling horses to India. For instance, Tweedie mentions that in the last quarter of the nineteenth century an unnamed Ottoman governor in Baghdad "was so fond of horses, or rather of the money which they represented that he never visited the bedū without bringing back several colts and fillies."[69] Although the export of horses had been banned by the very government he represented, the governor let it be known that the wealthier dealers could get a pass to ship their horses to Bombay if they bought two or three colts from him. The governor in question may have been ʿĀkif Pasha, vali of Baghdad in the 1870s, whom the Blunts met, and of whom they reported: "ʿĀkif if possesses the finest stud that has been got together in Baghdad for a number of years."[70]

In the last quarter of the nineteenth century, the Ottoman bureaucracy of Baghdad and Basra continued its counterattack against the by now thriving mercantile alliance of regional traders and British shippers. Through 1900, two parallel developments ran side by side: on the one hand, some regional traders, notably grain dealers, (see Chapter Five) had established themselves as state merchants; on the other, horse merchants deemed it more profitable to trade directly with British shippers and to divert their merchandise to tax-free havens, even though this ran counter to Ottoman economic policies. However, even though the trend seemed to be running in Britain's favor, the Ottomans were able to score some limited successes in their struggle to control the regional trade and production of livestock. The most important concerned the nineteenth century Ottoman practice of gradually weakening horse-breeding tribes and other tribes by settling them on government-allotted lands, curtailing their local resources, and imposing extraordinary duties on the most compliant shaikhs. The important Shammar tribe, reputed for its ʾaṣil (pure-bred)horses, was a case in point.

THE SHAMMAR HORSE TAX AND THE BEGINNINGS OF SEDENTARIZATION

The Shammar tribes in Iraq were originally from northern Arabia, or in the parlance of tribal geneologists, "from Tayy."[71] They were pastoralists, raising camels and horses; and the first of their shaikhs to be recognized as "Iraqī" was Fāris ibn ʾĀl-Muḥammad, who assumed the leadership of the Shammar Jarba in the 1790s. His son, Sufuk al-Farīsī, initially an early supporter of ʿAlī Pasha al-Laz, the Ottoman commander who defeated the last Mamluk pasha, Dāwūd, tried to play the Mamluks against the Ottomans without, as it turned out, much success; although he retained a semblance of independence, his death, reportedly at the command of the governor Najīb Pasha in 1847, brought about the near-immediate submission of important sections of the Shammar tribe to Ottoman authorities. Although the Shammar's submission was short-lived, the government's policy of forced tribal sedentarization was introduced in that period (1850–69) and gradually began to intrude upon the tribe's freedom of action. Naturally enough, the first restrictions imposed by Ottoman authorities were on the Shammar's control of pastoral resources, especially those concerning the livelihood of the tribe's horse-breeding sections.

In 1857, Farḥān was appointed by the governor, Muḥammad Rashīd Pasha, to be the shaikh of the tribe. His firmān (imperial edict of appointment, which he allowed the British Consul-General in Baghdad to read) stated the following: Farḥān was to have an Ottoman contingent of 500 matchlock men under his control, whom he was charged to feed and house; he was enjoined to "reduce the whole of his tribe to obedience"; he was responsible for guarding "all" the roads from ʿUrfa (northern Iraq) to Basra; he was to forego the imposition of duties on river craft and those exacted on tribal villages; and finally, Farḥān was to *"abolish the tax heretofore levied on the sale of horses of the Shammar."*[72] In return for these major concessions, the only promise exacted by Farḥān was to have his salary increased, but as the promise was not put into writing, the shaikh was not completely confident that this would materialize.

It must be noted that Farḥān was quite possibly the only contender for the leadership of the Shammar tribe because Farḥān's brothers, ʿAbdul-Karīm and Fāris, resisted Ottoman control until much later.[73] However, even though Shaikh Farḥān consented to most of the conditions imposed on him by the Ottomans, he was powerless to bring most of the Shammar along with him. In fact, until the 1880s, the majority of the Shammar, including tribesmen ostensibly loyal to Farḥān, never completely settled down to agricultural pursuits, even though by 1872 it was being asserted that Shaikh Farḥān "was allowed a handsome salary . . . [and] the government has already begun to build barracks for the troops, a suitable residence for the Governor, and a market [at Shirgāṭ, Farḥān's chosen quarters]."[74] Although most of the Shammar continued to plague the governments of Mosul and Baghdad with almost yearly rebellions until 1884, when the last of Shaikh Farḥān's brothers submitted to Ottoman authority, the latter shaikh never faltered in his loyalty to the authorities, and when he died in Baghdad in 1889, after a long stay in Istanbul, he was remembered as having been a courteous, Turkish-speaking gentleman whose only problem seemed to be that "none of his tribesmen obeyed him."[75]

While there is no evidence that Shaikh Farḥān was able to completely discontinue the horse tax levied by the chiefs of the Shammar on horse-breeders, especially since his writ seemingly ran no larger than Shirgāṭ (northern Iraq) and its environs, the Ottoman authorities continued to harry and harass pastoralist tribes, such as the Shammar and the ʿAnayza, until the turn of the century. While the horse-breeding clans and sections of the great pastoralist confederations may not have been the direct target of government wrath, the later Ottoman policy of breaking up and impoverishing tribes naturally decimated the herds on which pastoralists based their livelihood. Such tactics as forcing shaikhs to stop collecting revenues from the sale of horses may have been a temporary ploy (for evidence exists that the shaikhs of the Shammar remained firmly wedded to the horse trade well into the early twentieth century),[76] but it was an omen of things to come. Small wonder, then, that after Shaikh Farḥān's death, a British consul commented:

> We heard it bitterly remarked by many how, while accepting several thousand pounds a year of Turkish money under the pretence of settling his people at Qalʿāt Shirgāṭ on the Tigris, Ferhan had permitted, if not encouraged the plunder of flocks and merchandise. . . .[77]

Taken together, the policy of forced tribal sedentarization spelled trouble for the pastoral economy as a whole, and may have been yet another tactic in the overall Ottoman strategy of disrupting networks of regional production and trade.

THE POLICY OF NAVAL INSPECTIONS AND SEARCH AND SEIZE MISSIONS IN THE GULF

The second method by which the later Ottoman governors attempted to control the passage of horses to India had to do with the inspection by Ottoman authorities of European ships plying the Gulf; this tactic naturally supported the Ottomans' larger political design of hurting British trade as well as impairing the activities of regional merchants. Thus in July 1882 the official newspaper *al-Zawrāʾ*, which was published in Baghdad, carried a paragraph stating that, following the orders of the Interior Ministry in Istanbul each horse moved anywhere in the empire would henceforth be valued, and forty percent of its value be deposited at the nearest customs house, to be restored once its owner had furnished sufficient proof that it had not been transported to another destination for export.[78] According to British officials, this was yet another nail hammered into the coffin of legitimate trade, for due to the increased duties placed on horse dealers, smuggling and contraband were bound to increase. Moreover, the same dispatch intimated that, other than passing stringent new laws to prohibit the export of horses the Baghdad and Basra authorities were debating whether to start inspecting ships, particularily British steamers, for contraband horses.

This last piece of information threw British consuls in Baghdad, Basra, and Muhammara into a frantic correspondence with the Government of India as well as with each other; the more so that on June 9, 1883, the governor of Basra confirmed British fears by officially informing the consul at Basra that the Ministry of the Interior had instructed its subordinates in Iraq to start inspecting all horses boarded on European steamers, lest they be of Arab blood. Should any be so confirmed, the horses would be taken off the ships immediately and confiscated. Moreover, two Ottoman warships were to stationed at Fao and at Kuwait to prevent the export of equine cargo to India. Furthermore, the Vilayet Council also passed a decision forbidding the export of horses from Muhammara and Kuwait. British officials reported that while the Shaikh of Kuwait was reported to have complied with these instructions, nothing had been heard as yet from the ruler of Muhammara.[79]

Five days later, the British consul at Basra protested the Ottoman action in strong terms. Arguing that the search for Arab horses on British (and French) steamers by the Ottoman government set a bad precedent, he noted that if the right of inspection was conceded to the Ottomans, the Persian government concievably might ask for the same privilege, and the complications ensuing from from the claims and counter-claims from either side might jeopardize the whole export trade. Moreover, were the inspections to go through, a number of facets of international law would immediately enter the picture. One was the indisputed principle that "neutral ships make neutral goods" which stipulated that, once cargo from whatever provenance was loaded upon British or French or ships of any other nationality 'it was no longer associated with its original home port but fell into a different category altogether, and became the new owner's responsibility, whoever he was. The second legal principle underlined a thornier problem, that of the ultimate sovereignty of the Shaṭṭ al-ʿArab. Both the Ottoman and Qajar empires had long coveted the Shaṭṭ al-ʿArab waterway and throughout the nineteenth and early twentieth centuries made repeated attempts to stake total jurisdiction of the river. If the Ottomans were allowed to search and seize vessels plying the Shaṭṭ al-ʿArab, their actions might be construed as the illegal extension of a sovereignity still in dispute, prompting the Persian government to respond in kind, and the simmering conflict between the two governments might start yet another trade war on the river.

However, the sharpest British objections to the search of European shipping concerned the confused debate over what was an "Arabian" horse. An earlier generation of British horse specialists had insisted that there indeed was such a breed, and that it differed considerably from the Turcoman or Persian variety. In fact, the "pure-bred Arabian" was conceived to be a distinct category, and far superior to other breeds in the region.[80] Now the British were forced to concede that their equine categories were inflated, fanciful, and imprecise: for generations "Arab" horses had been bred on Persian soil, and only slightly differed from the horses bred in Iraqī tribal districts. Moreover, the whole notion of searching for "Arab" horses was bound to lead to an imbroglio in which Ottoman customs masters, British shippers and regional merchants could "fix" the origin, geneology and blood-lines of any horse they chose by means of false certification, or bribery.

While the British Consul-General in Baghdad, Major W. Tweedie (not coincidentally a horse fancier, who penned an entire book on the species after his retirement from government service) rejected the Ottomans' "extraordinary claim" to search merchant vessels in the Shaṭṭ al-ʿArab; he nevertheless took the precautionary move of requesting the Government of India to post a warship immediately at the mouth of Basra harbor in case of further trouble.[81] Although it is not clear whether Ottoman officials finally backed down as a result of this show of British military force, there is no further evidence of additional developments in this question. Still, it must be surmised that the whole issue of stopping and searching boats for "Arab" horses would not have commanded such attention from British officials had it not posed alarming consequences, both for the British and their on-and-off local allies, such as the shaikhs of Kuwait and Muhammara. Obviously, the Ottoman proposal to inspect ships for "illegal" cargo was aimed at hurting British interests as much as those of regional merchants for both parties colluded in the covert transport of horses to India, the British by docking their steamers at Muhammara (and indicating their intent to do the same in Kuwait) and regional merchants by driving their horses overland from Basra to Muhammara to escape Ottoman Customs duties. A focus on Kuwait will add some necessary detail to the discussion.

KUWAIT AND THE HORSE TRADE

Kuwait was also significant in the horse trade; the only difference being that, unlike Muhammara and Basra, it had not yet become a regular port of call for British steamships. However, horses were regularly shipped by way of sailing-boats from Kuwait. In June 1866, for instance, a British official requested the Secretary to the Government in Bombay to put pressure on the British Indian Steam Navigation Company to suspend their visits to the port, for fear of upsetting the Ottoman authorities at Basra.[82] By 1899, however, Shaikh

Mubārak of Kuwait (1896–1915) had begun to actively disassociate himself from Ottoman Basra. He imposed an import duty of five percent ad valorem on all goods arriving at Kuwait, the first such imposts on regional imports, whatever their origin.[83] Furthermore, he informed the British consul at Basra that he was even thinking of introducing a regular Customs department at the port.[84] Finally in July 1900, Mubārak, who had begun to smell easy profits in the shaikh of Muhammara's arrangement with regional traders, began to negotiate with the British shipping firm of Grey, Mackenzie and Company in order to secure Kuwait's services as a port for call for British steamboats.[85] The British consul noted in the same despatch that the subject of shipping horses from Kuwait dominated the entire negotiations, and may have acted as the primary motive for the discussions in the first place. A month later, the shipper George Mackenzie provided more light on the question. He stated that:

> In the course of the conversation [with Shaykh Mubārak], I brought up the question of the export tax of 5 liras per horse imposed by the Turkish government, necessitating the smuggling of a great number of horses across the frontier to Muhammara, thereby causing great inconvenience and risk to horsedealers, and I suggested the possibility of getting them to send their horses down to Koweit for shipment by mail-steamer, if he—the shaikh—had no objection to the steamers calling there. He at once expressed himself agreable to their calling if it could be arranged that their doing so would not bring about [Ottoman] quarantine restrictions at his port or at Fao or Bussorah against Koweit, which would hamper him and the trade of the port, especially in the date season. . . . He was fully alive to the proposed horse shipments which would create a demand for fodder and food for the horses and syces (grooms) but he also suggested the advantage it would be to the Koweit fishers to be able to ship their pearls direct from Koweit to Bombay, instead of doing so from Bahrain. He would doubtless be able to levy some duty on same. . . . In order to clinch the matter a day or two afterwards, I asked the shaikh directly what he would charge per horse (presuming the quarantine difficulty was got over), in the event of my arranging with the British India Company to send their steamers into Kuoweit, and also with the horsedealers to send their horses there for shipment to India. He asked what Khazʿal charged at Muhammara, and on my informing him 40 *krans,* he at once said that he would only charge 20 (20 kerans—5.12 rupees). . . . I must say I think his stipulation on this head no more than reasonable. . . .[86]

Neverthless, the time was seemingly not yet ripe for Mubārak to make his move. Barely a week later, the British Consul at Basra received word that the shaikh had withdrawn from the project of a weekly call by the British India Co's steamers at Kuwait. The British speculated that Mubārak's volte-face had occurred as a result of the none too subtle pressure put on him by one of the Porte's emissaries, Sayyid ʾAḥmad al-Naqīb, a leading notable of Basra, who was considered staunchly pro-Ottoman and anti-British.[87] Although at first the British refused to take Mubārak's rejection as a definite answer, the shaikh was adamant that he could not, for whatever reason, embark on the project for the moment. By January 1904, Shaykh Mubārak's ill-fated attempt to wrest economic control from Ottoman Basra had all but been forgotten, and the British Consul at Basra could report that horses from Najd were no longer exported to Kuwait, "as the trade has been deflected to Bussorah."[88]

CONCLUSION

By the turn of the century, however, the policies of the shaikhs of Muhammara and Kuwait had been vindicated. Much as the British had predicted, the horse trade continued unabated throughout the rest of the century and into the next; however, as a result of the Ottoman government's heavy imposition of fines and excessive imposts on horse traders, merchants no longer passed by way of Basra but regularly circumvented the port-town for Muhammara and Kuwait. Thus the official horse trade went through a slump, while smuggling increased by leaps and bounds. In November 1911 an Iraqī newspaper reported that

> The government has forbidden the export of horses to foreign countries, including India. Once the horse traders realized that the edict would hurt them, they began to send their horses by land instead of by sea. They would march them through Basra, then Zubair, then Kuwait or Muhammara. From then on, they would proceed by sailing-boat to India. And so the government, the [Ottoman] steamship administration, and the gümrük (customs) lost out on the profits that would normally accrue to them, were trade proceeding normally. For it is said that in the first week of September, six hundred horses were transported overland. The government should repeal this law that is working against the local population.[89]

-Seven-

The Growth of Regional Market Towns in Iraq, Kuwait, and Arabistan

The growth of market towns able to foster the exchange and distribution of regional goods over a wide area was an essential first step in the development of a regional market. Market towns of one form or another had existed in Iraq and the Gulf region for as long as there had been economic networks,[1] and as long as resident traders saw the need for establishing economic zones where they could control the supply and distribution of regional goods. The institution of such ports of trade over a relatively short period of time testifies to the vitality of regional trade networks and to the economic necessity that brought about the institution of such markets in the first place. While the historical growth of such towns as Zubara (Qatar/Bahrain) and Kuwait in the eighteenth century have already been alluded to, this chapter will trace the continuous development and redevelopment of commercial centers throughout the nineteenth century, particularily in Iraq. Our contention is that whereas in the eighteenth century the reason for building alternate commercial centers had been to systematize regional trade over a wide area, in the nineteenth century free ports were essentially built to resist outside control, especially Ottoman economic designs.

Because market towns served as the primary loci for the exchange of regional goods and functioned as all-important links between the countryside and the principal administrative centers in the region, they became vital economic assets for government agents or for tribal parties anxious to tax the entry of such goods and to monopolize their distribution. In the nineteenth century, the fate of these regional market towns became the principal focus of the relations between the Ottoman government and the rural hinterland. This chapter, then, will also describe and analyze the various factors that were brought to bear on governmental strategy in the countryside, as well as on the coast, the economic consequences of Ottoman control (or lack of it) over key market towns, and the resistance of regional traders to the adverse nature of governmental policies.

The principal problems for the Ottoman valis of Baghdad and Basra were how to control the free flow of regional trade and how to divert it more completely towards the Basra customs house in the face of resistance from other regional centers. Resistance took the form of contraband activities aimed at smuggling goods across fluid borders (See Chapter Six) and resulted in the creation or reinvigoration of secondary market towns in order to compete with Basra. A few activist governors of the early to mid-nineteenth century mounted military campaigns in order to destroy the hold of local merchants on rural market towns; but the military control of once-independent economic centers usually coincided with the development of secondary ports of trade, which more than made up for the loss of other markets. Thus throughout the period in question, the success of regional traders came to depend upon the establishment of independent market towns, to provide an alternative to government-controlled trade and to reroute goods and people to less monitored economic centers. Since this activity posed a direct challenge to the monopolist policies of governments in the region, Ottoman strategy began to hinge on the total subjugation of regional commercial centers, rather than on their partial destruction, for new venues of trade were forever springing up to take the place of older ones, thus calling for increased governmental efforts at control. In order to see how these developments affected the progress of regional trade in the nineteenth century, we must trace the origin of all these issues.

TRIBAL SŪQS AND FREE PORTS: SŪQ AL-SHUYŪKH, KUWAIT, KHAMISIYYA, ZUBAIR, AND MUHAMMARA

Sūq al-Shuyūkh

The earliest and most sustained Ottoman efforts to divert or destroy local centers of trade were expended on the market towns belonging to the Muntafiq, the largest tribal confederation in the south of Iraq, and one of the wealthiest.[2] Sūq al-Shuyūkh was the most famous, and certainly the most venerable, of the Muntafiq market towns, having been built in the early eighteenth century. It was also the chief administrative and economic center of the various tribal sections that made up the Muntafiq confederation, and functioned as the seat of the

Saʿdūn leadership. Because it was an important local trade center in the region, controlled by a powerful tribal confederation scattered over a large territory, Sūq al-Shuyūkh was a prize coveted both by tribal shaikhs and Ottoman administrators. Viewed in some ways as the key to the Muntafiq, the town became the linchpin of Ottoman efforts to control the regional trade of lower Iraq.

Sūq al-Shuyūkh was instituted under the forceful guidance of the then paramount shaikh, Thuwaini, in the heyday of Muntafiq power in Iraq.[3] The traditions of the town were those of the mobile market town; for at its inception, Sūq al-Shuyūkh was nothing more than an easily-assembled tent city in which the market place was the central focus, and the point of assembly for town as well as rural merchants. By 1762, however, the town, which had been built on the right bank of the Euphrates with its back to the desert, became the most important market for the Muntafiq, functioning as the focal node of a tribal shaikhdom that controlled a vast area of southern Iraq.[4] In addition, Sūq al-Shuyūkh's strategic location at the edge of the river allowed it to command all access routes into the town; thus, in 1804, a local traveller observed that when the Persian army invaded Basra in 1776, and fanned out to occupy the remaining countryside, the Muntafiq allowed the Persians to approach all the way into Sūq al-Shuyūkh, only to cut the bridges at night, stranding the Persian army in enemy territory and routing it once and for all.[5]

Historians generally agree that the first steps toward the eventual dissolution of the Muntafiq mashyakha (chiefdom) took place in the years 1851 to 1855, when a four-year struggle to impose an Ottoman garrison in Sūq al-Shuyūkh finally came to fruition.[6] As a result of the bitter civil war that nearly tore the Muntafiq confederation apart, Manṣūr, a contender for the leadership of the tribe and government nominee, became the paramount shaikh. However, the events that brought about Manṣūr's accession to the Muntafiq mashyakha illustrate how government efforts, even those culminating in the installation of a military detachment in rural market towns, were often less a victory for Ottoman policymakers than a personal truimph for the tribal shaikhs.

In 1850, the government of Baghdad believed it could finally mount a successful campaign to defeat the Muntafiq, and set events in motion by supporting a member of the tribal leadership, Farīs ibn al-ʿAjīl, for the leadership of the tribe.[7] Farīs was immediately opposed by his cousin, Manṣūr, who commenced a three-year war for the position of qāʾim-aqām (district governor) of Sūq al-Shuyūkh, the "capital" of the Muntafiq territories. After twice losing Sūq al-Shuyūkh to Farīs, Manṣūr finally occupied it and had Farīs put to death, although the latter had had the support of government troops and was considered to be, in some ways, "a shaikh of the people."[8]

The government which, for reasons of its own, had not seen fit to send a force to pacify the region during the two years of internecine fighting in the Muntafiq, finally bestirred itself, and under Namīq Pasha sent "a body of 3,000 Irregular Horse to Hillah [half-way to Sūq al-Shuyūkh], and detachments of artillery and regular infantry marching to their support."[9] At this point, the Muntafiq shaikhs again made a sudden volte-face, with Manṣūr joining the Ottoman side while his brother, Nāṣir, who had been Manṣūr's loyal lieutenant in the fight against Farīs, deserted to form another military front. With the appearance of yet another contender for the Muntafiq leadership in the person of Nāṣir, a further struggle for the mashyakha took place, with Manṣūr now fighting the government's battle (and, not coincidentally, his own).

Just as the Baghdad government was congratulating itself on finally having picked the right nominee and secured its advantage in the confused politics of the Muntafiq civil war, however, a quick resolution of the conflict occurred when, according to British sources

> the two brothers, who had apparently been such bitter enemies [stopped fighting] and shared the revenue . . . each one sending servants of their own to collect the outlying claims of the shaikh. Nāṣir . . . surrounded by the Saᶜdūn and Shebeeb shaikhs [was joined] by the entire Muntafiq while the Turks evacuated the country without making a single example of any of the rebel leaders; or receiving compensation for the sacrifices made either in money, territory, hostages or guarantees. The garrison at Sūq al-Shuyūkh can have no importance as with the whole surrounding country in favor of the shaikhs, its tenure is of no value and nearly entirely dependent upon the acquiescence of the Arabs. . . .[10]

The volte-face on the part of the two warring brothers left the Ottoman contingent sent to help Manṣūr in the lurch, while the Muntafiq chiefs sealed their rift very rapidly. Thus the Baghdad government, which had first espoused the case of the earlier contender, Farīs, was met with a fait accompli when Manṣūr bested Farīs, and killed him in the process. The next best government strategy, namely, to support Manṣūr against Nāṣir, was again dealt a serious blow when the competing brothers made peace with each other and immediately extended their immense political and military hold over all the Muntafiq domains, leaving the woefully unprepared Ottoman garrison at Sūq al-Shuyūkh to operate in the shadow of the newly-established Muntafiq concordat. In this case, then, it is obvious that policies of centralization were often met with open resistance and were adhered to only when they suited the political interests of the governing Muntafiq shaikhs. For it was one thing to pledge submission to a governor of Baghdad or Basra, and another thing entirely to use a governor's system of appointments to concretize one's own position in domestic affairs.

It is possible, however, that as a result of the government's final legitimization of his position, Manṣūr agreed to allow parts of the vast Muntafiq dīra to be subdivided, for after his installation as shaikh, the first alienation of Muntafiq lands to the government took place. Thus, the district of Samawa was separated from the rest of tribal territory, and Shaikh Manṣūr's *badal mithāl* (government share of the revenue) was adjusted correspondingly.[11] From that point onwards, the process of alienation of the Muntafiq lands was constant and irreversible, and every shaikh after Manṣūr complied with the Ottoman ruling that allowed more Muntafiq districts to be separated from the greater whole.[12] Although the alienation of tribal lands was never embarked upon willingly, for it was always perceived as forced usurpation of communally-owned lands by the Muntafiq shaikhs, and although the government's policy had its share of stops and starts, never truly gaining momentum until the accession of shaikh Nāṣir ibn Rashīd al-Saᶜdūn to the Muntafiq leadership in 1861–69, the whole process was indicative of the steady encroachment of governmental authority in the countryside. Even so, there are conflicting accounts on the sums paid out by the ruling Muntafiq shaikhs as badal to the Baghdad authorities in the years following the civil war between the Saᶜdūn shaikhs. Although the cession of Muntafiq lands continued apace, detaching important revenue-producing territories from the hold of the ruling shaikhs, there is some question as to whether the badal payment was either correspondingly decreased or augmented as a result. On the one hand, we have the account of the historian Yaᶜqūb Sarkīs, whose father was Nāṣir Pasha al-Saᶜdūn's accountant, stating that the *sharatname* (contract of tenancy) granted to Shaikh Nāṣir in 1866 stipulated that the yearly badal was decreased to 4,338,875 qurūsh, and the badal for three years would amount to 13,016,625 qurūsh, which Nāṣir was to pay in installments to the Treasury.[13]

On the other hand, there is the version recorded by ᶜAbbās al-ᶜAzzāwī which intimates that prior to 1869 and the final dissolution of the mashyakha, the badal of the Muntafiq shaikhs was increased.[14] This is reaffirmed by various British consuls in Baghdad, who were in the habit of recording the slightest change in the Muntafiq's relations with the government.[15] Even while making allowances for British exaggeration and misinformation (or even disinformation, particularily concerning the routine descriptions of "Turkish oppression" dutifully sent out by consular officers to their superiors), it is obvious that the yearly auction of communally-held Muntafiq territories did lead to a gradual dismemberment of the Muntafiq territory, and that its most visible indication was the changing amounts required of the Muntafiq leadership as badal.

Still, it must be borne in mind that the question of tribal subordination to civil authority was often less the result of governmental coercion than of shaikhly self-interest. The whole issue primarily concerned the relations of the paramount shaikhs with the government, and had absolutely nothing to do with the rest of the tribal confederation. Thus even though government agents were sometimes afforded the chance to appoint their favorites to office,[16] examples from the long and troubled history of Ottoman-Muntafiq relations reveal that centralization—that is, the installation of a military detachment in the chief market town, the setting up of a customs house, the establishment of schools, mosque-*madrasas* (religious colleges, town municipalities, and so on—was contingent upon first resolving the battle among family members for the tribal leadership. Only after a victorious shaikh had manifested his superiority over his opponent were the formal trappings of government office acknowledged, and then only in a nominal fashion.

For instance, there is some evidence to show that Nāṣir Pasha, the catalyst for the settlement of the Muntafiq tribes in government-sponsored market towns in the last quarter of the nineteenth century, believed that by accepting the post of mutaṣarrif (district governor) of the Muntafiq liwa in 1869, he was *temporizing,* and in fact, playing along with the government until he could work out more advantageous terms for himself. Namīq Pasha's earlier experiment, in which he tried to forge an administrative unit out of the Muntafiq directly responsible to the government, failed because

> The current Amir or head of the family, Manṣūr Pasha, was coerced into accepting this policy and was appointed Qaimmaqam, but his brother Nāṣir rallied the tribes and forced Namīq to abolish the post of Qaimmaqam and restore the paramountcy (mashyakha) of the family. Namīq had to do this, but he retaliated by nominating not Nāṣir but his cousin and rival, Fahad, to the mashyakha. . . .[17]

With such a precedent, Nāṣir Pasha could not but be cautious in his dealings with the Ottoman bureaucracy in Baghdad. When in 1869 the governor Midḥat Pasha gave him the choice of either becoming a mutaṣarrif of a newly-carved out liwa (administrative district) and accepting the same badal as before [which remained the same, even though a large amount of lands were appropriated by the government], or facing an all-out government-led assault on the Muntafiq, Shaikh Nāṣir decided to bite the bullet and accept the compromise, in the hopes that circumstances would change in the future, affording him more leeway in the governance of the Muntafiq.[18] Another internal reason for Shaikh Nāṣir acquiescing in Midḥat Pasha's offer must have had to do with the emergence of the ʾAlbū Muḥammad tribes, and their usurpation of power, particularily in Muntafiq-held territories. As explained in Chapter Four, from the mid-1850s onwards these tribes became the competitors of the Muntafiq in riverine trade, serving notice that the latter were no longer the only tribe that could collect riparian taxes for the government. This was yet another blow to the Saʿdūn chiefs' commercial fortunes, and forced the latter to reformulate their traditional strategies with regard to government power.

In this context, the institution of a customs administration in Sūq al-Shuyūkh may be viewed as less the result of an imposed settlement and more a question of an uneasy partnership. While there is no hard evidence to corroborate this point, it is clear that the establishment of a government customs house in the Muntafiq, let alone its smooth administration, could not have been undertaken without a modicum of support from the ruling shaikhs of the district. Although the exact date of the setting up of this institution is uncertain, the indications are that it was a regular feature of the town by the 1850s, as were the barracks and the mosque-madrasa(s) set up after the Ottoman occupation of Sūq al-Shuyūkh. However, it is certain that by 1852 the Muntafiq customs house was fully operational and was being farmed by the paramount shaikh, for the British trade report of 1852 claims that

> goods intended for the Suq [al-Shuyukh] market, after paying the 5% import duty as laid down in the [Balta Liman] Tariff are, if intended for the Upper Euphrates . . . subject to five separate imposts which are collectively farmed by the Muntafiq shaikhs for the large sum of 60,000 piastres. Those forwarded for sale at Sūq al-Shuyūkh are, however, only subject to the dues levied . . . at Sūq al-Shuyūkh. . . .[19]

In theory, a fully-maintained, efficient customs administration prevailed upon regional traders to pay completely the duties on transit goods. While there is no information as to whether customs duty in the Muntafiq was evaded, as seemed to be the rule in other districts (see Chapter Three), the installation of a gumrugjī (tr *gümrükci,* customs master) in Sūq al-Shuyūkh and the operations of a formal customs administration never completely achieved its intended purpose, at least not in the beginning. For if the idea behind the erection of a gümrük in Sūq al-Shuyūkh was the attempt to control trade in a more efficient manner in the Muntafiq districts (and to redirect most of the revenue of the region towards Ottoman coffers), the effect was nullified by the competition of more active regional ports. The case of Kuwait is instructive in this regard.

Kuwait

Irrespective of increasing Ottoman efforts to establish some control over regional trade by breaking the Saᶜdūn shaikhs' hold over southern Iraq, Kuwait provided a ready alternative to blocked regional routes, remaining important as a coastal outlet for goods from the interior of Najd and southern Iraq, and as a conduit for Indian and East African commodities. As a result, the unrestricted commercial opportunities in Kuwait continued to attract regional merchants in droves. Consular sources noted as much in their dispatches to the Foreign Office:

> [Regional] goods are brought up by petty traders or by resident merchants on commission from Basra itself, and the amount would be greatly increased were it not for the neighbourhood of the free port of Kuwait which, nominally under Turkish rule, although actually independent of the Porte, acknowledges no

> other authority but that of their elected shaikhs. . . . Its port [is] accessible to ships of the largest burden, [and] is free to every flag . . . [Kuwait's] merchants are large ship-owners and from the perfect security of life and property, its resident traders are among the wealthiest in Iraq. From the entire absence of any import dues, they are enabled most advantageously to compete with the Basra merchants, and their goods, from the comparative lowness of their price, have always the preference of the Sūq al-Shuyūkh market. . . .[20]

Ottoman control may have been more efficient at capturing some of the trade and agricultural revenues within the immediate surroundings of Sūq al-Shuyūkh; and it is even possible that the institution of a customs house may have had the opposite effect of the one intended. The customs house may in fact have proved detrimental to the trade of the Muntafiq districts by restricting the merchant's independence as well as his margin of profit through the imposition of additional taxes and duties. And as always, the existence of free ports such as Kuwait, where goods were hardly taxed at all,[21] allowed regional traders enhanced opportunities to undersell their competitors at Sūq al-Shuyūkh.

Nonetheless, it should be noted that the problems Kuwait posed to Ottoman-controlled inland markets such as Sūq al-Shuyūkh were not insurmountable. In fact, Kuwait seemed to have continued to play the role of an *alternative* market, never completely supplanting the more central function occupied by Sūq al-Shuyūkh, especially with regard to the transit trade flowing in and out of the region. The latter's demise was to come about only with the emergence of Khamīsiyya and especially, Nāṣiriyya, of which more later. In other words, Kuwait's free trade tradition had an immediate, albeit short-lived impact on merchants in Iraq. For while Kuwait may have siphoned off some of the transit trade from Sūq al-Shuyūkh at the mid-point of the century, the latter was resilient enough to withstand this temporary setback. This is indicated by the fact that by the last quarter of the nineteenth century, Sūq al-Shuyūkh had cornered an increased share of the area's production and trade, and its revenues formed a major portion of the total output from the Muntafiq districts, a point discussed in more detail further on.

The free trade tradition that gave rise to Kuwait, however, is an important one to explore, for the question of alternatives to government control of primary markets is an important one and deserves further study. Even though British consular sources gave Kuwait only a marginal entry in the broader pattern of Gulf trade,[22] the phenomenon of just such an alternative in the continuously flexible system of regional exchange throws a great deal of light on nineteenth-century commercial networks. Just as in the eighteenth century, the period between 1830–80 witnessed the emergence of a number of secondary or alternative trade centers which sprang up to take over the commerce of blocked or temporarily inaccessible market towns. Kuwait is the prime example of an eighteenth-century port-town that survived into the nineteenth century, primarily by serving the needs of regional merchants for coastal access and a free and unregulated market for regional goods. However, other settlements further in the interior—such as Khamīsiyya and Zubair—were also established (or reestablished) at the turn of the century, and began to function as secondary ports for merchants negotiating land passage into central Arabia. Naturally, one of the chief incentives for rerouting trade to such tribal market towns was the non-existence of customs duties, a facet of regional trade that was shared by all free ports, whether on the coast or in the interior. However, other characteristics of tribal markets included the fact that these were often instituted by entrepreneurial shaikhs who saw them as good investments, either because the new settlements were strategically placed on well-frequented trade routes or because they possessed numerous wells, owned by the shaikh-founder's tribe.[23] As a result, the new settlement was quickly transformed into an elite town, with most of the property claimed by the shaikh-founder's family and his retinue; because poor tribesmen could not afford housing, they were often the last to benefit from the establishment or renovation of these tribal markets. Finally, even though the founders of these towns physically transplanted themselves and their supporters (including the tribe's chief merchants) from the desert to the town, the paramount shaikhs never completely gave up their desert ways, always keeping one foot in the hinterland by usually leaving a wife in the countryside (as well as the wife's family). Thus they kept the channels open, in case the new settlement failed for any number of reasons.

Khamīsiyya

Khamīsiyya, the "pearl of the desert," owed its inception to just such a development. Built in 1881 in southern Iraq by one ᶜAbdullāh al-Khamīs, a shaikh from the Qāsim district in Najd, its main purpose seemed to be to control the passage of goods from central Arabia into the mid-Euphrates region of lower Iraq.[24] Al-Dakhīl, a tribal historian, pointed out that al-Khamīsiyya grew out of purely commercial reasons, for it was completely settled by Najdī merchants interested in carving out a significant alternative to Sūq al-Shuyūkh, still the most important tribal market in the Muntafiq region of lower Iraq.[25] While Sūq al-Shuyūkh's fortunes with regard to Ottoman policies of centralization have already been discussed, the only significant point to add here is that Khamīsiyya's founder, ᶜAbdullāh al-Khamīs, was an ally of Fāliḥ al-Saᶜdūn, the last of the rebel Muntafiq shaikhs to take on the Ottoman government in the disastrous campaign of 1880–81 (also called the "Battle of the Ra'is"). As a result of the Muntafiq defeat, heralding the final dissolution of the tribal principality, many of the Muntafiq shaikhs and their allies fled to the Shāmiyya desert. Faced with the fact that Sūq al-Shuyūkh had once again become the headquarters of an Ottoman military detachment—a development totally inimical to the spirit of regional trade —and chastened the following year by the spectacle of the Euphrates in full flood devastating the Muntafiq districts[26], shaikhs, and merchants set about building a new market town to replace Sūq al-Shuyūkh. Thus al-Khamīsiyya was born. Its creation served not only to underline the continuing flexibility of a regional market dependent on alternative or secondary commercial outlets, but as the century progressed, it came to take the place of other tribal markets, including, ultimately, Sūq al-Shuyūkh itself.[27]

Other than paying the customary tithe to the paramount shaikh and disbursing the shaikh's share in commercial partnerships,[28] no additional payment was enforced on merchants entering Khamīsiyya to trade in regional goods. Thus, the development of Khamīsiyya as a free port in the outlying tribal regions allowed it easy and regular access by merchants, shaikhs, and peasants alike. Merchants went about their commercial activities unhampered by governmental or military supervision, and the town gradually began to attract a sizable community. Admittedly, however, the somewhat tenuous nature of tribal market towns, and their vulnerability to human as well as natural catastrophes, made for short-lived economic gains. Khamīsiyya, for instance, finally succumbed to Ottoman control at the turn of the century, and no less a tribal "expert" than Gertrude Bell reported that the town had become the headquarters of an Ottoman military corps in the first quarter of the twentieth century.[29] Interestingly, one version of Khamīsiyya's decline ties it to the emergence of the Ottoman customs house. According to al-ʿĀṣī, after the Ottoman government began to send out roving inspectors to the interior to impose customs duties on all the goods entering and exiting the town, most merchants forsook Khamīsiyya for Basra, and began to buy and sell their goods in the latter town because, i̱n the words of one merchant, "prices were standardized."[30] In all likelihood, Khamīsiyya's merchants suffered from a vice prevalent in most tribal markets, namely, price-gouging. For even though ʿAbdullāh al-Khamīs took no customs duties per se, he was known to swoop down on the central market and demand instant "taxes" from merchants and shopkeepers. Ironically, most merchants now preferred to take their chances with the Ottoman authorities in Basra rather than suffer the uncertainties associated with tribal marts, thus signalling a transformation in the economic climate of late nineteenth century Iraq (and Arabia).

Nevertheless, the incidence and regularity of the establishment of these market towns is supportive of the thesis that regional collaboration created new markets in the full face of governmental opposition. The institution of Khamīsiyya, for instance, was a direct reaction to the collapse of Sūq al-Shuyūkh, and the installation of an Ottoman military detachment in the lower Euphrates. Its creation allows us to conclude that blocked access to commercial centers was usually met with flexible solutions; rather than decline and fade away, trade was reinvigorated by means of the replication of free ports in the interior, and the creation of new routes.

Zubair

Besides the institution of new towns to replace existing ones, an additional development was the refurbishment of older trading towns. For example, the fortunes of Zubair revived in the mid-nineteenth century, under the pressure of a more heterogeneous population and a more varied social base. Built originally around the tomb of one of the early Companions of the Prophet, the town of Zubair lay eight miles southwest of Basra, and commanded the access roads to Najd. Initially a sleepy hamlet whose sole claim to fame rested with its sacred shrines,[31] Zubair was provided with the incentive to change its whole tenor of life in the early to mid-nineteenth century. As a result of the emergence of the Wahhābī movement, a number of tribal conflicts erupted in central Arabia, which led to mass migrations of disaffected, anti-Wahhābī tribesmen to southern Iraq; one of the towns which these Najāda settled in was Zubair. With the influx of these new migrants, the population of Zubair swelled, and trade began to flourish correspondingly.[32] The improvement in Zubair's fortunes was so marked that by the mid-nineteenth century, it not only gained the reputation of being the haven of the richest merchants in the region, but also drew extravagant praise from consular officials, who termed it "an opulent town."[33] Because Zubair commanded land passage into Najd and functioned as a ready alternative to Wahhābī domination of trade routes into central Arabia,[34] it developed quite rapidly into an important regional market. Significantly, the town also enforced a free economic climate, devoid of customs barriers. Consular officials waxed lyrical on its enormous advantages:

> Nominally dependent upon Turkish rule, [Zubair] acknowledges no shaikh unless a nominee or favorite of their most influential families and the supreme Government of Basra, unequal to the task of subjugation, tacitly acknowledges its sense of its own weakness and acquiesce in their nomination, although deploring the weakness which compels them from interfering more directly with the administration of government in the town, the possession of which they have so long and so secretly coveted. But this inability to extend the pernicious effects of Turkish rule to Zobeir has been in the highest degree beneficial to the mercantile interests of Basra. From the security engendered by its free and unrestricted form of government, it is a favorable route of the Bedu. . . . All resort there in large numbers during the winter and spring months to exchange supplies of grain, coffee, henna. . . . They come and go unmolested by Turkish officials and with their goods unhampered by restrictive exactions, the inevitable concomitant of their fiscal policy. . . .[35]

However, a number of problems having to do with the struggle for control of the political leadership of the town began to emerge in the early nineteenth century, which presaged the attempted takeover of Zubair by Ottoman officials. Again, the pattern of conflict and cooperation that marked developments at Sūq al-Shuyūkh is much in evidence with regard to Zubair. Here, too, Ottoman attempts to bring Zubair in line with government policies ended with mixed results.

Zubair's population was repopulated with Najdī settlers from the districts of Washm, Sudair, and especially from Ḥirma and Ḥarīmla.[36] The settlers from Ḥirma and Ḥarīmla quickly infiltrated Zubairī politics, forming powerful factions to influence the election of local shaikhs. Although local historians would have us believe that the leadership of Zubair was most often composed of democratically elected shaikhs representing a reconstituted, cohesive tribal "republic,"[37] events were not quite that simple. The traditional leaders of Zubair, and members of the family most often associated with Zubairī politics, were the Zuhairs, important merchants originally from Najd but in the nineteenth century having footholds in Aleppo and Basra as well. Even though they hailed originally from central Arabia, they looked askance at the new immigrants, and moved rapidly to offset the latter's mounting influence in the town. As a result of political friction between the two sides, factional divisions became common in Zubair, resulting in a wave of political assassinations in 1824 and 1827.[38] For a time, the Zuhair family retained its ascendancy in local politics, then in the period between 1830 to 1833, the anti-Zuhair faction reassembled themselves into a powerful coalition comprising disenfranchised Najdī merchants, shaikhs of the Muntafiq, the deputy governor of Basra, and the ruling ʾamīr of Kuwait, Shaikh Jābir. This coalition led a siege against the town, which only ended when the Muntafiq entered the town by stealth at night, and arrested ʿAbdul-Razzāq al-Zuhair and his brothers, thus extinguishing the family's power for several decades.[39]

Nevertheless, by the 1870s, the Zuhair family had made a comeback, in part due to expedient alliances made with Ottoman governors.[40] While these alliances were often made for political purposes, and were often broken the minute the Zuhair leadership felt the time was opportune to shake off Ottoman tutelage, they undoubtedly instilled a precedent. Clearly, such lapses in the local control of the town's affairs gave the Ottoman governors of Basra the incentive to interfere in Zubairī politics even more than was their usual wont. Thus while the Zuhairs seemed able to resist a too-close alliance with the Ottomans for part of the time, they were often dragged into local offshoots of the power struggle between Najdī settlers and Ottoman policymakers, and frequently suffered as a result.

In any event, the Zuhairs managed to stave off renewed challenges to their leadership until the mid-1870s. However, in 1874, the first direct Ottoman intervention took place, which resulted in a pitched battle between Ottoman troops and local forces outside the walls of the town. After that, for some reason the sources do not make quite clear, the Zuhairs shifted to a pro-Ottoman stance.[41] Part of the problem may have had to do with the capitulation of the Zuhair leadership to the Ottoman army even before the siege of Zubair began—a debacle which finally installed an Ottoman governor in the town and brought an end to unrestricted local control of Zubair. The Najdī element remained strong, however, long after the imposition of Ottoman control,[42] allowing only the strictest adherence to *Shafʿī* interpretations of commercial law, and forbidding the settlement of Christian or Jewish merchants until the beginning of the twentieth century. The evidence, slight as it is, nevertheless leads us to the conclusion that local forces continued to balance their interests against Ottoman designs up to the turn of the century.

In the examples given above—Sūq al-Shuyūkh, Kuwait, Khamīsiyya, and Zubair—a number of characteristics stand out clearly. First, none of these market towns operated in a vacuum. On the contrary, all of the commercial centers under discussion were interdependent and interacted within a regional context, subject to diverse forces emanating from within a wider region. Second, all of these market towns owed their initial raison d'être to the fact that they provided opportunities for an untaxed economic haven to tribal and urban merchants alike. Their smooth operation owed much to the laissez-faire attitude of regional merchants themselves. Third, as the case of Khamīsiyya illustrates, these free ports were often survival mechanisms, built to reinforce the tribal sector against the enveloping sweep of governmental centralization which, more often than not, was a city phenomenon. Lastly, Ottoman efforts to recapture regional markets were only partially successful, and when imposed, control was often nominal. Thus the period from 1830 to 1900 witnessed the recurring struggle to undermine regional centers in the face of continuous attempts by merchants to recreate these same centers elsewhere.

The struggle for Iraqī market towns occupied most of the efforts of late nineteenth century administrators, taking convoluted turns that culminated in mixed results. Nonetheless, Ottoman authorities were also anxious to restore other trading centers to their control; as it turned out, however, Ottoman centralist policies were equally uneven with regard to markets traditionally in the Ottoman sphere of interests, but which were now rapidly slipping out of their grasp. Muhammara is a case in point.

Muhammara

Up to the first third of the nineteenth century, Muhammara—and the districts to the north and east of it, the domain of the Kaʿab tribes—was considered to be under Ottoman jurisdiction. Ottoman valis in Iraq considered the area around the Haffar River and the whole length and breadth of the Shaṭṭ al-ʿArab as Ottoman territory, first given in grant to Basra notables by Sulṭān Selim in 1512, and later, in the eighteenth century, farmed out to Kaʿab shaikhs by Mamluk pashas.[43] It has been argued throughout this book that throughout the nineteenth century legal jurisdiction often did not correspond to practical reality, and that territorial sovereignty and political borders were murky issues, little appreciated either by tribesman, merchant, or ʿalim. It must be noted, however, that the Kaʿab tribes did pay heed to government demands for revenue; the only difference was that they paid their taxes to *both* the Ottoman and the Qajar authorities, using their political acumen to conciliate potentially aggressive adversaries and to ward off military campaigns from either government. Thus, even though British consular officials, themselves wary of Ottoman designs on Muhammara, confirmed Ottoman rights over the port (at least up to 1837), the actual occupants of the land, the Kaʿab tribes, paid taxes regularly to both governments and straddled the fence politically with regard to which sovereign power had the ultimate say in their districts. Moreover, throughout the eighteenth century and the early part of the nineteenth, the Kaʿab annexed adjoining territories at will, vacated others to which they had been assigned for tax purposes by the Ottoman government, and practiced a form of squatters' rights on lands which they had forcibly taken from other tribal parties or from the central government. Thus it is doubtful whether either the Ottoman or the Qajar government could claim de facto sovereignty over Muhammara and its adjoining districts, even though as far as the Ottomans were concerned, title to the land had been acquired as early as the sixteenth century.[44]

In 1837, an abrupt shift occurred in Muhammara's fortunes. The town had grown from a mud fort into an important market, vying for prominence both with Huwaiza (further north) and Basra. Under Shaikh Jābir al-Mirdāw, the port town soon began to siphon off some of the trade from both of these centers, leaving the Ottoman government of ʿAlī Pasha al-Lāz with no other recourse but to invade and occupy Muhammara. In the words of Rawlinson, the British Resident at Baghdad,

> ʿAlī Pasha of Baghdad, desirous of protecting Bussorah from any further injury to its revenues, considering Shaikh Jābir in no other light than as a servant of the Chaab [sic] and believing that the land on which Muhammara had been built was unequivocally Turkish property, marched against the place in 1837, took it by assault and plundered all of the merchandise that had been stored in its warehouses. . . .[45]

Because of the Ottoman invasion, a whole chain of events unfolded, which eventually resulted in the reoccupation of Muhammara by Persian troops and the subsequent opening up of negotiations on the frontier problem between Qajar Iran and Ottoman Turkey. While the frontier commissions dragged on, allotting jurisdiction of geographically hazy borders to either Ottoman Turkey or Qajar Iran, conditions on the ground very often negated the diplomatic gains wrested by either empire. For while in 1847 the Treaty of Erzerum awarded Muhammara, Abadan (Jazīrat al-Khiḍr), and the coastal strip of the eastern Shaṭṭ al-ʿArab inhabited by Persian-affiliated tribes to the Qajar state, in return for a free hand by the Ottomans in Kurdistan and northern Iraq, Shaikh Jābir al-

Mirdāw, and later on his sons Mizᶜal and Khazᶜal, successfully kept the Persian government at bay till the beginning of the twentieth century.

Looking at the question from the point of view of the Ottoman governors of Basra, these three shaikhs were responsible for transforming Muhammara into Basra's most serious commercial rival in the nineteenth century. While the evidence indicates that Muhammara's rise to commercial prominence only came about in the period between 1890 and 1900, that is to say, after the opening of the Karun River to British steamships,[46] the port continued to be portrayed as a direct threat to Basra's revenues, at least in the perception of Ottoman bureaucrats. In fact, under the adroit economic management of Shaikhs Mizᶜal and Khazᶜal, the enhanced position of Muhammara soon made it a point of contention between Ottoman authorities, British consuls, and governors of Arabistan. The Ottomans were so worried about Muhammara's commercial potential that they sent missions from Istanbul to gauge the damage that might be done to Basra's trade.[47] And their efforts at creating a modern navy to be stationed at the mouth of Basra harbor may be seen as a defensive move to counterbalance Muhammara's increased attraction as a secondary port of shipment for Gulf trade.[48]

But it was the free port aspect of Muhammara that worried the Ottomans most. The shaikhs of the town could afford to clear regional goods duty-free because they had become the customs masters of the town from 1840 onwards; they paid a sum of £8,000 to the Qajar government for the privilege, but it was calculated that they stood to gain profits equal to or surpassing that figure.[49] In the 1880s, for example, Shaikh Khazᶜal was not only legally entitled to import a variety of goods duty-free into Muhammara but, as a result of farming out the customs house at Ahwaz to the shaikhs of the Bawi tribe, the latter could export their wheat without paying any duties, "a hidden subsidy"[50] which Shaikh Khazᶜal undoubtedly profited from as well. Moreover, since it was illegal to import firearms into Persia, Shaikh Khazᶜal could score an additional coup by "legitimately confiscating all smuggled firearms which were shipped for his political rivals, [which were then] distributed to his own supporters."[51] For these, and other reasons, the ruler of Arabistan was adamantly against any revision of the customs agreement between him and the central government.

Moreover, not only were the Ottomans (and Persians) disturbed by Muhammara's functions as a free economic zone; British shippers, who faced an uphill struggle to ply their trade on the rivers of Muhammara, were also thwarted in their commercial designs. In Shaikh Mizᶜal's time (1881–97), the British firm of Stephen Lynch and Company faced countless commercial obstructions imposed by the governor of Muhammara himself, chiefly because the latter wanted to keep the monopoly of riverine transport in his hands and the control of Muhammara's wheat reserves as his prerogatives.[52]

Because Muhammara was viewed as Basra's most dangerous competitor in the Gulf, the town became the object of Ottoman sanctions in the nineteenth century. The sanctions consisted of the following two-pronged strategy: first, the Ottoman bureaucracy of Basra tried to impose customs duty on Muhammara, and second, they attempted to tax all ships entering the Shaṭṭ al-ᶜArab, and in some cases, those proceeding only to Muhammara. Thus in October 1893, the British Consul-General in Baghdad sent an urgent despatch to his superiors, notifying them that the Ottoman authorities in Basra had decided to levy import and export duties on Muhammara, which the British generally viewed as a clear breach of the status quo in the Gulf. At the same time, the consul let it be known that the local government in Basra was obliging Indian vessels to undergo twenty-four hours' observation in the cholera-infected port of Fao, even though some had arrived from a "clean" port like Karachi. However, under heavy British pressure, the muscle-flexing at Muhammara was discontinued a month later, and the Ottomans withdrew their insistence on collecting duty at the port. Redoubling their efforts, Ottoman authorities now focused their attention on the issue of the quarantine, and attempted to exploit loopholes in internationally-drafted agreements on health and sanitation measures in order to detain Indian-owned, Muhammara-bound ships entering the Shaṭṭ al-ᶜArab.[53]

Sensing a danger to their commercial position, British authorities undertook stern measures to curb this new Ottoman policy. On 24 October 1894, the consul at Basra memoed to the consul at Baghdad that the Ottoman authorities in Basra were insisting on the production of customs certificates from British-Indian merchants sailing into the Gulf; that, in the absence of these, merchants had to leave their ships either at Fao or Muhammara and find persons of sufficient standing to furnish security that the customs receipts would be duly produced; and that, once ships were left idling in the Gulf, they were invariably at the mercy of "pirates" who demanded "blackmail" on goods brought from India. The consular official, Belville, intimated that it was only the presence of the British man-of-war, the *Lapwing,* that provided protection for British-Indian merchants, and that the vessel should be more or less permanently stationed at Basra to keep river brigands (and perhaps Ottoman customs masters) at bay throughout the date season.[54] Nevertheless, at least up to 1898, Ottoman customs masters kept up their policy of harassing British-Indian vessels by forcing them to pay a double duty as soon as they entered the Shaṭṭ. Eventually, however, Ottoman efforts to dislocate British trade, as well as Muhammara's finances, proved only partially successful, and, again under British pressure, were finally discontinued by the early twentieth century.

The final, and most telling, blow occurred in 1902 when Shaikh Khazᶜal formally submitted to a Persians customs administration. The change had been coming for some time. As a result of the gradual dissolution of customs farming throughout Persia from 1897 onwards, the central government decided to institute a system of direct revenue collectior.. Although Shaikh Khazᶜal resisted the change at first, he was eventually forced to accept the imposition of a Belgian-administered customs department, of which he was to become the titular head, in return for which he was to be compensated by the grant of "virtual title to the bulk of the remaining crown estates in the province."[56] Even though the agreement went some way towards placating the shaikh, the fact that Khazʿal had accepted the external supervision of Muhammara's financial administration indicated that he had been bypassed by the new developments; it indicated that the beginnings of a centralized national government was in the offing and that Khazʿal was no longer master of his fief. In fact, the shaikh was the last of the truly independent shaikhs of ʿArabistan.

The imposition of a centralized customs administration in Muhammara dealt a severe blow to Ottoman policies of centralization and further aggravated the nature of government control in the region. Efforts to control interior markets and free ports were problematic and, more often than not, highly uneven. They succeeded in some places (such as Sūq al-Shuyūkh and much later, in Khamīsiyya) but failed dismally in others. In order, therefore, to capture a portion of the regional trade circulating in interior markets, Ottoman authorities decided on a novel, and more aggressive approach. This consisted in the establishment of government-sponsored towns in the interior, which forms the subject of the next section.

GOVERNMENT TOWNS: ʿAMĀRA AND NĀṢIRIYYA

ʿAmāra

That Ottoman authorities resorted to another settlement policy in the late nineteenth century is attested to by the proliferation of government towns in the riverine areas of southern Iraq. The two best examples are those of ʿAmāra and Nāṣiriyya. Undoubtedly, the most successful venture on the Tigris was ʿAmāra, a town that developed out of military camp *(urdū)* to become a major center for riverine trade and export-oriented agriculture.[56] Rebuilt in 1862 on an ancient site by Ottoman engineers, ʿAmāra grew so rapidly that it attracted many hundreds of settlers from within Iraq and from across the Shaṭṭ al-ʿArab, specifically from Arabistan.[57] The Ottoman authorities in Iraq deliberātely threw the district open to any farmer who wanted to avail himself of a free plot of land and accessability to water; moreover, they devised "easy customs regulations as well as other facilities," so much so that, as late as 1891 [three years after the Karun River was officially opened up for traffic], most of Muhammara's foreign trade was still being channeled through ʿAmāra itself.[58] In fact, the latter town became such a successful venture that in the 1880s, it was estimated that close to 1,000 families had migrated from Dizful (northern Arabistan) alone.[59]

ʿAmāra served as a successful channel by which the Ottomans could recapture some of the trade that was being rerouted elsewhere, and showed that the Ottoman policy of creating new markets instead of expanding their energies on recapturing older ones was vindicated. For whereas the older markets of Sūq al-Shuyūkh, Zubair, and Kuwait were difficult to control and to reassimilate into the Ottoman fold, ʿAmāra was strategically placed on the Tigris and able to oversee all of the cargo-laden traffic on the river. Moreover, the town boasted an active customs administration and a quay to unload goods passing downstream, which served to capture a share of the transit trade as well or better than the inland markets.[60] ʿAmāra also contributed towards the transit trade by growing two important cash crops, rice and grain. The Ottomans favored rice over all other food grains in the 1870s, to the point where they forbade by imperial fiat the sale of rice lands in Iraq as detrimental to the imperial treasury.[61] By the late nineteenth century, ʿAmāra had become such valuable agricultural land that it was incorporated into Sulṭān Abdul-Hamid's domains as the property of the Crown; and as a result, it became one of the better-managed districts of lower Iraq.

The British focus on ʿAmāra was equally significant. British traders rarely ventured inland to buy or barter goods from the tribes or rural merchants, but ʿAmāra's improved facilities for transport and its situation on the river made it easily accessible to foreign merchants and therefore conducive to better business. In addition, the British firm of Stephen Lynch and Company had bought choice property on the waterfront in the early part of the century (Miʿqal, near Basra),[62] and was rapidly making inroads in riverine trade. By the end of the nineteenth century, Lynch and Company was busy solidifying its hold on the Tigris. ʿAmāra served foreign interests well, because its peasants grew grain and rice—the two principal cash crops of the riverine Arabs—which British merchants had begun to trade in and ship heavily in the 1860s. For all these reasons, the town began to function as a *point d'appui* for British merchant houses eager to become established in direct trade with the regional merchants that flocked to the new markets of ʿAmāra.

Notwithstanding the town's ideal location, and its superb facilities for the export of regional goods, however, ʿAmāra's tribal periphery—which was responsible for the production of cash crops—was often a problem in itself. Throughout the nineteenth century, ʿAmāra's most important tribal confederations, the ʾAlbū Muḥammad and the Banū Lām were constantly warring against each other, or fighting among themselves. The chief cause for tribal disturbances on the eastern Tigris was, of course, land, and more importantly, the ownership of choice grain or rice-growing property. Here, however, the role that Ottoman authorities played with regard to the control and redistribution of property was radically different from that of the Muntafiq. Suffice to say that in the 1860s, the governor of Baghdad, Namīq Pasha, tried to disestablish the traditional system of landholding by introducing annual auctions of leases, in order to create dissension among the shaikhs, and so gradually loosen their hold over the tribal districts. But "the end result was near-anarchy, the tribes refused to pay the new land rents, and raids and interference with the river traffic increased."[63]

As a result, Namīq established a defensive belt of garrison towns along the river, including ʿAmāra. While the tribes of ʿAmāra were the first to appreciate the merits of export agriculture (having seen its benefits in the form of larger profits), the fact that the Ottoman administration could manipulate the annual auction of leases and reward only those shaikhs that followed the Ottoman line made for increased friction between tribal chiefs. This may also have caused trouble for British shippers who not only faced obstacles to their trade thrown up by rebellious shaikhs on the river, but also extraordinary delays in the shipment of cash crops to India and Europe. Nevertheless, Ottoman bureaucrats had an easier time controlling trade routes leading to and from ʿAmāra, simply because the town's unparalleled situation on the river, and its lack of a major hinterland made for more direct access to production.

Nāṣiriyya

Another successful venture was the creation in 1870 of Nāṣiriyya, in the Muntafiq districts. As recounted above, Shaikh Nāṣir al-Saʿdūn (who gave his name to the new settlement) had been prevailed upon by Midḥat Pasha, governor of Iraq from 1869 to 1871, to accept the title of mutaṣarrif of the Muntafiq, which now became a liwā (a subdivision of a province). As a result of Shaikh Nāṣir's cooperation in the settlement of the Muntafiq tribes, a number of small towns were built (of which Nāṣiriyya was the most important), and it was in this period that the government first began to alienate communally-held lands to the Muntafiq shaikhs.[64]

Nāṣiriyya became the showpiece of a successfully-managed tribal administration in southern Iraq. Built by a Belgian engineer and staffed by Ottoman bureaucrats of various ethnic origins, it became a *markaz-qaḍāʾ* (headquarters) of the Muntafiq sanjaq in the 1880s, and its shaikhs were correspondingly transformed into pashas. Moreover, a division of niẓām troops was headquartered there, under the command of an ʾamīr liwā. Interestingly, Nāṣir Pasha's chief accountant was Niʿmatullāh (Naʿūm) Sarkīs, an Aleppo-born Christian who had become the second largest proprietor in the town after the shaikh.[66] With the inception of Nāṣiriyya, the older market of Sūq al-Shuyūkh began a steep decline, from which it was never to recover. At first, however, Sūq al-Shuyūkh held its own, and even outstripped Nāṣiriyya's revenues. Since the volume of trade of both towns was duly registered in Turkish customs ledgers, a quick survey of Turkish statistics will show this development more fully. In the period between 1868 and 1872, the years in which Nāṣir, the paramount shaikh of the Muntafiq assumed the governership of the mutaṣarrifiyya of the district, Sūq al-Shuyūkh's trade figures in their totality were consistently higher than in any other district in the province of Basra, with the exception of Basra itself. Thus over a period of four years, the revenues of the Muntafiq came to 88,508 qurūsh, while that of the newly-established qaḍāʾ of Nāṣiriyya amounted to 26,973 qurūsh, the *nahiyas* of Wasit to 12,283 qurūsh, and that of al-Shatra to 31,781 qurūsh. This effectively allowed Sūq al-Shuyūkh to contribute 55.5% of the revenues of the province.[66] It should be kept in mind that these statistics were calculated and registered at a later period, that is, after the paramount shaikhs of the Muntafiq began to collaborate more fully in the collection of revenue, and to set up wider alliances with government officials. Moreover, inspite of the fact that Ottoman governmental intrusion in Muntafiq affairs led to disruptions in the traditional system of revenue-gathering, bringing about a rapidly growing rift between the Saᶜdūn shaikhs and the peasants of the Muntafiq, the growth of a new intermediary class of rich peasants, the *sarkals,* brought the Muntafiq districts more closely within the Ottoman orbit, and thus facilitated the collection of a measure of the annual taxes in kind for the state.[67]

By the 1880s, however, the importance of Nāṣiriyya had become so pronounced that it attracted settlers from all over the Muntafiq, as a result of which the population swelled to 55,000 inhabitants, a remarkable feat in the twelve years of its existence.[68] Soon, Nāṣiriyya began to surpass Sūq al-Shuyūkh, the older "capital" of the Muntafiq, in terms of prosperity and population, and in fact eventually subsumed it altogether. In effect, Nāṣiriyya sealed Sūq al-Shuyūkh's fate, for by becoming the headquarters of the vast Muntafiq liwāᵓ, it redirected Sūq al-Shuyūkh's trade and siphoned off the administrative talents and commercial skills of rural bureaucrats and resident merchants alike. While Sūq al-Shuyūkh did not exactly "die on the vine," it clung to a tenuous existence so that by the beginning of the twentieth century, a noted authority on Najdī affairs could say of the town:

> In the year 1871, the Suq became a qaḍāᵓ and [from that period onwards] it began to decline . . . so that in 1897, it even became a *mudiriya* [lesser administrative district] even though it still possessed a Qaimmaqam. And this was because of its decline and its lack of prosperity, and its regression. . . . The reasons [for this state of affairs] was that the Arab tribes stopped frequenting it, as well as the unhealthiness of its soil, and the many diseases that infected its inhabitants because it was close to the marshes. . . .[69]

A sad indicator of Sūq al-Shuyūkh's decline was that its population decreased to 4,000 in the last quarter of the nineteenth century. In Shaikh Thuwainī's time, in the 1780s, the town had had a population of 12,000, and was better maintained, so that the flood waters of the Euphrates and the malarial climate of the marshes failed to make a dent in its fortunes.[70] When Nāṣiriyya took over Sūq al-Shuyūkh's position, it finally brought an end to that most vital of market towns, emphasizing in the process that the Ottoman struggle to control economic centers in the interior was a long, arduous and costly venture, undertaken with little guarantee of success or material rewards. There can be no doubt that the process was helped along by shaikhs interested in making the most of government alliances for their own reasons, for without important support from the local stratum, all centralization efforts in the nineteenth century would have been doomed.

CONCLUSION

The complexities of governmental intrusion in the free play of regional trade in the nineteenth century have been imperfectly pieced together in the past, and have led to some wooly generalizations made by state-focused historians, which seem not altogether appropriate to the socioeconomic dynamics of a *region*. Some historians have posited the argument that the economies of nineteenth century Iraq, Arabia, and the Gulf were based on subsistence agriculture, which failed to generate enough surplus to propel these economies into the take-off stage for capitalism. "Simple" trade relations coupled with subsistence agriculture were not enough incentives for the development of an independent bourgeoisie.[71] A corresponding thesis is that Iraqī productivity was largely frittered away through tribal uprisings, governmental corruption, and fragmentation of political control. As a result, the rural sector—composed of undifferentiated tribes—enveloped the cities and suffocated any form of nascent urbanism. The growth and extension of cities did not occur until the advent of Midḥat Pasha, the "reformist" governor of Iraq, as "dozens of settlements spread throughout tribal areas during the last quarter of the nineteenth century, gradually tilting the rural balance in favor of the urban areas."[72]

The argument that conditions in both provinces mitigated against the emergence of a productive rural and urban sector, which hampered the growth of indigenous capitalism and the spread of towns, leads to the concomitant thesis that Arabia and Iraq were unequipped to create an entrepreneurial and administrative infrastructure on their own. As a result, the development of towns in the countryside had to await the renewed resolve of Ottoman governors and Saʿūdī modernizers, as well as the emergence of centralized political control in the Arabian interior and the Iraqī countryside. However, this chapter has shown that contrary to the standard interpretation, merchant capital was indeed ploughed back into the region, and reinvested especially into the building of towns. Even as early as the mid-eighteenth century, regional entrepreneurs built towns as enduring as Kuwait and Sūq al-Shuyūkh; by the nineteenth century, the proliferation of free ports both in the desert as well as on the coast continued to siphon off regional trade towards local markets and away from Ottoman-controlled venues. In fact, some independent market towns were even built at the height of Ottoman centralization in the countryside. Khamīsiyya was just such a venture, having been established in the same period when the most powerful tribal confederation in southern Iraq, the Muntafiq, had been broken by the force of Ottoman arms. Thus while the last decades of the nineteenth century have usually been described as the period in which the goals of "Ottomanization" proceeded at full tilt, marking the last time in which local forces could influence turn of events in the region, Khamīsiyya disproves that point in rather spectacular fashion. While it may have been the last gasp of the regional market, and established too late to make an impact, its institution serves notice that independent market towns were being built at the height of Ottoman centralization for purely mercantile reasons. Even though Khamīsiyya was soon taken over by an Ottoman garrison, the fact that it was built at all is an illustration of the resilience of the regional market, which took its cue from the local forces of production and capital in the region.

Afterword

By 1900, the regional market that had been established in Iraq, Arabia, and the Gulf had been subsumed into the global economy. The autonomy of regional merchants had been shattered and their independence of action irredeemably impaired. Instead of controlling the distribution and exchange of regional commodities, local merchants now became valuable intermediaries who bargained, paid for, and shipped the product to British-controlled Bombay or Manchester on behalf of European firms. In the words of Batatu:

> the bulk of the once-independent Moslem merchants, if they had not gone under, had—even when competing against commission agents and trading in English machine-made goods on their own accounts, or helping only indirectly in the propagation of these goods—become in essence merchant-intermediaries or client-merchants, mere cogs on the rim of England's imperial economic wheel. . . .[1]

It is our contention that the transformation that reduced regional tujjār into "merchant-intermediaries" or "client-merchants" has been unduly stressed in the secondary literature on nineteenth-century Iraq, Arabia, and the Gulf. Little attention has been paid to the inception and organization of a regional market that bought, sold, and transported agricultural goods and livestock to India before the advent of steam engines or rail transportation. Certain features of the regional market, notably the emergence of free ports and the institution of trade monopolies, deserve further study because they were developments indigenous to the region, and seem to have coexisted in an uneasy but nonetheless working symbiosis. While the total control of trade and transport by pre-industrial states and societies most probably was never an issue seriously entertained by local rulers of the period (the permeability of frontiers, and the instability of the political climate mitigated against such a reality), the temporary control of routes and revenue may have well been within the realm of the possible. Thus, the question must be posed as to whether the institution of a regime of monopolies, short-lived though it may have been, formed an essential component of long-distance commerce, and eventually sowed the seeds for the formation of an regional market. In this respect, a reading of the revisionist literature on the Indian Ocean is fundamental to the reformulation of indigenous systems of trade and transport in Iraq, Arabia, and the Gulf.

Second, "modernization" theorists have made too much of the impact of the West on the region. Not enough has been said of the resistance movements and oppositional currents that slowed, if only for a brief historical moment, the entry of British capital in the region. In fact, British efforts to control regional trade in the nineteenth century were met with a variety of responses, some violent, others less so. One reaction was the spread of hostilities in the riverine areas of Iraq, as shaikhs and merchants fought against the introduction of British steam transport on the twin rivers. Other confrontational methods employed were urban insurrections against the export of food, and the circumvention of the articles of the Balta Liman Treaty by means of tax evasion at customs houses. But perhaps the most important strategy of all was the establishment and renovation of market towns by merchants and rural notables at certain critical periods in the regional economy's development, which gave local trade additional impetus in the face of foreign challenges.

Third, the question of governmental centralization in the nineteenth century has been given undue weight by historians. Judging from the evidence collected in this book, Ottoman behavior in the provinces of Iraq, and later in the northern Gulf, never really approximated the classic version of the "brutal Turk" prevalent in Orientalist literature (or that of Arab textbooks of the early twentieth century, for that matter). No Ottoman official could afford to alienate the important sectors of Iraqī/Gulf society by excessive coercion, extortion, or venality; there were always ways to escape official mistreatment or to alleviate governmental excess. One method—sometimes used only as a last resort—was for merchants physically to uproot themselves to other markets in the region, following, in the tradition of other tribal clans and sections who chose to "secede" from their settlements of origin when climatological or military adversity destroyed their options, and join the large transnational community scattered from coastal Arabia to western India. While the diasporic merchant communities of the Indian Ocean may have had divergent reasons for coalescing into self-contained societies across Asia, they shared elements with other heterogeneous communities in ambivalent self-exile in that they were

> deployed in transnational networks built from multiple attachments, and they encode practices of accommodation with, as well as resistance to, host countries and norms. Diaspora is different from travel (though it works through

> travel practices) in that it is not temporary. It involves dwelling, maintaining communities, having collective homes away from home (and in this it is different from exile, with its frequently individualistic focus). Diaspora discourse articulates, or blends together, both roots and routes to construct what Gilroy describes as alternate public spheres, forms of community consciousness and solidarity that maintain identifications outside the national time/space in order to live inside, with a difference. Diaspora cultures are not separatist, though they may have separatist or irredentist moments. . . . Thus the term diaspora is a signifier, not simply of transnationality and movement, but of political struggles to define the local, as distinctive community, in historical contexts of displacement.[2]

Over and above the fact that fleeing merchants depleted the government's resource base, and added to the already large deficit in the provincial treasury, government officials could not but tread lightly with the tax- and revenue-producing elements in society. The local machinery of government was, in many ways, oiled by provincial notables and merchants, to whom Mamluk and later Ottoman officials turned to for indispensable assistance and succour. If the vali were to recompense himself for having paid a large *badal* to Istanbul for the post of governor of Baghdad or Basra (an important priority for all officeholders in nineteenth-century Iraq), he had to enter into local alliances: for without local support, no government official could hope to extract the bare minimum of revenue from the provinces of Iraq.

One of the reasons for this lopsided equation was the reality of government tenure in Iraq. In terms of economic influence, the vali was far less influential than local merchants in any number of economic activities. For instance, the control of the grain-producing districts adjoining Baghdad was in the hands of grain merchants and rural shaikhs; if the vali were to make any sort of profit from the grain trade, he had to choose his local allies well. Even then, he was invariably at a disadvantage. The evidence relating to the Najīb Pasha's tenure in government shows that the vali was only one of many tax-farmers/monopolists of the province, and not necessarily the richest one. He was as much in need of local allies as state-affiliated merchants needed him. In fact, the question then poses itself: *why* did state-affiliated merchants answer to the vali in this instance? In view of the paucity of material, we can only surmise an answer. Quite simply, it may have been the governor's ill-equipped, poorly paid but nonetheless adequate fighting force that allowed the vali an edge over his competitors. For even though the standard of the niẓām troops had been considerably improved from the middle of the nineteenth century onward, the Sixth Army Corps was still considered to be a rag-tag army by its end: ill-clothed, ill-shod, and barely able to muster full company strength in a defensive war against tribal irregulars. Nonetheless, they could still be very effective against unarmed merchants and landholders, who almost always were at the government's mercy in these situations. However, force was always used as a last resort. Guile, flattery, and persuasion were preferred; only when that failed did the poisoned cup of coffee become a real alternative in the troubled relations between Ottoman valis and tribal shaikhs.

Notes

INTRODUCTION

1. K. N. Chaudhuri. *Trade and Civilization in the Indian Ocean: An Economic History from the Rise of Islam to 1750.* Cambridge: Cambridge University Press, 1985, 34–79.

2. For an exposition of this argument, see the late Muḥammad Salmān Hasan's "The Role of Foreign Trade in the Economic Development of Iraq, 1864–1964: A Study in the Growth of a Dependent Economy" in M. A. Cook, ed. *Studies in the Economic History of the Middle East* (London: Oxford University Press, 1970) and his *Al-tatawur al-iqtisadi fi al-Iraq; Al-tijara al-kharijiyya wa al-tatawur al-iqtisadi, 1864–1958,* (2 vols., Sidon and Beirut: Al-Maktaba al-Asriya li al-Tibaʿa wa al-Nashr, 1965).

3. Philip D. Curtin. *Cross-Cultural Trade in World History.* Cambridge: Cambridge University Press, 1984, 3.

4. Arasaratnam. "Recent Trends in the Historiography of the Indian Ocean, 1500 to 1800" in *The Journal of World History,* Vol. I, no. 2, 1990, 226.

5. Ibid., 228.

6. Sanjay Subrahmanyam. "The Portuguese, the port of Basrur, and the rice trade, 1600–50" in Sanjay Subrahmanyam, ed. *Merchants, Markets and the Early State in Early Modern India.* Delhi: Oxford University Press, 1990, 19.

7. An international symposium on "The State, Decentralization and Tax-Farming, 1500–1850: The Ottoman Empire, Iran and India" was held in Munich on 2–5 May 1990.

8. See Chaudhuri, op. cit.; and by the same author, *Asia Before Europe.* Cambridge: Cambridge University Press, 1991.

9. André Wink. "Review Article: World Trade, Merchant Empires and the Economy of the Indian Ocean" in *The International History Review* XV, i, February 1993.

10. Chaudhuri. *Trade and Civilization,* 21.

11. Edmund M. Herzig. "Hormuz" in *Bulletin of the British Society for Middle Eastern Studies.* Vol. 12, no. 1, 1985, 11.

12. Ibid., 8.

13. Subrahmanyam. op. cit., 18–47.

14. Ibid., 44.

15. Sanjay Subrahmanyam and C. A. Bayly. "Portfolio Capitalists and the Political Economy of Early Modern India" in *Subrahmanyam*. op. cit., 259.

16. Ibid., 247.

17. Ibid., 262.

18. Dina Rizq Khoury. "Merchants and Trade in Early Modern Iraq" in *New Perspectives on Turkey*, nos. 5–6, Fall 1991, 70–82.

19. Ibid., 70.

20. Anne Pérotin-Dumon. "The Pirate and the Emperor: Power and the Law on the Seas, 1450–1850" in James D. Tracy, ed. *The Political Economy of Merchant Empires: State Power and World Trade, 1350–1750*. Cambridge: Cambridge University Press, 1991, 200–6.

21. Ibid., 222.

22. C. A. Bayly. *Imperial Meridian: The British Empire and the World, 1780–1830*. London and New York: Longman, 1989.

23. Ibid., 54–55.

24. Ibid., 72.

25. Niewenhuis believes that "the wider integration of market and agricultural products was blocked by bad transportation and hindered by natural and political factors. Periods of succession, plagues or warfare could demolish all the movements realized before." See Tom Niewenhuis. *Politics and Society in Early Modern Iraq: Mamluk pashas, Tribal Shaykhs and Local Rule Between 1802 and 1831*. The Hague: Martinus Nijhoff Publishers, 1982, 111.

26. See Curtin. op. cit., 32–42; and Chaudhuri *Trade and Civilization*, 20.

27. See al-Haidari's description of the rich merchant al-Haj Nuʿman al-Pachachi: ". . . And he amassed more money than any other person in his time." ʾIbrāhīm ibn Sabghatullah al-Haidari. *Kitab ʿunwan al-Majd fi Bayan Ahwal Baghdad Basra wa Najd*. (Basra: Dar Manshurat al-Basri, n.d.), 100.

28. See Hasan, op. cit., 34–35, 71, 87–89 and Charles Issawi, "Notes on the Trade of Basra, 1800–1914" in *Journal of Turkish Studies*, Vol. 10, 1986, 167–74.

29. For an example of the "dependency" argument, see Hasan, op cit., 346–72.

1. A REGIONAL WORLD: 1745–1900

1. On this subject see, for instance, the interesting article by Michael Bonner. "The Naming of the Frontier: ʿAwasim, Thughur and the Arab Geographers" in *Bulletin of the School of Oriental and African Studies*, Vol. LVII, Pact I, 1994, 17–24.

2. See al-Haidari. *Kitab unwan al-majd*, 179–80, 190–93.

3. For an analysis of these fundamental Islamic concepts, see James P. Piscatori. *Islam in a World of Nation-States*. Cambridge: Cambridge University Press, 1986, 40–75.

4. William H. McNeill. *Europe's Steppe Frontier, 1500–1800*. Chicago: University of Chicago Press, 1964; and *The Great Frontier: Freedom and Hierarchy in Modern Times*. Princeton: Princeton University Press, 1983.

5. Peter Sahlins. "Natural Frontiers Revisited: France's Boundaries since the Seventeenth Century" in *The American Historical Review*, Vol. 95, no. 5, December 1990,

1423–35; and R. J. W Evans. "Essay and Reflection: Frontiers and National Identities in Central Europe" in *The International History Review,* Vol. XIV, no. 3, August 1992.

6. Ibid., 1426.
7. Ibid., 1433.
8. Ibid., 1435.
9. Evans, op. cit., 480–81.
10. Ibid., 482.
11. Ibid., 484–85.
12. Ibid., 489.
13. Ibid., 491.
14. Ibid., 493.
15. Ibid., 495.
16. MacNeill. *Europe's Steppe Frontier,* 13.
17. Ibid., 33–47.
18. Ibid., 54–66.
19. Ibid., 89.
20. According to shaikh Yasin al-ʿUmarī, he only "recorded the biographies of wazirs, ʿulamāʾ, ʾamīrs and poets . . . because the others were but merchants and members of artisanal corporations and there is no advantage to recording the latter's biographies." See Shaikh Yasin al-ʿUmarī. *Ghayat al-maram fi tarikh mahasin Baghdad Dar al-Salam.* Baghdad: Basri Press, 1968, 322.
21. Shaikh ʿUthmān ibn Bishr. *Unwan al-majd fi tarikh Najd.* Vol. 1, Riyāḍ: Maktabat al-Riyāḍ al-Haditha, n.d. 121–22, 130–31, 133–34, 135–38, 141–46.
22. Ibid.
23. Al-Haidari devotes a great deal of space describing Abadan, Dawraq [Fallahiya] and Muhammara, all towns in Arabistan. Moreover, his regional history encapsulates the districts of Najd, Kuwait, Basra and Muhammara in a regional framework that had little to do with the more rigid political boundaries usually associated with either Iraq or Iran. See al-Haidari. op. cit., 179–83. See also ʾAḥmad Nur al-Din al-Ansari. "Al-nasra fi akhbar al-Basra," Parts I–II, edited by Yūsuf Izzidin in *Majallat al-Majmaʿ al-Ilmi.* Vols. 17–18, 1969, 198–99.
24. Shaikh Husain ibn Ghannam. *Tarikh Najd aw rawdat al-afkar wa al-afham li-murtad hal al-Imam wa ghazawat dhuwa al-Islam.* Vol. 1 (Riyāḍ: Privately published by shaikh Abdul-Muhsin ibn ʿUthmān Aba Butain, 1949), 10.
25. I am indebted to my colleague at U.C.L.A., Dr. ʿAbdullāh Mutawa for this aphorism.
26. The most important work on this subject is still in dissertation form. See Uwaidah Metaireek al-Juhany. "The History of Najd Prior to the Wahhābīs: A Study of Social, Political and Religious Conditions in Najd During Three Centuries Preceding the Wahhābī Reform Movement." Ph.D. dissertation, University of Washington, 1983.
27. Ibid., especially al-Juhany's Chapters Three to Six.
28. Ibid., 108–12.
29. Ibid., 115.
30. Ibid., 126–30.
31. Ibid., 130.
32. Ibid., 136–41.

33. Ibid., 153–54.

34. ʾIbrāhīm ibn Salih ibn Isa. *Tarikh baʿḍ al-hawadith al-waqiʿa fi Najd wa wafiyat baʿḍ al-aʿyan wa anssabahum wa bina' baʿḍ al-buldan*. Riyāḍ: Dar al-Yamama press, 1966, 30.

35. Ibid., 31.

36. Ibid., 36–53.

37. For the clearest description of this phenomenon, see Peter Lienhardt. "The Authority of Shaykhs in the Gulf: An Essay in Nineteenth Century History" in *Arabian Studies II*, MCMLXXV, 63.

38. *Arabian Gulf Intelligence: Selections from the Records of the Bombay Government*. London: Oleander Press, 1985, 94.

39. ʾAḥmad Mustafa Abu-Hakima. *The Modern History of Kuwait: 1750–1965*. London: Luzac and Company 1983, 4.

40. As late as 1852, Kuwait was noted for its lack of custom dues. See F.O. 78/907, Taylor to Foreign Office, Basra, 1 May 1852.

41. ʿUthmān ibn Sanad al-Basri. "Kitab sabaʾik al-ʿasjad fi akhbar ʾAḥmad Najl Rizq al-Asʿad." Unpublished Ms. Or. 7565, British Library, London; and Abu Hakima, op. cit., 63–76.

42. For instance, Zamil Muḥammad al-Rashīd believes that "like their kinsmen at al-Zubarah and al-Bahrayn, Al-Sabah (the rulers of Kuwait) benefited greatly from the decline of al-Basrah and the diversion of trade and commerce into the maritime states on the Gulf shores, which made al-Kuwayt an entrepot for exported and imported goods." This view is corroborated by Jacqueline Ismael, who adds that the Persian siege of Basra in 1775 which resulted in the occupation of Basra, brought about a shift of trade routes to Kuwait, made all the more important by the parallel transfer of the British Factory from Basra to Kuwait. Finally, Thabit ʿAbdullāh shows that, although Basra's trade went through a boom in the 1760s, the Persian occupation of the city in 1776 brought about a sharp commercial decline. See Zamil al-Rashīd. *Suʿudi Relations with Eastern Arabia and Uman (1800–1871)*. London: Luzac and Company, 1981, 41; J. Ismael. Kuwait: *Social Change in Historical Perspective*. Syracuse: Syracuse University Press, 1982, 32–33; and Thabit ʿAbdullāh. "The Political Economy of Merchants and Trade 1722–1795." Unpublished Ph.D. dissertation, Georgetown University, 1993, 187–89.

43. Charles Issawi believes that "From the last decades of the seventeenth century, the privateers and pirates of Muscat and Oman ranged freely over the waters of the Persian Gulf . . . their depradations were supplemented by those of British and other European privateers, whose activities reached their peak during the great wars of the seventeenth and eighteenth centuries. Bahrain, the richest island in the Gulf, was alternately occupied by Arabs and Persians. And at the close of the eighteenth century, the rising Wahhābī state broke through to the Persian Gulf. . . ." According to him, Gulf trade could not but suffer as a result. See Charles Issawi, ed. *The Economic History of the Middle East, 1800–1914*. Chicago and London: The University of Chicago Press, 1966, 296.

44. ʿAbbās al-ʿAzzāwī. *Ashaʾir al-Iraq*. Vol. I. Baghdad: Baghdad Press, 1937, 19.

45. Ibid., 76–79.

46. Ibid., 85–99.

47. A battle took place between the Muntafiq and the Khazāʿil over Samawa which ended in the Muntafiq's favor; by 1726, the district formed part of the recognized dira of the Muntafiq, awarded annually by Ottoman/Mamluk pashas to Muntafiq shaikhs as part of the annual badal. See Maan Hamdan ʿAlī, ed. *Mabahith Iraqīyya fi al-jughrafya wa al-tarikh wa khitat Baghdad.* Baghdad: Dar al-Rashi, 1981, 171.

48. Ibn Isa. op. cit., 1966, 74.

49. Al-Haidari, op. cit., 113.

50. Anonymous. *Kitab lamʿ al-shihab fi sirat al-shaikh Muḥammad ibn ʾAbdul-Wahhāb.* Edited by Shaikh Abdul-Rahman ibn ʿAbdul-Laṭīf ibn ʿAbdullāh Al al-Shaikh. Riyāḍ: Dar al-Malik ʿAbdul-Azīz, 1394/1974, 61.

51. Shaikh Rasul Al-Kirkukli. *Dawhat al-wuzaraʾ fi tarikh waqaiʿ Baghdad al-zawraʾ.* Translated from the Turkish by Musa Kadhim Nawras. Beirut: Dar al-Katib al-Arabi, n.d., 211.

52. Ibid., 211.

53. Al-Haidari, op. cit., 108.

54. *Kitab lamʿ al-Shihab,* 62.

55. Ibid., 62 and al-Azzawi. *Ashaʾir,* 137–41.

56. Ibid., 156.

57. Albertine Jwaideh. "Aspects of Land Tenure and Social Change in Lower Iraq During Late Ottoman Times" in Tarif Khālidi, ed. *Land Tenure and Social Transformation in the Middle East.* Beirut: American University of Beirut, 1984, 334.

58. Paul Dresch. *Tribes, Government and History in Yemen.* Oxford: Clarendon Press, 1989, 343.

59. See Richard N. Schofield, ed. *The Iraq-Iran Border, 1840–1958.* Vol. I. Oxford: Archive Editions, 1989, 311.

60. Ibid., 161.

61. Tareq Y. Ismael. *Iraq and Iran: Roots of Conflict.* Syracuse: Syracuse University Press, 1982, 2.

62. Sayyar al-Jamil. *Al-ʿuthmāniyun wa takwin al-Arab al-hadith: min ajil bahth ruʾyawi muʿasir.* Beirut: Muʾassissat al-Abhath al-Arabiyya, 1989, 327–49.

63. ʿAbdul-Azīz M. Awad. "The Gulf in the Seventeenth Century" in *Bulletin for the British Society for Middle East Studies,* Vol. 12, no. 2, 1985, 124.

64. Ibid., 130.

65. Donald Edgar Pitcher. *An Historical Geography of the Ottoman Empire.* Leiden: E. J. Brill, 1972, 141.

66. See the chapter on Markets.

67. Robert Mantran. "Réglements Fiscaux Ottomans: La Province de Bassora" in *Journal of the Economic and Social History of the Orient,* December 1967.

68. Ibid., 269–70.

69. See the discussion in al-Kirkukli, op. cit., 16–92. Although freeborn sipahis, the era of these two governors marks the beginning of Mamluk rule in Iraq, for they were the first governors of Iraq to staff their households with Mamluk youths, usually bought in Russian Georgia, converted to Islam, and trained in the arts of war and civil administration in Baghdad.

70. Ibid., 155.

71. Thabit ʿAbdullāh, op. cit., 107–10, 189–91.

72. However, during periods of Ottoman-Persian conflict, the import of Gilani silk usually went through a decline. See Dina Khoury, op. cit., 68; see also Thabit ʿAbdullāh, op. cit., 109.

73. One of the articles of the peace treaties between Ottoman Iraq and Safavid Persia also stipulated that Persian pilgrims and merchants be afforded every protection. See Al-Kirkukli, op. cit., 76.

74. Abdul-Rahman al-Suwaidi. *Hadiqat al-zawraʾ fi sirat al-wuzaraʾ*. Vol. I. Edited by Safaʾ al-Khulusi. Baghdad: Zaim Press, 1962, 94–96; and al-Kirkukli, op. cit., 17. Al-Suwaidi wrote his history at the behest of a Mamluk patroness, Khadija Hanum, Hasan Pasha's granddaughter.

75. Al-Kirkukli, ibid., 75–76; and Schofield, op. cit., 161.

76. Introduction to al-Suwaidi, op. cit., 18.

77. Al-Kirkukli, op. cit., 17.

78. Hamid Algar. "Shīʿīsm and Iran in the Eighteenth Century" in Thomas Naff and Roger Owen, eds. *Studies in Eighteenth Century Islamic History*. Carbondale: Southern Illinois University Press, 1977, 296.

79. This was entirely in keeping with the best of Ottoman legal-commercial traditions. See Mantran, op. cit., 226.

80. Al-Suwaidi notes that, whereas a number of infrastructural projects were financed from funds from al-bait al-mal (the state treasury), the Wazir Hasan Pasha also repaired and renovated bridges and aqueducts "from his own pocket." See al-Suwaidi, op. cit., 68.

81. "Even from the fallahat who entered Baghdad to sell eggs, one egg would be taken." Ibid., 68.

82. Ibid., 27.

83. Ibid., 29.

84. Ibid., 31–32.

85. ʿAlī Shakir ʿAlī. *Tarikh al-Iraq fi al-ahd al-ʿuthmāni, 1638–1750: dirasa fi ahwaluha al-siyasiyya*. Ninevah: Maktabat 30 Tammuz, 1985, 109.

86. Ibid., 70.

87. Dina Khoury, op. cit., 70.

88. ʿAbbās al-ʿAzzāwī. "Al al-Shawy" in *Lughat al-Arab,* Vol. 9, January-October 1931, 45.

89. This, in fact, happened in 1766–69 during the height of the civil war in Baghdad, when ʿAbdullāh's son, Suleimān, who also held the post of Bab al-Arab, became one of the leaders of the "Arab" camp. See Abdul-Rahman al-Suwaidi. *Tarikh hawadith Baghdad wa al-Basra*. Edited by Imad Abdul-Salam Rauf. Basra: Basra University Press, 1980, 86–138.

90. Ibid., 48.

91. Niewenhuis, op cit., 126–28.

92. The following discussion relies heavily on the first-hand report of Yaʿqub ibn Niʿmatullah ibn Hagop ibn Sarkis ibn Hagop Jan ibn Maqsud, a member of the ʿAbbūd family, important merchants heavily involved in the Basra-India route. See Yaʿqub Sarkis. *Mabahith Iraqīyya fi al-jughrafya wa al-tarikh wa al-athar wa khitat Baghdad*. Vol. I, Baghdad: Sharikat al-Tijara wa al-Tibaʿa, 1935–1981, 8–26.

93. Ibid., 19–20.

94. Niewenhuis, op. cit., 76–77.

95. Stephen Helmsley Longrigg. *Four Centuries of Modern Iraq*. Oxford: Clarendon Press, 1925, 160.

96. Niewenhuis, op. cit., 19–22.

97. Al-Suwaidi, *Hadiqat al-zawra*ʾ, 49.

98. Ibid., 49.

99. Ibid., 33.

100. Ibid., 72.

101. See "Kafir" in EI 2.

102. Ibid.

103. According to Ibn al-Ghannam, a pro-Wahhābī historian, "this issue (i. e the belief in tawhid) is what distinguishes between unbelief and Islam." See Ibn al-Ghannam. op. cit., 106.

104. Aziz al-Azmeh. *Islams and Modernities*. London and New York: Verso, 1993, 105. See also Elizabeth Sirriyeh. "Wahhābīs, Unbelievers and the Problems of Exclusivism" in *Bulletin of the British Society for Middle East Studies*. Vol. 16, no. 2, 1989, 125.

105. The earliest known historian of the Wahhābī movement, Shaikh Husain ibn Ghannam (d. 1810) was an alim-historian who was born in al-Ahsa, and whose family traced its roots to the Banu Tamim tribe. His history, entitled *Rawdat al-Afkar wa al-Afham,* is a catalogue of the corrupt practises prevalent not only in central Arabia but in the Hijaz, Oman, Yemen, Egypt and Iraq prior to the development of the Wahhābī daʿwa (for instance, saint worship, the veneration of tombs, trees and rocks); he also lists the geneology of the Imam, explains the principles of his daʿwa in detail, and writes down the early history of the first Saʿūdī state (ending in 1797). For ibn Ghannam's biography, see ʿAbdullāh Al-Shebl. "Aham al-masadir al-Najdīyyah li tarikh al-dawlah al-saʿūdīyyah." Unpublished Ph.d dissertation, Alexandria University, Egypt, 1988, 99–154.

106. Ibn Ghannam. *Rawdat al-Afkar,* Vol. II, 13–14.

107. Ibid., 14.

108. Shaikh Muḥammad Hamad al-Bassam al-Tamimi (d. 1831). "Kitab al-durar al-mafakhir fi akhbar al-Arab al-awakhir." Unpublished Ms. Add. 7358, British Library, folio 67.

109. Shaikh ʿUthmān ibn Sanad (d. 1826), who composed *Mattaliʿ al-Saʿūd fi tayyib akbar al-vali Dāwūd,* was a Najdī scholar and Sufi who had made Basra his home. For the biography of Ibn Sanad, see Hamad al-Jasir, "Muʾarrikhu Najd" in *Al-Arab,* Vol. 10, Year 5, Rabiʿ al-Thani/June 1391/1971, and Imad Abdul-Salam Rauf. *Al-Tarikh wa al-Muʾarrikhun al-Iraqīyun fi al-Asr al-ʿUthmāni*. Baghdad: Dar al-Arabiyya Press, 1983, 171–75.

110. Al-Haidari, op. cit., 227.

111. Ibid., 227.

112. See Rauf, op. cit., 171–75 and 881.

113. Ibn Sanad, op. cit., 30.

114. John O. Voll. "Wahhābīsm and Mahdism: Alternative Styles of Islamic Renewal" in *Arab Studies Quarterly*, Vol. 4, nos. 1 and 2, 1980, 121.

115. For a particularily detailed analysis of these charges, see *Kitab lamʿ al-shihab,* 29–31, and Ibn al-Ghannam. *Rawdat al-afkar,* Vol. I, 25–50.

116. *Kitab lam^c al-shihab,* 44–45. Although this book has been attributed to an anonymous author, most probably a Shīʿī resident of eastern Arabia, new evidence points to the theory that the author may have been a local assistant to Captain Robert Taylor, a British official who spent most of his life (1788–1852) in the Gulf. Although his account of the religious practises of the Imam Muḥammad ibn ʾAbdul-Wahhāb is fanciful and somewhat imprecise, the author's detail on the organization of state finances, defence matters and political alliances is quite the best account of internal affairs in the emergent Saʿūdī state. Even so, the book has come under virulent criticism from a leading member of the Al al-Shaikh family, a descendant of shaikh Muḥammad ibn ʾAbdul-Wahhāb, for presenting a fraudulent picture of the personality, actions and beliefs of the Imam. For more information on the author, note the conflicting studies of ʿAbdul-Waḥīd Raghib, Michael Cook and shaikh Abdul-Rahman Al al-Shaikh, the editor of the manuscript itself. See the Introduction to *Kitab lamʿ al-shihab. . . ,* g.; al-Raghib. "Kitab lamʿ al-shihab" in *Al-Darah,* no. 2, year 2, 1976, 239–41; and Michael Cook. "The Provenance of the lamʿ al-shihab fi sirat muḥammad ibn ʾAbdul-Wahhāb" in *Journal of Turkish Studies,* Vol. 10, 1986.

117. Shaikh ʿUthmān ibn Bishr (d. 1871), the author of *ʿUnwan al-Majd,* was a noted alim from al-Jalajil in the Sudair district, who was a fervent partisan of the Wahhābī cause, and especially of the teachings of its founder, Shaikh Muḥammad ibn ʾAbdul-Wahhāb. Having studied in Darʿiyya in his youth, he was an eye-witness to the emergence of the embryonic Saʿūdī state and so resolved to write a history of its rulers. His wealth of detail on the military campaigns undertaken by ʿAbdul-Azīz ibn Saʿūd and of his son, Saʿūd in Najd, the Hijaz, eastern Arabia, Oman and Iraq is extremely valuable, and forms the core of most of the secondary histories of the Wahhābī movement. Ibn Bishr's work has received lavish praise from scholars of the Wahhābī movement in present-day Saʿūdī Arabia, and no less than the premier historian of Najd, Hamad al-Jasir has called Ibn Bishr's work "the best history written on the subject." See Al-Jasir. "Mu'arrikhu Najd," op. cit.

118. *Kitab lamʿ al-shihab,* 44–45.

119. Ibn Bishr, op. cit., 12–13.

120. ʿAbdullāh Mutawa. "The Ulama of Najd from the Sixteenth to the Mid-Eighteenth Century." (Unpublished Ph.D. dissertation, U.C.L.A., 1989), 53–56.

121. There is evidence, however, that the Bani Khālid ʾamīrs were less interested in plunder than the sharifs of Mecca, and that they tried to build longer-lasting alliances with the people of Najd. See Mutawa, ibid., 41–52.

122. *Kitab lamʿ al-shihab,* 52.

123. Ibn Bishr, op. cit., 79.

124. Ibid., 80.

125. *Kitab lamʿ al-shihab . . . ,* 52.

126. Ibid., 52.

127. Al-Azmeh. op. cit., 109–10.

128. Ibn Bishr, op. cit., 175.

129. Ibid., 129. No figures are available for the taxes paid by other tribes or districts.

130. Ibid., 175.

131. Ibid., 129.

132. Ibid., 129 and 175.

133. Ibid.

134. The first military campaign against the Saᶜūdī state was initiated by shaikh Thuwaini of the Muntafiq in 1796–97. Among his chief supporters were the deposed ᵓamīrs of the Bani Khālid tribe, Muḥammad al-ᶜUrayᶜir and Barrak. The campaign came to an abrupt halt when shaikh Thuwaini was assassinated. See al-Kirkukli, op. cit., 204.

135. *Kitab lamᶜ al-shihab,* 76.

136. The historian who was the most critical of the Wahhābī "heresies" was ᶜUthmān ibn Sanad al-Basri, a tribal alim and protége of the last Mamluk Pasha, Dāwūd (1817–1831). See the abridged version of his magisterial history, *Mukhtassar tarikh al-Shaikh ᶜUthmān ibn Sanad al-Basri al-musamma bi matalliᶜ al-Saᶜūd bi-tayyib akhbar al-vali Dāwūd,* by Amin ibn Hasan al-Hulwani, 1833, 22–30.

137. There is evidence that the Wahhābī daᶜwa made followers of important Sunni ᶜulamāᵓ in Iraq, such as the noted shaikh ᶜAlī al-Suwaidi. In turn, the latter may have been instrumental in influencing the religious principles of the ruling Mamluk Pasha of his day, Suleimān the Little (1807–1810). Whatever the merits of this view, it is important to note that the salafi ᶜaqida, on which the Wahhābī daᶜwa based its main precepts, had, of course, existed in Iraq from the earliest days of the Islamic conquest. See ᶜAbbās al-ᶜAzzāwī. *Dhikra Abi Thanaᵓ al-Alusi.* Baghdad: Sharikat al-Tijara wa al-Tibaᶜa, 1958, 35–40.

138. For instance, Husain Khalaf al-Shaikh Khazᶜal gives it a mere two pages. See *Tarikh al-Jazira al-Arabiyya fi ᶜasr al-shaikh Muḥammad ibn ᵓAbdul-Wahhāb.* (also entitled *Hayat al-shaikh Muḥammad ibn ᵓAbdul-Wahhāb).* Beirut: Dar al-Kutub, 1968, 330–32.

139. Ibn Bishr, op. cit., 81–82.

140. Ibid., 109.

141. Ibid., 109.

142. As a Katib in the Baghdad diwan, shaikh Rasul al-Kirkukli, a Turcoman who only wrote in Turkish, was privy to the correspondence between the Mamluk valis in Baghdad, their commanders in the field and the Saᶜūdī generals who waged the battle against Iraqī towns and villages on the frontier. Because he was less versed in dogma than this peers (or chose not to enter into the doctrinal issues surrounding the Wahhābī-Mamluk wars), his history is confined to the more formal, and exterior aspects of the Saᶜūdī campaigns in Iraq. More reticent than Ibn Sanad, he was the epitome of a good bureaucrat who never critiscized his masters directly; however, by confining himself to a factual narration of the deprivation suffered by the Mamluk armies in Najd, he was able to convey his disillusionment far better than if he had attempted a direct critique of the Baghdad administration. By letting the facts speak for themselves, al-Kirkukli's history emphasizes the lack of preparation and more importantly, the failure of will in the Mamluk camp; thus, for him, the history of the Mamluk campaigns in Najd is one of abysmal defeat. See al-Kirkukli, op. cit., 204.

143. Ibn Sanad. op. cit., 22.

144. Ibid., 23.

145. For an examination of ᶜAlī al-kahyā's aborted campaign from an Iraqī perspective, see al-Kirkukli, op. cit., 205–10. See also *Kitab lamᶜ al-shihab,* op. cit., 130. According to the anonymous author, ᶜAlī Pasha "the Georgian" also recruited tribesmen from the Muntafiq under their new leader, Ḥumūd, and "Turks, Kurds and Khazāᶜil Arabs."

146. Al-Kirkukli, ibid., 208. Perhaps because he was a Mamluk bureaucrat, al-Kirkukli had access to documents exchanged between the two sides.

147. Ibid., 209.
148. Ibn Sanad, op. cit., 25–26.
149. Ibid., 26.
150. Ibid., 26.
151. Ibid., 26–27.
152. *Kitab lam*ᶜ *al-shihab,* op. cit., 130–32.
153. Ibid., 76.
154. Ibid., 80–81.
155. Al-Rashīd, op. cit., 47.
156. *Arabian Gulf Intelligence,* op. cit., 432.
157. Al-Rashīd, op. cit., 50.
158. Ibid., 305.
159. Ibid., 396.
160. For example, see Ibn Bishr, op. cit., 31–47.
161. Ismael, op. cit., 22.
162. Ibid., 22.
163. Michael Cook. "The Expansion of the First Saᶜūdī State: The Case of Washm" in C. E. Bosworth, et. al, *The Islamic World from Classical to Modern Times: Essays in Honor of Bernard Lewis*. Princeton: The Darwin Press, 1988, 669.
164. Ibid., 678.
165. Vincenzo Maurizi. *History of Seyd Said, Sulṭān of Muscat; Together with an Account of the Countries and Peoples on the Shores of the Persian Gulf, Particularily of the Wahabees*. Translated from the Italian. London: John Booth, 1819, 42.
168. Ibn Bishr, op. cit., 216.
169. Quoted in Yaᶜqub Sarkis. *Mabahith Iraqīyya,* 55.

2. THE STRUCTURE OF THE REGIONAL MARKET OF IRAQ, ARABIA, AND THE GULF, 1745–1900

1. Muḥammad ibn ᶜAbdullāh Abdul-Qadir al-Ansari. *Tuhfat al-mustafid bi tarikh al-Ahsa al-qadim wa al-jadid*. Riyāḍ: n.d., 1962, 121.
2. ᶜAbdullāh M. Mutawa. "The Ulama of Najd from the Sixteenth Century to the Mid-Eighteenth Century" (Phd. dissertation, U.C.L.A., 1989), 68.
3. Ibid., 304.
4. ʾIbrāhīm ibn ᶜUbaid Abdul-Muhsin. *Tadhkirat ᶜuli al-nahi wa al- ᶜurfan bi-ayyam Allah al-Wahid al-diyan wa dhikr hawadith al-zaman*. Vol. 1 (Riyāḍ: Nur Printing Press, n.d.), 104.
5. Husain ibn Ghannam. *Tarikh Najd,* 95–221; and ᶜAbbās al-ᶜAzzāwī. *Dhikra Abu Thana' al-Alusi*. Baghdad: Sharikat al-Tijara wa al-Tibaᶜa, 1958, 35–40.
6. ʾIbrāhīm Fasih ibn Sabghatullah al-Haidari. *Kitab ᶜunwan al-Majd,* 186–202.
7. Mahmoud Shukri al-Alusi. *Tarikh Najd*. Edited by Muḥammad Bahjat al-Athari. Cairo: Salafiyya Press, 1928.
8. There had been a strong commercial relationship between Basra and Huwaiza from as early as the sixteenth century onwards. See Imad ʾAḥmad al-Jawahiri. "Al-Dawr

al-tarikhi li al-Basra ʿala al-khalij al-Arabi ma bain 1500–1600" in *Dirasat al-Khalij wa al-Jazira al-Arabiyya,* vol. 13, January 1978, 83.

9. Al-Haidari, op. cit., 179–80; 241.

10. See the pioneering dissertation of Uwaideh Metaireek al-Juhany.

11. Carlo Guarmani. *Northern Najd: A Journey from Jerusalem to Anaiza in Qasim.* Translated by Lady Capel-Cure, with Introduction and Notes by Douglas Carruthers (London: The Argonaut Press, 1938), 39–40.

12. Charles M. Doughty. *Travels in Arabia Deserta.* With an Introduction by T. E. Lawrence. Vol. 1. New York: Dover Publications, 1979, 664.

13. F.O. 78/907, Taylor to F.O., 1 May 1852.

14. W. G. Palgrave. *A Personal Narrative of a Year's Journey Through Central and Eastern Arabia, 1862–1863.* London: Darf Publishers Ltd., 1985, 118.

15. Al-Alusi, op. cit., 21–22.

16. ʿAbdullāh Mutawa, op. cit., 28 ft.

17. Shaikh ʿUthmān ibn Bishr. *Unwan al-majd fi tarikh Najd,* 98.

18. Salih Muḥammad Al-Abid. *Dawr al-qawassim fi al-khalij al-Arabi, 1742–1820.* Baghdad: Ani Press, 1976, 134.

19. Philip Curtin, *Cross-Cultural Trade in World History,* 2–14.

20. G. E Lorimer. *A Gazeteer of the Persian Gulf, Oman and Central Arabia* (Calcutta: Government Press, 1908), 665–67.

21. Anonymous. *Kitab tarikh kayf kana dhuhur Shaikh al-Islam Muḥammad Ibn ʾAbdul-Wahhāb.* Edited by ʿAbdullāh Salih al-Uthaymin, Riyāḍ, 1983.

22. Anonymous. op. cit., 92.

23. *Arabian Gulf Intelligence,* 17–18.

24. Ibid., 110–11.

25. Georges Douin. *L'Egypte et La Syrie en 1833: La Mission du Baron de Boislecomte.* (Cairo: Societe Royale de Geographie d'Egypte, 1927), 166–67.

26. F.O. 78/907, Taylor to F.O., Basra, 1 May 1852.

27. H. R. P Dickson. *The Arab of the Desert.* Edited by Robert Wilson and Zahra Freeth (London: George Allen and Unwin, 1983), 10–12.

28. Ismael. *Kuwait: Social Change in Historical Perspective,* 46–47.

29. Alan Villiers. "Some Aspects of the Arab Dhow Trade" in Louise E. Sweet, ed. *People and Cultures of the Middle East,* vol. 1. (New York: The Natural History Press, 1965), 155.

30. F.O. 78/907, Taylor to F.O., Basra, 1 May 1852.

31. One eventually did. In 1871, shaikh ʿAbdullāh accepted the Ottoman title of Qaim-Maqam (sub-district governor), "and Kuwait became an administrative unit of the Ottoman Empire." This was reversed in 1896 with the appearance of shaikh Mubārak. See Ismael, op. cit., 45–46.

32. *Arabian Gulf Intelligence,* 296.

33. Pierre de Vaucelles. *La Vie en Irak il y a Un Siècle.* Paris: Editions A. Perdone, 1963, 5.

34. ʾAḥmad Nur al-Ansari. "Al-nasra fi akhbar al-Basra" in *Majallat al-majmaʿ al-ilmi,* vol. 18, 203–5; 297–301.

35. Al-Ansari was originally from Arabistan, and therefore he strongly deplored the manner in which regional merchants were treated by the governors of Basra. Ibid., 297–301.

36. Thabit A. J ʿAbdullāh. "The Political Economy of Merchants and Trade in Basra," 187.

37. See F.O. 78 /907, Taylor to F.O., Basra, 1 May 1852.

38. Harry St. John Philby. *Arabia of the Wahhābīs*. (New York: Arno Press, 1973), 218.

39. Al-Haidari. op. cit., 162.

40. Denis de Rivoyre. *Obock, Mascate, Bouchire, Bassorah*. (Paris: Plon et Cie., 1883), 182.

41. Mostafa Ansari. "The History of Khuzistan, 1878–1925: A Study in Provincial Autonomy and Change." (Ph. D dissertation, University of Chicago, 1974), 51.

42. F.O. 195/367, Rawlinson to Canning, Baghdad, 19 May 1852.

43. De Rivoyre. op. cit., 266

44. Ibid., 209–10.

45. Al-Haidari, op. cit., 171.

46. Ibid., 172.

47. J. B Rousseau, quoted in Charles Issawi, ed. *The Economic History of the Middle East*, 135–36; and Husain Muḥammad al-Qahawati. *Dawr al-Basra al-tijari fi al-khalij al-Arabi*. Baghdad: Irshad Press, 1980, 23–24.

48. Grattan Geary. *Through Asiatic Turkey: Narrative of a Journey from Bombay to the Bosphorous*. (New York: Harper and Bros., 1878), 13.

49. Shaikh Muḥammad ibn Musa al-Nabhani. *Al-tuhfa al-Nabhaniya fi tarikh al-Jazira al-Arabiyya*. Vol. 9, Basra: Basra University Press, n.d., 114.

50. F.O. 78/907, Taylor to F.O., 1 May 1852.

51. Ibid.

52. Ibid.

53. Ibid.

54. Ibid.

55. William Tweedie. *The Arab, His Horse and His Country*. (Calcutta: Government Press, 1894), 85.

56. Al-Jawahiri. op. cit., 84–88.

57. Mustafa Abdul-Qadir al-Najjar. *Al-tarikh al-siyasi li-imarat ʿArabistan al-ʿArabiyya*. (Cairo: Dar al-Maarif, 1971), 57.

58. F.O. 708/907, Taylor to F.O., 1 May 1852.

59. F.O. 195 /272, Rawlinson to Wellesley, Baghdad,11 March 1847, and F.O. 195 /318, Rawlinson to Cowley, Baghdad, 5 January 1848.

60. In 1850, Consul Abbot estimated that most of the merchants of Muhammara were natives of Bushire, Behbehan, Shuster, Dizful, Basra and Kuwait. Quoted in Abbas Amanat, ed. *Cities and Trade: Consul Abbot on the Economy and Society of Iran, 1847–1866*. London: Ithaca Press, 1983, 90.

61. Shahbaz Shahnavaz. "Britain and the Opening of the Karun River Circa 1873–1910" (Ph. D dissertation, Oxford University, 1980), 15.

62. Arnold Wilson. *South-West Persia: A Political Officer's Diary, 1907–1914*. London, New York and Toronto: Oxford University Press, 1941, 38.

63. Ibid., 72. What is of additional significance is that, other than making maps for the Intelligence branch of the India Government, Wilson's main mission seemed to be to open the caravan road into central Iran in order that British goods might penetrate the country in the same way that Russian commodities were flooding the market by way of the northern route.

64. Ansari. op. cit., 51.

65. Amanat, op. cit., 91–92.

66. One of the problems that British officials faced when compiling their annual trade reports for the Foreign Office was that, very frequently, they were not allowed to see the revenue figures of the Mosul, Baghdad and Basra Customs Houses. British officials were therefore forced to rely on the statistics of British shipping firms, which undoubtedly gave them a skewed picture of trade in the Iraqī provinces as a whole. See, for example, F.O. 78/3778, Tweedie to Wyndham, Baghdad, 6 October 1883.

67. The report is referenced as F.O. 78 /907, Taylor to F.O., Basra, 1 May 1852. Surprisingly, it doesn't show up either in Charles Issawi's economic history of the Fertile Crescent, nor in his later article on the trade of Basra. See Issawi. *The Fertile Crescent, 1800–1914: A Documentary Economic History*. (Oxford: Oxford University Press, 1988), 173–99; and Issawi. "Notes on the Trade of Basra," op. cit., 167–74.

68. The shāmī was a silver currency, originally minted under the name of the Qirsh al-Hamidi by the imperial Mint in the era of Sulṭān Abdul-Hamid I (d. 1788). It was renamed shāmī in Iraq because of its provenance, Bilad al-Sham. The shāmī was also known as the Qirsh ʿayn (or the Qirsh Rumi); in fact, both terms were used concurrently in the countryside. Although it made way for the government-backed Constantinople piaster in other parts of Iraq, the shāmī remained the tribesman's coin of choice until the early twentieth century. See ʿAbbās al-ʿAzzāwī. *Tarikh al-nuqud al-Iraqīyya*. Baghdad: Sharikat al-Tijara wa al-Tibaʿa, 1958, 149–51.

69. See Issawi, *The Fertile Crescent*, 134–36; and Issawi, "The Trade of Basra," 172.

70. A Lac is a unit of 100,000. See Al-Azzawi, op. cit., 40.

71. F.O. 78/907, Taylor to F.O., Basra, 1 May 1852.

72. Yaʿqub Sarkis. *Mabahith Iraqīyya fi al-tarikh wa al-athar wa khitat Baghdad*. vol. 1. Baghdad: Maktabat al-Tijariya, 1955, 74–81.

73. Ismael. op. cit., 54–59.

74. *Arabian Gulf Intelligence*, op. cit., 109.

75. Quoted in Issawi. *The Fertile Crescent*, 109.

76. Mahdi Jawad Habib al-Bustani. "Dirasat li-wathaʾiq ʿuthmāniyya ghayr manshura" in *Dirasat fi al-Tarikh wa al-Athar: Majallat Jamʿiyyat al-Muʾarikhin wa al-Athariyin fi al-Iraq*. vol. 13, 1987, 99.

77. ʾIbrāhīm ibn Salih ibn Isa. *Tarikh baʿḍ al-hawadith al-waqiʿa fi Najd wa wafiyat baʿḍ al-aʿyan wa ansabihum wa binaʾ baʿḍ al-buldan*. Riyāḍ: Dar al-Yamama, 1966, 205–6.

78. Doughty. op. cit., Vol. II, 376.

79. Ibid., 389.

80. Ibid., 382.

81. Ibid., 383, 386.

82. F.O. 195 /2164, Crow to the Government of India, Basra, 28 November 1904.

83. Philby. op. cit., 275–76.

84. Ibid., 276.

85. Palgrave, op. cit., 93.

86. Ibid., 93.

87. Carlo Guarmani. *Northern Najd,* 92.

88. Ibid., 33, ft.

89. Al-Haidari, op. cit., 165.

90. Ibid., 165.

91. al-Azzawi. op. cit., Vol. 8, 68; and al-Nabhani. op. cit., 124–33.

92. G. E Lorimer. *Gazeteer of the Persian Gulf,* 2372–73; F.O. 195/1935, Whyte to Foreign Office, Basra, 15 June 1896 and al-Haidari. op. cit., 164.

93. Haifa ʾAḥmad al-Nakib. "A Critical Study of Sayyid Ṭālib Pasha al-Nakib in the Setting of His Time and Environment, on the Basis of Arabic and Foreign Documents" (Master's Thesis, University of Leeds, 1973), 33.

94. Ibid., 33–34.

95. Lorimer, *Gazeteer.* 1446.

96. For a comparison, see Juan Cole. "Mafia, Mob and Shiism in Iraq: The Rebellion of Ottoman Karbala, 1824–1843" in *Past and Present, 1986.* See also De Rivoyre, op. cit., 230–34.

97. Suleimān Faiḍi. *Fi ghamrat al-niḍal.* (Baghdad: Sharikat al-Tijara wa al-Tibaʿa, 1952), 51.

98. Ibid., 52.

99. According to Sir Nicholas O'Conor, the British Ambassador in Istanbul, Sayyid Ṭālib's candidature was "strongly supported by the palace clique," by which the Ambassador was probably referring to shaikh Abul-Huda al-Sayyadi, Sulṭān Abdul-Hamid II's chief advisor. See *Foreign Office Confidential Print: The Affairs of Kuwait, 1896–1905.* Vol. II, (London: Frank Cass and Company Ltd., 1971), 63–64

100. Ibid., 52.

101. F.O. 195 / 2163, Crow to O'Conor, Basra, 28 March 1904.

102. Yaʿqub Sarkis, op. cit., 46–52.

103. Ibid., vol. 1, 13–20.

104. Ibid., 20.

105. De Rivoyre. op. cit., 189–90.

106. Ibid.

107. *Lughat al-Arab,* Vol. II, August 1912.

108. Thabit ʿAbdullāh. op. cit., 129–30.

109. Ibid., 170.

110. Philby, op. cit., 193.

111. Mohammed Almana. *Arabia Unified: A Portrait of Ibn Saʿūd.* London: Hutchinson Benham, 1980, 191.

112. Ibid., 169.

113. Tweedie. op. cit., 309.

114. George Curzon. *Persia and the Persian Question.* Vol. II, London: Longmans' Green and Company 1892, 325–26.

115. F.O. 78/4358, Chevenix-Trench to the Foreign Office, Basra, 29 May-6 July 1891.

116. Ibid.

117. The anonymous author of *lamʿ al-shihab* mentions that there was a shaikh ʾIbrāhīm ibn ʿAbdul-Razzāq living in the famous port-town of al-Zubara in the 1780s; after the Saʿūdī invasion of al-Zubara, shaikh ʾIbrāhīm and many of the leading merchants of Zubair fled to parts unknown. See *Kitab lamʿ al-shihab fi Sirat Muḥammad ibn ʾAbdul-Wahhāb*. Edited by shaikh Abdul-Rahman Al al-Shaikh. Riyāḍ, 1962, 78. See also Al-Haidari, op. cit., 167–68.

118. Ibid., 168–70.

119. Ibid., 171.

120. *Arabian Gulf Intelligence* . . . , 39–40.

121. Alan Villiers. *Sons of Sinbad*. (New York: Charles Scribner and Sons, 1940), 271.

122. Ibid., 370.

123. *Arabian Gulf Intelligence*, 39–40.

124. Alan Villiers made a journey in just such a vessel to East Africa and India, and he indicates that at the end of 1939, there were close to 106 sailing-ships registered in Kuwait that still sailed to Bombay or Tanganyika. See Alan Villiers. "Some Aspects of the Arab Dhow Trade," 155.

125. F.O. 708/907, Taylor to Foreign Office, Basra, 1 May 1852.

126. The following discussion will be based on Villiers, op. cit., 46–47. See also F.O. 78/907, Taylor to Foreign Office, Basra, 1 May 1852.

127. Fernand Braudel. *The Wheels of Commerce*. Vol. II. (New York: Harper and Row, 1979), 361–66.

128. F.O. 708/907, Taylor to Foreign Office, Basra, 1 May 1852.

129. Braudel, op. cit., Vol. II, 125–29.

130. F.O. 78/907, Taylor to Foreign Office, Basra, 1 May 1852.

131. Vital Cuinet. *La Turquie d'Asie* (4 Vols.; Paris: Leroux, 1892), IV, 236.

132. Ibid., 237.

133. Ibid., 178–79.

134. Ibid., 203.

135. At its most refined, this argument has been used to distinguish between "archaic" characteristics of one economy and the near-capitalistic features of another. For instance, Braudel makes a distinction between the Ottoman and Indian economies in the eighteenth century. He rightly places emphasis on the shortage of currency in the Ottoman "world-system" but calls the import of specie from Europe an "archaic" feature. Thus "money, the sinews of western trade, usually made only fleeting appearances in the Turkish economy . . . [and] the West was correspondingly free to use its monetary superiority in the Levant market and even, when circumstances permitted, to deal in money itself." The fact that the Ottomans had little money in circulation allows Braudel to conclude that the Ottoman system was forced to rely on its "uncapitalistic" sectors, i. e food and textiles. On the other hand, the Indian economy was permeated with the money economy. Thus "the term that springs to mind, perhaps an excessive one, is that of a national market: the Indian subcontinent, for all its size, had a degree of coherence in which the money economy was an important or essential element." However, Braudel only credits India with a "certain capitalism" or "a peculiar form of capitalism" that still was not strong enough to withstand the impact of the West. See Fernand Braudel. *The Per-*

spectives of the World: Civilization and Capitalism, 15th.–18th. Centuries. Vol. III. Translated by Sian Reynolds (New York: Harper and Row, 1984), 473.

136. Willem Floor. "The Dutch on Khark Island: A Commercial Mishap" in *International Journal of Middle East Studies,* Vol. 24, August 1992, 449. Interestingly, Thabit ʿAbdullāh's evidence points to completely different conclusions. According to his sources, as a result of the highly insecure economic climate in Basra in the mid to latter part of the eighteenth century, the British East India Company forbade its agents from buying with credit. See Thabit ʿAbdullāh, op. cit., 138.

137. In 1898, for instance, British consuls noted that "it might be necessary to patrol the [Shaṭṭ al-ʿArab] river with British gunboats to guard our interests [from "local" pirates in Muhammara] . . . [for] the time when these outrages usually occur . . . is in the date season, August to November, when the Masters of native craft come up the river with a large amount of cash for the purchase of dates." See F.O. 78/907, Taylor to the Foreign Office, Basra, 1 May 1852, and F.O. 195/2020, Mockler to Currie, Baghdad, 6 June 1898.

138. Ibid.

139. Ibid.

140. Ibid.

141. I.O.R.L./P&S/7/41, Plowden to the Secretary of the Government of India, Baghdad, 3 June 1884.

142. Ibid.

143. In 1846, British trade reports indicated that a large imbalance had occurred in Iraq's balance of trade as a result of a century or more of currency shortages. This was occasioned by the great export of specie to India and Europe to pay for Iraqī imports. Because there was not enough of a surplus of regional goods for export, currency had to be shipped to Bombay instead to pay for textiles, sugar and tea. This was to be a recurrent problem for the provincial treasury throughout the nineteenth century. See F.O. 424, Rawlinson to Canning, Baghdad, 3 February 1846.

144. Tweedie, op. cit., 270.

145. Guarmani, op. cit., 33–34.

146. Hanna Batatu. *The Old Social Classes and the Revolutionary Movements of Iraq.* (Princeton: Princeton University Press, 1978, 63–152.

147. Louise Sweet. "Camel Raiding of North Africa Bedouin: A Mechanism of Ecological Adaptation" in Louise E. Sweet, ed. *Peoples and Cultures of the Middle East* Vol. I (New York: The Natural History Press, 1965), 270–89.

148. In general, prices for horses fluctuated widely: Upton talks of a price between £50 and £70 for a "pure-bred Arabian" while indicating that exceptional mares could be bought for as high a price as £100, while Tweedie mentions the more reasonable price of £55 per horse. Doughty's standard was the camel, to wit: "the best brood mares of pure blood are valued in the Arab tribes . . . at twenty-five camels, that is £130 at least or at most £150, and the worst at five camels." See R. D. Upton. *Gleanings from the Desert of Arabia* (London: Kegan Paul and Company, 1881), 201, 391–93, 396; Tweedie, op. cit., 270, and Doughty, op. cit., Vol. II, 419.

149. According to the Basra trade report of 1852, "Baghdad, Basra, the whole of Irak is nearly entirely dependent upon the Indian trade; that trade has been steadily decreasing for some time in value. Highly unprofitable branches that formerly existed have

dwindled away and the total trade, not including India and the value of the pearl imports of all the ports put together, does not equal that of the Yemen trade twenty years ago. . . ." See F.O. 78/907, Taylor to Foreign Office, Basra, 1 May 1852.

3. REGIONAL TRADE, OTTOMAN CENTRALIZATION, AND THE BRITISH ECONOMIC CHALLENGE

1. Al-Jawahiri. "Al-dawr al-tarikhi li al-Basra," op. cit., 84–87.

2. Ibid., 84–87.

3. Ibid., 86–91.

4. Suraiya Faroqhi. "Introduction" in *New Perspectives on Turkey,* nos. 5–6, Fall 1991, 1–2.

5. Robert Mantran. "Reglements Fiscaux Ottomanes," op. cit., 224–70.

6. Palmira Brummett makes the important point that, similar to the economic policies of the other great empires of the sixteenth century, the Ottoman Empire competed to "control the custom revenues of the east-west trade," using seapower to achieve its objectives. See her "Competition and Coincidence: Venetian Trading Interests and Ottoman Expansion in the Early Sixteenth Century Levant" in *New Perspectives on Turkey,* nos. 5–6, Fall 1991, 48.

7. Dina Rizq Khoury. "Merchants and Trade," op. cit., 60.

8. Tariq Nafiᶜ al-Hamdani. "Al-Tanzimat al-iqtisadiya al-ᶜuthmāniya fi Wilayet al-Basra iban al-nisf al-thani min al-qarn al-sadis ashr" in Abdeljelil Temimi, ed. *La Vie Economique des Provinces Arabes et Leurs Sources Documentaires a l'Epoque Ottomane.* Tome 1 and 2. Zaghouan: C.E.R.P.A.E.O., 1986, 563–64.

9. Ibid., 564–65.

10. Longrigg. *Four Centuries of Modern Iraq,* 32–33.

11. Jon E. Mandaville. "The Ottoman Province of al-Ahsa in the Sixteenth and Seventeenth Centuries" in *Journal of the American Oriental Society, 1970,* 488; 502. See also Muḥammad ibn ᶜAbdullāh Al Abdul-Qadir al-Ansari. *Tuhfat al-mustafid bi tarikh al-Ahsa fi al-qadim wa al-jadid.* Edited by Hamad al-Jasir. Vol. 1. Riyāḍ: Riyāḍ Press, 1960, 121. The latter places the Ottoman occupation as late as 1555.

12. Al-Ansari, Ibid., 121–22.

13. Mandaville, op. cit., 488–98.

14. Ibid., 490.

15. Ibid., 493.

16. This is Mandaville's point. Ibid., 496–513.

17. Al-Ansari, op. cit., 123.

18. Mandaville, op. cit., 506–7.

19. Ibid., 510.

20. By and large, Iraqī scholars have divided Ottoman rule into two sharply defined phases: pre–1869 and post–1869. Prior to the entry of the Vali Midḥat Pasha in Baghdad in 1869, political life in Ottoman Iraq is considered to have been one of stagnation and drift; after the vali's installation in office, there is dynamism in the air. Not only is Midḥat Pasha viewed as the sole catalyst of the period but the Tanzimat edicts, first promulgated in 1839, are seen as nothing short of revolutionary, for they are deemed

to have introduced radical changes in the region that would transform it for the next three-quarters of a century. For a certain generation of Iraqī historians, both Midḥat Pasha and "his" laws are therefore irrevocably linked together by virtue of their reformist agendas, and 1869 is seen as the pivotal year of the "new" nineteenth century, in which a whole generation came to the fore, imbued with reformist ideas of social justice and freedom. Detailing the history of these reforms, as well as analysing the contribution of the man who set them in motion then becomes a systematic endeavor for a whole school of Iraqī historians. See ʿAbbās al-ʿAzzāwī. *Tarikh al-Iraq bayn ihtilalayn*. Vol. 7, Baghdad: Sharikat al-Tijara wa al-Tibaʿa al-Mahduda, 1955, 159–269; ʿAbdul-Razzāq al-Hilali. *Dirasat wa tarajim Iraqīyya;* and Yaʿqub Sarkis. *Mabahith Iraqīyya fi al-jughrafya wa al-athar wa khitat*. Baghdad.

21. Suleimān Fāʾiq [Bey]. *Tarikh Baghdad.* Translated from the Turkish by Musa Kadhim Nawras. Baghdad: Maarif Press, 1962, 105–10.

22. Ibid.

23. Al-Azzawi, op. cit., 10–14.

24. Ibid., 10.

25. ʿAbdī Pasha, who became vali in 1849, was thought to have belonged to a clique which numbered among its ranks many of the leaders of the "old Georgian guard." See F.O. 195/334, Rawlinson to Canning, Baghdad, 18 July 1849.

26. Ibid., 18.

27. Ibid., 12.

28. Ibid., 12.

29. Fāʾiq, op. cit., 105–10.

30. Niewenhuis, *Politics and Society in Early Modern Iraq,* 51–53.

31. H. A. R Gibb and Harold Bowen. *Islamic Society and the West.* Vol. 1. London: Oxford University Press, 1958, 44; and Mantran, op. cit., 224–70.

32. F.O. 78/656, Rawlinson to Canning, Baghdad, 5 August 1846.

33. For an interesting description of the badal in the nineteenth century Ottoman Empire, see David Urquhart. *Turkey and its Resources.* London: Saunders and Otley, 1833, 107–10.

34. F.O. 78/656, Rawlinson to Canning, Baghdad, 5 August 1846.

35. Abou El-Haj, op. cit., 56.

36. F.O. 195/367, Kemball to Canning, Baghdad, 19 November 1851.

37. Gibb and Bowen, op. cit., 12–13.

38. F.O. 78/656, Rawlinson to Canning, Baghdad, 5 August 1846.

39. Much of the information that Al-Azzawi cites in his Tarikh with regard to al-Mosulī can be attributed directly to an anonymous history of early nineteenth century Baghdad, to which al-Azzawi refers as al-*Tarikh al-majhul.* See al-Azzawi, Ibid., 53–56.

40. Ibid., 54.

41. Al-Mosulī was dismissed from office and recalled to Istanbul at the same time as the vali, ʿAlī Riḍā Pasha al-Lāz, i.e, in 1842. See Al-Azzawi, op. cit., 55; and F.O. 78/656, Hector to Rawlinson, Baghdad, 30 July 1846.

42. Quoted in J. G. Lorimer. *A Gazeteer of the Persian Gulf,* 1620.

43. Ibid., 1621.

44. Thabit A. J ʿAbdullāh. "The Political Economy of Merchants," 61–62.

45. M. E. Yapp, "The Euphrates Expedition" in C. E. Bosworth, et. al. *The Islamic World from the Classical to Modern Times: Essays in Honor of Bernard Lewis*. Princeton: The Darwin Press, 1988, 895–912.

46. Roger Owen. *The Middle East in the World Economy, 1800–1914*. London and New York: Methuen, 1985, 276–78.

47. C. A. Bayly. *Imperial Meridien,* 9–10.

48. Ibid., 10.

49. Donald Quataert and Caglar Keyder. "Introduction" in *New Perspectives on Turkey,* Spring 1992, 3.

50. Sevket Pamuk. *The Ottoman Empire and European Capitalism, 1820–1913*. Cambridge: Cambridge University Press, 1987, 23.

51. F.O. 78/656, Rawlinson to Aberdeen, Baghdad, 27 April 1846.

52. Ibid., 6.

53. See, for instance, Resat Kasaba's article, "Open-Door Treaties: China and the Ottoman Empire Compared" in *New Perspectives on Turkey,* no. 7, Spring 1992, 71–73.

54. Roderic H. Davidson. "Britain, the International Spectrum, and the Eastern Question, 1827–1841" in *New Perspectives on Turkey,* no. 7, Spring 1992, 29.

55. Issawi, *The Economic History of the Middle East . . . ,* 38–39.

56. F.O. 195/237, Rawlinson to Canning, 12 June 1844.

57. F.O. 195/237, Rawlinson to Canning, Baghdad, 3 September 1845.

58. Ibid.

60. Bruce Masters indicates that these berāts started to be granted by Sulṭān Selim III (1789–1809) by at least 1806. See his "The Sulṭān's Entrepreneurs: The Avrupa Tuccaris and the Hayriye Tuccaris in Syria" in *International Journal of Middle East Studies,* Vol. 24, no. 4, November 1992, 579–97.

61. C236. Political and Secret Library. J. A Saldanha. *Precis of Turkish Arabia,* 1801/1905, 39.

62. F.O. 78/656, Rawlinson to Canning, Baghdad, 5 August 1846.

63. The text of the Convention is reprinted in Issawi, *Economic History of the Middle East,* 38–40.

64. F.O. 78/656, Rawlinson to Canning, Baghdad,5 August 1846.

65. Ibid.

66. Ibid.

67. Ibid.

68. F.O. 78/3015, Nixon to Layard, Baghdad, 25 January 1879.

69. Owen, *Middle East in the World Economy,* 108–9.

70. Quoted in Yaᶜqub Sarkis. *Mabahith Iraqīyya . . . ,* Vol. 2, 289.

71. F.O. 424, Rawlinson to Canning, Baghdad,3 February 1846.

72. Abbas Amanat, *Cities and Trade,* vi.

73. F.O. 424, Rawlinson to Canning, Baghdad, February 3, 1846; and F.O. 78/656, Hector to Rawlinson, Baghdad, 30 July 1846.

74. F.O. 78/656, Rawlinson to Canning, Baghdad, 5 August 1846.

75. 2.2 bedras equalled one qirsh in 1860–61. See Suleimān Fāʾiq. *Tarikh Baghdad.* 173–74.

76. F.O. 78/957, Rawlinson to Foreign Office, Baghdad, 14 June 1853.

77. See Abdul-Rahman ibn ᶜAbdullāh al-Suwaidi. *Tarikh hawadith Baghdad wa al-Basra*. Edited by Abdul-Salam Rauf. Basra: Basra University Press, 1980, 66; Al-Ansari. "Al-Nasra fi Akhbar al-Basra," op. cit., 203–5; and Suleimān Fāʾiq. *Tarikh Baghdad*. Trans. from the Turkish by Musa Kadhim Nawras. Baghdad: Maarif Press, 1962, 174.

78. Mahdi Jawad al-Bustani. "Watha'iq ᶜuthmāniyya ghayr manshura ᶜan Basra wa ustuluha wa silatuha bi al-khalij al-Arabi fi awasit al-qarn al-tasiᶜ ashr" in *Al-Wathiqa* (Bahrain), no. 17, July 1990, 110.

79. Ibid., 107–9.

80. Ibid., 108.

81. Ibid., 109.

82. F.O. 195/272, Rawlinson to Welleseley, Baghdad, 3 March 1847.

83. F.O. 195/367, Rawlinson to Canning, 25 February 1852.

84. F.O. 195/367, Rawlinson to Canning, 25 February 1852.

85. Al-Bustani. "Watha'iq ᶜUthmāniyya, 111.

86. Ibid., 112.

87. Ibid., 112.

88. According to a published sijjil of the Basra civil court, shaikh Fahd al-Mughamis of the Muntafiq sold all the lands in the village of Miᶜqal to the British Resident in Basra, John Latouche in 1780; the lands were then transferred to the Lynch firm. See Mustafa Kazim al-Madamgha. *Nusus min watha'iq al-ᶜuthmāniya ᶜan tarikh al-Basra fi sijillat mahkamat al-sharᶜīyya fi al-Basra*. Basra: Basra University Press, 1982, 47. See also Shaikh Abdul-Qadir Bashaᶜyan al-Abbasi. *Al-Basra fi adwaruha al-tarikhiyya*. Basra: Dar al-Basri, 1961, 91–92.

89. Ibid., 92.

90. al-Bustani. "Dirasa li-Watha'iq ᶜUthmāniyya," 89–107.

91. Ibid., 98–99.

92. Ibid., 106–7.

93. F.O. 195/949, Nixon to Elliot, Baghdad, 29 March 1871.

94. Zamil Al-Rashīd. *Suᶜudi Relations With Eastern Arabia And Uman, 1800–1870*. London: Luzac, 1981, 127.

95. Lorimer. op. cit., 1130.

96. Longrigg, op. cit., 302–3.

97. Longrigg, op. cit., 303.

98. Al-Ansari, op. cit., 186.

99. Sayyid Dāwūd al-Saᶜdī. "Al-tariq min al-ahsa ila al-Riyāḍ" in *Lughat al-Arab*, Vol. 3, July 1913–1914, 118–25.

100. Al-Ansari, op. cit., 186–88.

101. Vital Cuinet. op. cit., 315–16.

102. F.O. 195/2096, Wratislaw to O'Conor, Basra, 3 June 1901.

103. F.O. 602/19, From Richards to O'Conor, Damascus, 3 November 1902.

4. RIVER ROUTES

1. See chapter one.

2. The second Saʿūdī state was reconsolidated under the auspices of Turki ibn ʿAbdullāh (1823–34) and his son Faiṣal (d. 1865). See R. Bayly Winder. *Saʿūdī Arabia in the Nineteenth Century*. (New York: St. Martin's Press, 1965.

3. See Salman Hasan. *Al-tatawur al-iqtisadi fi al-Iraq,* 87–89; Charles Issawi. "Middle East Economic Development, 1815–1914: The General and the Specific" in M. A Cook, ed. *Studies in the Economic History of the Middle East* (London: Oxford University Press, 1970), 400–1; and Roger Owen. *The Middle East in the World Economy,* 183.

4. A notable exception to this trend is ʿAlī Abdullatif Ahmida. *The Making of Modern Libya: State Formation, Colonization and Resistance, 1830–1932*. Albany: State University of New York Press, 1994.

5. Charles Issawi. *An Economic History of the Middle East and North Africa,* New York: Columbia Press, 1982, 47–48.

6. For the classic discussion of "protection" costs, see Niels Steensgard. *Carracks, Caravans and Companies: The Structural Crisis in European-Asian Trade in the Early Seventeenth Century*. (Copenhagen: 1973), 39–40.

7. Khwaja Abdul-Qadir. *Waqai-Manazil-Rum: Diary of a Journal to Constantinople*. Edited by Mohibull Hasan. (London: Asia Publishing House, 1968), 46.

8. Nieuwenhuis, *Politics and Society,* 133.

9. Muḥammad ʾAḥmad Mahmoud. "Ahwal al-ashaʾir al-Iraqīyya al-Arabiyya wa ilaqatuha bi al-hukuma, 1872–1918" (Master's thesis, Baghdad University, 1980), 15.

10. F.O. 78/656, Hector to Rawlinson, Baghdad, 30 July 1846.

11. F.O. 195/521, Kemball to Redcliffe, Baghdad, 5 August 1857.

12. The Finnish explorer, Georg August Wallin noted in 1845 that tribal agriculturalists in the Syrian desert sometimes gave presents of clothing to their bedu protectors; while in 1862–63, the British traveller, W. G. Palgrave paid four shillings to cross the dira of Tallal ibn al-Rasheed, shaikh of Jabal Shammar. See Wallin. *Travels in Arabia*. Cambridge and New York: The Oleander Press, 1979, 122, and Palgrave. *Personal Narrative,* 57.

13. Abdul-Rahman al-ʿUrayni. "Al-hayat al-ijtimaʿiyya lada badiyat Najd wa athar al-daʿwa al-salafiyya fiha mundhu al-qarn al-ashir al-hijri wa hatta suqut al-Darʿiyya" (Master's thesis, Al-Imam Muḥammad ibn Saʿūd Islamic University, Riyāḍ, 1984), 290–99.

14. Muḥammad ʾAḥmad Mahmoud. op. cit., 16.

15. Rifaat ʿAlī Abou-El-Haj. "Taxation, Trade, Production and Society in 16th Century Mosul" in Abdeljelil Temimi, ed. *La Vie Sociale dans les Provinces Arabes a l'Epoque Ottomane*. Vol. 3, Tunis, 1988. I used this article while still in manuscript form.

16. F.O. 195/301, Rassam to Wellesley, Mosul, 25 May 1847.

17. Abou-El-Haj, op. cit.

18. F.O. 78/656, Hector to Rawlinson, Baghdad, 30 July 1846.

19. F.O. 195/521, Kemball to Redcliffe, Baghdad, 19 August 1857.

20. F.O. 78/656, Hector to Rawlinson, Baghdad, 30 July 1846.

21. F.O. 78/656, Hector to Rawlinson, Baghdad, 30 July 1846.

22. F.O. 195/318, Rawlinson to Canning, Baghdad, 6 December 1848.

23. F.O. 78/656, Hector to Rawlinson, Baghdad, 30 July 1846.

24. F.O. 602/33, Rawlinson to Parsigh, Baghdad, 15 November 1846.

25. Thabit, A. J. ʿAbdullāh. "The Political Economy of Merchants and Trade in Basra," 61–62.

26. M. E. Yapp. "The Euphrates Expedition," op. cit., 895–912.

27. F.O. 78/656, Hector, et al., to Rawlinson, Baghdad, 24 October 1846.

28. See the discussion in the Introduction to James D. Tracy, ed. *The Political Economy of Merchant Empires: State Power and World Trade, 1350–1750.* Cambridge: Cambridge University Press, 1991.

29. Covering Letter appended by Rawlinson to Hector's despatch referenced below as F.0. 78/656, Baghdad, 24 October 1846.

30. F.O. 78/656, Hector et al., to Rawlinson, Baghdad, 24 October 1846.

31. F.O. 195/367, Jones to Rawlinson, Basra, 2 February 1852.

32. Eventually, the mashyakha was granted to Fahd by the Ottomans, and he was replaced by Nāṣir al-Saʿdūn in 1863. See Suleimān Fāʾiq. *Tarikh al-Muntafiq.* Translated from the Turkish by Muḥammad Khulussi al-Nāṣiri. (Baghdad: Maarif Press, 1961), 27–51.

33. ʿAbbās al-ʿAzzāwī. *Tarikh al-Iraq bayn ihtilalayn.* Vol. 7, 93–98; 35.

34. Al-Azzawi. Ibid., 97.

35. Fāʾiq. op. cit., 27–51.

36. Al-Azzawi, op. cit., 99–100.

37. F.O. 195/367, Rawlinson to Canning, Baghdad, 19 May 1852.

38. F.O. 195/521, Taylor to Kemball, Basra, 17 April 1856.

39. F.O. 195/521, Taylor to Kemball, Basra, 17 April 1856.

40. F.O. 195/521, Kemball to Redcliffe, Baghdad, 19 August 1857.

41. That the Muntafiq leaders no longer commanded the men or matériel to engage another tribe on their own had become an open secret. For instance, after the bloody civil war in the Muntafiq dira, shaikh Bandar was only able to win a battle against the Rabīʿa tribe because he was accompanied by a small party of Turkish irregular cavalry. See F.O. 195/521, Taylor to Kemball, Basra, 17 April 1856.

42. F.O. 195/521, Kemball to Redcliffe, Baghdad, 19 August 1857.

43. F.O. 195/521, Kemball to Redcliffe, Baghdad, 19 August 1857.

44. It was reported that shaikh Manṣūr "even looked to aid from the Chaab tribe to enable him to meet his opponents in the field." See F.O. 195/334, Kemball to Canning, Baghdad, 24 September 1850.

45. The previous section has relied upon Yaʿqub Sarkis's account; the latter's father, Niʿmatullah or Naʿum was the Muntafiq shaikh Nāṣir al-Saʿdūn's khazandar (treasurer) in the crucial first years of the Mutassarafiyya. See Yaʿqub Sarkis, 74–81.

46. F.O. 195/442, Jones to Redcliffe, Baghdad, 30 May 1855.

47. Grattan Geary. *Through Asiatic Turkey,* 15–16.

48. To quote Ṛoger Owen, "sea-borne exports . . . tripled between 1880–1884, and 1910–1913." See Owen, op. cit., 274.

49. For example, in 1897 Shaikh Ajil ibn Rokan, commonly called ibn Majlad, the chief of the Dhamshah branch of the ʿAnayza tribe, having developed a grudge against the authorities at Aleppo who had expelled the tribe from its traditional dira, directed his tribe to "forcibly intercept boats coming down from Birjik laden with wheat for Baghdad . . . on which [tribesmen] exacted blackmail on each boat at the rate of £1 in money and two bags of wheat. . . . The owners of the wheat have now complained to the vali of Baghdad for assistance." See F.O. 195/1978, Extract from Diary of H. B. M.'s Consul-General, Baghdad to the Secretary to the Government of India, Foreign Office Department, 29 September 1897.

50. Eric Hobsbawm. *Captain Swing: A Social History of the Great Agricultural Uprising of 1830* (New York: W. W. Norton and Company, 1968), 283–88.

51. F.O. 195/949, Nixon to Elliot, Baghdad, 29 March 1871.

52. Winder, op. cit., 250.

53. F.O. 195/1478, Plowden to Dufferin, Baghdad, 17 April 1884.

5. THE GRAIN TRADE

1. Amanat, *Cities and Trade*, 75–118; Ismael, *Kuwait: Social Change in Historical Perspective*, 32–36; and F.O. 78/704, Rawlinson to Palmerston, Baghdad, 28 May 1847.

2. Issawi, *The Fertile Crescent.*

3. Geary, *Through Asiatic Turkey*, 13–14.

4. Afaf Lutfi al-Sayyid Marsot. *Egypt in the Reign of Muḥammad ʿAlī.* Cambridge: Cambridge University Press, 1984, 236.

5. Vernon John Puryear. *International Economics and Diplomacy in the Near East: A Study of British Commercial Policy in the Levant.* Stanford: Stanford University Press, 1935, 181.

6. Ibid., 182–83.

7. Ibid., 118.

8. Ibid., 124.

9. F.O. 195/272, Kemball to Cowley, Baghdad, 18 August 1847. One tghar equalled two tons.

10. F.O. 195/318, Rawlinson to Canning, Baghdad, 16 August 1848.

11. Ibid.

12. Ibid.

13. F.O. 195/318, Rawlinson to Canning, Baghdad, May 20, 1848.

14. Ibid.

15. Ibid.

16. al-ʿAzzāwī, *Tarikh al-Iraq bayn ihtilalayn.* Vol. 7, 111–13.

17. F.O. 371/624, Kemball to Bulwer, Baghdad, 28 September 1859.

18. F.O. 371/624, Hector to Bulwer, Baghdad, 29 February 1860.

19. Issawi, *The Fertile Crescent*, 279.

20. Ibid., 280.

21. Ibid., 348.

22. F.O. 195/237, Rawlinson to Canning, Baghdad, 8 January 1845.

23. Ibid.

24. F.O. 195/237, Rawlinson to Canning, Baghdad, 16 April 1845.

25. Ibid.

26. F.O. 195/272, Kemball to Cowley, Baghdad, 18 August 1847.

27. F.O. 195/237, Rawlinson to Canning, Baghdad, 8 January 1845. In fact, dates, rice and wheat were being exported in small quantities to Muscat, Mauritius and India.

28. F.O. 78/656, Rassam to Canning, Mosul, 10 July 1846.

29. F.O. 195/334, Rawlinson to Canning, Baghdad, 23 May 1849.

30. Ibid.

31. F.O. 195/334, Rawlinson to Canning, Baghdad, 20 June 1849.

32. F.O. 371/624, Kemball to Bulwer, Baghdad, 28 September 1859.
33. F.O. 371/624, Hector to Bulwer, Baghdad, 29 February 1860.
34. Al-Ansari, "Al-Nasra fi Akhbar al-Basra," Part 2, Vol. 18, 299.
35. Ibid.
36. Ibid.
37. Ibid.
38. Ibid.
39. Ibid., 205.
40. Suleimān Fā'iq. *Tarikh Baghdad,* 174.
41. Ibid., 175.
42. F.O. 371/624, Kemball to Bulwer, Baghdad, 12 October 1859.
43. F.O. 78/2650, Nixon to Derby, Baghdad, 18 September 1877.
44. Ibid.
45. F.O. 78/2846, Muḥammad to Nixon, Baghdad, 7 October 1877.
46. F.O. 195/142, from the Agents of Gray, Mackenzie and Company to Captain E. A. Fraser, Basra, 9 November 1877.
47. Ibid.
48. Roger Owen. *The Middle East in the World Economy,* 183. In fact, exports soared from £230,000 in 1870–1875 to nearly £800,000 in 1875–1880.
49. F.O. 78/2615, Nixon to Gray, Mackenzie and Company, Baghdad, 3 December 1877.
50. F.O. 78/2615, Nixon to Layard, Baghdad, 3 December 1877 .
51. Geary. op. cit., 19
52. Ansari, "The History of Khuzistan," 143.
53. Ibid.
54. F.O. 78/4364, Mockler to White, Baghdad, 21 November 1891.
55. al-Qahawati, *Dawr al-Basra,* 343.
56. Ibid., 342–43.
57. F.O. 371/624, Kemball to Bulwer, Baghdad, October 12, 1859.

"[Because] there has been a further rise in the prices of wheat and barley at Baghdad, a resolution has been taken by Omer Pasha . . . interdicting the export and hoarding of grain, and requiring the sale of stores now existing in the city. If these orders be seriously enforced, with respect to the miri or government grain, and the grain in the hands of monopolists, and if the obstacles be suspended which have been hitherto opposed to the importation of grain from the districts, some amelioration may be expected to ensue. . . ."

58. F.O. 78/2846, Muḥammad to Nixon, Baghdad, 7 October 1877.
59. F.O. 78/2872, Nixon to Derby, Baghdad, 21 September 1878.
60. F.O. 195/142, From Grey, Mackenzie and Company to Fraser, Basra, 9 November 1877.
61. F.O. 78/2650, Nixon to the Secretary of State for Foreign Affairs, Baghdad, 18 September 1877.
62. F.O. 78/2872, Nixon to Derby, Baghdad, 21 September 1878.
63. Al-Qahawati, op. cit., 344.
64. Ansari, op. cit., 237.
65. Al-Qahawati, op. cit., 340.

66. Upton, *Gleanings from the Desert of Arabia,* 391–98.
67. Salman Hasan, *Al-Tatawur al-Iqtisadi fi al-Iraq,* 171.
68. F.O.195/2242, Crow to Barclay, Basra, January 3, 1907.
69. Ibid.
70. Ibid.
71. Ibid.
72. Al-Qahawati, op. cit., 348.

6: THE HORSE TRADE

1. Hasan links the development of sea transport and the rise in European demand for wool and hides to the changes taking place in the Iraqī economy. According to Hasan, those two interrelated developments led to the destruction of the bedu economy, which depended primarily upon the breeding of livestock. Thus the price of animal products such as wool and hides rose from 548,000 Iraqī dinars in 1878 to 924,000 Iraqī dinars in 1939. The price of grain went up from 70,000 Iraqī dinars to 188,000 Iraqī dinars from 1890 to 1911. See Salman Hasan, *Al-tatawur al-iqtisadi fi al-Iraq,* 172.

2. For instance, in 1895–96 a certain horse dealer form Mosul named Ali ibn Ṭālib made it his specialty to buy "big horses with good bone and substance, combined with quality" for the Civil Veterinary Department in India; he became so successful at identifying, and meeting British demand for horses that officials in India used his services over those of other dealers. See *The Annual Administration Report on the Civil Veterinary Department in India for the Year 1895–96,* 4–5.

3. Frauke Heard-Bey. *From Trucial States to United Arab Emirates: A Society in Transition.* London and New York: Longmans, 1982, 24–27.

4. F.O. 78/907, Taylor to Foreign Office, Basra, 1 May 1852.

5. Duarte Barbosa. *A Description of the Coasts of East Africa and Malabar in the Beginning of the Sixteenth Century.* London: The Hakluyt Society, 1850.

6. Simon Digby. "The Horse and the Elephant in the Armies of the Delhi Sultanate Their Sources of Supply," paper presented at the Conference of War, Technology and Sociology in the Middle East, School of Oriental and African Studies, University of London, 22–24 September 1970, 11.

7. Indications are that the Portuguese trade in Arabian and Persian horses continued with much vigor until the early part of the seventeenth century, especially between the Portuguese colony of Goa and Yemen, Oman, lower Iraq and the coastal ports or bandars of Iran. However, by 1726 or after, Arabian horses had become essential to Mamluk armies in Iraq. For the Portuguese connection, see C. R. de Silva, "Empire, Horses and Trade: An Examination of Portuguese Control over the Trade in Arab and Persian Horses across the Arabian Sea during the Sixteenth Century," paper presented at the Second International Conference on Indian Ocean Studies, Perth, Western Australia, 2–12 December 1984, 1. For evidence of Mamluk 1 Ottoman reliance on Arab horses, see Yasin ibn Khairallah al-ᶜUmarī. *Zubdat al-athar al-jaliyya fi al-hawadith al-ardiyya.* Edited by Imad Abdul-Salam al-Raouf (Najaf: ʾAdab Press, 1974), 169. In 1791, a shaikh of the Ubaid tribe sent the Pasha of Baghdad ten Arab horses as presents these had entered his stable as war booty.

8. William Heude. *A Voyage Up the Persian Gulf and a Journey Overland from India to England in 1817.* (London: Longmans', 1819), 134–36.

9. The Marquess of Anglesbury. *A History of the British Cavalry.* Vol. II (London: Leo Cooper, 1975), 437.

10. Ibid.; and J. M. Brerton. *The Horse in War.* (London: David and Charles Ltd., 1976), 91. See also Lady Anne Blunt. *Bedouin Tribes of the Euphrates.* Vol. II (London: John Murray, 1879), 243–76. The author's husband, the famous traveller Wilfred Scawen Blunt devoted a whole chapter in the book to the "distinctive" features of the pure-bred Arabian horse.

11. Muḥammad Hamad al-Bassam al-Tamini. "Kitab al-durrar al-mafakhir fi akhbar al-Arab al-awakhir" (British Library, London: Ms. Add. 7358), folios 90–100; al-ᶜAzzāwī. *Asha'ir al-Iraq.* (Vol. 1., 177, 224–33); *Rihlat al-Munshi al-Baghdādī.* Edited by ᶜAbbās al-ᶜAzzāwī (Baghdad: Tijara Press, n.d..), 54; F.O. 195/1409, Tweedie to Granville, Baghdad, 1 November 1882, and Tweedie, *The Arabian Horse,* 84, note.

12. Throughout the eighteenth century, the Shammar of Iraq continued in their efforts to dislodge the Wahhābī hold over central Arabia. In 1790, a battle took place between the Shammar and allied tribes on the one hand, and the forces of ᶜAbdul-ᶜAzīz ibn Saᶜūd on the other, in which the shaikh of the "Iraqī" Shammar, Mislat ibn Mutlaq al-Jarba, was killed near Ha'il. See ᶜUthmān ibn Bishr. *Unwan al-Majd fi Tarikh Najd,* 87 and Al-Azzawi. op. cit., Vol. 4, 137–41.

13. al-Suwaidi. *Tarikh Baghdad,* Vol. I, 34. For instance, in 1728, a battle took place between the Shah of Persia, Ashraf Khan and the vali of Baghdad, the Mamluk ᵓAḥmad Pasha in which "the Muslims (i.e., the Ottoman/Mamluk camp) overcame the heretics *(al-muliḥidūn)* and captured their camps, their supplies, their weapons and their horses. . . ." See al-ᶜUmarī, op. cit., 86.

14. Al-Suwaidi, op. cit., 36.

15. Suleimān Abu Laila (1750–1762) is thought to have paid little or no revenue to the Porte, in part because "his expenses were higher than his income." See Tom Niewenhuis, *Politics and Society in Early Modern Iraq,* 80.

16. Al-Umari, op. cit., 120.

17. Ibid., 125.

18. Ibid., 129.

19. Suleimān Fāᵓiq. *Tarikh al-Mamalik* Baghdad (Translated from Turkish by Muḥammad Najib al-Armanazi. Baghdad: Maarif Press, 1961), 64.

20. Ibid., 60.

21. Yaᶜqub Sarkis, *Mabahith Iraqīyya,* Vol. 3, 318.

22. Akif Pasha vali of Baghdad in the 1870s, was reputed to have one of the two best horse studs in town, the other belonging to an Indian nawāb called ᵓAḥmad Agha. Lady Anne Blunt, op. cit., Vol. 1, 200–5.

23. Ibn Bishr. op. cit., 98–99.

24. Ibid., 98.

25. Ibid., Vol. I, 31–98.

26. For the first example, see Ibn Bishr, op. cit, Vol. 1, 35, 109. For the second, see ᶜal-Umari, op. cit., 169.

27. Al-Tamimi, op. cit., folios 90–100.

28. Al-ᶜAzzāwī, *Tārīkh al-ᶜIrāq bayna ᵓIḥtilālayn,* Vol. 8, 12–13.

29. Upton, *Gleanings from the Desert of Arabia,* 188.

30. lbid, 366–96.

31. Jeanne Dieulafoy. *La Perse, La Chaldee et La Susianie.* Paris: Librairie Hachette, 1887, 634–35; and al-ʿAzzāwī. *ʿAshāʾir . . . ,* Vol. I, 381.

32. One of the ʾamīrs of the Saʿūdī state, Saʿūd ibn ʿAbdul-ʿAzīz, alone possessed 1,400 pure-bred Arabian stallions. See Ibn Bishr. *ʿUnwan al-Maid,* Vol. I., 173.

33. Tweedie, op. cit., 293–94.

34. Ibid., 294.

35. Ibid., 290.

36. Upton. op. cit., 391–93, 396.

37. F.O. 195/2214, Ramsey to Clark, Baghdad, 17 May 1906.

38. H. St. John Philby, *Arabia of the Wahhābīs,* (New York: Arno Press, 1973), 274.

39. Charles Doughty. *Wanderings in Arabia* .An abridgement of *Travels in Arabia Deserta* (2 vols.; New York: Thomas Seltzer, 1924), Vol. II, 254.

40. Muḥsin Ghayyāth al-ʿAjīl. *Al-saḥāfī, al-siyāsī, al muʾarrikh al-Najdī Suleimān ibn Ṣāliḥ al-Dakhīl.* (Baṣra: Baṣra University Press, 1982), 165.

41. Ibid., 164.

42. Doughty, op. cit., Vol. II, 217, 233.

43. See Carl R. Raswan. *Black Tents of Arabia* (Boston: Little, Brown and Company, 1935), 135–36.

44. Upton, op. cit., 220.

45. ʿAbdul-ʿAzīz al-Qassāb. *Min dhikrayātī.* (Beirut: Faḍl Press, 1962), 8.

46. Tweedie mentions that one of the most successful horse merchants was ʿAlī al-Khuḍairī "whose home is in Baghdad"; the latter imported the famous racehorse, Euphrates, into Bombay. See Tweedie, op. cit., 271.

47. Tweedie. op. cit., 299, note.

48. Ibid., 300.

49. Doughty, op. cit.

50. Tweedie, op. cit., 300.

51. Ibid., 307.

52. F.O. 195/237, Rawlinson to Canning, Baghdad, 3 September 1845.

53. F.O. 78/656, Rawlinson to Canning, Baghdad, 5 August 1846.

54. F.O. 195/803 B, Kemball to Lyons, Baghdad, 5 September 1866.

55. Owen, *The Middle East in the World Economy,* 277.

56. Whether delays with regard to British goods were part of an overt Ottoman policy or sprang from local initiative cannot be confirmed. However, from about the middle of the century, British consuls kept up a steady stream of complaints to their superiors, intimating that lost merchandise or an extraordinary amount of red tape was not only proof of official incompetence but of governmental willfulness in the face of foreign representatives. See, for example, F.O. 781/4285, Tweedie to H.B.M.'s Ambassador, Baghdad, 7 October 1890.

57. For instance, in 1858, the Ottoman authorities chartered a British ship, and entered into partnership with local traders to send a cargo of dates and horses to India Because this was considered enticement on the part of the Ottomans, the British were convinced that pressure had been put on local merchants to ship their wares on Ottoman

vessels. See F.O. 195/577, Extract of a Letter from H.M.'s Vice-Consul at Bussorah to H.M.'s Consul-General at Baghdad, 26 November 1858.

58. F.O. 195/803B, Kemball to Lyons, Baghdad, 5 September 1866.

59. F.O. 195/803B, Kemball to Lyons, Baghdad, 5 September 1866.

60. F.O. 195/803B, Gonne to the Secretary to the Government of India, Simla, 15 October 1866.

61. Al-Qahawātī, *Dawr al-Baṣra,* 383–84.

62. Lorimer, *A Gazeteer of the Persian Gulf,* 2337–38.

63. In the mid-1870s, British consuls were not allowed to see Ottoman trade statistics and had to compile their trade reports from information given them by British shipping firms, thus drawing their data from a limited source. See F.O. [785/3778], Tweedie to Wyndham, Baghdad, 6 October 1883.

64. F.O. 195/803B, Kemball to Lyons, Baghdad, 5 September 1866.

65. F.O. 195/803B, Kemball to Lyons, Baghdad, 5 September 1866.

66. India Office Record Library/Political and Secret (hereafter I.O.R.L./P.&S.). Extract from the Diary of the Political Agent in Turkish Arabia for the Week Ending July 22, 1882.

67. F.O. 195/1445, Tweedie to Wyndham, Baghdad, 2 July 1883.

68. F.O. 602/17, Wratislaw to O'Conor, Basra, 19 July 1900.

69. Op. cit., 296.

70. Lady Blunt, op. cit., 200–7.

71. Al-Azzawi. *Asha'ir al-ʿIrāq,* Vol. I, 130–44.

72. F.O. 195/521, Kemball to Redcliffe, Baghdad, 4 February 1857.

73. In fact, shaikh ʿAbdul-Karīm continued to do battle with the Ottoman government until he was caught and hanged by Midḥat Pasha. See F.O. 195/1409, Tweedie to Foreign Office, Baghdad, 1 November 1882.

74. F.O. 195/949, Rassam to Elliot, Mosul, 4 January 1872.

75. Al-ʾAzzawi *Tarikh . . . ,* Vol. 8, 103.

76. ʿAjīl Pasha al-Yāwar, shaikh mashayikh of the Shammar, was considered to be one of the chief breeders and seller of horses in the early twentieth century. See Ernest Main. *In and Around Baghdad.* Baghdad: The Times Press, n.d., 19. See also Al ʿAzzāwī. *ʿAshāʾir . . . ,* 373.

77. Tweedie, op. cit., 72.

78. I.O.R.L./P&S/ 33, Extract from the Diary of the Political Agent in Turkish Arabia for the Week Ending July 22, 1882.

79. I.O.R.L./P&S/7/ 37, Translation of Letter no. 287, dated June 9, 1883, from H.E. the Governor of Basra to H.B.M.'s Consul at Basra.

80. See the discussion in Upton, op. cit., 200–398; Tweedie, op. cit., 21, 84–85, 272, and Blunt, op. cit., 117–18, 205–7.

81. I.O.R.L./P&S/ 7/37, no. 65, Tweedie to the Secretary of the Government of India, Baghdad, 22 June 1883.

82. F.O. 602/2, Kemball to the Secretary to the Government in Bombay, Baghdad, 26 June 1866.

83. *Foreign Office Confidential Print: Affairs of Kuwait,* 71.

84. Ibid., 71.

85. F.O. 602/17, Wratislaw to O'Conor, Basra, 19 July 1900.
86. Foreign Office Confidential Print . . . , 38–39.
87. Ibid. . . . , 45.
88. Ibid., 7–8.
89. *Lughat al-ʿArab,* Vol. IV, November 1911, 198.

7. THE GROWTH OF REGIONAL MARKET TOWNS IN IRAQ, KUWAIT, AND ARABISTAN

1. Curtin, *Cross-Cultural Trade in World History,* 2–14.
2. The best sources on the Muntafiq remain Yaʿqub Sarkis, *Mabahith Iraqīyya;* and Albertine Jwaideh. "Aspects of Land Tenure and Social Change in Lower Iraq During Late Ottoman Times" in Tarif Khalidi, ed. *Land Tenure and Social Transformation in the Middle East.* Beirut: American University of Beirut Press, 1984.
3. Muhsin al-Ajeel, ed. *Al-suhafi, al-muaʾrikh,* 73–74.
4. Ibid., 74–75.
5. Mirza Ṭālib Khan. *Rihlat Ṭālib Khan ila al-Iraq wa-Awrupa, 1799.* Translated from the French by Dr. Mustafa Jawad. Baghdad: Iman Press, 1969, 405.
6. See, for example, Sarkis, op. cit., Vol. I, 73–81.
7. F.O. 195/334, Kemball to Canning, Baghdad, 24 September 1850; F.O. 195/Kemball to Canning, Baghdad, 6 November 1859; F.O. 195/334, Jones to Kemball, Baghdad, 12 December 1850 and F.O. 195/367, Taylor to Kemball, Basra, 9, October 1851.
8. Ibid.
9. F.O. 195/367, Rawlinson to Canning, Baghdad, 24 February 1852.
10. Ibid.
11. Sarkis, op. cit., Vol. 1, 74–75.
12. Ibid., 73–79.
13. Ibid., 73–79.
14. al-ʿAzzāwī. *Tarikh al-Iraq bayna ihtilalayn.* Vol. 7, 150, 157.
15. F.O. 195/521, Kemball to Redcliffe, Baghdad, 9 January 1856.
16. Note the negotiations that took place between Ottoman authorities and the shaikhs of the Shammar, another important tribe. Although in theory there were other contenders for the post of shaikh al-mashayikh of the Shammar, Farhan was given the position because he could pay the sums expected of him. See F.O. 195/521, Kemball to Redcliffe, Baghdad, 4 February 1857.
17. Albertine Jwaideh. "Midḥat Pasha and the Land System of Lower Iraq," in *St. Antony's Papers,* no. 16. *Middle Eastern Affairs,* no. 3. London: Chatto and Windus, 1963, 114.
18. Al-Azzawi, op. cit., 193–94.
19. F.O. 78/907, Taylor to the Foreign Office, Basra, 1 May 1852.
20. Ibid.
21. This continued to be the case until the latter part of the nineteenth century. See F.O. 78/907, Taylor to Foreign Office, Basra, 1 May 1852.

22. Statistics on Kuwait were usually included in British trade reports on Basra; for the most part, they are meager indications of the volume of Kuwait's imports and exports. See especially F.O. 78/907, Taylor to the Foreign Office, Basra, 1 May 1852.

23. I owe a debt of gratitude to Dr. William Charles Young, my colleague at U.C.L.A., for points brought up in the following discussion.

24. Different dates are given for the establishment of the town. According to a present-day writer, Jasim al-ᶜĀṣī, the town may have been built in 1887; however, Suleimān al-Dakhil, who witnessed for himself many of the events described, says that it was built in 1881. See Jasim al-ᶜĀṣī. "Al-Khamīsiyya: madina mahjura" in *Al-Turath al-shaᶜbi,* Vol. 6, no. 6, 1975, 260; and Al-Ajeel, op. cit., 67–69.

25. Al-Ajeel, op. cit., 68.

26. Ibid., 68.

27. Ibid., 68.

28. Ibid., 69.

29. Gertrude Bell, *The Arab of Mesopotamia.* Basra: Government Press, 1916, 27.

30. Al-Asi, op. cit., 266.

31. Zubair was the burial place of two important early Muslims, the Sufi Hasan al-Basri and Zubair ibn al-ᶜAwwam, one of the Companions of the Prophet. See al-Haidari, *Kitab ᶜunwan al-Majd,* 161.

32. Al-Juhany, "The Social History of Najd Prior to the Wahhābīs," 223–24.

33. F.O. 78/907, Taylor to the Foreign Office, Basra, 1 May 1852.

34. Al-Juhany, op. cit., 224.

35. F.O. 78/907, Taylor to the Foreign Office, Basra, 1 May 1852.

36. ibn Bishr, *ᶜUnwan al-majd fi tarikh Najd,* Vol. 2, 45–46.

37. al-Nabhani, *Al-tuhfa al-Nabhaniyya,* 123.

38. Ibn Bishr, op. cit., 26–32.

39. Ibid., 45–46.

40. In 1860, the mutasallim of Basra turned the tables on his erstwhile allies, the Muntafiq shaikhs and joined Suleimān ibn ᶜAbdul-Razzāq ibn Zuhair in a successful attempt to dislodge the Muntafiq as well as cal-ᶜUjmān tribes from their preponderant position in the date groves surrounding Basra. See Abdul-Muhsin, *Tadhkirat uli al-nahi,* 120–21.

41. This is further suggested by the post of Qasim Pasha al-Zuhair who seems to have coveted the post of vali of Basra in 1880 but ended up instead as a member of the first Ottoman parliament (al-Mabcuthan) in 1881. By joining a nascent "Ottomanized" elite in lower Iraq, he was following the only path left to deracinated notables and aᶜyan in the latter part of the nineteenth century. See Abdul-Qadir Bashaᶜyan al-Abbasi. *Basra fi adwaruha al-tarikhiya.* (Basra: Dar al-Basri, 1961), 58; and al-Azzawi, op. cit., Vol. 8, 68.

42. Prior to the battle, the Zuhair leadership asked for assistance from the governor of Basra and, during the ensuing melée, opened the gate of the town to the Ottoman army and allowed it to loot and ransack at will. See Al-Nabhani, op. cit., 120, 128.

43. F.O. 195/237, Rawlinson to the Foreign Office, Baghdad, 6 January 1844.

44. Ibid.

45. Ibid.

46. Shahnavaz, "Britain and the Opening of the Karun River," 252.

47. F.O. 195/272, Rawlinson to Wellesley, Baghdad, March 1847.

48. F.O. 195/367, Rawlinson to Canning, 25 February 1852, and Ibid.
49. Ansari, "The History of Khuzistan," 160.
50. Ibid.
51. Ibid.
52. F.O. 78/458, Report of a Journey up the Karun River by Captain Chevenix-Trench, Basra, April 1891.
53. F.O. 195/1799, Mockler to Ford, Baghdad, 30 October 1893, and F.O. 195/1799, Extract from the Diary of H.M.'s Consul, Basra, for the Week Ending November 30, 1893.
54. F.O. 78/4552, Belville to Mockler, Baghdad, 25 October 1894.
55. Al-Ansari, op. cit., 172.
56. Al-Azzawi, op. cit., vol. 8, 68.
57. Shahnavaz, op. cit., 128–29.
58. Shahnavaz, op. cit., 128.
59. Ibid.
60. ʿAbdul-Razzāq al-Hassani. *Al-Iraq qadiman wa hadithan*. Sidon: Irfan Press, 1956, 190–91.
61. Jwaideh. "Aspects of Land Tenure . . . ," 343.
62. Al-Qahawati, *Dawr al-Basra,* 209.
63. Jwaideh, "Midḥat Pasha and The Land System," 114.
64. Jwaideh. "Aspects of Land Tenure," 346.
65. Denis de Rivoyre. *Les Vrais Arabes et Leur Pays,* 233.
66. Sarkis, op. cit., 265–72.
67. Jwaideh, "Aspects of Land Tenure . . . ," 346.
68. Vital Cuinet. *La Turquie d'Asie.* Vol. 4, 303.
69. Al-Ajeel, op. cit., 75.
70. Ibid., 75–76.
71. Helen Lackner. *A House Built on Sand: A Political Economy of Saʿūdī Arabia.* London: Ithaca Press, 2.
72. Phebe Marr. *The Modern History of Iraq.* Boulder and London: Westview Press, 1985, 23.

AFTERWORD

1. Hanna Batatu. *The Old Social Classes and the Revolutionary Movements of Iraq: A Study of Iraq's Old Landed and Commercial Classes and of its Communists, Baʿthists and Free Officers.* Princeton: Princeton University Press, 1979, 243.

Bibliography

PRIMARY SOURCES

Foreign Office, Great Britain (F.O.). Series 78, 1846–1891; Series 195, 1845–1907; Series 371, 1859–1880.

Abdul-Qadir, Khwaja. *Waqai-Manazil-Rum: Diary of a Journal to Constantinople.* Edited by Mohibul Hasan. London: Asia Publishing House, 1968.

Annual Administration Report on the Civil Veterinary Department in India for the Year 1895–96.

Anonymous. *Kitab lamᶜ al-shihab fi sirat Muhammad ibn Abdul-Wahhab, (*Riyad: Dar al Malik Abdul-Aziz, 1974).

Anonymous. *Kitab tarikh kayf kan zuhur Shaikh al-Islam Muḥammad ibn ʾAbdul-Wahhāb.* Edited by ᶜAbdullāh Salih al-Uthaymin. Riyāḍ: 1983.

Al-Ajeel, Muhsin. *Al-Suhafi, al-siyasi, Al-muʾarrikh al-Najdī Suleimān ibn Salih al-Dakhil.* Basra: Basra University Press, 1982.

Al-Ansari, ʾAḥmad Nur al-Din. "Al-Nasra fi Akhbar al-Basra," Parts 1 and 2. Edited by Yūsuf Izzidin. *Majallat al-majmaᶜ al-ilmi,* vols. 17–18, (Baghdad, 1969).

Al-Basri, ᶜUthmān Ibn Sanad. "Kitab sabaʾik al-ᶜasjad fi akhbar ʾAḥmad Najl Rizq al-Asᶜad." Unpublished Ms. Or. 7565, British Library.

———. *Mukhtassar tarikh al-shaikh ᶜUthmān ibn Sanad al-Basri al-musamma bi matalliᶜ al-Saᶜūd bi-tayyib akhbar al-vali Dāwūd.* Abridged by Amin ibn Hasan al-Hulwani, 1833.

Al-Haidari, ʾIbrāhīm Fasih ibn Sabghatullah. *Kitab unwan al-majd fi bayan ahwal Baghdad wa al-Basra wa al-Najd.* Basra: Manshurat al-Basri, n.d.

Al-Kirkukli, Rasul. *Dawhat al-wuzaraʾ fi tarikh waqaᶜi Baghdad al-Zawraʾ.* Trans. from the Turkish by Musa Kadhim Nawras. Beirut: Dar al-Katib al-Arabi, 1963.

Al-Saᶜdi, Dāwūd. "Al-Tariq min al-Ahsa ila al-Riyāḍ" in *Lughat al-Arab,* vol. 3, July 1913–1914.

Al-al-Shaikh, Abdul-Rahman, ed. *Kitab lamᶜ al-shihab fi sirat Muḥammad ibn ʾAbdul-Wahhāb.* Riyāḍ: Dar al-Malik ᶜAbdul-Azīz, 1974.

Al-Suwaidi, Abdul-Rahman. *Tarikh Baghdad aw hadiqat al-zawra' fi sirat al-wuzara'*. Edited by Safa' al-Khulusi, Baghdad: Zaim Press, 1962.

———. *Tarikh hawadith Baghdad wa al-Basra*. Edited by Abdul-Salam Rauf. Basra: Basra University Press, 1980.

Al-Tamimi, Muḥammad Hamad al-Bassam. "Kitab al-durrar al-mafakhir fi akhbar al-Arab al-awakhir." Unpublished Ms. Or. Add. 7358, British Library.

Al-Umari, Yasin bin Khairallah. *Ghayat al-maram fi tarikh mahasin Baghdad dar al-salam*. Baghdad: Basri Press, 1968, p. 322.

———. *Zubdat al-athar al-jaliya fi al-hawadith al-ardiyya*. Edited by Imad Abdul-Salam Rauf. Najaf: Adab Press, 1974.

Barbosa, Duarte. *A Description of the Coasts of East Africa and Malabar in the Beginning of the Sixteenth Century*. London: The Hakluyt Society, MDCCCL.

Blunt, Lady Anne. *Bedouin Tribes of the Euphrates*. Vol. I and II. London: John Murray, 1879.

Bidwell, Robin, ed. *Foreign Office Confidential Print: The Affairs of Kuwait, 1896–1905*. Vol. II. London: Frank Cass and Company Ltd., 1971.

Cuinet, Vital. *La Turquie d'Asie*. Vol. IV. Paris: Leroux, 1892.

Curzon, George. *Persia and the Persian Question*. Vol. II. London: Longman's Green and Company, 1892.

De Rivoyre, Denis. *Obock, Mascate, Bouchire, Bassorah*. Paris: Plon et Cie., 1883.

———. *Les Vrais Arabes et Leur Pays: Bagdad et Les Villes Ignorees de l'Euphrate*. Paris: Librairie Plon, 1884

Dieulafoy, Jeanne. *La Perse, La Chaldee et La Susianie*. Paris: Librairie Hachette, 1887

Doughty, Charles M. *Travels in Arabia Deserta*. With an Introduction by T. E Lawrence. Vol. 1. New York: Dover publications, 1979.

Douin, Georges. *L'Egypte et La Syrie en 1833: La Mission du Baron de Boislecomte*. Cairo: Societe Royale de Geographie d'Egypte, 1927.

Fā'iq Bey, Suleimān. *Tarikh al-Muntafiq*. Trans. from the Turkish by Muḥammad Khulussi al-Nāṣiri. Baghdad: Maarif Press, 1961.

———. *Tarikh al-mamalik al-Gulamend fi Baghdad*. Trans. from the Turkish by Muḥammad Najīb al-Armanazi. Baghdad: Maarif Press, 1961.

———. *Tarikh Baghdad*. Trans. from the Turkish by Musa Kadhim Nawras. Baghdad: Maarif Press, 1962.

Geary, Grattan. *Through Asiatic Turkey: Narrative of a Journey from Bombay to the Bosphorous*. New York: Harper and Bros., 1878.

Guarmani, Carlo. *Northern Najd: A Journey from Jerusalem to Anaiza in Qasim*. Trans. by Lady Capel-Cure. London: The Argonaut Press, 1938.

Heude, William. *A Voyage Up the Persian Gulf and a Journey Overland from India to England in 1817*. London: Longman's, 1819.

Ibn Isa, 'Ibrāhīm. *Tarikh ba'd al-hawadith al-waqi'a fi Najd wa wafiyat ba'd al-a'yan wa ansabihum wa bina' ba'd al-buldan*. Riyāḍ: Dar al-Yamama, 1966.

Ibn Bishr, 'Uthmān. *Unwan al-majd fi tarikh Najd*. Vol. 1, Riyāḍ: Maktabat al-Riyāḍ al-Haditha, n.d.

Ibn Ghannam, Husain. *Tarikh Najd al-musamma rawdhat al-afkhar wa al-afkham*. Vols. I and II. Riyāḍ: Al-Ahliya Press, 1949.

Maurizi, Vincenzo. *History of Seyd Said, Sulṭān of Muscat; Together with an Account of the Countries and Peoples on the Shores of the Persian Gulf, Particularily of the Wahabees.* Trans. from the Italian. London: John Booth, 1819.

Palgrave, W. G. *A Personal Narrative of a Year's Journey Through Central and Eastern Arabia, 1862–1863.* London: Darf Publishers, 1985.

Tweedie, William. *The Arab, His Horse and His Country.* Calcutta: Government Press, 1894.

Upton, R. D. *Gleanings from the Desert of Arabia.* London: Kegan Paul and Company, 1881.

Urquhart, David. *Turkey and its Resources.* London: Saunders and Otley, 1833.

Wallin, Georg August. *Travels in Arabia.* Cambridge and New York: The Oleander Press, 1979.

Ph.D. Dissertations and Masters' Theses:

ʿAbdullāh, Thabit. "The Political Economy of Merchants and Trade in Basra, 1722–1795" Unpublished Ph.D. dissertation, Georgetown University, 1992.

Al-Juhany, Uwaidah Metaireek. "The History of Najd Prior to the Wahhābīs: A Study of Social, Political and Religious Conditions in Najd During Three Centuries Preceding the Wahhābī Reform Movement. " Unpublished Ph.D.dissertation, University of Washington, 1983.

Al-Mutawa, ʿAbdullāh. "The Ulama of Najd from the Sixteenth Century to the Mid-Eighteenth Century." Unpublished Ph.D. dissertation, U.C.L.A., 1989.

Al-Nakib, Haifa ʾAḥmad. "A Critical Study of Sayyid Ṭālib Pasha al-Nakib in the Setting of His Time and Environment. " Unpublished Master's Thesis, University of Leeds, 1973.

Al-Urayni, Abdul-Rahman. "Al-hayat al-ijtimaʿiyya lada badiyat Najd wa athar al-daʿwa al-salafiyya fiha mundhu al-qarn al-ashir al-hijri wa hatta suqut al-Darʿiyya." Unpublished Master's Thesis, al-Imam Muḥammad ibn Saʿūd Islamic University, Riyāḍ, 1984.

Ansari, Mostafa. "The History of Khuzistan, 1878–1925: A Study in Provincial Autonomy and Change." Unpublished Ph.D. dissertation, University of Chicago, 1974.

Fattah, Hala. "The Development of the Regional Market of Iraq and the Gulf, 1800–1900." Unpublished Ph.D. dissertation, U.C.L.A., 1986.

Mahmoud, Muḥammad ʾAḥmad. "Ahwal al-ashaʾir al-Iraqīyya al-arabiyya wa ilaqatuha bi al-hukuma, 1872–1918." Unpublished Master's Thesis, Baghdad University, 1980.

Shahnavaz, Shahbaz. "Britain and the Opening of the Karun River, circa 1873–1910." Unpublished Ph.D. dissertation, Oxford University, 1980.

SECONDARY SOURCES

Abdul-Muhsin, ʾIbrāhīm ibn Ubaid. *Tadhkirat ʿuli al-nahi wa al-urfan bi-ayyam Allah al-wahid al-diyan wa dhikr hawadith al-zaman.* Vol. I. Riyāḍ: Nur Printing Press, n.d.

Abou El-Haj, Rifaat ʿAlī. "Taxation, Trade, Production and Society in 16th Century Mosul" in Abdeljelil Temimi, ed. *La Vie Sociale dans les Provinces Arabes à l'Epoque Ottomane.* Vol. 3, Tunis, 1988.

———. *Formation of the Modern State: The Ottoman Empire, Sixteenth to Eighteenth Centuries*. Albany: State University of New York Press, 1991.

Abu-Hakima, ʾAḥmad Mustafa. *The Modern History of Kuwait: 1750–1965*. London: Luzac and Company 1983.

Ahmida, ʿAlī Abdullatif. *The Making of Modern Libya: State Formation, Colonization and Resistance, 1830–1932*. Albany: State University of New York Press, 1994.

Al-Abid, Salih Muḥammad. *Dawr al-Qawassim fi al-khalij al-arabi, 1742–1820*. Baghdad: Ani Press, 1976.

Al-Ansari, Muḥammad ibn Abdul-Qadir. *Tuhfat al-mustafid bi tarikh al-Ahsa al-qadim wa al-jadid*. Riyāḍ: n.d., 1962.

Al-Asi, Jasim. "Al-Khamīsiyya: madina mahjura" in *Al-Turath al-shaʿbi*. Vol. 6, no. 6, 1975.

Al-Azzawi, Abbas. "Al-Al-Shawy" in *Lughat al-Arab*, vol. 9, January–October 1931.

———. *Tarikh al-Iraq bayn ihtilalayn*. Vols. 7 and 8. Baghdad: Tijara and Tibaʿa Press, 1935.

———. *Dhikra Abi Thanaʾ al-Alusi*. Baghdad: Sharikat al-Tijara wa al-Tibaʿa, 1958.

———. *Tarikh al-nuqud al-Iraqīyya*. Baghdad: Sharikat al-Tijara wa al-Tibaʿa, 1958.

Al-Azmeh, Aziz. "Wahhābīte Polity" in Ian Richard Nettleton, ed. *Arabia and the Gulf: From Traditional Society to Modern States*. London and Sydney: Croom and Helm, 1986.

Awad, ʿAbdul-Azīz M. "The Gulf in the Seventeenth Century" in *Bulletin for the British Society for Middle Eastern Studies*, vol. 12, no. 2, 1985.

Al-Bustani, Mahdi Jawad Habib. "Dirasa li-wathaʾiq ʿUthmāniyya ghayr manshura" in *Dirasat fi al-tarikh wa al-athar: majallat jamʿiyyat al-muʾarikkhin wa al-athariyyin fi al-Iraq*. Vol. 13, 1987.

———. "Wathaʾiq ʿuthmāniyya ghayr manshura ʿan Basra wa ustuluha wa silatuha bi al-Khalij al-Arabi fi awasit al-qarn al-tasiʿ ashr" in *Al-Wathiqa* (Bahrain), no. 17, July 1990.

Al-Hamdani, Tariq Nafiʿ. "Al-Tanzimat al-iqtisadiya al-ʿuthmāniya fi wilayet al-Basra iban al-nisf al-thani min al-qarn al-sadis ashr" in Abdeljelil Temimi, ed. *La Vie Economique des Provinces Arabes et Leurs Sources Documentaires à l'Epoque Ottomane*. Tome 1 and 2. Zagouan: CERPAEO, 1986.

Al-Hasani, ʿAbdul-Razzāq. *Al-Iraq qadiman wa hadithan*. Sidon: Irfan Press, 1956.

Al-Jamil, Sayyar. *Al-ʿuthmāniyun wa takwin al-Arab al-hadith*. Beirut: Muʾassissat al-Abhath al-Arabiyya, 1989.

Al-Jawahiri, Imad ʾAḥmad. "Al-Dawr al-tarikhi li Basra ala al-Khalij al-Arabi ma bain 1500–1600" in *Dirasat al-Khalij wa al-Jazira al-Arabiyya*. Vol. 13, January 1978.

Arabian Gulf Intelligence: Selections From the Records of the Bombay Government. London: The Oleander Press, 1985.

Al-Madamgha, Mustafa Kazim. *Nusus min watahaʾiq al-ʿUthmāniya ʿan tarikh al-Basra fi sijillat mahkamat al-sharʿīyya fi al-Basra*. Basra: Basra University Press, 1982.

Al-Nabhani, Muḥammad ibn Musa al-Nabhani. *Al-Tuhfa al-Nabhaniya fi tarikh al-Jazira al-Arabiyya*. Vol. 9. Basra: Basra University Press, n.d.

Al-Najjar, Mustafa Abdul-Qadir. *Al-Tarikh al-siyasi li-imarat Arabistan al-Arabiyya*. Cairo: Dar al-Maarif, 1971.

Al-Rashīd, Zamil Muḥammad. *Suᶜudi Relations with Eastern Arabia and Uman (1800–1871).* London: Luzac and Company, 1981.

Al-Shaikh Khazᶜal, Husain. *Tarikh Al-Jazira al-Arabiyya fi asr al-Shaikh Muḥammad ibn ʾAbdul-Wahhāb.* Beirut: Dar al-Kutub, 1968.

Al-Qahawati, Husain Muḥammad. *Dawr al-Basra al-tijari fi al-Khalij al-Arabi.* Baghdad: Irshad Press, 1980.

Al-Qassab, ᶜAbdul-Azīz. *Min dhikrayati.* Beirut: Fadhul Press, 1962.

Algar, Hamid. "Shīᶜīsm and Iran in the Eighteenth Century" in Thomas Naff and Roger Owen, eds. *Studies in Eighteenth Century Islamic History.* Carbondale: Southern Illinois University, 1977.

ᶜAlī, Shakir ᶜAlī. *Tarikh al-Iraq fi Al-ahd al-ᶜUthmāni, 1638–1750: Dirasa fi ahwaluha al-tarikhiyya.* Ninevah: July 30 Press, 1985.

Almana, Mohammed. *Arabia Unified: A Portrait of Ibn Saᶜūd.* London: Hutchinson Benham, 1980, p. 191.

Amanat, Abbas, ed. *Cities and Trade: Consul Abbot on the Economy and Society of Iran, 1847–1866.* London: Ithaca Press, 1983.

Arasaratnam, [. . .]. "Recent Trends in the Historiography of the Indian Ocean, 1500 to 1800" in *Journal of World History,* vol. 1, no. 2, 1990.

Batatu, Hanna. *The Old Social Classes and the Revolutionary Movements of Iraq.* Princeton: Princeton University Press, 1978

Bayly, C. A. *Imperial Meridian: The British Empire and the World, 1780–1830.* London and New York: Longman, 1989.

Bonner, Michael. "The Naming of the Frontier: ᶜAwasim, Thughur and the Arab Geographers "in *Bulletin of the School of Oriental and African Studies,* Vol. LVII, Pact I, 1994.

Braudel, Fernand. *The Wheels of Commerce.* Translated by Sian Reynolds. Vol. II. New York: Harper and Row, 1979.

———. *The Perspectives of the World.* Vol. III. New York: Harper and Row, 1984.

Brerton, J. M. *The Horse in War.* London: David and Charles Ltd., 1976.

Brummet, Palmira. "Competition and Coincidence: Venetian Trading Interests and Ottoman Expansion in the Early Sixteenth Century Levant" in *New Perspectives on Turkey,* nos. 5–6, Fall 1991.

Chaudhuri. *Trade and Civilization in the Indian Ocean: An Economic History from the Rise of Islam to 1750.* Cambridge: Cambridge University Press, 1985

———. *Asia Before Europe.* Cambridge: Cambridge University Press, 1990.

Cole, Juan. "Mafia, Mob and Shiism in Iraq: The Rebellion of Ottoman Karbala, 1842–1843" in *Past and Present,* 1986.

Cook, Michael. "The Provenance of the Lamᶜ al-Shihab fi Sirat Muḥammad ibn ʾAbdul-Wahhāb" in *Journal of Turkish Studies,* vol. 10, 1986.

———. "The Expansion of the First Saᶜūdī State: The Case of Washm" in C. E Bosworth, et. al. *The Islamic World from Classical to Modern Times: Essays in Honor of Bernard Lewis.* Princeton: The Darwin Press, 1988.

Curtin, Philip D. *Cross-Cultural Trade in World History.* Cambridge: Cambridge University Press, 1984.

Davidson, Roderic H. "Britain, the International Spectrum, and the Eastern Question, 1827–1841" in *New Perspectives on Turkey,* no. 7, Spring 1992.

Dresch, Paul. *Tribes, Government and History in Yemen.* Oxford: Clarendon Press, 1989.

Eickelman, Dale F., and Piscatori, James, eds. *Muslim Travellers: Pilgrimage, Migration and the Religious Imagination.* Berkeley and Los Angeles: University of California Press, 1990.

Evans, R. J. W. "Essay and Reflection: Frontiers and National Identities in Central Europe" in *The International History Review,* Vol. XIV, no. 3, August 1992.

Faidhi, Suleimān. *Fi Ghumrat al-Nidal.* Baghdad: Sharikat al-Tijara wa al-Tibaʿa, 1952.

Floor, Willem. "The Dutch on Khark Island: A Commercial Mishap" In *International Journal of Middle Eastern Studies,* vol. 24, August 1992.

Hasan, Muḥammad Salman. *Al-Tatawur al-iqtisadi fi al-Iraq: Al-tijara al-kharijiyya wa al-tatawur al-iqtisadi, 1864–1958.* Vol. I. Sidon: Al-Maktaba al-Asriyya li al-Tibaca wa al-Nashr, 1965.

Heard-Bey, Frauke. *From Trucial States to United Arab Emirates: A Society in Transition.* London and New York: Longman's, 1982.

Herzig, Edmund M. "Hormuz" in *Bulletin of the British Society for Middle Eastern Studies.* Vol. 12, no. 1, 1985.

Hobsbawm, Eric. *Captain Swing: A Social History of the Great Agricultural Uprising of 1830.* New York: W. W. Norton and Company, 1968.

Hodgson, Marshall. *The Venture of Islam: Conscience and History in a World Civilization.* Vol. III. Chicago and London: The University of Chicago Press, 1974.

Ismael, Tareq Y. *Iran and Iraq: Roots of Conflict.* Syracuse: Syracuse University Press, 1982.

Issawi, Charles, ed. *The Economic History of the Middle East, 1800–1914.* Chicago and London: The University of Chicago Press, 1966.

———. "Middle East Economic Development, 1815–1914: The General and the Specific" in M. A. Cook, ed. *Studies in the Economic History of the Middle East.* London: Oxford University Press, 1970.

———. *An Economic History of the Middle East and North Africa.* New York: Columbia Press, 1982.

———. "Notes on the Trade of Basra, 1800–1914" in *Journal of Turkish Studies,* vol. 10, 1986.

———. *The Fertile Crescent: A Documentary History.* Oxford: Oxford University Press, 1988.

Ismael, Jacqueline. *Kuwait: Social Change in Historical Perspective.* Syracuse: Syracuse University Press, 1982.

Jwaideh, Albertine. "Midḥat Pasha and the Land System of Lower Iraq" in *St. Antony's Papers no. 16. Middle Eastern Affairs no. 3.* London: Chatto and Windus, 1963.

———. "Aspects of Land Tenure and Social Change in Lower Iraq During Late Ottoman Times" in Tarif Khalidi, ed. *Land Tenure and Social Transformation in the Middle East.* Beirut: American University of Beirut Press, 1984.

Kasaba, Resat. "Open-Door Treaties: China and the Ottoman Empire Compared " in *New Perspectives on Turkey,* no. 7, 1992.

Khoury, Dina Rizq. "Merchants and Trade in Early Modern Iraq" in *New Perspectives on Turkey,* nos. 5–6, Fall 1991.

Lackner, Helen. *A House Built on Sand: A Political Economy of Saʿūdī Arabia.* London: Ithaca Press, 1978.

Lienhardt, Peter. "The Authority of Shaykhs in the Gulf: An Essay in Nineteenth Century History" in *Arabian Studies II,* MCMLXXV.

Longrigg, Stephen Helmsley. *Four Centuries of Modern Iraq.* Oxford: The Clarendon Press, 1925.

Lorimer, G. E. *A Gazeteer of the Persian Gulf, Oman and Central Arabia.* Calcutta: Government Press, 1908.

McNeill, William H. *Europe's Steppe Frontier, 1500–1800.* Chicago: University of Chicago Press, 1964.

———. *The Great Frontier:Freedom and Hierarchy in Modern Times.* Princeton: Princeton University Press, 1983.

Main, Ernest. *In and Around Baghdad.* Baghdad: The Times Press, n.d.

Mandaville, Jon. "The Ottoman Province of al-Ahsa in the Sixteenth and Seventeenth Centuries" in *Journal of the American Oriental Society,* 1970.

Mantran, Robert. "Reglements Fiscaux Ottomans: La Province de Bassora" in *Journal of the Economic and Social History of the Orient.* December 1967.

Marr, Phebe. *The Modern History of Iraq.* Boulder and London: Westview Press, 1985.

Marsot, Afaf Lutfi al-Sayyid. *Egypt in the Reign of Muḥammad ʿAlī.* Cambridge: Cambridge University Press, 1984.

Masters, Bruce. "The Sulṭān's Entrepreneurs: The Avrupa Tuccaris and the Hayriye Tuccaris in Syria" in *International Journal of Middle Eastern Studies,* vol. 24, no. 4, November 1992.

Niewenhuis, Tom. *Politics and Society in Early Modern Iraq: Mamluk pashas, Tribal Shaykhs and Local Rule Between 1802 and 1831.* The Hague: Martinus Nijhoff, 1982.

Owen, Roger. *The Middle East in the World Economy, 1800–1914.* London and New York: Methuen, 1985.

Panzac, Daniel. "International and Domestic Maritime Trade in the Ottoman Empire during the Eighteenth Century" in *International Journal of Middle East Studies,* vol. 24, May 1992.

Pamuk, Sevket. *The Ottoman Empire and European Capitalism, 1820–1913.* Cambridge: Cambridge University Press, 1987.

Pitcher, Donald Edgar. *An Historical Geography of the Ottoman Empire.* Leiden: E. J. Brill, 1972.

Puryear, John Vernon. *International Economics and Diplomacy in the Near East: A Study of British Commercial Policy in the Levant.* Stanford: Stanford University Press, 1935.

Pérotin-Dumon. "The Pirate and the Emperor: Power and the Law on the Seas, 1450–1850" in James Tracy, ed. *The Political Economy of Merchant Empires.* Cambridge: Cambridge University Press, 1991.

Philby, Harry St. John. *Arabia of the Wahhābīs.* New York: Arno Press, 1973.

Piscatori, James P. *Islam in a World of Nation States.* Cambridge: Cambridge University Press, 1986.

Raswan, Carl. *Black Tents of Arabia.* Boston: Little, Brown and Company, 1935.

Sahlins, Peter. "Natural Frontiers Revisited:France's Boundaries Since the Seventeenth Century" in *The American Historical Review,* vol. 95, no. 5, December 1990.

Sarkis, Yaʿqub. *Mabahith Iraqīyya fi al-tarikh wa al-athar wa khitat Baghdad.* 3 vols. Baghdad: Maktabat al-Tijariyya, 1955.

Schofield, Richard N. *The Iraq-Iran Border, 1840–1958.* Vol. I. Oxford: Archive Editions, 1989.

Steensgaard, Niels. *Carracks, Caravans and Companies: The Structural Crisis in European-Asian Trade in the Early Seventeenth Century.* Copenhagen, 1973.

Subrahmanyam, Sanjay. "The Portuguese, the port of Basrur and the Rice Trade, 1600–1650" in Subrahmanyam, ed. *Merchants, Markets and the Early State in Early Modern India.* Delhi: Oxford University Press, 1990.

Wink, André. "Review Article: World Trade, Merchant Empires and the Economy of the Indian Ocean" in *The International History Review,* XV, February 1993.

Vaucelles, Pierre de. *La Vie en Irak il y a Un Siecle.* Paris: Editions A. Perdone, 1963.

Villiers, Alan. *Sons of Sinbad.* New York: Charles Scribner and Sons, 1940.

———. "Some Aspects of the Arab Dhow Trade" in Louise E. Sweet, ed. *Peoples and Cultures of the Middle East.* Vol. I. New York: The Natural History Press, 1965.

Wilson, Arnold. *South-West Persia: A Political Officer's Diary, 1907–1914.* London, New York and Toronto: Oxford University Press, 1941.

Winder, Bayly R. *Saʿūdī Arabia in the Nineteenth Century.* New York: St. Martin's Press, 1965.

Yapp, M. E. "The Euphrates Expedition" in C. E Bosworth, et. al. *The Islamic World from the Classical to Modern Times: Essays in Honor of Bernard Lewis.* Princeton: The Darwin Press, 1988.

Index

Abadan (town in Arabistan), 198
ʿAbbud family, 81, 110, 150
Abdullah Pasha, 39
Abdul-Wahhab, Imam Muḥammad, 41, 42, 45, 46, 47, 64, 165
Abou el-Haj, Rifaat, 100
Aḥmad Pasha (governor of Iraqi provinces), 33, 163
Al-ʿAhsa (eastern Arabia), 29, 49, 51, 53, 54, 56, 63, 64, 65, 66, 67, 68, 94, 95, 96, 114, 116, 119, 120, 121, 123, 137, 162, 165, 166
Al-Alusi, Maḥmud Shukri, 64, 66
Al-Badr family, 82, 169
Al-Bassam family, 44, 77, 78, 150, 169
Albu Muḥammad tribes, 132, 133, 134, 135, 136, 190
Aleppo, 9, 79, 93, 96, 196
Al-Ḥaidari, shaikh Ibrahim ibn Sabghatullah, 30, 64, 71, 83, 212n.
Al-Ḥijaz, 41, 43, 52, 66, 114, 124, 135, 140
Al-Ḥirma (town in Arabia), 24, 196
ʿAli al-Kahya (Mamluk commander), 52, 54, 55
Al-Juhany, ʿUwaidah, 23, 24
Al-Kirkukli, shaikh Rasul (Iraqi Mamluk historian), 53, 54, 55, 215n.
Al-Laz, ʿAli Riza Pasha (vali of Iraq), 98, 101, 112, 178, 198
Al-Mandil family, 82
Al-Qasim (district in Arabia), 53, 65, 66
Al-Qaṭif (eastern Arabia), 32, 53, 84, 116, 120
Al-Qawasim tribes, 56, 57, 60
Al-Rashid shaikhs, 66, 78, 79, 121, 137, 138, 169
Al-Sabah, shaikh Abdullah, 119
Al-Sabah, shaikh Mubarak, 121, 122, 182, 183
Al-Saʿdi, shaikh Dawud, 120
Al-Saʿdun, shaikh Bandar, 134, 135
Al-Saʿdun, shaikh Manṣur, 132, 187, 188, 189, 190
Al-Saʿdun, shaikh Naṣir, 119, 122, 136, 188, 189, 190, 203
Al Saʿud, shaikh ʿAbdul Aziz ibn Muḥammad (second ruler of the Saʿudi state), 30, 48, 50, 53, 55, 61, 165
Al Saʿud, shaikh ʿAbdul Aziz ibn Abdul-Raḥman (later first King of Saudi Arabia), 121
Al Saʿud, shaikh ʿAbdullah ibn Faiṣal (contender for the Saʿudi throne and Ottoman ally), 118, 119, 137
Al Saʿud, shaikh Muḥammad (first amir of the Saʿdi state), 46, 47, 48
Al Saʿud, shaikh Saʿud ibn ʿAbdul-Aziz (third ruler of the Saʿudi state), 54, 55
Al-Shabib family (ruling family of the Muntafiq tribal confederation), 29, 188
Al-Shabib, shaikh Thuwaini ibn ʿAbdullah, 52, 53, 54, 55, 126, 187, 204
Al-Shawi, shaikh ʿAbdullah, 38
Al-Shawi, shaikh Jasim, 39
Al-Shawi shaikhs (paramount shaikhs of the ʿUbaid tribes), 38, 164
Al-Suwaidi, shaikh ʿAbdul-Rahman, 36, 40, 216n.
Al-Thamer, shaikh Ḥumud, 39, 98
Al-ʿUqair (port in eastern Arabia), 65, 67, 68
ʿAmara (town in eastern Iraq), 201, 203

ʿAnayza tribes, 23, 25, 30, 119, 126, 135, 162, 166, 167, 179
Arabia (Najd), 1, 2, 7, 8, 9, 10, 11, 13, 14, 20, 21, 22, 23, 24, 25, 26, 29, 30, 32, 41, 42, 45, 46, 50, 58, 63, 64, 65, 66, 67, 68, 72, 86, 89, 90, 103, 105, 119, 120, 121, 122, 124, 137, 162, 194, 195
ʿArabistan (Khuzistan), 1, 8, 13, 22, 65, 71, 72, 79, 82, 93, 119, 140, 154, 201
Asfar family, 81

Bab al-Arab (Mamluk title), 38
Baghdad, 6, 9, 21, 22, 31, 32, 34, 36, 37, 38, 41, 46, 53, 66, 70, 71, 72, 74, 75, 76, 77, 79, 82, 84, 88, 91, 92, 94, 96, 98, 99, 100, 101, 102, 103, 104, 105, 107, 109, 110, 112, 113, 116, 117, 119, 122, 127, 128, 129, 131, 136, 140, 141, 142, 145, 147, 148, 149, 151, 152, 153, 157, 164, 165, 168, 169, 173, 177, 178, 179, 180, 186, 188, 198, 200, 209
Baḥrain, 26, 27, 32, 56, 58, 61, 74, 82, 84, 95, 111, 114, 160, 185
Balta Liman Treaty (Anglo-Turkish Convention), 11, 92, 99, 102, 106, 107, 108, 110, 111, 113, 122, 128, 130, 140, 141, 154, 171, 172, 173, 191, 208
Banu Khalid tribes, 23, 27, 30, 47, 51, 53, 59, 66, 82, 95, 165
Banu Lam tribes, 36, 37, 116, 126, 128, 162
Baṣra, 6, 8, 9, 11, 21, 26, 27, 29, 31, 32, 33, 34, 37, 41, 57, 63, 64, 65, 68, 69, 70, 71, 72, 73, 74, 75, 76, 77, 79, 80, 81, 82, 83, 84, 85, 86, 89, 91, 92, 93, 94, 95, 96, 97, 100, 101, 104, 105, 111, 112, 114, 115, 116, 117, 118, 119, 122, 127, 128, 129, 130, 131, 140, 141, 145, 149, 150, 151, 152, 157, 169, 170, 173, 176, 177, 178, 180, 182, 183, 186, 187, 188, 194, 195, 196, 197, 199, 200, 202, 209
bayʿa (oath of allegiance), 41, 43, 49, 58
Bayly, C. A., 6, 7, 105
Blunt, Lady Anne, 79, 177
Bombay, 1, 9, 70, 77, 83, 88, 105, 116, 123, 149, 150, 160, 161, 168, 170, 171, 172, 174, 177, 182, 207
Braudel, Fernand, 85, 86, 226n.
British East India Company, 57, 76, 102, 103, 104, 117, 130
Buraida (town in Arabia), 25, 65, 140, 167, 170

Chaudhuri, K. N., 1, 2, 4
Cook, Michael, 59, 60

Darʿiyya (capital of the first Saʿudi state), 24, 25, 47, 48, 49, 51, 58
dates, 27, 31, 47, 71, 73, 79, 83, 85, 86, 87
Dawud Pasha (last Mamluk ruler of Iraq), 39, 40, 45, 97, 98, 132, 164, 165, 178

Evans, R. J. W., 15, 16, 17, 18, 19, 20

Faiq, Suleiman (Iraqi Mamluk historian), 112, 132, 164
fatwa (legal opinion), 34, 35, 48
France, 15, 16, 17
frontier(s), 13, 14, 15, 16, 17, 19, 20, 23

Gulf, 2, 4, 6, 7, 10, 11, 13, 14, 20, 21, 23, 25, 32, 41, 42, 51, 56, 58, 63, 65, 67, 76, 85, 89, 90, 91, 92, 95, 101, 102, 103, 105, 116, 130, 139

hujjaj (pilgrims), 34, 48, 55
Harford Jones, 103, 104
Hasan Pasha (governor of the Iraqi provinces), 33, 34, 35, 36, 37, 40
Herzig, Edmund, 4, 5
Hilla (town in southern Iraq), 155, 187
Hormuz, 4, 95, 160
horses, 11, 27, 30, 65, 66, 73, 78, 79, 82, 88, 89, 90, 93, 106, 159, 160, 161, 162, 163, 164, 166, 167, 168, 169, 171, 172, 174, 175, 176, 177, 178, 179, 180, 181, 182, 183
Ḥuwaiza (town in Arabistan), 8, 65, 72, 198

Ibn Bishr, shaikh ʿUthman (Najdi historian), 47, 48, 50, 51, 52, 53, 60, 218n.
Ibn Ghannam, shaikh Huṣain (Najdi historian), 43, 217n.
Ibn Sanad, shaikh ʿUthman (Iraqi Mamluk historian), 44, 45, 51, 52, 53, 55, 217n.
Iiltizam(s) (tax farms), 74, 94, 99
India, 8, 9, 11, 21, 22, 27, 65, 74, 86, 87, 92, 93, 104, 105, 111, 113, 139, 156, 161, 162, 173, 181

Indian Ocean, 1, 2, 3, 4, 5, 6, 7, 8, 20, 28, 95, 130
Iran, 1, 4, 20, 24, 33, 34, 35, 70, 111, 115, 198
Iraq, 1, 2, 4, 5, 7, 9, 10, 11, 13, 14, 20, 21, 22, 23, 24, 25, 27, 28, 29, 31, 32, 33, 34, 35, 40, 41, 42, 45, 46, 50, 58, 63, 64, 65, 66, 67, 68, 72, 73, 75, 76, 78, 84, 89, 90, 91, 92, 96, 97, 98, 102, 104, 105, 107, 111, 113, 114, 116, 119, 125, 130, 135, 136, 144, 154, 156, 159, 163, 167, 174, 185, 202, 209
Ismael, Jacqueline, 58
Istanbul, 93, 94, 99, 100, 108, 113, 115, 116, 121, 127, 128, 129, 165, 176, 179

Jabal Shammar (district in northern Arabia), 49, 66, 78, 121, 138, 162

Kaab tribes (of Arabistan), 32, 65, 73, 79, 115, 197, 198
kafir (kuffar) (unbelievers), 42, 44
Karbala, 29, 51, 56, 60, 69, 70, 78, 80
Khamissiyya (town on the Iraqi-Najdi "frontier"), 8, 186, 193, 194, 197, 201, 205, 206
Khazᶜal, shaikh of Arabistan, 82, 83, 177, 182, 199, 201
Khazᶜil tribes, 37, 148, 162, 166
Khoury, Dina, 5, 38
khuwwa (brotherhood tax), 6, 30, 31, 47, 49, 50, 60, 126
kufr (unbelief), 42, 43
Kuwait, 1, 8, 13, 21, 22, 26, 27, 29, 42, 46, 51, 54, 58, 59, 63, 64, 65, 68, 71, 72, 75, 76, 78, 79, 84, 86, 87, 97, 114, 119, 121, 137, 150, 168, 176, 180, 181, 182, 183, 185, 186, 191, 192, 196, 197, 205
Kurds, 31, 39, 164

Lynch shipping firm, 83, 104, 131, 152, 153, 171, 199

Mamluks, 14, 23, 30, 33, 34, 35, 36, 38, 39, 40, 41, 51, 52, 54, 55, 59, 76, 79, 81, 97, 98, 99, 112, 132, 135, 162, 163, 164, 178, 197
Maᶜshuq Pasha (Vali of Basra), 114, 118
McNeill, William, 14, 18, 19, 20, 21
Mecca, 47, 48, 66, 72, 120
Midhat Pasha (Vali of Iraq), 108, 118, 119, 190, 203, 205
Mosul, 6, 22, 31, 33, 34, 122, 126, 127, 129, 141, 145, 162
Muhammad Ali (ruler of Egypt), 52, 104, 106, 130, 140
Muhammara, 8, 22, 63, 65, 72, 73, 80, 82, 85, 86, 114, 115, 117, 156, 169, 176, 177, 181, 183, 187, 197, 198, 199, 200, 202
Muntafiq district, 11, 51, 72, 74, 75, 126, 135, 187, 189, 190, 192, 203, 204
Muntafiq *mashyakha*, 75, 131, 132, 133, 135, 187, 188
Muntafiq shaikhs (al-Shabib and al-Saᶜdun), 38, 72, 79, 93, 94, 117, 122, 126, 132, 134, 137, 164, 165, 187, 188, 193, 196
Muntafiq tribes, 29, 37, 39, 51, 88, 116, 119, 132, 162, 165, 166, 190
Mutair tribes, 23, 50, 64, 65, 162, 166

Nadir Shah, 31, 34, 35
Najaf, 69, 70
Najib Pasha (Vali of Baghdad), 100, 112, 115, 128, 129, 141, 142, 143, 144, 145, 146, 147, 148
nakhoda(s) (ship captains), 84, 128
Naqib family, 70, 79, 80, 120, 182
Naqib, Sayyid Talib, 79, 80
Nasiriyya (town in southern Iraq), 192, 201, 203, 204
Nixon, Consul-General, 151, 152, 153

Ottomans, 31, 32, 57, 68, 70, 75, 79, 80, 88, 90, 91, 92, 93, 95, 96, 98, 99, 101, 102, 107, 110, 115, 118, 129, 135, 137, 147, 151, 162, 163, 174, 181, 186, 194, 199, 200
Ottoman Empire, 31, 34, 94, 104, 105, 106, 115, 130, 140, 160, 198

Pamuk, Sevket, 105
Perotin-Dumon, Anne, 6
Persians, 31, 32, 48, 57, 68, 69, 70, 73, 92, 103, 111, 134, 176, 187, 199
Portuguese, 4, 5, 6, 32, 92, 93, 95

qapudan Pasha (admiral of the Ottoman fleet), 70, 94
Qatar, 22, 26, 59, 120, 185

Ras al-Khaima, 56, 57
Rawlinson, Consul-General, 73, 107, 108, 111, 112, 113, 115, 128, 129, 130, 131, 141, 144, 145, 171, 172, 198
Riyaḍ, 66, 120

Saᶜdun (shaikh of the Banu Khalid tribes in eastern Arabia), 96
Safavid(s), 3, 4, 7, 14, 20, 31, 32, 34, 35
Sahlins, Peter, 15, 16, 17, 18, 19, 20
Saᶜid Beg (later Pasha, Iraqi Mamluk governor), 39, 81, 98
Sassoon family, 152, 169
Saᶜudi *imara* (state), 23, 30, 41, 46, 47, 48, 49, 51, 52, 56, 57, 58, 59, 60, 61, 64, 66, 67, 89, 123, 124, 166
Shah Safi, 35
shami (local currency), 66, 74, 87
Shammar tribes, 23, 30, 32, 38, 50, 119, 126, 128, 129, 135, 162, 166, 177, 178, 179
Sharif(s) of Mecca, 47, 48
Shatt al-Arab, 26, 36, 65, 69, 70, 71, 72, 73, 83, 84, 93, 116, 117, 156, 180, 197, 198, 200, 201
Subrahmanyam, Sanjay, 5
Suleiman Abu Laila (Iraqi Mamluk governor), 40, 163
Suleiman Pasha the Great (Iraqi Mamluk governor), 39, 40
Sultan Murad IV, 31, 35
Suq al-Shuyukh (town in southern Iraq), 8, 29, 72, 74, 75, 86, 134, 170, 186, 187, 188, 190, 191, 192, 193, 194, 195, 197, 201, 203, 204, 205
Syria, 25, 29, 46, 50, 92, 160, 174

takfir (the act of labelling someone an unbeliever), 42
tanzimat (Ottoman regulations), 97
Tweedie, Major, 170, 176, 181

Ubaid tribes, 38, 162, 164
Uman, 50, 52, 56, 60, 66, 69, 116, 174
Unaiza (town in Arabia), 65, 77, 78, 140, 167, 170
Uqaylis (Uqaylat), 39, 169
Ushayqir (town in Arabia), 24, 77
Utub (Utbi) tribes, 26, 59, 61
ᶜUyuyna (town in Arabia), 24, 25, 77

Villers, Alan, 84

Wahhabis, 22, 23, 24, 27, 28, 29, 41, 42, 43, 44, 45, 46, 48, 49, 51, 54, 56, 57, 60, 65, 66, 67, 78, 119, 137, 166, 195

Yemen, 50, 66, 74, 78, 87, 91, 103, 160

Zafir tribes, 12, 29, 50, 64, 119, 162, 166
zakat (Islamic tax), 50, 51,
Zubara (town in Qatar), 26, 27, 51, 56, 58, 59, 185
Zubaid tribes, 126, 128, 129, 132, 147
Zubair (town in southern Iraq), 8, 21, 29, 54, 64, 71, 72, 75, 76, 79, 80, 82, 86, 113, 167, 170, 186, 193, 195, 196, 197
Zuhair family, 79, 196